Each One Another

Each / One

Another

The Self in Contemporary Art

Rachel Haidu

The University of Chicago Press
Chicago and London

The University of Chicago Press, Chicago 60637
The University of Chicago Press, Ltd., London

Published 2023

Printed in China

32 31 30 29 28 27 26 25 24 23 1 2 3 4 5

ISBN-13: 978-0-226-82341-6 (cloth)
ISBN-13: 978-0-226-82342-3 (e-book)
DOI: https://doi.org/10.7208/chicago/9780226823423.001.0001

Library of Congress Cataloging-in-Publication Data

Names: Haidu, Rachel, author.
Title: Each one another : the self in contemporary art / Rachel Haidu.
Description: Chicago : University of Chicago Press, 2023.
| Includes bibliographical references and index.
Identifiers: LCCN 2022024439 | ISBN 9780226823416 (cloth) | ISBN 9780226823423 (ebook)
Subjects: LCSH: Self (Philosophy) in art. | Self (Philosophy) in the performing arts. | Arts, Modern—21st century—Psychological aspects. | Performing arts—21st century—Psychological aspects.
Classification: LCC NX650.S437 | DDC 704.9/49126—dc23/eng/20220720
LC record available at https://lccn.loc.gov/2022024439

♾ This paper meets the requirements of ANSI/NISO Z39.48-1992 (Permanence of Paper).

Contents

List of Illustrations vii
Introduction 1

I / *Shape*

Philip Guston
Late Work 23

Amy Sillman
Recent Work 57

II / *Character*

James Coleman
Retake with Evidence 99

Steve McQueen
Shame 120

III / *Role*

Anne Teresa De Keersmaeker
Work/Travail/Arbeid 157

Yvonne Rainer
The Concept of Dust, or How do you look when there's nothing left to move? 179

Acknowledgments 192
Notes 195
Index 233

Illustrations

Gabriele Münter, *Portrait of a Young Woman*, 1909 17

Philip Guston, *Yellow Light*, 1975 26

Philip Guston, *The Coat*, 1977 27

Jules Olitski, *Unlocked*, 1966 36

Jules Olitski, *Wet Heat Company*, 1963 37

Denise Hare, Guston's studio, 1975 40

Philip Guston, *Untitled (Light Bulb)*, 1968 41

Philip Guston, *Shoe*, 1968 42

Phillip Guston, *Untitled (Shoe)*, 1968 43

Philip Guston, *Untitled (Nail)*, 1968 44

Philip Guston, *Driving Around*, 1969 45

Philip Guston, *Green Rug*, 1976 48

Philip Guston, *Ancient Wall*, 1976 49

Philip Guston, *The Street*, 1977 52

Philip Guston, *Dawn*, 1970 53

Amy Sillman, *The Shape of Shape*, Museum of Modern Art, 2019 60

Elizabeth Murray, *Her Story*, 1984 62

Ellsworth Kelly, *Green Curve with White Panel*, 1989 63

Amy Sillman, *Fatso*, 2009 64

Amy Sillman, *Untitled*, 2010–11 65

Amy Sillman, *A Shape That Stands Up and Listens #8*, 2012 68

Amy Sillman, *A Shape That Stands Up and Listens #10*, 2012 69
Amy Sillman, *A Shape That Stands Up and Listens #11*, 2012 71
Amy Sillman, installation shot, entrance to *Mostly Drawing*, Gladstone 64, 2018 75
Amy Sillman, installation shot, last room of *Mostly Drawing*, Gladstone 64, 2018 77
Amy Sillman, *SK42*, 2017 79
Emil Nolde, *The Burial*, 1915 80
Amy Sillman, *Dub Stamp*, 2018 85
Yvonne Rainer, original manuscript for "A Quasi Survey of Some 'Minimalist' Tendencies in the Quantitatively Minimal Dance Activity Midst the Plethora, or an Analysis of *Trio A*," 1966 91
James Coleman, *Retake with Evidence*, 2007 (Harvey Keitel) 100
James Coleman, *Box (ahhareturnabout)*, 1977 101
James Coleman, *Retake with Evidence*, 2007 (Harvey Keitel) 103
James Coleman, *Retake with Evidence*, 2007 (Harvey Keitel) 104
Model for set, *Retake with Evidence*, 2007 107
Steve McQueen, *Shame*, 2011 (Michael Fassbender) 126
Steve McQueen, *Shame*, 2011 (Carey Mulligan) 128
Steve McQueen, *Shame*, 2011 (Michael Fassbender) 128
Steve McQueen, *Shame*, 2011 (Michael Fassbender) 129
Steve McQueen, *Shame*, 2011 (Michael Fassbender) 129
Steve McQueen, *Shame*, 2011 (Michael Fassbender, Deedee Luxe) 130
Steve McQueen, *Shame*, 2011 (Michael Fassbender) 131
Steve McQueen, *Shame*, 2011 (Michael Fassbender) 131
Steve McQueen, *Shame*, 2011 (Michael Fassbender) 137
Steve McQueen, *Hunger*, 2008 (Michael Fassbender) 137
Anne Teresa de Keersmaeker, *Work/Travail/Arbeid*, 2015 (Marie Goudot), Wiels, 2015 158
Anne Teresa de Keersmaeker, *Vortex Temporum*, 2013 (Cynthia Loemij, Carlos Garbin) 159
Anne Teresa de Keersmaeker, *Work/Travail/Arbeid*, 2015 (Marie Goudot, Boštjan Antončič), Museum of Modern Art, 2017 160
Anne Teresa de Keersmaeker, drawing of a floor pattern with names of the dancers assigned to pentagon circles for *Work/Travail/Arbeid*, 2015 160
Anne Teresa de Keersmaeker, *Work/Travail/Arbeid*, 2015 (Bryana Fritz), Wiels, 2015 161
Anne Teresa de Keersmaeker, *Work/Travail/Arbeid*, 2015 (Cynthia Loemij, Marie Goudot), Wiels, 2015 163

Anne Teresa de Keersmaeker, *Work/Travail/Arbeid*, 2015 (Carlos Garbin, Cynthia Loemij, Marie Goudot, Boštjan Antončič), Museum of Modern Art, 2017 163
Anne Teresa de Keersmaeker, *Vortex Temporum*, 2013 (Cynthia Loemij, Georges-Elie Octors, Marie Goudot, Jean-Luc Plouvier, Michaël Pomero, Boštjan Antončič, Dirk Descheemaeker) 165
Anne Teresa de Keersmaeker, *Work/Travail/Arbeid*, 2015 (Marie Goudot, Samantha van Wissen), Museum of Modern Art, 2017 168
Anne Teresa de Keersmaeker, *Work/Travail/Arbeid*, 2015 (Jean-Luc Plouvier, Carlos Garbin), Tate Modern 170
Anne Teresa de Keersmaeker, *Work/Travail/Arbeid*, 2015 (Jean-Luc Plouvier, Carlos Garbin), Museum of Modern Art, 2017 171
Yvonne Rainer, *The Concept of Dust, or How do you look when there's nothing left to move?*, 2015 (David Thomson, Yvonne Rainer, Emmanuèle Phuon, Keith Sabado, Patricia Hoffbauer, Pat Catterson), Museum of Modern Art, 2015 180
Yvonne Rainer, *The Concept of Dust, or How do you look when there's nothing left to move?*, 2015 (Yvonne Rainer, Patricia Hoffbauer, Pat Catterson), Museum of Modern Art, 2015 181
Yvonne Rainer, *The Concept of Dust, or How do you look when there's nothing left to move?*, 2015 (Emmanuèle Phuon, Patricia Hoffbauer, David Thomson, Yvonne Rainer), Museum of Modern Art, 2015 184
Yvonne Rainer, *The Concept of Dust, or How do you look when there's nothing left to move?*, 2015 (Pat Catterson, Patricia Hoffbauer, Keith Sabado, David Thomson), Museum of Modern Art, 2015 185
Jacques Tati, *Playtime*, 1967 185
Yvonne Rainer, *The Concept of Dust, or How do you look when there's nothing left to move?*, 2015 (Yvonne Rainer, Keith Sabado, Patricia Hoffbauer, David Thomson, Pat Catterson), Museum of Modern Art, 2015 188

Introduction

When I was writing my first book, on Marcel Broodthaers, the artist's widow asked that I delete one phrase from the text, and that phrase was "the subject." I had to laugh: she was both out of line and completely correct. What was this "subject" that stood in for so much? What kind of work was it doing? If it went away, what would I use in its place? I have never forgotten this little trial, and questions raised by her demand have informed much of the discussion that follows. However, this book is not about semantics, nor is it about doing away with "the subject." It is about ideas of interiority and oneness that persevere despite their displacement by theories of subjecthood. It begins with the simple observation that while standard narratives of postmodernism may have occluded art's role as a vehicle for experiences of selfhood—from roughly the 1960s through the 1990s—a number of artists have returned to that project.[1] I have written it in the hope we can learn from these works about how to think more perceptively and generously about interiority, about our separation from one another as individuated beings, and about how we relate to each other in spite of or perhaps through both interiority and separateness. This book assumes that what we can know best about this promissory concept of the self is what we expect and want from it—and how it deceives or disappoints us—rather than what "it" is.

The term "self" opens up all kinds of questions about both the subject and the self. "Selfhood" defers to an inkling that subjecthood, as it has been described by theorists and philosophers, leaves remainders: ideas or fantasies of uniqueness, interiority, and even the boundedness of our separate and separable selves. These remainders, or what is left "for us" by our construction as subjects, are what I refer to as the "self." Theories of structure and the subject have not eradicated these ideas and fantasies. Recent turns—for example, to and away from affect theory, as with ongoing investigations into the interior lives of those whose subjectivity has been denied—provide some evidence that these remainders are persistent.[2] This persistence raises the question: What *are* selves in light of our attachment to questions of identity, alterity, and historical memory? Or, closer to what can be addressed in the present project: What relations can art disclose about separability, interiority, and uniqueness, given the ways that reproductive structures produce and erase us as subjects?

Each One Another responds to a sense that those interior lives that feel like they are *each our own*—possessed by each of us—are a part of what makes us separate from *one another*. It answers a sense that we live inside our heads, where we talk to ourselves in a kind of primordial, endless back-and-forth. It responds to the injunctions to relate to another, or others, by placing that right to silence (which has been a tactic of civil disobedience practitioners) inside relations between intimates. It tries to get at questions of oneness and separateness through our ideas of unity. It looks to the ways our shell-like bodies can be pierced or made apparent to us through aesthetic experience—rather than by allowing those questions to rest on structural frameworks. And it tries to examine the transitory movement between selves that takes place as we shift between the many intersecting and simultaneous roles we are assigned or solicit. It is, in other words, about the sense—which we get from living in our heads—that we are *each one another*.

Theories of the subject remind us that we are perpetually inside reproductive structures: social and economic classes; racialized, colonial, and imperial fictions; constructs of gender and sexuality; "family romances." Here I want to complement the work of addressing structural violence that those theories undertake by focusing on the shared sense that we are each our own story, or as the philosophers Judith Butler and Adriana Cavarero have put it, our own "account" or "narrative." Yet this is not an argument about escaping those structures. Instead I am interested in getting at what selfhood might consist in, by thinking about the work done with paint, video and sound, and dance—work that is largely outside our self-accounts or -narratives (as writers such as Butler and Cavarero consider them). Even when language is involved, I am more interested in the form through which we encounter that language—the form of the soliloquy, or the conversation inside an actor's "head" that we encounter through our own shell-like bodies—than the account itself. I am also interested in how a film uses chromatic, sonic, and perspectival interruptions to that shell-like exterior through which we receive our apparently innate sense of being "one." These aesthetic inventions, for me, are key to understanding and generating the silences or refusals to *account for* that can constitute intimate and public politics.

While such aesthetic possibilities are lodged in techniques unavailable to us in the course of our ordinary day-to-day, they point us back toward quotidian experiences that are often so mundane as to be utterly sublimated. For example: in identifying oneness with bounded shapes, we each see ourselves as *one*. What can shape in paintings tell us about this state of oneness? How can we think more complexly about our own perceived oneness? Can we shift how that oneness operates by looking at how painted shapes contend with their own boundaries, their interactions with other elements in painting, and their displacements, fragmentations, multiplications, and reappearances? What about the ways that shapes not only signify (a sphere looking like an apple, for example) but suggest qualities—like the abjection of a droop or the perkiness of an upward-pointing tip?

Finally: every time we watch dancers perform, we are watching them step temporarily into roles—formal, lasting choreographic patterns in time and space. Can we use the vehicular form of the role to rethink both our attachments to oneness and our relations to one another—even to masses of others? To underline and revalue the transitory processes through which we are constantly shifting? By considering the forms that art brings to these questions—shape in painting, character in moving images, and role in dance—I want to complicate ideas of oneness, interiority, and distinctness, showing how artists cleave open the ways we see ourselves. Inside these refractions of our assumptions about the self lie unexamined processes that are quite different from those addressed in analyses of subjecthood.

In the 1970s and '80s, as artists launched into "postmodernism" and its conceptions of the subject, Bernard Williams and Charles Taylor published *Problems of the Self* and *Sources of the Self*, respectively. Both chose to short-shrift then-ascendant theories of subjecthood and instead exhibited deep attachments to philosophical questions and histories predating the 1960s. Taylor, for example, proposes historical arguments underpinning the notion that "we have to determine our place in relation to the good," while Williams reaches such moral and political questions as whether "everyone ought exclusively to pursue his [*sic*] own interests" only after shifting through logical arguments about the conceivability of a singular individual.[3] While the former seeks frameworks open to theisms and other "non-anthropocentric good," the latter, utterly anthropocentric in focus, is concerned with questions of identity that rest entirely with an idea of "a peculiar sense in which a man is conscious of his own identity"—albeit an identity based in a presocial and prepolitical sense of self.[4] These works of moral philosophy and intellectual history present a kind of counterweight to the psychoanalytic references to selfhood one finds in the vivid, sophisticated writings of Leo Bersani, Christopher Bollas, and Adam Phillips. In Bersani and Phillips's text on barebacking, for example, we find an almost ecstatic reach for "self-divestiture" and "self-expansiveness" as possibilities opened to subjects entered into a regime of "pure love" and quasi-mystical surrender.[5] Or, in Bollas, a more traditional description of the therapeutic process as one of recovering the self become object *to itself*: "The patient can now occupy that position that the analyst has been occupying; the analysand can now receive his own discourse. . . . The discourse is now uttered to an internal other, that other constituted in the patient through identification with the function and psychosomatic trace of the analyst."[6] Though the terms frequently seem interchangeable, Bollas uses "subject" to describe the patient in the therapeutic process and "self" to imagine the possibilities opened to the patient through analysis.[7] Thus does the self occasionally persist within psychoanalytic discourse as a conception of individuated being that is held by the subject even as the subject apprehends its development qua subject. It is from that standpoint—albeit without the armature of psychoanalytic theory itself—that I depart.[8]

Most relevant to this project instead are the recent works by Butler and Cavarero that take up the rhetoric of the "self" without necessarily accounting for how that self differs from the subject that grounds feminist philosophy more broadly (including Butler's vastly important earlier work). I address Cavarero's and Butler's work in the second part of this book, on moving images and characters, where I shift away from their framing of selfhood in the ethics of a face-to-face encounter. First of all, art history gives us more complex ways to consider the extra-linguistic dynamic of that encounter. Moreover, art (as usual) gives us license to rebel against many immediately available moral and political precepts: a sense of self that is grounded in an experience that offers itself as *other* than that ruled by the norms (or even ideals) of social life seems to me to be worth examining.[9] It is the possibility of reaching an understanding of what the self can be constituted in—lying outside dialogue and linguistic "accounting"—that interests me. Put another way: it is the way that the promissory nature of art combines with the promissory nature of the self that fascinates me and drives this investigation.

As early as 1980, Julia Kristeva pointed out that what is externalized by the subject becomes the constant challenger to that subject and its claims to separateness and indeed separability, its "borders" and boundaries. What she names "the abject" is internalized by the subject and enacted in its very *ideas* of the divide or border between the external and the internal ("I expel *myself*, I spit *myself out* . . . within the same motion through which 'I' claim to establish *myself*"[10]). This book begins, alongside Kristeva, with the notion of separability as it is constituted in ideas of unity. A perceptible unity, whether it appears to us as melody or object of vision, appears to *take shape*. Its very existence as a unity is defined by its edges, or the simple fact that it appears to have edges—a beginning and an end or, as Kristeva would put it, a marked absence of formlessness. Studying the bounded object at its most basic—as literal shape—I look at how these shapes present as analogues to a self. A triangle that loses one corner is no longer the same shape it was before the corner went missing. This logic recurs in the discourse of the subject. Once I perceive myself as the effect of structures beyond myself, I become heterogeneous to myself as a pregiven unity. In the world of structures, holisms are suspect, and yet the subject's "remainder" is a given. In this book, I am not interested in restituting wholeness to the self. Nor is the point to regress to ideas of selfhood that predate or pretend to dismantle theories of the subject. It is instead the very framework of holisms and boundaries that are the materials and objects of my investigation. They are the vehicles through which we can understand uniqueness and substitutability, separability and collectivity, and even the way that interiority relates to structures that seem to threaten the autonomy of "one's" self—all the while lying "outside" it *in order to* constitute it from without.

These concepts—between the sensing self and the idea of that which lies beyond it, and related ideas of interiority and separability, uniqueness and replaceability—are explored in each of the three parts of this book. In the first section, on shapes, I address how two painters explore shapes and wholeness. Shapes' wholeness, I argue, can mitigate the acts of reference that shapes often enact—especially in painting, where those acts of reference often seem to distinguish abstraction from figuration. For example, I argue that the shapes in Philip Guston's late works often overpower references to mere objects and to history. Consider his figures that are alternately Klansmen, the artist himself, and various chimera. The shapes of their hoods—whether perkily alert or bathetically droopy—draw us into the framework of expressivity. Shape as such overpowers received ideas, bringing us further into history's fullness, its deeper address of *each* of us. Painting's signifying work, I argue, is stronger in that expressive fullness than in its narrations or even its reclamation of figuration. Shapes become Guston's vehicle of choice for addressing history. In the work of Amy Sillman, by contrast, painting's claims to expressivity simultaneously surface and break down as she both draws with paint (disclosing a relation to Guston) and uses printmaking procedures to break up shapes as wholes. In so doing, Sillman reframes the wholeness once ascribed to shapes as she gives the viewer a place to look simultaneously at shapes *and* at structures (of repetition and difference, and ultimately of affect and expressivity). Sillman's pictures, in other words, grant a position from which to "see" structures as well as how they produce the totalities we can see figured as shape.

Since at least the mid-twentieth century, structure has played an outsize role in our consideration of the subject or indeed its remainder in selfhood because of the ways that language and linguistics have dominated theoretical considerations of who we are. Language is the master narrative of subjecthood: some theories of the subject hold that we are produced as subjects *through* language (Lacan) or its immanent relation to ideology (Althusser). Even as such theories are critical of totality, they have nevertheless generated narratives about subject and self. I am not at all interested in resisting the substance of these theories, but in asking questions about what they sideline. For example: How do our ruminations—our interior, often silent conversations with ourselves—picture language for us? These interior monologues, after all, are at the core of theories of the subject from Rousseau to Husserl to Derrida.[11] And what of our refusals to speak out loud? When one refuses to speak, do other means of producing the self open up?

These questions turn me from shape to another figure for the self: character. As throughout this book, I proceed in twos: two successive chapters structured around two artists of successive generations whose works I believe speak to each other. In part II, "Character," I contend with two outliers among cinematic "characters." One is inside a work of art made for exhibition, where we once might not have expected to meet a narrative character. In a now-famous video installation by James Coleman featuring Harvey Keitel, the theatrical soliloquy takes center stage (literally, in a work that is almost as much about the soundstage we see as it is about a famous actor, his words, and the format—a vast, projected image with sound). The entanglement of the convention of the soliloquy—through which the actor speaks his thoughts aloud, the shell of his body becoming a kind of new "fourth wall"—with the ruins of an imperial civilization is the object of the film. It is also a lesson in how characters can reveal the self. (In this case, the character is a version of Oedipus, the ur-character of the West/North.) What does the character allow us to understand about our own "fourth wall," that divide between our interior self and the "rest" of the world, a world upon which our language is dependent? What can a character's boundaries tell us about how we relate to that "'rest' of the world"?

Similar questions about the boundedness of a character reappear in a work by Steve McQueen, whose main character refuses to tell us what we would like to understand about his interior life. In the space opened up by that refusal, the film reaches the spectator in her seat through other means. By using color filters and unexpected audio registers, McQueen makes us aware of how we are "pierced" by the work unfolding before us, particularly by our identification (or lack thereof) with the character onscreen. Chroma and sound become ways to understand how the self surmounts—or appears to surmount—the limits of our dialogic self, the one entwined with others through not only conversation but touch and sensation, apprehension of a shared world.[12] McQueen pierces our sensoria, our ears and eyes, especially as if to draw out a distinction between narrative and linguistic ways of knowing a character. The framework (film) through which dialogue and perspectival vision have become enshrined as the classic mechanism for subject production finds an escape valve that can only exist in the aesthetic realm, past the possibilities of "language" per se.

The final part of this book takes up the question of the separable and the collective self. Here, the cipher for selfhood is the role in dance. Roles are what enable a choreographer to make a dance into a formal object that can survive successive performances: a dance role can be performed by this dancer or her successors, by this dancer *or* that one. Roles can also build on an individual dancer's body or style or predilections.[13] Or, as I discuss, a role might even be built on the bounded and individuating unities (e.g., a melody or a particular rhythm) that make up a musical composition. That is the concept behind several of Anne Teresa de Keersmaeker's dances. In one titled *Work/Travail/Arbeid*, adapting her 2013 dance *Vortex Temporum* to a museum's spaces and rhythms, de Keersmaeker expands the scope of a dance that already takes as its subject the manner in which space and time converge in musicality. In particular, de Keersmaeker tunes her audiences' sensoria to the full spectrum of sound (rather than the integer-like distinctions between notes) at the basis of the composition. That spectrum in turn provides a basis for an array of dancers' roles, each built on a given instrument's score. These spectral differences mean that the roles themselves comment on the distinctions that exist between dancers—or rather, on the linked issues of difference and separability.

De Keersmaeker's dance allows me to circle back to the dancer-choreographer whose body of work is at the very heart of this project: Yvonne Rainer. A lecture she gave decades ago, when I was in graduate school, tuned me to the "remainder" of subjectivity that structuralist and phenomenological concepts of the subject leave behind. Since then I have wanted to address this remainder in a way that would sit alongside Rainer's films and dances, including her first narrative film, *Lives of Performers*, with its metacritique of the distinction between characters and performing subjects. Frankly it is impossible to think of Rainer's work as if it were simply another exemplar of this book's project: her work is its substrate. It is also impossible to ignore how Rainer has continuously confronted both structuralism's romance with difference and philosophy's romance with dance. As Butler writes about the conclusion of Hegel's early essay "Love" (1797–98):

> Dance seems to give a concrete meaning to the idea of an animated and animating law. Indeed, dance seems to be singled out grammatically, evincing that moment when bodies come alive in a rule-bound way, but without precisely conforming to any law. . . . [Hegel] is trying to imagine some operation of love that goes beyond the dyad and property. . . . What Hegel seeks through the idea of animating law (or enlivening form) is something close to a dance, the dance of lovers (not presumptively dyadic), understood as a rhythm between a finite series or sequence, understood as spatially elaborated time, and what cannot be captured within its terms, the infinite.[14]

In a project on that which exceeds subjecthood—on the remainders of the overdetermination of our selves by structures and laws and history—it makes sense to end by imagining that the laws themselves become "animated," part of the life that we imagine exceeds them. In the work that ends this book, we find Rainer's dancers "doing themselves": releasing into her highly referential choreography the subtleties of highly individuated ways of moving. Yet these individuated dancers are also compellingly choreographed into groups that transcend the terms of that dancerly individuation I have described as roles. If individuation has long been indissociable from the manner in which property relations deform our living relations to one another, then it is Rainer's genius to transform dance—such an enshrined cultural "escape" from those social relations—into a form of work that reimagines collectivity and relationality.

It should be clear by now that just as a section on shapes asks questions about when a shape becomes quasi-characterological, full of totalizing meaning, a section on roles also asks questions about when a role starts to take on characterological dimension. Roles are built—as I explain—on shapes both physiological and melodic: shapes can recur in a dancer's body and in our ears, sometimes simultaneously. In other words, figures for the self constantly cross into one another, infusing each other despite the "medium-specific" logic through which they appear in this book. I try not only to extend one argument across these medium-specific sections but to show how each artist complicates the boundaries of her medium. Through Guston's reliance on comics in his late, figurative painting and their incursions on painterly "space," painting as a singular, privileged practice is diffused. Same with Sillman's extraordinary investment in printmaking and drawing as complications within and without painting. Artists' films already encompass and absorb ways that theater and narrative film present bodies onscreen as characters. Those studied here use characters as only one form of evidence of how a moving image treats the bounded, physical, and psychic entities in the audience, interrupting narrative reliance on the characterological "whole" with effects of scenery, chroma, and sound that remind us of film's roots in spectacle. Dance seems wedded to musical reinventions of the "whole" such as melody or rhythm. But dance is also dependent on dancers' bodies. Dance work argues with the primordial space-time of performance just as it argues with its own notational, historically, and spatially transcendent modes of figuring composition. It is an art form with a capacity to wonder how a given entity (a composition, a role) can supersede instances of performance or indeed the individuality of performers. New forms of collectives can be imagined by a dance invested in the formal rigor of roles, just as they can arise in response to musical compositions that argue with how musical scales create and reflect integer-like notions of individuality. We need not melt away the boundaries of a medium to get at what it offers to our thought and pleasure, but we do need to think constructively about boundaries themselves.

Finally, a complicating theme throughout this book is the question of history, which I explore through the notion of modes. I borrow this term from Northrop Frye, who, more than a half century ago, proposed as the subject of his "First Essay" (subtitled "Historical Criticism: Theory of Modes") a discussion of "Fictional Modes," "Tragic Modes," "Comic Modes," and "Thematic Modes." His goal was to counter the ways in which criticism attaches itself to "one of a miscellany of frameworks outside" literature. Frye was on a warpath against what he perceived as a takeover of criticism by concerns and expertise belonging to "theology, philosophy, politics, science, or any combination of these."[15] For me, hybridity is a precondition for thought and work, but I too am attached to the idea that forms of art offer modes of knowing distinct from other modes of experience even as they cross-pollinate. For Frye, these modes of knowing are innately historical, and despite his denial of his own historical moment (and the conditions for art making), I agree with that precept. In the following pages, I turn to the tragic and also to two modes that are left out of Frye's analysis—the tragicomic and the melodramatic. For me, all three modes allow us to understand how contemporary artists position the self in a shared present. Modes not only hypostatize what is most convention-borne about art—how art relies on its own habits and practices—but show us how figures of selfhood are threaded through experiences that belong to a viewership that is both collective and historical. We can only see "through" a lens loosely defined through our historical moment, but artworks have the capacity to name what is unnamable in that moment. Also: through modes we see not only with reference to the singular self but also with reference to others who we know join us in a mode of seeing—who laugh with us, for example, or join us in tragicomic despair. A mode like the tragicomic signifies a kind of gravesite for other forms of collectivity; it marks the end of the tragic hero who can be seen as such "by all." But in so doing it does not answer whether the self can supersede its investment in its own singularity or uniqueness or interiority to become collective: it merely provides that horizon of collectivity to which all selves are ultimately tied.

I

Shape

I'm old!
I'm old and I'm sad!
I'm old and I'm sad!
And that sadness has a shape!

SARAH MICHELSON

As the choreographer and dancer Sarah Michelson repeats "And that sadness has a shape!" she is herself making a shape.[1] She makes it not only out of her body but out of our—her audiences'—placement in her performance space; out of the repetition of her pose and those lines; and out of the relation between those spoken—*yelled*—lines and the shape of her body. She doesn't say those lines just once in her work *May 2018 /*; she says them again and again. Each time, she makes a shape out of her body: the same shape time after time, bending at the hips so that she is in a pronounced sideways L, glaring back at the part of the audience—sitting on mushroom-shaped stools scattered around the performance space—who are behind her. In other words, her sadness may have "a" shape, but it's a very specific one, repeated, unvarying, and connected to our position in her space, listening to her words.

Her shout underscores her insolent posture to make a kind of cartoonish, exaggerated L shape rife with potent affective qualities: angry and sad, wry and reckless, despairing and desirous. Above all, it is performed very explicitly *for us*, her audience, in this anniversary performance in a space she's worked in before.[2] Her vindictive, furious pseudobirthday speech enacts part of the claim she's shouting, identifying the literal shape of her body with the metaphorical shape of her sadness. But when she claims she's "old and sad" and bends over, the shape of her body totals those claims and makes them look suddenly, insolently, powerfully sexy. The reflexiveness of this gesture—in which she watches us watch her bend over—tells us everything about how shape works. Shape here is not a one-way street, a mere "gestalt," but a conscious, even complex maneuver of concept, viewer, line, body, and everything that gives that line *sense*: the sexy configuration of performer and audience, the volleyed weight of "I'm old and I'm sad!," the persona of that choreographer-performer, the shout itself.

Michelson in these moments is behaving like a figure in a comic strip whose exaggerated contours perform an affective and situational idea. Such an idea, in the comics, takes graphic form by absorbing into itself relations to the space it is in; whether the objects shown are telegraphically "zoomed into," part of a neomythical or fantastical landscape or simply part of a conventionally represented landscape. Through such spatial maneuvers, the comics form takes into account the space occupied by its viewer and the relation between graphics and text and the "common place" between them that is generated by an acknowledgment of the viewer's readerly attention. Michelson similarly exploits our focalized attention, our embeddedness in a shared space, and our linguistic responsiveness in order to telegraph ideas about shape and subjectivity. The latter—the conditions that our attentiveness, physical embeddedness, and language provide to our experience—are managed inside a hypothesis about the former. Or, more provocatively (and more usefully, for our purposes): the former—shape's capacity to define our attention, to embed our presence within a spatial dynamic, to re-form our relation to affective statements like "I'm sad" or the implied yet incontrovertible sexiness with which "her" sadness is defined—tells us something about subjectivity. In Michelson's work, the particular subjectivity being considered is not only "hers" ("I'm old and I'm sad!"), but that implied by an artist's return to a space marked by the transformation of Manhattan's Lower East Side and, indeed, an entire city whose management of sexuality has become both emancipatory and grimly reifying.[3] In other words, the subjectivity that is both on display and "our own," in this performance, is both historically conditioned *and* known intimately, or interiorized. "I'm old and I'm sad" is one thing; once she can say "And that sadness has a shape!" the relation between interiority and shape opens up. Would *we* recognize the shape of her sadness? Is it the same as our own? What relation does shape have to intimacy, to expression, to publicness? In short: what is the relation between her feeling, which we understand through the term "sad," and shape?

Shapes appear self-defining, constituted as entireties unto themselves. But in fact, like other signs, they are constituted through difference and likeness: *this* circle is not (or is not identical to) *that* one. (We arrive at the question of two or more identical shapes in the next chapter.) A triangle is different from a circle, and this triangle, with its acute angle, is different from that one, with its obtuse angle. However, shapes, especially those we find in works of art—that is, those shapes that have been formed by people rather than resulting from biological or mathematical laws—can seem to already hold their meanings, whether or not they are referential. A given shape will strike a viewer as having or even *totalizing* its meaning: it rounds or sags or sits straight up. It balloons weightlessly or slumps heavily. Inside these narrow ranges of meaning, shape can convey even without communicating directly what a given shape "is": shapes can produce a sense or feeling about themselves on an intuitive level, one that seems to address their viewers at a level of interiority that is the subject of this section. They can do so without reference, and to me, this is what is most interesting about shapes. They seem to address the perceptive, intuitive, interior self without even naming a shared idea like "sadness" or indeed any concrete referent. And finally, they can *stand in* for the self, to the degree that shapes rely on the ways they seem to imprint on us as wholes, as "gestalts." *This* self is not *that* self. Each one indeed separate, and *other*—aside from the seemingly identical repetitions of this or that shape.

In Amy Sillman's recent reinvention of painting through processes of printmaking, we are shown how shape can both militate against its own claims on uniqueness and disrupt the organic ways it seems to project feeling, especially insofar as feeling can appear to signify as a "whole," nuanced or otherwise, in itself.[4] Indeed, shapes in Sillman's paintings provide a prime vehicle for her to test the apparently more immediate idea that painting conveys expression or expressiveness. For a painter whose decades-long experimentation has already demonstrated the affective possibilities of shape, Sillman's recent work is most striking for the ways it complicates both the sense that *that sadness* [or lustfulness or rage or . . .] *has a shape* and the idea that a shape must be singular to be expressive.

In her investigation into the expressivity of shape and the effects that printmaking can have on "singular" shape, shapes constituted in their difference from one another, Sillman upends the linear ways that we understand expressivity to work. Rather than understanding expression as a straight line from the artist-communicator onto the canvas or paper and into the room in which the work is shown (and the bodies within), her recent works derive their force from the processes by which the shapes are divided, multiplied, fragmented, repeated, and layered. The fact that she is able to generate a sense of affective force from within this overdetermining process shows us that shapes are less dependent on their oneness, their singularity and wholeness, than they might at first appear. In her hands, they confront the structuralist approach to meaning and its reliance on difference. Shape becomes a function of repetition and reinscription, dismantling and deformation. By investing painting with printmaking's complexity, Sillman points to the archived manner in which emotionality and affect are marshaled to "manage the ongoing present," as Lauren Berlant has described.[5]

Philip Guston's work on shape takes a different tack, with a similar—if more overt—attention to his own (and his paintings') historical conditions. By making his late, figurative painting fundamentally about the expressivity of shape, he revises what figuration does in history painting. We are consumed not merely with scene, iconography, and figure but with the totalizing ways that a shape amalgamates and conveys sensory information. In this way, his late shapes operate in a very different way from signs—or at least, differently from how structuralism has taught us that signs operate. Rather than gaining their meaning through their differences from one another, Guston's shapes often multiply across a canvas as a sea of bobbing balloon heads or a rumpus of right-angled knees. In his huge shape panoramas of the late 1970s but also in his earlier, small paintings of "common objects," Guston's shapes operate through increases in number, in degrees of meaning, and ultimately, through intensification.[6] In the study of logic, "intension" is the set of attributes belonging to all and only those things to which the given term is applied; it is also the "formal distinctness" with which a concept lets itself be understood *through* those attributes. A particular shape, such as the bean shape of many of his heads, puckered in the middle and ballooning on two sides, gains "intension" by becoming the connotatively rich dimension of a human head that is so empty it balloons and puckers, its shape redefining its meaning. Not merely leading toward a figural or tropological expansion of the term "head," which would aim for a hermeneutics of truth and cognition ("this is what heads are"), shapes intensify in order to overcome the singularity (or even polyvalence) of meaning. A head shape that is balloningly empty is no longer merely about "heads" but about how we see shapes. Shapes thereby argue that painting can describe a situation beyond reference, even when—as in Guston's case—they are figurative.

Shapes, Guston shows us, work the intensional over and above even the recognizability of certain figures: in his late paintings, Klansmen and corpses are recognizable, but it is the baffled hollowness of their tipped-back, stiffened, conical hoods that gives us a sense of the historical conditions Guston painted. It is those conditions that he was painting, rather than merely the scenes of his time. Toward the end of my chapter on Guston, I explore the genre through which I think his shapes demand to be read. Tragicomedy reminds us that the tragic (genocide, apocalypse, murder) does not survive its repetition intact; as it slowly dawns on us that we have been here before, we realize our own pathetic, denuded state. No longer "full subjects," we are left with no more than the "recognition of the fact that the tragic is ultimately but a mask of the really miserable, a mask that cannot survive its own repetition."[7] That repetitiveness that we witness across his late paintings—in the piles of corpse legs or shoe soles, the flotsam of heads floating at sea—is about a condition of subjecthood that is deprived of any kind of immediate relation to history and thus rooted, inextricably, within "the really miserable." It is with us still as it was with him *again*.

In this section, I am specifically interested in exploring how shapes both avow and disavow that highly subjective sense by which we might understand a circle to droop with some kind of expressiveness or significance, some kind of weighty unhappiness, for example. When shapes become signifying in Guston's painting—when rectangles become mordantly plank-like or circles bob insouciantly because of the ways they are painted—they do so by joining shapehood to other pictorial aspects: textures, weight, solidity, color. They need not signify representationally to do this (the rectangle need not become a gravestone), but they need to pull *on* the effort of representation, its connotative or intensive depths. Getting us into the question of those depths is a question of both expressivity in painting and the rules of painting, and that is where Sillman joins our story. As so many painters had already demonstrated by 1910, painting that tends toward abstraction is composed of shapes and their ambiguity regarding representation: shapes perform for the sake of compositional issues as well as toward representation. Sometimes a shape will inhabit an expressive idea of "feeling" and perform structural work to reference objects in the world, even as it draws our attention to the architectonics of a picture and whatever other formal projects are at hand. The hard outlines around many of Gabriele Münter's shapes in her portraits—*Portrait of a Young Woman* (1909) for instance—show us shapes entering bilateral symmetries and improbable architectures. They are part of compositional systems as well as referential ones, chromatic and planar systems as well as figural ones. A suspicion that this is true of Expressionists in general leads me to a discussion of Expressionisms (including Neo-Expressionism) in my chapter on Sillman.

A painter like Sillman, however, is interested in the ways that painting can be interfered with by what might seem like extrapainterly procedures. The medium that provides us with perhaps the most straightforward

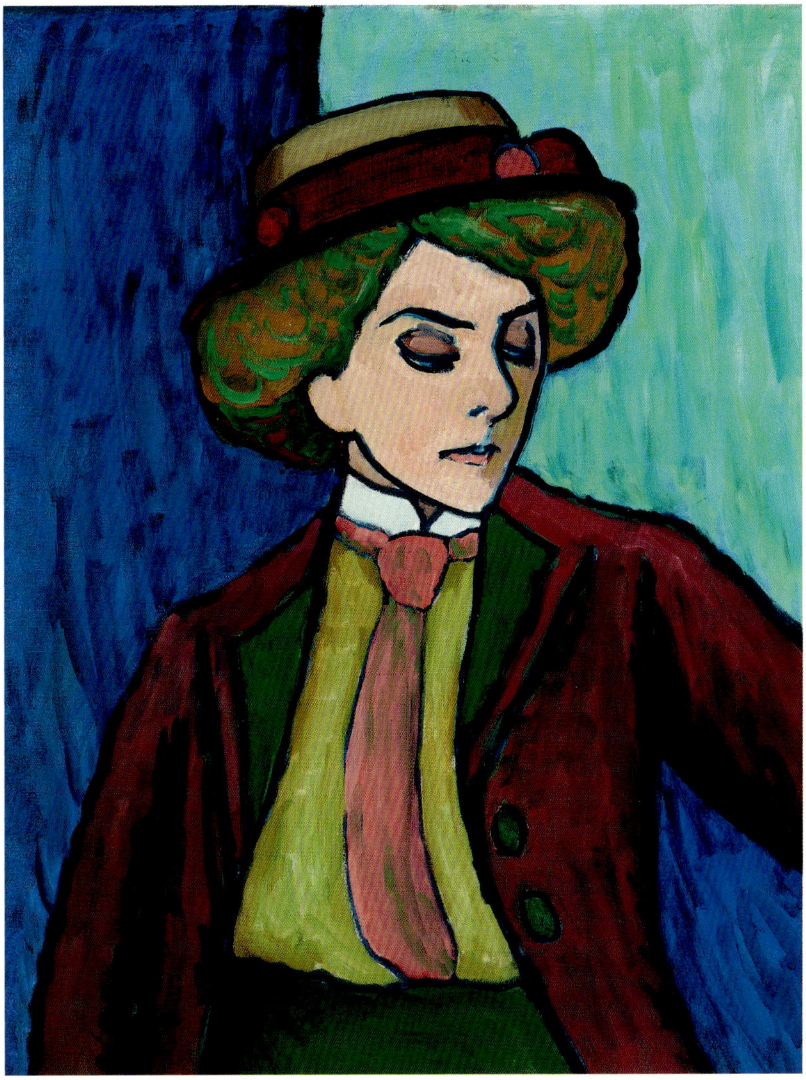

Gabriele Münter (German, 1877–1962), *Portrait of a Young Woman (Bildnis einer jungen Dame)*, 1909. Oil on canvas, 27 × 19 in. (70.17 × 48.26 cm). Milwaukee Art Museum, gift of Mrs. Harry Lynde Bradley, M1966.164. Photo: John R. Glembin. © Artists Rights Society, New York / VG Bild-Kunst, Bonn.

demonstration of shape's primordiality is collage. A circle, cut out and pasted—missing and possibly presented anew—shows the way that collage works as a system (cut and paste; repeat). It also shows us the first and second properties of shapes: unity (a shape is defined by its own edges, its oneness) and transposability. In cutting out shapes, possibly leaving their negatives behind and/or possibly placing the missing shape on the paper or other surface, collage allows shapes to produce effects of repetition, displacement, reproducibility, and absence. In Sillman's experiments with collage and, therefore, with shape, unity is foregrounded. By extension, so are the rhythms and ramifications of processes of transposition and disappearance. In her works that use and build off collage and even printmaking procedures, Sillman attacks the totalizing unity of shape and only returns it as such, dismantled, to painting, where such unities are usually immanent. (In a painting, a shape cannot be dissociated from the space around it, the textures and colors that set it off, its relation to other shapes, etc.) Guston, in his moment, shows us that it is shape's capacity to become totalizing—demonstrating the affective force of whatever bloats it, tips it over—that allows it to gain a connotative or even characterological depth or richness. Sillman's dismantling of its capacity to become a totalizing unity shows us from where that depth and richness emerge.

The idea of a correlation between a self and a shape was in force in the American mid-century, when Gestalt theory gave a kind of prima facie idea of shapehood: a shape is what imprints itself as a whole on our minds. Gestalt formalized the relation between the subject and object as a relation between two *wholes*, yet it did not account for the ways we have come to understand the subject as fragmented, or indeed, as deploying its own fictive unity in order to make other systems such as gender, race, or capital cohere. Gestalt theory, even when it began to try to accommodate complexly developed subjects, could not concern itself with what "motivates" the subject's relation to an object; it had to stay true to both the object's and the subject's constitutions as single wholes.[8] From there came the theory's limits and its irrelevance to the conception of fragmented or internally multiple subjects.[9] I depart from an interest in that very threshold, where shapes assert themselves as unified, and yet we are enjoined to understand what happens to a nonunified subject. The self operates as the repository of the subject's fantasies and working fictions—fantasies of unity, of the immediacy and authenticity of felt and expressed emotional states, for example. Shapes are a way to get *at* the unity of the self, to figure out something more about what it relies on, from its ideas of distinctness and separateness to its capacity as a vehicle for emotions and expression. If Gestalt made a double intervention—once into the field of psychology and a second time into the field of aesthetics—then aesthetic production, at least from the 1960s forward, has responded in ways that enable new manners of thinking through how shapehood relates to the self.

But I also, in the second part of this section, invert this logic in order to better understand how shapes tell us about the alleged difference between self and subject through what appears to be their opposite: formlessness. For if formlessness appears as the opposite of shapes, it is also that which demonstrates that the subject is both dependent on that formless "excess" and to a large degree overdetermined by it. Julia Kristeva and Judith Butler have both assigned the notion of formlessness to that which lies outside the subject in the structures that generate subjects. Kristeva, in her 1980 *Pouvoirs de l'horreur*, defines the abject as that which looms both within and beyond the subject and participates in—is in fact the excess *of*—the same master/slave dialectic that produces the subject.[10] Butler, in *Bodies That Matter*, reminds us that "the construction of the human is a differential operation that produces the more and the less 'human,' the inhuman, the humanly unthinkable. These excluded sites come to bound the 'human' as its constitutive outside, and to haunt those boundaries as the persistent possibility of their disruption and rearticulation."[11] Shape is particularly interesting because it seems to be the opposite of formlessness or failures of articulation. And because shape also has a seemingly inherent relation to interiority—think of (discredited) Rorschach tests, for example, or of the idea of the "expressive" shapes mentioned above—it seems to correlate only to formed subjects, not to the formless. In other words, shape, as a category of articulated forms, seems to reject all that is formless within the subject as well as on the pictorial surface.

In fact, as I'll argue, enhanced understanding of shape developed in this section might help us rethink how formlessness can describe that which lies outside the category of the subject, or that which makes up the category of subjects deemed nonsubjects.[12] As many recent theories ask: What of "interiority" can survive the crumbling of a distinction between the self and the formless—that state of abjection into which so many of us tumble or find ourselves permanently buried?[13] On another, aesthetic plane: the relation of shape to formlessness dips into something else, the *expressivity* of the formless. Consider the gestural Abstract Expressionist painting (such as that which Guston abandoned in his return to figuration) and its declared repudiation of closed forms—that is, shapes that entail powerful and sometimes overdetermining outlines. Thinking about shape and formlessness together invites us to consider how the frameworks of expressivity and formlessness might stand in for "feeling" or indeed the haunting of the subject/nonsubject. Despite how the distinction between subject and nonsubject grounds many discourses (from Butler's work on gender to Afro-pessimism), ideas of selfhood persevere (for example in the works of Fred Moten and Maggie Nelson.

Still, the idea of treating shapes as individual unities or even in relation to formlessness does not quite do justice to the ways that shape relates to the self or subject. I will be using the term "unary" to describe those shapes that operate as what Heinrich Wölfflin calls "closed forms."[14] *Unary* means more than a bounded figure: in psychoanalytic theory, it describes the totalizing work of consolidation that takes place when a subject misidentifies a single trait (*einen einzigen Zug*) for the totality of an other.[15] A child, identifying as powerful a small gesture or feature of her mother, makes that feature or gesture the "unary" trait. The most famous example of unary perception is that which the male infant undergoes in the mirror stage, mistaking his mother's "lack" for her defining, terrifying feature. But the unary trait can also play into how a subject identifies as "herself": thinking of her work ethic, for example, she might allow that single trait to overwhelm her, becoming almost comically slavish to the one idea she has of her self. Not insignificantly for the discussion that follows, Walter Benjamin called the unary trait the key to comedy, and hence to characterhood generally. (According to him, it is comedy that demonstrates characterhood's "erroneous connection to . . . fate.")[16] The unary, in this discussion, describes the totalizing power of shape to sometimes name a referent but at other times to give a shape a single, "identifying" quality that I am calling characterological, for its apparent claim on qualities we recognize as subjective. Thus, shape might show an *abject* droop, a *planking* heaviness, a *ballooning* weightlessness. Its unariness may not be all that a given shape has, but it names the way our perception is drawn to that shape and its seemingly inherent characteristics.

The very possibility that shape could do that much, and that "that much" could mean something to the viewer about herself and possibly our historical condition, came to me over months of looking at Guston's late paintings. The ballooning of those idiot heads sketched in paint; the weighted oval-rectangles of so many shoe soles; the plumbing-like right-angled knobs of all those knees and elbows in his paintings of the 1970s seemed to testify to the powers of such repeated shapes to do a kind of supplemental work well beyond their referents. At the same time, the referents themselves—KKK hoods, cars, corpses, an artist's studio, a desolate exurban landscape—were emblems of a mass existence that Guston was painting as our own. One can't ignore, in those late paintings, *what* it is that he is painting: an American nightmare, haunted by images of the Kent State massacre, the Holocaust, the murders of civil rights protestors, lynchings, the persistency of the Klan and its encompassing ideological and psychic stronghold. The manner in which he paints all of this draws on both the graphic immediacy of cartoonish shapes *and* on the limits of representation as established by "abstract painting" (but equally part of its prehistory, from Titian through Turner). In canonical works like *Flatlands* or *Dawn*, vast empty swaths of brushy surface present a new kind of space for his shapes to dominate, teeter within, or perhaps collapse. Both figure and shape are crucial in these paintings, and yet they test their power against a ground that is familiar from his extensive work in highly gestural, abstract painting. In their manner of totalizing what appears to be "their own," immanent meaning—of showing us how intensively a shape can work, and substituting that intensive wholeness for the compositional "part" that a shape conventionally plays—Guston's shapes mitigate the ways that figures work, insisting that there is another dimension in which we must read them. Shapes, here, build on the signifying work that figures make possible and then build well beyond, into a sense of how we see, as if "from within" a self that knows expressivity when she sees it.

Guston's 1970s can be pictured as an America spastically dividing its attention between post–civil rights racial retrenchment, the war waged in Vietnam, and the crises of governance and public confidence that followed the collapse of Richard Nixon's administration; an America dogged by memories of the World Wars and nightmares of a nuclear holocaust: an America rejoined to absurd notions of "foundational" processes after having, in the late 1960s, flexed its embrace of the present and the just. All of these American scenes pose questions about the limits of representation: how to describe in a time following a cruelly optimistic period of change? In 1966, describing how Bertolt Brecht's drama *The Life of Galileo* put a (further) end to classical tragedy, Raymond Williams explains that "the more moved we are" by the loyalty that the character Galileo demonstrates to the ruling group that maintains him, "the more ashamed we must be."[17] For shame arises as a structure of feeling in a culture when its agents realize they are not, for example, heirs to an actual revolution. Tragedy as a classical dramatic form does not exist in the revolutionary or postrevolutionary times that Williams diagnosed as his (and Guston's) own.[18] Instead it is the commonness of tragedy, its wheeling omnipresence, which might be what allowed Guston to overspend on shape in the first place, giving his shapes a kind of awkward wholeness, letting them pull on and then almost overcome the figures they compose.

Guston gives his shapes the kind of telegraphic immediacy that comes from the comics, inside frames that zoom in and out, sometimes magnifying a simple set of shapes, sometimes repeating them manically. By drawing on comics, he erects the notion of a mass rhetoric, and even a notion of "the mass" itself. He pulls a national consciousness into his version of painterly expressivity even as he makes his shapes do things that others' do not. This is a response to both what we call shape and what I am calling the "self," that which is left "for us" by our construction as subjects (or by our understanding of how subjects operate). Understanding how shapes function as totalities—unities whose meanings can be perceived only by an interior, intuitive self—leads us toward an understanding of how selfhood operates. It is this compensatory idea of interiority that we cannot abandon, even as it calls our attention to the ways that one's interiority, that sense of "oneself" as deeply inside, is made *of* the crisis, or slow-burning catastrophe, of a collective historical lot.

Philip Guston

Late Work

> Because I am so impatient with the universalizing impulses of the modernist tradition, I am tempted to say that Kelly's purpose is to defeat the generality—the dreary impersonality—of the square. And impersonality doesn't have a chance in the vicinity of his curves and other irregular forms. These are his the way the shape of his skull and the tone of his voice are his.
>
> CARTER RATCLIFF, 2002

With these few lines, Carter Ratcliff produces one theory of shape.[1] The anaphoric, four-times-repeated "his" in the last sentence allows us to understand how Ellsworth Kelly's shapes triumph over a particular failure. That failure belongs to shape, specifically its capacity for generality and emptiness, its lack of personality, its aptitude for being kidnapped and abused by modernist boringness. Kelly's shapes, according to Ratcliff, represent *him*, and it is only through that identification that they conquer modernism's "dreary impersonality." In Ratcliff's account, Kelly's shapes *are* specificity and personality; others' squares and curves are relegated to a neutral, "universalizing" generality as well as the "impersonality" of modernism and structuralism and their implications for us all. What does it mean to lend Kelly's shape biomorphic and even biological resonance ("his skull and the tone of his voice")? In his theory of shape Ratcliff regenerates conventions of authorship that are in direct and intentional opposition to geometry and its universality. These conventions also reject that other horizon of ideas such as "the author function" that evacuate notions of style and personhood from authored works.[2] In underscoring his own antimodernist position, in which Kelly's shapes serve not modernism's "universalizing" impulses but a far more personal, even *personality-driven*, notion of shape, Ratcliff also reminds us that such empty universalism is tied to the *generic*, "the dreary impersonality of the square." Antistructuralist critique and geometric rationalism are unusually aligned in a passionate argument in which Kelly's shapes serve as an artistic signature, similar to the way some speak of "Picasso's line" or "Warhol's line." They also provide a vehicle for us to "see" artistic individuation; it is in becoming such a vehicle that Kelly's shapes anchor his artistic practice.

Ratcliff confronts the trajectory of modernist art history that has privileged a singular lineage of shapes—geometric shapes, "deductive structures," and the like—with connoisseur-style advocacy and something else. That something else is the idea that shapes might betray not only a sense of their author but the *cause of individuality itself*. That cause seems strengthened by its opposition to the postmodernist author function and its close relation, the modernist subject. For Ratcliff, Kelly's shapes point us to a notion of particularizing individuation in opposition to the "dreary . . . universalizing" world of subjects and their squares. Shapes both represent the maker-self and a sense of selfhood that riffs off shape's potential for the particular, the specific. "*His* curves," as a notion, both signifies the specificity of Kelly's "own" kinds of curves and signals a broader argument against the impersonality of curves and straight lines elsewhere.

Sometime at the beginning of the present millennium, the figures of Philip Guston's late painting—his hooded Klansmen, shoe-sole graveyards, and hairy insomniacs—became irresistible. Possibly, as I suggest, this has to do with a rhyming between our historical moment and his own. It might also result from the inevitable weakening of certain master narratives opposing, for example, Expressionism's excesses and modernism's austerity or, indeed, as in Ratcliff's peculiar couplings, poststructuralism's author functions and connoisseuring critics' formalisms.[3] Guston's modernistic, expressionistic, almost vengeful figurations are deeply invested in the figure of the author, as well as his own epoch—both of which are frequent subjects in his work of the 1970s. And it is those late, figurative paintings in particular that have been "rediscovered" by art students and art dealers, artists and art historians.[4] They have become a model for contemporary painters such as Nicole Eisenman and Amy Sillman, who in their different ways respond to his invitation to luxuriate in certain forms of painterly "badness," a deliberate wrongness they explore and politicize, appropriate and historicize.[5] More importantly for our purposes, they take seriously how his provocative, cartoonish, and often enormous late paintings reconsider and magnify complex formal issues relating to color, shape, and figuration. From the concentric rings of Eisenman's *Weeping Woman* (2007)—pinpointed blue circles inside larger eye orbitals inside a black-contoured bust—to Sillman's *Nose Job* (2014), with its interlocked green balls and whalelike shape cradled by a Gustonian pointed finger, these contemporary painters have isolated and energized the problematic of shape. That they have done so inside a "turn to figuration" or its semblances is key to their Gustonian heritage and to the challenges of confronting shape. In the next chapter I focus on how Sillman's treatment of shape develops a set of ideas about the "interior" spaces of the self and its relations to the structuralist concerns with authorship and subjectivity that Ratcliff repudiates. For Sillman, questions of interiority are an inevitable part of painting's complex legacy. She confronts them head-on and by integrating collage, drawing, and printmaking into her address of painterly shape, shows us how rich painterly investigations of interiority—understood as both "the psychological" and as a set of spatial concerns—can become.

But in this chapter on Guston I propose shape painting as a form of history painting. I focus on how shapes generate a sensitivity to the historical moment that draws on or speaks to an understanding of the self. It is through an emphatically historical frame that Guston's shapes address ideas of the self—its individuation, its separateness from others, its claims to interiority—in a way that an interpretive focus on figures and the figurative cannot. Hence this chapter's position in the text: it seeks to coax open the discourse on representation just enough to let a certain revisionary discourse on selfhood to edge in.[6] By the same token, this chapter's insistence on history should alert readers that what might otherwise seem like a purely formal category (shape) will here become something quite different.[7] In describing Guston's late, figurative painting as being about shapes—when they are so evidently picturing a bloody period of antiwar protests and civil rights, of memories and resurgences of holocaust—I am claiming that shapes in these works are edging past what representation and figuration do for painting's viewers. In returning us via formal questions to history, they make room for what can seem like the representation of "tragedy [as] a time of chaos and suffering" as well as, in Williams's key point, an understanding that the tragic is truly no more than a means to understand the "'structure of feelings' [*sic*] that condition social life."[8] And yet as they point us to the tragic as

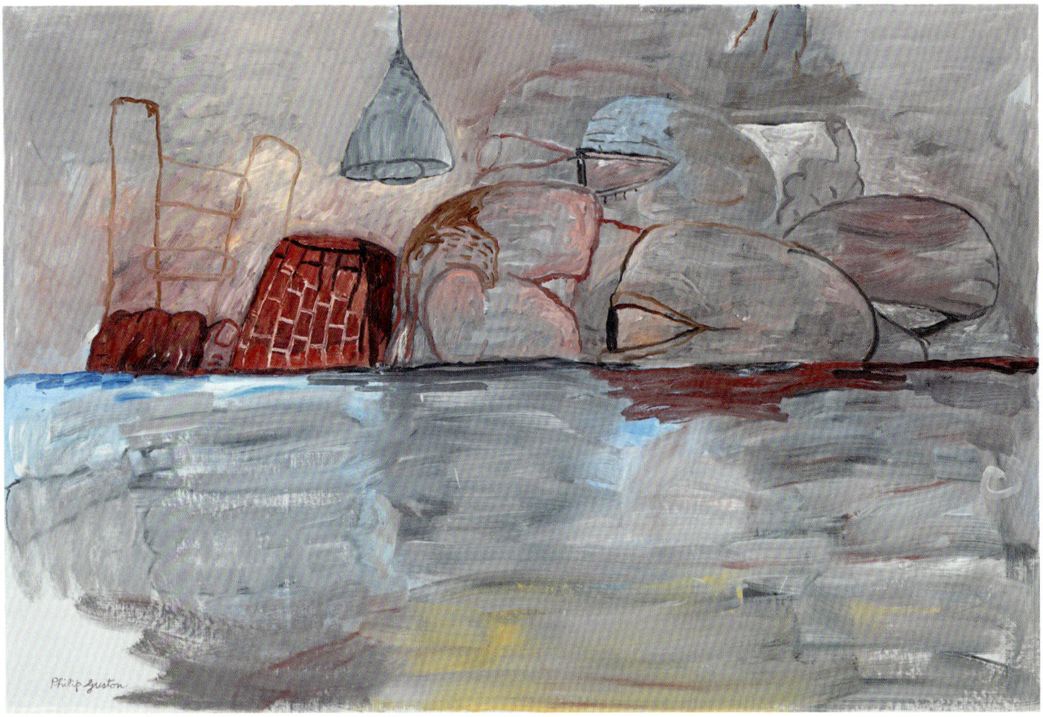

Philip Guston, *Yellow Light*, 1975. Oil on canvas, 67½ × 96¾ in. (171.4 × 245.8 cm). Promised gift of Musa Guston Mayer to the Metropolitan Museum of Art. Photo: Genevieve Hanson. © The Estate of Philip Guston, courtesy Hauser and Wirth.

a condition for getting at that "structure of feeling," they also hold up a framework of immiseration in which tragedy reveals itself, too obviously, as repetition and continuation. Not, in other words, as tragedy, but as tragicomedy. That is how Guston's paintings are comic without being funny: their tragicomedy reveals the condition for our understanding of both the world and our own structure of feeling.[9]

What does shape look like in Guston's late paintings, made in the lead-up to and after his provocative 1970 show at the Marlborough Gallery? Let us look for a moment at two very different compositions from later in the decade: 1975's *Yellow Light* and 1977's *The Coat*. *Yellow Light* is a large oil painting (171.4 × 245.7 cm), far airier than the dry, brown *The Coat* (172.7 × 200.7 cm). The "yellow light" in the former emerges from the bottom center of a silvery sea that meets, in the exact center of the canvas, a black horizon line, a rusty spillage, some leaning brick structures beneath a lamp, and a sea of heads—semitransparent, gray-pink with elements of ocher and black—across the right top quadrant of the canvas. These heads are described by their outlines as bean-shaped half circles, as they are in many of Guston's other paintings. We do not see whole heads, but monocular half profiles with unpromisingly low, flat, or absurdly convex foreheads. In the upper left is a leaning outline of an edifice, two ungainly vertical rectangles connected by two

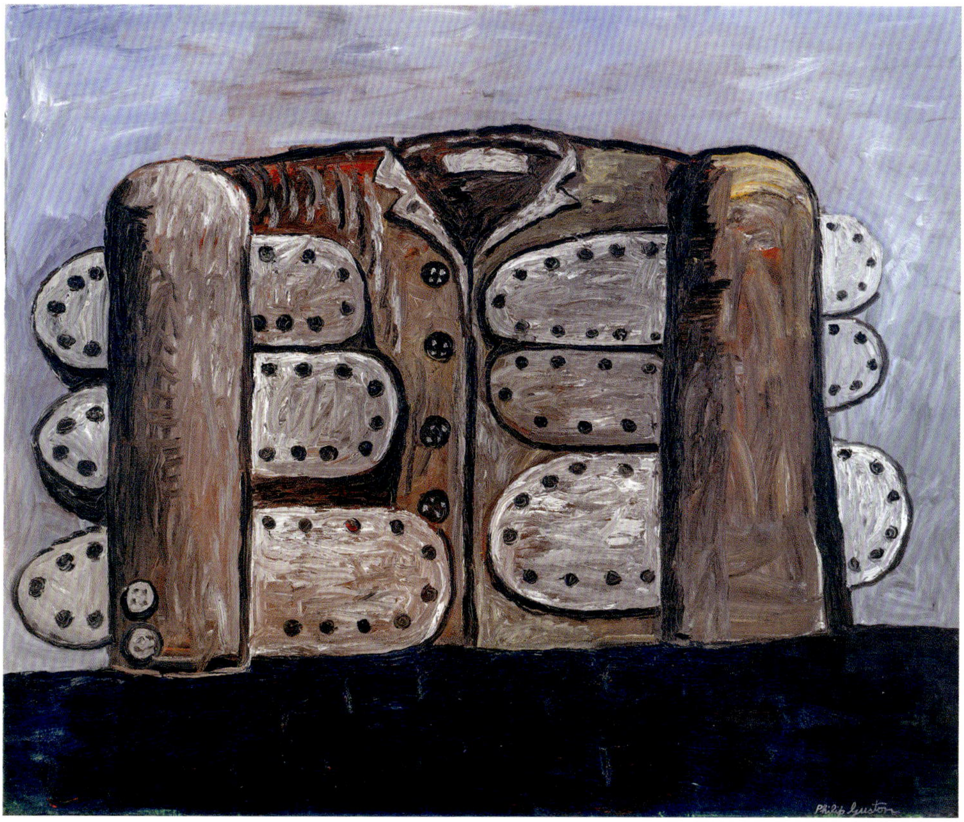

Philip Guston, *The Coat*, 1977. Oil on canvas, 68 × 79 in. (172.7 × 200.7 cm). Private collection. © The Estate of Philip Guston, courtesy Hauser and Wirth.

shorter lateral ones. In those mustardy sketches in paint lie the succinct phrasing of a question that Guston pursues throughout this painting and many others: to what extent is shape merely its own boundary or outline, and to what extent is it also everything that painting can use to fill in those outlines?

What fills in a painted shape is not just the colors inside the shape's boundaries—"his curves," as Ratcliff wrote, momentarily eclipsing how color works in Kelly's paintings. As soon as colors and brushstrokes "fill in" shapes in paintings like Guston's that pull on figurative painting's traditions, we find other elements coming into play: weight, transparency or opacity, surface texture, and so on. (Arguably, exactly the same happens in Kelly's painting, despite the evenness of their color, the opacity of the paint, the "generic" qualities he is also pouring into his painting.) Shape, in other words, has to negotiate whether it is *also* all those other aspects—the weighty gravitational sag of a collapsing edifice, like the red brick building in *Yellow Light*, for example—or whether it is just its own boundaries and outlines, the outer perimeter of any given shape, its most "neutral" or impersonal state. *Yellow Light* is a treatise on this bifurcated definition of shape: it gives us some empty shape outlines—that open, sketchy edifice on the left; on the right, another outlined head and a pointing finger—as if to test how neutral an outline can be; then fills in many other possibilities: silvery bulb heads, pendulous lamp, mounded red brick nub, and so on.

There are also other, half-erased shapes in the "sea" below the horizon line, echoing the question and perhaps allegorizing it. They raise a separate issue: to what extent is shape not only in direct relation to the sign (e.g., "head") it helps compose, but also the erasure and absence of that sign?[10] I am calling this erasure by degrees "the subfigural": that realm of suggestion that shapes draw on when we see them as one or more or even *no* "signifieds." If a sign in painting is a figure—something whose solidity as a represented entity is doubled by the painterly disclosure that this was painted for you, a figure—then it also corresponds, albeit imperfectly, to linguistic signs (head, shoe, lamp).[11] Guston's work makes explicit that this correspondence between the figural and linguistic sign is unsound. Sometimes a tablet shape looks like a painting, at other times like a thick tombstone, at other times like a half-erased rectangle. (These conflations, existential and anguished, are also often parodic, even punning lamentations: part of Guston's update to painting's constant crisis of morbidity.)[12] The relation between simple shape, "common object," and linguistic sign, as I explore below, is not a linear or clean set of relations (as was pictured, for example, by Saussure's chalkboard sketches and their selection for the publication of the *Cours de linguistique générale*).[13] An outlined shape holds more than figural possibilities: forward-facing, abject, plank-like canvas; weighty, grave, tablet-tombstone; sometimes, the partial edging-out of the object altogether, to become a ghost of a rectangle. A single shape becomes subfigural when it constitutes a figural set of meanings but resists becoming a stable signifier and possibly begins dissipating the figural action altogether.

It also registers as "subfigural" in a seemingly different situation, in which a single sign—for example, "head"—takes on various different shapes and argues with their connotative range. In *Yellow Light*, the two rightmost bean-shaped heads become translucent and weightless flotsam; just to their left, in the center of the canvas, a mustard-ocher head startles, suddenly alert, pointedly denser. With its rosy, sculptural corners, that head uses a different range of textures, weight, colors, and opacity to draw heads as a different kind of shape. Its partners to the right are outlines: loose, bendy, pneumatic. It—a sketch getting very painterly—both approaches solidity and describes how a painter gets there. But more essentially it poses the question: Is the outline or indeed the *shape* separable from its weight and solidity, or its translucency and weightlessness? How do we see a shape as an object of perception: Is it always a whole, and if so, does it always gather into itself that "other" sensorial information? *Yellow Light* lavishes attention on these questions. I follow them to ask, finally: How do these shapes themselves—*separately from figuration*—represent a quality of selfhood, a set of ideas about individuation, separateness, and wholes? What can shape deliver that figures cannot?[14] If, in particular, they are pointing to their own time as one of "chaos and suffering," can they show us the ways that social life is internalized and understood, however intuitively, as a structure of feeling? Can they even point us past that condition, to a sense of how the comedic underlines this moment we share, robbing what is truly tragic of its singularity even as it leaches oneness—a sense of discreteness—from the ongoing historical present?

In *The Coat*, a buttoned work shirt in the deep, muddy brown ineluctably associated with labor camps, faces the viewer hieratically. It is flanked by two rows of three shoe soles, each of which are themselves pinned by two pillar-like sleeves. The coat is an architecture, using shapes to describe a highly pronounced, regular symmetry. We get rhythms of long and short: bifurcated, straight-edged ovals; circles (buttons and nail holes); an empty, dark triangle at the shirt's neck. This layout is utterly frontal, built out of shapes painted in a narrow chromatic and tonal band. Everything is *a* plane, out of depth; the black band at the bottom is too desolate to be any *thing*; it is a stage. These are shapes marshaled to provide repetition, symmetry, and structure.

The Coat's shapes are united by circumnavigating lines that at times break up amateurishly, as if to show the painting's viewer how painting is connected to the work of drawing (and rather rough drawing at that). Those broken, heavy lines reinforce the empty, forward-facing hieraticism of the painting's centered and vertically stacked shapes; those lines pull *The Coat*'s shapes deeper into the world of shapes as such and further from the world of fulsome illusion. *The Coat*'s shapes insist on a space that is alien to most figurative painting: it is so frontal and totemic as to defeat its own claims on deep, recessive space. That is also how *The Coat*, with its stacks of shoe soles and paired sleeve pillars, evokes history: uneasily but with all the might of a monument. History is present in that heavily coded chromatic scale and in the painting's scale—at 177 × 200 cm or almost 6 × 6 feet, a picture that dominates the human viewer. Forcing us to step back, it pictures or enacts History, with a capital H.

But at the same time, *The Coat* allows its assemblage to maximize a kind of planarity and graphism that bespeaks another logic altogether. The coat, sleeves, and sole stacks make a rickety and punning (*sole/soul*) wall, a grouping smashed together to point explicitly at how graphic/

pictorial and linguistic/allegorical spaces coexist. As in (but very differently from) Magritte's fables, coexistence is only peaceable at a certain level of decorous explicitness ("this is a pun"); the power of Guston's shapes makes that peaceability slide right out. It is not "what" you see but how brutally and finally you see. It is these stacked and pillared, repetitive shapes that build that brutality and finality into a deafening wall silence. And also, incongruously, tragicomically, a cartoonish architecture of signs both graphic and verbal, zoomed-in-upon to giganticize what we sense has become narratively significant.

The Coat's sleeves, buttons, and shoe soles, like *Yellow Light*'s heads and lamp, relate not through narrative or allegorical compositions that are familiar to us from most history painting, nor through the kinds of abstraction that would empty such signs of their signifying load (if not their symbolic value: see Miró's existentially overflowing shape painting of the mid-1920s forward). On the contrary, what they do is to raise the possibility of a system in which "the symbolic assemblage 'speaks' for itself."[15] That is, the shapes together rest on the forced unity of the signs as a whole, which in some cases empties out their figural meanings and in others exaggerates their symbolic load. Often, Guston's late paintings do *both*, letting clocks and paintbrushes coexist in a way that points simultaneously to a kind of existential angst and to their compositional logic as sticks, circles, and planes. These "figurative" paintings describe an indifference to—or hyperbolization of—the distinction between pictorial space and linguistic space. They produce a kind of space that relies on its own ability to both figure forth symbols and empty out signs, resulting in shapes that describe their own connotative richness even as they accentuate their status qua shapes. Shapes in Guston's shape system "fill up," as it were, with the intensional impressions of morbidity or perkiness, abject collapse or wretched, ballooning emptiness, even as they represent *and* refuse the work of signs.

Guston's shapes borrow from the ways that mass-produced comics use shapes telegraphically, to volley a specific meaning as legibly and unambiguously as possible. In comics, this often happens when a sign is placed in a graphic space deprived of the illusionist details that would normally fill up a representational sign. But even while comics radically reinvent graphic space, when their panels denature illusionist spaces—for example, by zooming in on a detail, making the "background" briefly irrelevant—they do not merely turn that seemingly "abstract" space of the sign into a vacuum. On the contrary, what they do is allow the sense of general spatial fluidity to enhance the telegraphic qualities of the drawn shapes and signs. Comics not only introduce language and thought bubbles, panels and gutters, but innovate and depend on a variety of other spatial operations that negotiate the distinctions between representational space and other kinds of space. (These spaces include the protocinematic, the televisual, etc.)[16] Like Roland Barthes's understanding of myth, comics are a "second language, in which one speaks about the first [language]"—or, in the case of comics, languages.[17]

In the Barthesian system, by infusing the pseudorepresentational spaces of myth with this second order of signification, myth opposes History.[18] Myth, like comics, would have little need for a perfectly "illusionist" space, because it creates its own self-enclosing logic.[19] For Guston, such a metalanguage is precisely what history—in his moment—demands. Though *Coat* is far from the most cartoonish of Guston's paintings, some of its aspects call up the comics and illustrative work Guston did concurrently with his return to figuration. (For example: cartooning Richard Nixon and his cabinet in the series *Poor Richard* in the summer of 1971, or "illustrating" numerous books of poetry.)[20] There are the heavy-handed gestures at creases in the left-hand shoulder of the coat, evoking ways an artist like R. Crumb connotes vulgarity (cheap clothes) or overused expressions (a creased forehead). There is the coat's gigantism: taking up almost the entire frame, it instantly evokes the kind of "panel-to-panel transitions" that comics artist and scholar Scott McCloud discusses, in which the reader is either telescoped in to a single subject or detail, or oriented "from subject-to-subject while staying within a scene or idea."[21] *The Coat* shows us a coat that has become meaningful in some larger, cumulative way; it has been magnified heroically or indeed, *post*heroically.[22] To talk about Guston's shapes is to talk not only about their range of figural or subfigural meanings and the pictorial spaces they generate, but about how those pictorial spaces relate to those of comics and by extension, to those ideas about history that comics can leverage, parody, or address.[23]

Comics space relies on the recognizability of drawn signs. It also—like advertising and other instances in mass media—dramatizes their symbolic load, allowing those signs to become utterly freighted. The space that surrounds such signs uses the telegraphic economy of the cartooned line to tell us more than what a sign *is*; it tells us about how that sign behaves, how we should perceive it. "The line drawing is purely conventional symbolism," writes Ernst Gombrich, noting one particularity of comics' graphic forefather, caricature.[24] When emphasizing the power of shape by drawing a given shape one way or another (a triangle as sagging or jaunty, for example), an artist can convey shape's intensive range; its ability to give character to whatever it is figuring. This manner of making shape not only a whole but a drag on signification is Guston's crucial takeaway from comics. His shapes allow the signs in his painting to become superburdened by their own symbolic—not just representational—load, even as they emphasize their own separateness and autonomy as shapes. This move, which I describe in the psychoanalytic language of the unary, inaugurates a painting that emphasizes graphic simplicity and mythic grandiosity simultaneously. It takes painting outside its traditional spaces, toward comics and their "badness," in order to refute "figurist" conformism, which would narrow how we read space.[25] It also allows shapes to mediate the figure, or what Guston himself disdains as "the recognizable." His shapes produce a space that is not merely figurative or figural but is instead almost overwhelmingly symbolic, and additionally—as I argue in the last section of this chapter—*both* tragic and comic. Guston's painting, in the staginess of his mythographic space and his attention to low or "bad" genres, describes the havoc wreaked on the scene of representation by historical repetition.[26] Simple figuration is not the option: its dismantling has already—historically—occurred.

Massive symbolic work is taking place in *Yellow Sea* and *The Coat*: an empty work shirt, just like a sea of floating heads, invokes mass, mechanized murder. Here, repetition—bean heads, circle buttons, oval soles—evokes work and death camps as acutely as the signs themselves. But Guston's shapes both generate that meaning *and* move out of a merely signifying function. And they do so with a conscious evocation of how the look of the "low" or the "bad" refers us to the scale of the mass—mass distribution as well as mass execution. *The Coat*'s overwhelming size magnifies its explicit cartoonishness, but also its deliberate over-reliance on the cartoon and its mass audience. Its shapes fit into what Bill Berkson describes as "deliberate stubbiness and raggedy elongations common to classic comic-strip characters—traits that keep them close to the ground."[27] (*The Coat* might well evidence Guston looking at Spiegelman's *Portrait of the Artist as a Young Man* in his 1977 *Breakdowns: From Maus to Now*. That image is centered on a very different kind of shirt, elegantly opened at the neck as its dashing but exhausted wearer downs the Lichtensteinian contents of an inkwell.) The kind of intentionally amateurish, drawn-in-paint outline we find in *The Coat*, like the central, parodically masculine, ocher-colored head in *Yellow Sea*, evokes comics' adulation of "badness" not just to bring a sense of the comic into play but to demonstrate how devastating "the comic" can be.

A Brief Genealogy of Shape

Just as a shape is lodged in its distinctness from other shapes, we are lodged in our own apparent separateness from others; just as shapes coincide and proliferate—a profusion of circles or squares becoming possible at any time—we belong to multitudes. These analogies between self and shape are overdetermined by ideologies of separateness and sovereignty that are themselves historical. The European Gestaltist theories of shape, in particular, must confront other twentieth-century ideas and ideologies of the subject, including the psychoanalytic, the structuralist, and the decolonial. The implications of these other ideologies—that the subject is necessarily fragmented, overdetermined, and anything but sovereign—mean that the Gestaltist ideology, with its dependence on the idea of the *whole*, cedes territory. Yet, shapes themselves persist, demanding that we either understand them as wholes or, better, understand what their implications for holism *are*.

In his 1924 article "Gestalt Theory," Max Wertheimer lays out some of the critical foundations of Gestalt theory and its ramifications for how we think of wholes. "The fundamental 'formula' of Gestalt theory might be expressed in this way. . . . There are wholes, the behavior of which is not determined by that of their individual elements, but where the part-processes are themselves determined by the intrinsic nature of the whole. It is the hope of Gestalt theory to determine the nature of such wholes."[28] A little later he narrates the question of what he means by "wholes" in relation to musical melodies:

> Is it true that when I hear a melody I have a sum of individual tones (pieces) which constitute the primary foundation of my experience? Is not perhaps the reverse of this true? What I really have, what I hear of each individual note, what I experience at each place in the melody is *a part which is itself determined by the character of the whole*. What is given me by the melody does not arise (through the agency of any auxiliary factor) as a secondary process from the sum of the pieces as such. Instead, what takes place in each single part already depends on what the whole is.[29]

What Gestalt theory does—very emphatically in its applications to aesthetic experience—is to prioritize the notion of the whole imprinting itself on the individual. One can argue that the notion of melody presumes a notion of wholeness and that Gestalt theorists rely on the accessibility of such wholes in authored compositions in order to naturalize the concept.[30] But I am less interested in advancing an argument against Gestalt theory than in understanding how its conceptions of wholes—and by extension, shapes as wholes—produce a sense of analogy between what we observe and who we are as we observe. As Wertheimer acknowledges, "Once constituted, the Ego is a functional part of the total field. Proceeding as before we may therefore ask: What happens to the Ego as a part of the field?"[31] In other words, Gestalt theory not only argues that experience is imprinted on us through wholes that totalize their parts. It also understands that we project ourselves as wholes—each one of us an "Ego"—inside this experience. Wholeness becomes something that we share, as subjects, with the objects of our experience.

Gestalt theory becomes central to 1960s art when Robert Morris writes, in the first part of his series "Notes on Sculpture," that "certain forms do exist which . . . do not present clearly separated parts for these kinds of relations to be established in terms of shapes. Such are the simpler forms which create strong gestalt sensations. Their parts are bound together in such a way that they offer a maximum resistance to perceptual separation."[32] Though indebted to mainstream Gestalt theory, the essay goes on to presume something quite different from Wertheimer's open-ended concern for "what happens to the Ego." Describing what happens once the Gestalt is "established" (i.e., "all the information about it" is absorbed, or in his terminology, "exhausted"), Morris gestures at that familiar but indeterminate subject known as *one*: "One is then both free of the shape and bound to it. Free or released because of the exhaustion of information about it, as shape, and bound to it because it remains constant and indivisible."[33] This "one" is never defined: is it the viewer, the artist, the Gestalt subject, or another kind of idealized subject? All we know about it is the mere fact of its pseudosovereignty: that it is "bound to" and "free from" shape because shape is itself *one*, indivisible, and constantly such. Shape enters the conversation as a measure of the Gestaltist whole but also as a measure of "one," thanks to its own wholeness.

Morris was not only reading Gestalt theory, of course. The posthumous publication of Ludwig Wittgenstein's *Philosophical Investigations* was of primary importance for Morris and colleagues including Hollis Frampton and Carl Andre. Taken at the time as a masterpiece of cognitive science and—perhaps more faithfully to its author's intentions—a metaphysical probing of how language functions, the *Investigations* examine how signs can be understood through their constant and quotidian use, as can be summarized in the epithet "We want to *understand* something that is already in plain view."[34] The section concerned with shape addresses whether an internal cognitive change, something that happens inside the mind, is truly "interior." The most famous example of this is provided by the duck/rabbit image; once the individual viewer (Wittgenstein's subject is always an individual viewer) has seen the duck and *then* sees the rabbit (or vice versa), that viewer has divorced the figure from a singular meaning. Thus, just because a sign resembles something does not mean it signifies that thing; the difference between resemblance and identity is absolute for Wittgenstein. Moreover, his theory demands that the viewer/reader affirm that there is a question about where meaning exists in the world. If meaning is not *in* the image, and is not stable *in us*, then where—in what space—do we locate meaning?

After discussing the duck/rabbit image, Wittgenstein considers apparently neutral geometric shapes—those that Ratcliff derided as having "dreary impersonality." For Wittgenstein, the fact that a simple shape can easily refuse to settle into a single meaning allows geometric shapes to provide the clearest examples of the philosophical quandary of signification. Observing that a simple triangle "can be seen as a triangular hole, as a solid, as a geometrical drawing, as standing on its base, as hanging from its apex, as a mountain, as a wedge, as an arrow or pointer, as an overturned object which is meant to stand on the shorter side of the right angle, as a half parallelogram, and as various other things," Wittgenstein ruins the notion of both a purely "geometric" shape *and* a purely signifying shape.[35] No shape is a simple thing: even the barest outline of a triangle suggests a multitude of possible readings. But by the same token, no shape is *not* a potential or already-signified thing: no shape actually evacuates the possibility of signification.

Crucially, Wittgenstein also presents shapes as preexisting totalities: though we cannot see shapes "exactly as they are" because every shape gives way to being seen in a multitude of ways, shapes themselves are *objects*. "How is it possible to see an object according to an interpretation?—The question represents it as a queer fact; as if something were being forced into a form it did not really fit. But no squeezing, no forcing took place here."[36] Shapes can have no "correct" signification; even a shape that follows clear geometrical laws refuses the possibility of a single signification. But also, a shape is always a single unit, and as such, a definite *object*. Once fragmented—once a line leaves a triangle, for example, so that the two remaining lines are connected at only one point—a shape transforms into another shape, becomes a different object of perception. Shape both refuses to do the *mere* work of signification, to become the epiphenomenon of something else, and depends utterly on its own holism. A shape is always a whole; a theory of shapes is always a theory of wholes.

For the philosopher Wittgenstein, shape was a constant by which meaning could be measured or considered; for the theorist of perception Wertheimer, shape is a mechanism and a model for thinking about how meaning is produced. The difference is slight but important. For Wertheimer, the interest lies in how the totality before us unfolds even as it, as totality, mirrors each of us as separate totalities. For Wittgenstein, how shape means *as such* is the question, and we are simply vehicles trying to understand how that unfolding of meaning takes place. If the holism of shapes operates as a given in these theories, the status of the viewer—idealized or particular, whole or fragmented—is not under investigation. And perhaps that is because theories of the subject almost inevitably lead to an understanding of the subject's holism as a fiction, even a necessary fiction.

This problem of wholes and its correlative, the problem of totalization, are central to the question of shape as we will understand it in Guston's painting. It is shapes that "totalize" meanings for the viewer, especially when we understand those paintings as history paintings rather than simply figurative paintings. Shape is what forced critics Clement Greenberg and Michael Fried, in the late 1960s, to turn away from a purist understanding of abstraction that would barely admit the viewer as a subject, let alone the "anthropomorphizing" aspect of her perceptual apparatus. Despite their resistance to admitting the anthropomorphic that lies inside modernist painting, Greenberg and Fried did admit the perceptual action exerted by shapes on the viewer. Both, in essays published in 1966 and 1967, described Jules Olitski's extralong and narrow canvases as "stamp[ing] themselves out as shapes." (Fried echoes that phrase with another: "make themselves felt as shapes with such force.")[37] The notion of seeing shapes "stamped out" as such is Gestaltist, but both critics countered that perceptually laden approach to shape by the concept of the "deductive structure" that would allow those shapes to refer us to the "inclosing shape" of the canvas—something timeless and unchanging (despite its radical alteration in Olitski's hands).

Yet Greenberg did provide one outlying link that connects to our interests in shape: "Olitski's art begins to call attention at this point, as no art before it has, to how very much *this shape is a matter of linear drawing*, and as such, an integral determinant of the picture's effect rather than an imposed and external limit"[38] (emphasis added). Perhaps he was thinking less, at that moment, of Olitski's elongated vertical canvases than of works like *Demikovsky Green* or *Wet Heat Company*, both from 1964. In the latter, a small green ball bounces lightly inside a white swath dominated by an enormous rusty curve that is somehow also weightless, but buttressed by a heavier, curving rectangular nipple. These works of Olitski's from the mid-1960s foretell the degree to which Guston's shapes will work intension—for example, bounciness inhering in circular shapes. In such works, it is stains of acrylic color that show us shape as "a matter of linear drawing" most emphatically (as opposed to the "long brush-strokes of color that run along two or three sides of a given painting" that Fried cites). But perhaps it

Jules Olitski (American, born Soviet Union, 1922–2007), *Unlocked*, 1966. Water-miscible acrylic on canvas, unframed: 140½ × 19 in. (356.8 × 48.2 cm); framed: 141 $^{9}/_{16}$ × 20 in. (359.5 × 50.8 cm). Gift of Mr. and Mrs. Robert Eichholz. National Gallery of Art, Washington, DC, 1978.39.1. © 2021 Estate of Jules Olitski / licensed by VAGA at Artists Rights Society, New York.

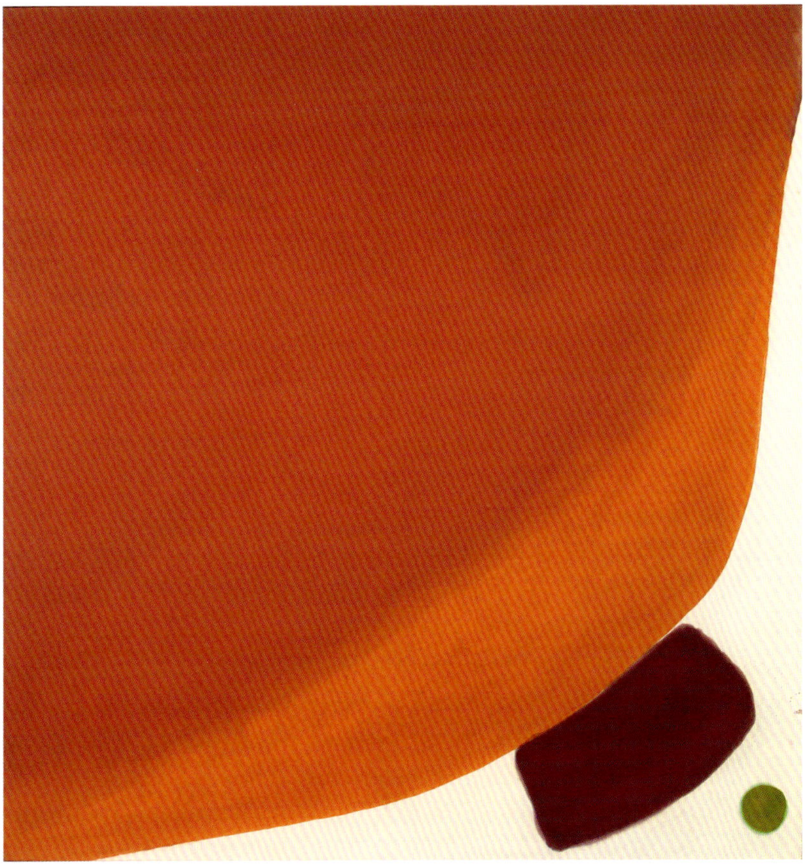

Jules Olitski, *Wet Heat Company*, 1963. Magna acrylic on canvas, 87 × 80 in. (221 × 203.2 cm). Digital image courtesy of Yares Art. © 2021 Estate of Jules Olitski / licensed by VAGA at Artists Rights Society, New York.

is the very anthropomorphic quality—the manner in which they echo the painted shapes' embodied, phenomenological effects on us—that make some of Olitski's shapes, as "a matter of linear drawing," so important to what Guston and Sillman share: both are willing to diffuse gestural abstraction with the somewhat unusual (if also "modernist") move of drawing shapes with paint.[39] That drawn-in-paint shape is what links the explorers of shape painting to the framework of history painting. For it is inside shapes often drawn in paint—sketched or outlined with a loaded paintbrush—that Guston reintroduces, in his work of the late 1960s and 1970s, what he calls "the image" and what I have been calling, after Robert Slifkin, the figure: that recognizable painted sign whose function as a sign both acknowledges a human viewer (as one who reads sign systems) and opens up the question of how that viewer sees.

Before we turn back to Guston, and specifically to his earliest drawings-in-paint that suggest both sign and shape—and the negotiation between them—let us remember that shapes have the capacity to denote the distinction between not only the formless (in gestural abstraction or Olitski's sprays and spills) and the formed, but a graphic echo of the conceptual distinction between subjects and nonsubjects. This is the crucial framework that emerges in T. J. Clark's 2013 book *Picasso and Truth*, which ends with a stirring and timely examination of the artist's 1937 masterwork of history painting, *Guernica*. For Clark, Picasso resolves how to represent the "incommensurable" time of death in *Guernica* through his use of scale. "Certain kinds of death break that human contract" ("some kinds of death . . . are a special obscenity") through which "we" unthinkingly orient our time toward inevitable death.[40] Just as collaged pieces in Picasso's earlier works index "'surface' retrieved," scale allows Clark to see the painter think "about what, in painting, kept the world close to the picture plane."[41] This kind of twinning of a formalist ("picture-plane"-oriented) set of concerns with the painter's absorption in contemporary events and their destruction of the world—and possibly a secure place for painting—is familiar to modernist discourse, particularly regarding this moment in painterly practices.[42] What I propose is that what Guston of the 1970s shares with Picasso in the 1930s is "recognizable" shape as the privileged means of expressing anguish over history in the making. If this choice is acute in 1937 given the historical masses whose extinction was already going on and would continue to go unmarked, that might be our signal that for considering *when* shape overtakes figure even—or *especially*—in history painting. One need only look to *Guernica*'s imitation of the collage system—the figures, rendered universally as shapes with internal markings, appear as if cut out against their pitch-darkened background, which itself sports further outlined shapes of arrows, upturned beaks, and graph-paper grids—to see how much the shape as cutout, shape become emphatically linear, mattered to Picasso's desire to bring history to his viewers.[43]

It is precisely this kind of closed shape, framed by Guston as the question of a figure's recognizability in his painting, that the artist described again and again throughout the 1970s. As his "figurative painting" generated interview after interview, postmortem after postmortem, he responded with different versions of a logic that refuses the recognizability of shapes as figures: "I have often wondered why I find an image that is easily recognizable to be so intolerable in a painting. My answer is that it's intolerable—and also irrelevant—because it's too abstract."[44] This is the opposite of what we normally imagine when we oppose figuration and abstraction. The image that "vanishes into recognition" doesn't mean *enough*. Further, that question of intolerability should prickle our attention: what about an image can become intolerable in its tethering to meaning, to recognition? Or rather, to reframe what has become a dead-end question about representation: When we stop merely recognizing the figure in a shape, what do we understand about the process of the figure's tethering to meaning that might help us reframe who "we" are?

Throughout his analysis, Clark gestures at the well-worn realm of thinking about "bare" or "precarious life,"[45] but the "we" to whom his analysis consistently refers is understood as quite other to those dying obscene deaths. Indeed, that "we" is the same modernist viewer that Fried and Greenberg address, utterly persuaded by the way that the medium of painting structurally rephrases the question of what is being seen. The question we might raise regards the position of the viewer and how figuration and shape painting work differently. Guston's paintings of KKK hoods look forward to the continuation of Hannah Arendt's diagnosis: "If a human being loses his political status, he should, according to the implications of the inborn and inalienable rights of man, come under exactly the situation for which the declarations of such general rights provided. Actually, the opposite is the case. It seems that a man who is nothing but a man has lost the very qualities that make it possible for other people to treat him as a fellow-man."[46] Already sensing, perhaps, that the figural does not go far enough toward treating the distinction between a "man" with political status and "bare life"—or, the viewer of a painting and the corpses piled like so many sticks into the tin-cup cars driven by Guston's KKK "hoods"—Guston overwhelms the figural work that his shapes do with the *other* work they do, to upend signifying procedures and their relation to "the subject" and to pull, instead, on our sensible selves.[47]

Common Objects

> He began to paint with acrylic on small panels, and he painted what he called common objects. In the beginning, they were identifiably books, though more like ancient tablets with incised vertical lines or horizontal ledgers. These books reached phantasmic proportions and metamorphosed into buildings, bread, and sometimes canvases. The old impulse to caricature revived. Guston's "common objects" of 1968 were things huddled on the bottom of an abstract place, or they were exactly and primitively centered on the canvas.
>
> DORE ASHTON, 1976

The "common objects" that Guston began painting in 1968 showed more than simply a return to figurative painting, which would prove to be the seemingly indisputable ground on which his 1970 exhibition at the Marl-

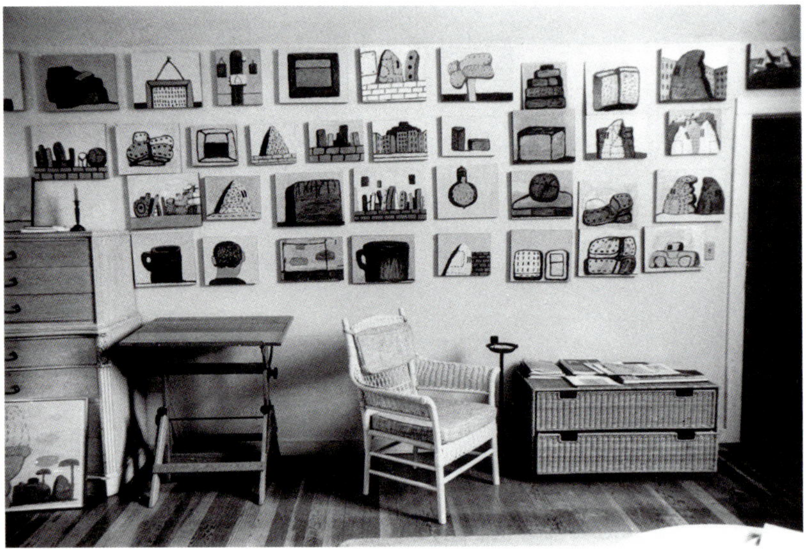

Denise Hare, Guston's studio, 1975. © Denise Hare.

borough Gallery would be judged (in its moment, harshly). In the photograph by Denise Hare accompanying Ashton's text in its 1976 publication, we find small paintings hung in a grid in Guston's Woodstock studio. The paintings in the photograph seem, at first glance, to illustrate Ashton's description: "He began to paint with acrylic on small panels, and he painted what he called common objects."[48] Hare's photograph, however, is of the smaller oils that began coming in 1968; the first group of "common objects" that Guston painted, in 1967, were indeed on wood panels in acrylic, but not particularly small; most range from 16 × 20 to 30 × 32 inches. They were already of "monstrous proportions," single objects dominating panels bigger than those smaller oils in the Hare photograph, ranging in size from 10-inch squares to 12 × 16–inch rectangles, formats in which he would continue experimenting into 1972.[49]

It is in painting these common objects that Guston's shape painting first raises representational questions. At what point do we decide that a stick is not a leg or that it is; that a canvas is not a book *or* a tablet?[50] Or: what is it about Guston's shapes that produces one outcome and not the other? In *Untitled (Light Bulb)*, 1968 (a 12 × 14 in. oil), a stemmed circle, somewhat off-center, is in the middle of the canvas, occupying a pinkish space that is otherwise bare. With a heavy black outline and a brassy yellow stem, this shape announces itself as a light bulb. But this light bulb also wears the same pink, pore-stippled skin that we will come to know in his later paintings of bodies and body parts (*Painting, Smoking, Eating*, 1973; *Green Rug*, 1976; *Ancient Wall*, 1976, etc.)—and already know from *Untitled (Shoe)*. In other words, it is *Untitled (Light Bulb)*'s shape that

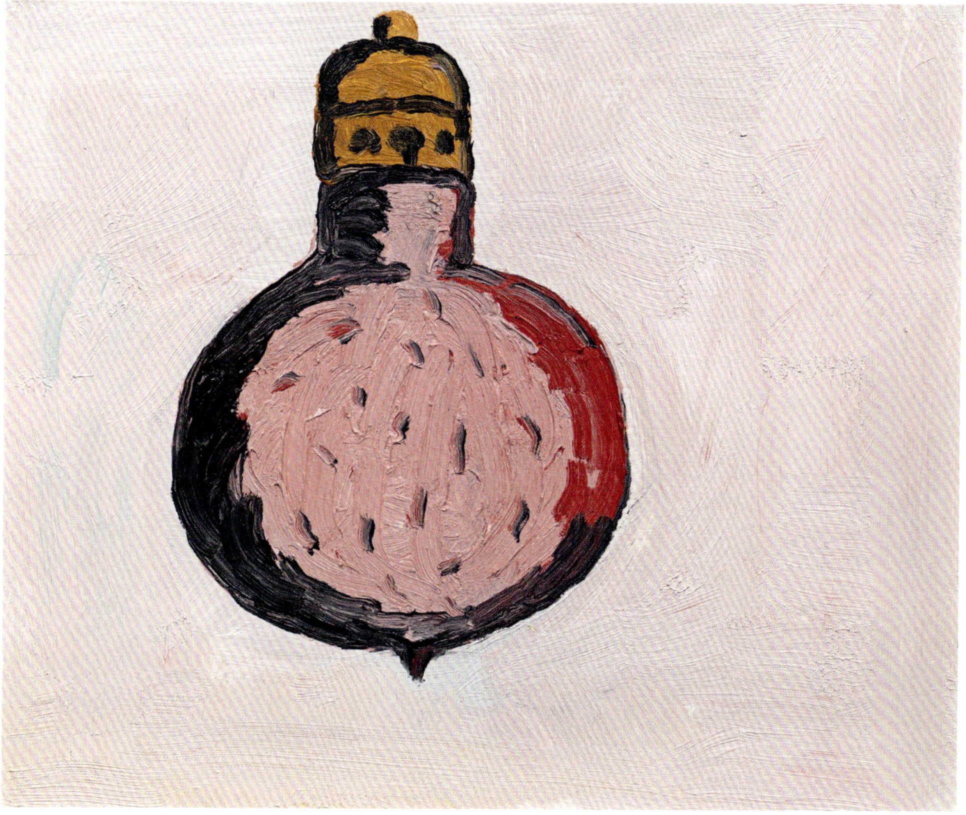

Philip Guston, *Untitled (Light Bulb)*, 1968. Oil on panel, 12 × 14 in. (30.5 × 35.6 cm). Promised gift of Musa Guston Mayer to the Metropolitan Museum of Art. Photo: Genevieve Hanson. © The Estate of Philip Guston, courtesy Hauser and Wirth.

overtakes its pink color and pockmarked covering; the stemmed globe shape vies with the knobbiness of flesh and allows us to see a transparent electrical object that is *also* a chunk of meaty corpus.

In order to fight the tendency of the painted object to "vanish into recognition," Guston's shapes consistently assert themselves against other pictorial elements, yet insist on their separateness from these other painterly elements. When Rudolf Arnheim, author of the 1954 painting bible *Art and Visual Perception*, answers the question "How does the sense of sight take hold of shape?" by pathologizing "visual agnosia" as an "incapacity to grasp a pattern as a whole," he opposes the question of shape's simplicity to the complications offered by the other sensory information offered by a picture. The power of shape's simplicity—"The smaller the amount of information needed to define a given organization as compared to the other alternative, the more likely that the figure will be so perceived"—is its ability to overwhelm other sensory information in order to convey the wholeness of the pattern or structure.[51] Arnheim's chapter on shape is organized around the question of simplicity, or what he calls "parsimony," and characterizes under the subheading "*A Whole Maintains Itself*."[52]

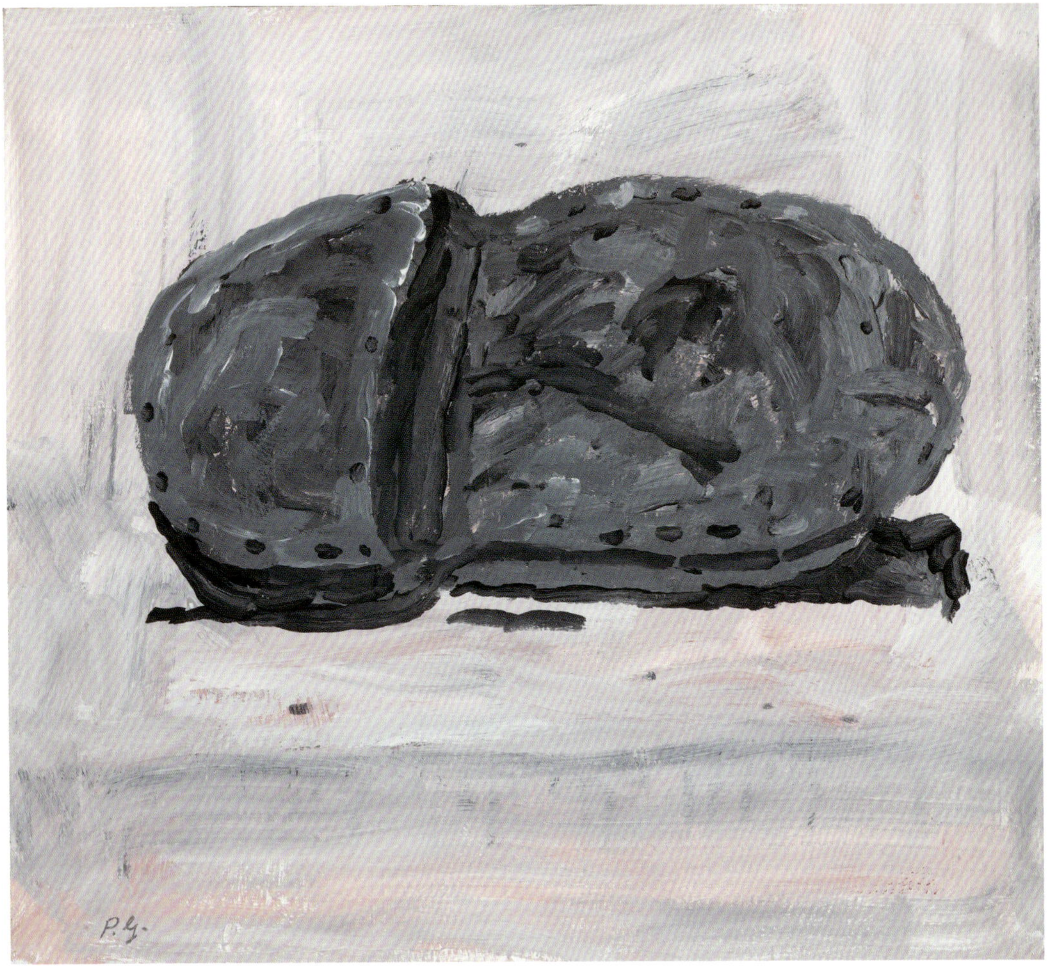

Philip Guston, *Shoe*, 1968. Acrylic on panel; unframed: 30 × 32 in. (76.2 × 81.3 cm); framed: 30 × 33 × 1 in. (78.42 × 83.82 × 4.13 cm). Collection of the Modern Art Museum of Fort Worth, gift of Musa and Tom Mayer. © The Estate of Philip Guston, courtesy Hauser and Wirth.

In Arnheim, Gestalt theory found an evangelist. But Guston's impulse is not to make a "good" painting or even one that "relates" to the "humbler and more common activity of the eyes in everyday life."[53] When he uses shape to defeat the impulse to see something else, he turns away from modalities of painting that insist on recognizability.

Let's look at two of the early acrylics, both from 1968: *Shoe*, showing the shoe sole only, and *Untitled (Shoe)*, showing a shoe in profile made into a curvilinear mountain or building or vase, its ankle/tower/spout exaggeratedly elongated. Only the iconographic hints—stitching around the heel and the toe; dots where the laces might be threaded—"confirm" that this mountain/building/vase is a shoe. The *shape* has become something altogether exaggerated, molded around another idea: What if the vaguely triangular shape of a shoe in profile were thickened by a clumping footfall or the tawdriness of the worn leather? (Iconographically, this is a chal-

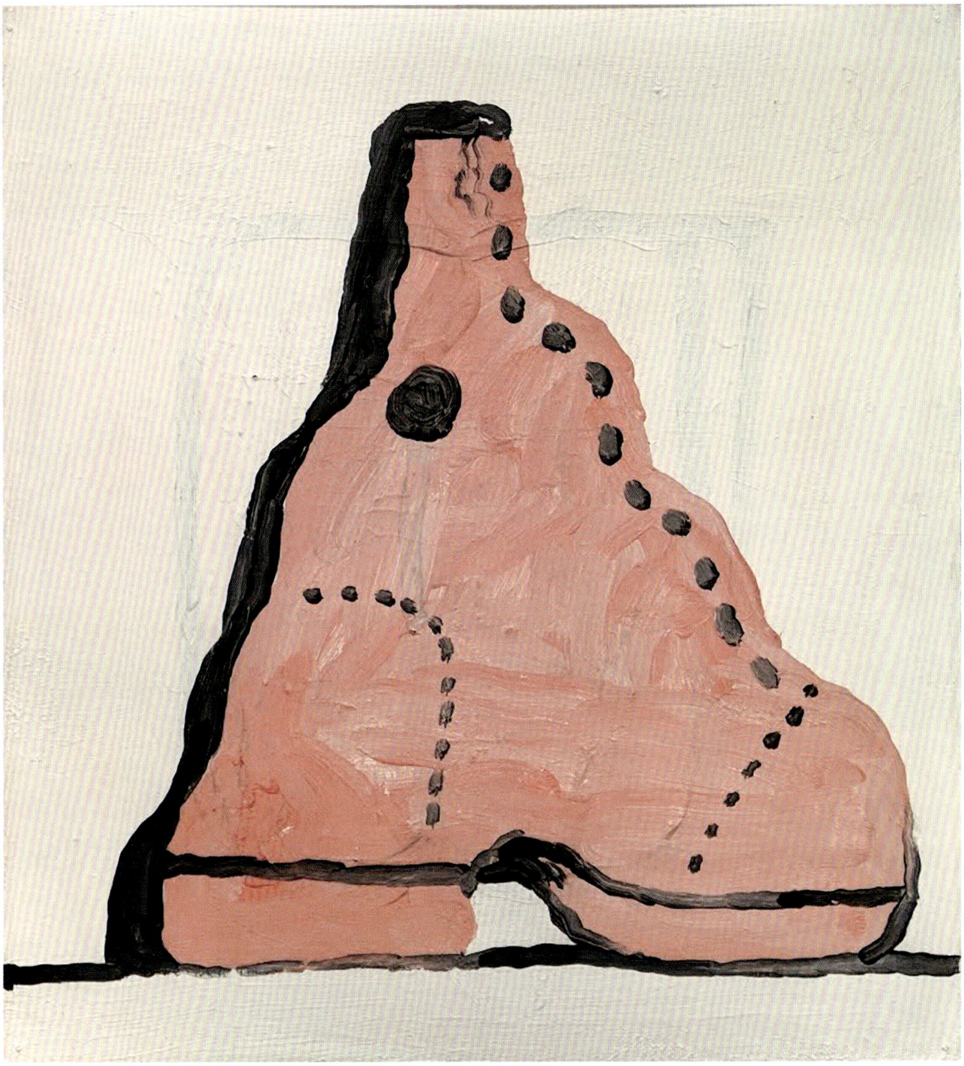

Philip Guston, *Untitled (Shoe)*, 1968. Acrylic on panel, 20 × 18 in. (50.8 × 45.7 cm). Private collection. © The Estate of Philip Guston, courtesy Hauser and Wirth.

lenge to the past: here, van Gogh and Heidegger are met by Chaplin and a kind of overturning of *Manhatta*, of the glamour of high-rises and busy workdays: the work-shoe as pinko icon is revived but made ugly according to a new set of aesthetic norms.) Or what if we emptied the shape of the notion of shoe and just looked at its peculiar architecture, its pink skin, ungainly but sturdy volume? If *Shoe* is Cézannesque, a bendy black plane tipping over, with the barest hint of a foregrounded table edge brushed in blue under the cast of pinks and white, *Untitled (Shoe)* looks much more like what we have come to expect from Guston's figurative works: a comics-informed, heavily outlined object whose semiotic meaning is often in question, but superseded anyway.

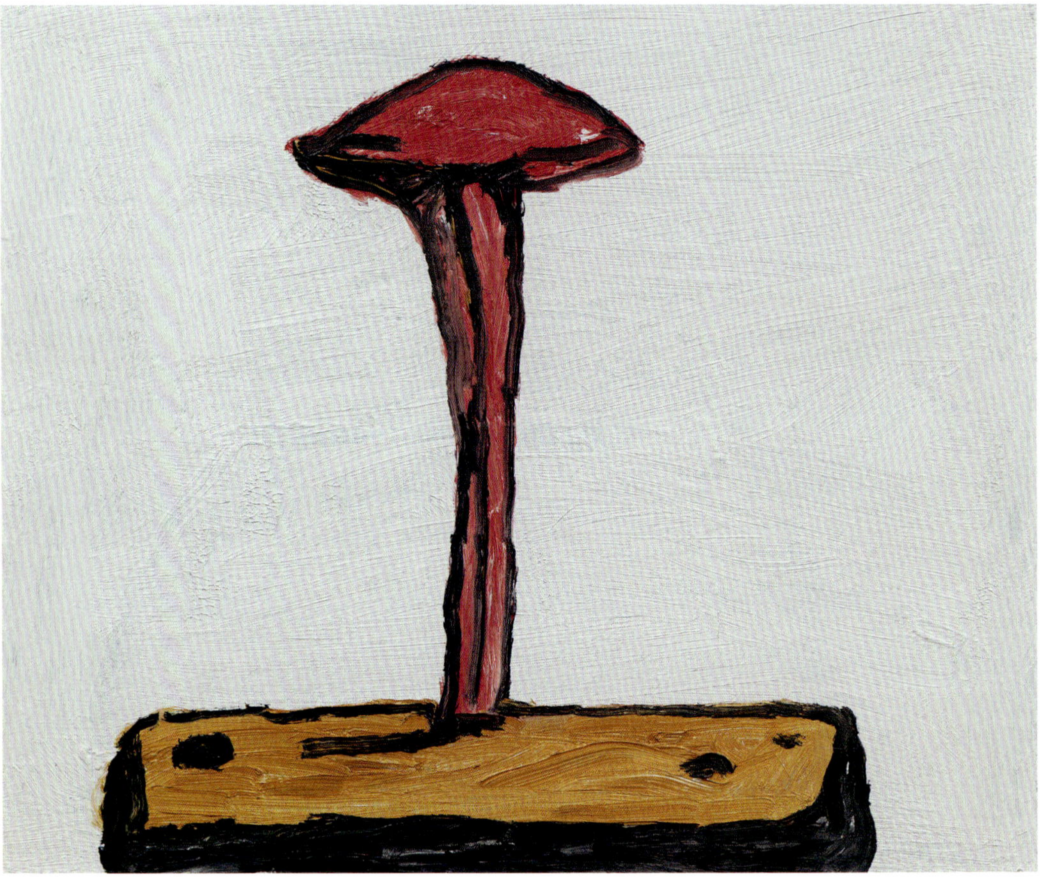

Philip Guston, *Untitled (Nail)*, 1968. Oil on panel, 12 × 14 in. (30.5 × 35.6 cm). Promised gift of Musa Guston Mayer to the Metropolitan Museum of Art. Photo: Genevieve Hanson. © The Estate of Philip Guston, courtesy Hauser and Wirth.

The small oils that follow are preoccupied, as Ashton asserts, with the everyday: toast, bricks, a smoking cigar butt, a nail in a two-by-four, a shoe, a chair, a light bulb. Some simply depict a solitary object, a cigar or a shoe or a chair; many depict arrangements of some kind. A gigantic nail emerges from a wood two-by-four; another nail pins a painting to a wall with a cord, generating a triangle between the two. Every represented "common object" emphasizes the ways that figuration builds out of simple shapes—or, in contrast, shows how simple shapes can take over from the figure. The big nail dwarfing its two-by-four is also in the direct center of the canvas, and very *red*: its floral, colored shape rather than its function as a nail is the painting's subject. This flowering nail shape will eventually become the steering wheel that inserts itself midway through the long exploration of Klansmen hoods that will preoccupy the next few dozen small oils. Guston is not merely making small, experimental paintings of common objects. He is exploring how these shapes, often outlined in black or as monochromatic volumes,

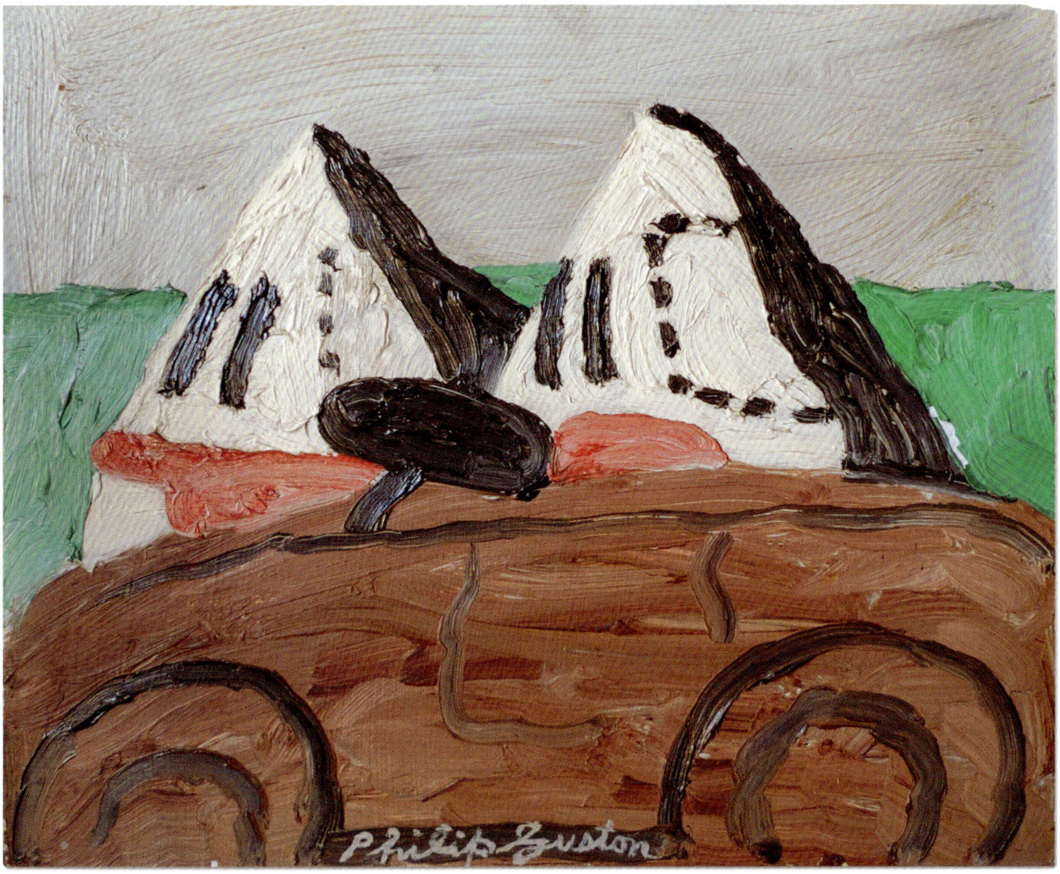

Philip Guston, *Driving Around*, 1969. Oil on panel, 10 × 12 in. (25.4 × 30.5 cm). Collection of Jolie Stahl. © The Estate of Philip Guston, courtesy Hauser and Wirth.

can dominate the center or "front" of his small, squarish canvases. He is figuring out how to get them to convey a grandiose, mythic sense of scale, solitariness, and significance—even in these small formats. As his canvases grow to acquire the scale of his later, giant paintings, that mythic grandiosity becomes even more significant, for their relation to the problem of ongoing history becomes more explicit. Throughout, he is working out the kinks of whether his figures are more interesting when they play with semiotic meaning *or* the capacity of shapes to put forward new formal questions: How did a sole become plank-like, and thereby redefine not "sole" but the particular breaking open of that bifurcated oval shape? How did a nail become not only a flowery shape but a steering wheel and thereby break its attachment to "wheel," becoming instead a bendy oval laid on top of two pyramidal, stitched "hoods"? And at the same time, new possibilities vis-à-vis history painting and its viewer: Can a plank-like sole, in redefining how shape operates, reach into the sense of unity that in each of us responds to the unity that is shape? A shape that plays with its own innate capacity for totalization—the way that a circle can seem heavy and therefore deathly, or if it is a sphere, bathetically bubbly—toys with our ability to project totality, a sense that this thing's wholeness is like "our own." These are shapes that mirror the subject's compensatory desire for totality, show us what our sense of interiority demands from us. In pointing toward the figure but overcoming it (by hollowing out a head or sinking a shoe sole), they give shape a role to play in a kind of history painting less invested in representing history than in making us feel its ongoing costs.

How does shape get to be the privileged element that gathers together information including weight, volume, surface texture, and color, as well as the relevance of that information to the composition? In Guston's painting, the telegraphic quality of many of his shapes derives from the compressed nature of comics graphics as a response to the gestural formlessness of painting as he had practiced it throughout the postwar period. Shapes submitted to newsprint presses or comics publishing achieve a special degree of boundedness and fixity. Through outline or monochromatic color, comics shapes convey a graphic flatness that is alien to most "painterly" compositions, or indeed to painting's own conventions, often tied to qualities of "movement and the play of light and shadow."[54] Another way of describing the "comics" quality of Guston's shapes is that he marshals what Heinrich Wölfflin named the "anti-painterly," or linear, "closed form," which emphasizes symmetry, centering, and fixity in order to reify form's relations as *picture*. Just as the "painterly style does not shape things in themselves but represents the world as a seen world, namely, as it actually appears to the eye . . . the linear style is a style of plastically perceived definition."[55] Yet in its translation as "closed form," Wölfflin draws "the linear style" away from the notion of the palpable or multisensory, and toward a mode of reflexivity.[56] Closed form is "bounded within itself and always points back to itself, just as, conversely, the style of open form always suggests something beyond itself and wants to appear unbounded, even though there will always be a hidden boundary and it is precisely that which makes the closed character possible in the aesthetic sense."[57] That way that classicism not only folds painting back on itself but allows the possibility of fixity to become a point of fascination is what Guston is experimenting with in his early "common objects" paintings. It is not semiological multivalence or even the Cézannesque possibilities that open up once objects become less interesting than their formal translation. It is in a way the opposite. To find a sole become plank-like or to see a head balloon is to see in a totalized way, and to celebrate that totalization: to go utterly along with it.

Totalization and Repetition

By the mid-1970s, Guston's paintings of single, iconic shapes or objects start turning their totalizing capacities toward multiplication, proliferation, and the crowding-out of other dimensions for reading shape (e.g., semiotically). Closed form and its allegedly "anti-painterly" aspect, coupled with the "badness" that Guston draws on through comics, allows Guston's shapes to reach new levels of complexity. In the "common objects" paintings, the shapes were centered and singular. Eventually, in works like *Source* (1976), such simple, centered shapes would gain grandiosity through scaling up. But by the middle of the decade they had also started to multiply all over his canvases. A single pair of tubular right-angled legs (in *Green Rug*, 1976), becomes dozens later that year (*Ancient Wall*, 1976). The pair of shoe soles that proliferates into a half-dozen shadows in *Green Rug* in turn becomes a pile of corpse soles—this time only heels—clambering around the bottom of *Ancient Wall*, pushing forward out of the picture plane. Totalization—and the ways Guston mobilizes it around shapes—is a kind of revenge that the "closed form" wreaks on painting as a means of addressing the world.

Totalization finds a psychoanalytic translation. The unary, in psychoanalysis, is that extreme reduction of the other to what Lacan calls, after Freud, the *einziger Zug*—the "sole (absolute, complete, unique, etc.) trait (stroke, etc.)." In Freud's analysis of Dora, the cough by which his patient imitated her father was a means of identifying (regressively) with him.[58] He is reduced to one single, totalizing trait. Similarly, the castration complex itself is a unary misrecognition of the mother for her phallic lack; the mirror stage—the ground zero of totalization—lets the baby perceive itself as a masterful whole despite its incapacitating limits. Lacan—and differently, Klein and Winnicott—attacked this notion of a preexisting whole that would find its corollary in the unified ego by investigating the early processes through which an infant moves, from either "part object" processes of identification and disidentification, or indeed through the structures of signification such as language and visuality. But what is key for our purposes is not the process by which a subject is "made," but how the concept of totality leverages shape, or more specifically, the notion of the whole as shape and the shape as whole, in a way that lets us better understand what our own assumptions about wholeness mean to our ideas of selfhood.

In *Green Rug*, shape employs a kind of totemic force not merely to argue with the figural but to make itself central, to use its power to anchor the painting. Guston's shapes in *Green Rug* cross a black canvas whose brushy mix of shiny and matte black paint underscores the

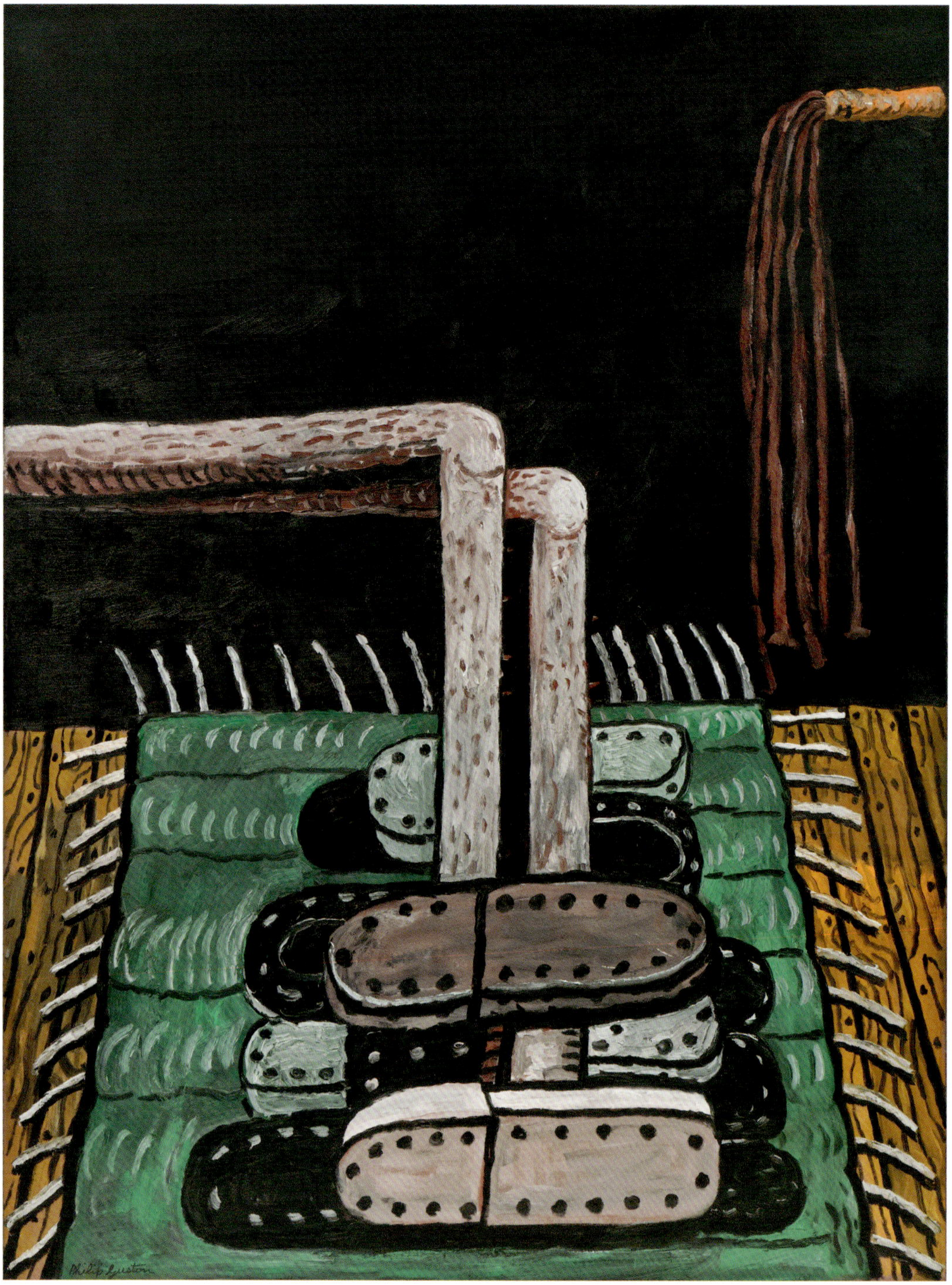

Philip Guston, *Green Rug*, 1976. Oil on canvas, 94 × 68½ in. (238.8 ×174 cm). The Museum of Modern Art, New York, gift of Edward R. Broida in honor of Ann Temkin. Digital image © The Museum of Modern Art / licensed by SCALA / Art Resource, New York. © The Estate of Philip Guston, courtesy Hauser and Wirth.

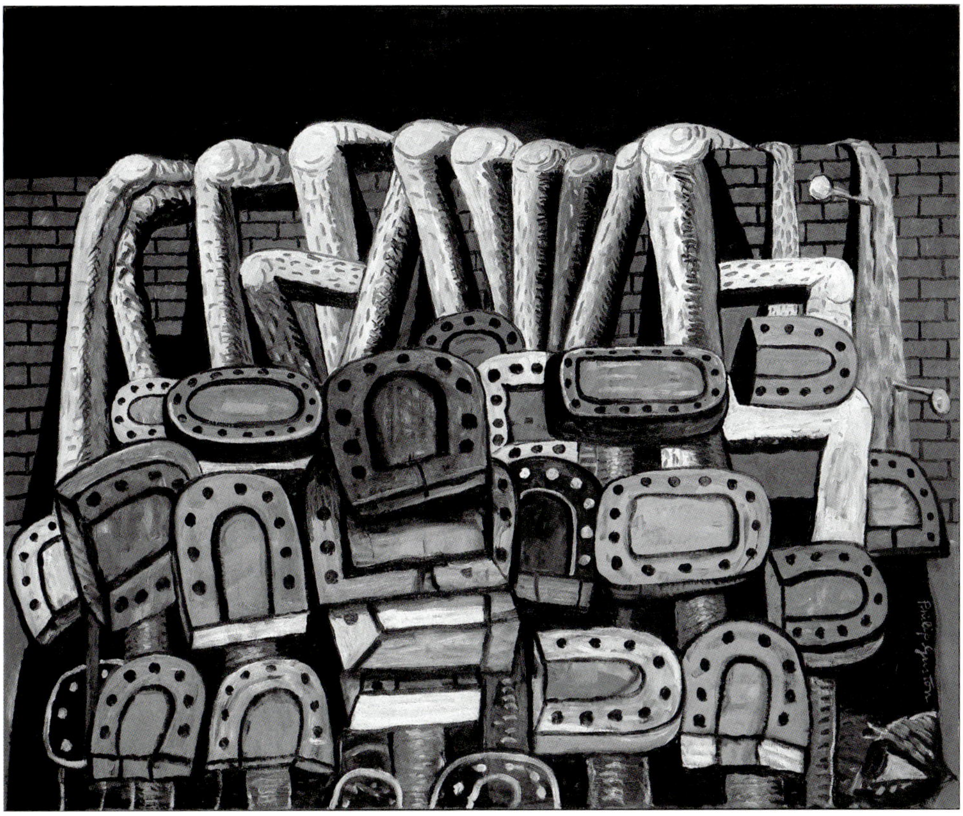

picture's mythic, vacuum-like space. Two sticklike legs are joined like plumbing pipes, ending in two pink shoe soles and a graveyard of their black and minty green-gray shadows. A margin of black space between the two legs is at the exact center of the vertical canvas. These narrowed pipe legs hinge open to let a long triangle of negative space open what is otherwise an extraordinarily planar, nonrecessional space; it is a castrated space, to go along with the disturbing crisscross of the shoes. The shoe soles and legs face the viewer and angle away from a green rug levitating off a wooden floor, threatened by a cat-o'-nine-tails in the upper right corner. Like a hyperbolic nightmare of painterly tectonics, *Green Rug* refuses the conventions of recessive space. What it presents in place of such space is shapehood, excessive and exaggerated. Each shape's separateness is deeply stressed by a thick black outline or its definition against a black ground. Each is set into a composition that wants their holistic identities, their separateness, and their repetition as shapes to dominate, even tyrannize the picture.

Philip Guston, *Ancient Wall*, 1976. Oil on canvas, 80 × 93 in. (203.2 × 237.8 cm). Regents Collection Acquisition Program, 1987. Lee Stalsworth. Hirshhorn Museum and Sculpture Garden, Smithsonian Institution. © The Estate of Philip Guston, courtesy Hauser and Wirth.

The pink pair of shoe soles splits into further pairs: all together, four black-edged, half-rounded rectangles. Each has a separate orientation—the darker pair faces slightly up, while the lower, lighter pair faces just slightly toward the bottom of the canvas. And each suggests depth and weight differently. The top pair floats, whereas the bottom pair weighs down. The top, with a white stripe around its bottom edge, hankers after light and reflectiveness (like the rightmost knee), whereas the bottom stays chalkily uniform. These are shapes that gesture at the other elements of painting—at light and weight, for instance. But those other elements fail to tie them to their semiotic or "representational" functions in what would have been—in a different picture—a recessive space with conventionally arranged questions of weight, texture, color, and gravity. Everywhere across *Green Rug*, Guston distinguishes his painting from such conventional distributions: from the rug's hilly rows to the mix of shiny and matte paint in the black background. Then he uses repetition to insist on the totality of each shape. Gray and black half circles fill up the rest of the rug, as if it were a graveyard not of shoe soles (they are barely perceptible as such) but of graphic echoes of the half circle closed by its drawn diameter. The degrees of these curvatures are consistent; the right angles formed with their hard edges are unvarying. Guston is demonstrating something that has little to do with how shape gathers together other elements into wholes to serve semiotic or even "painterly" purposes. In his work such repetitions and stoppages argue for the power of shape divorced from whether it is "signifying" weightlessness or solidity—let alone a referent.

Shoe soles, like heads, recur across so many late paintings: *Room* (1976); *Discipline* (1976); *The Coat* (1977); *Sleeping* (1977); *Entrance* (1979). Even the ghostlike outlines in *Waking Up* (1975) bring back this early subject from the "common objects" acrylics (there are five paintings of shoe soles in the black-and-white Woodstock studio picture, more than any other subject except hoods). Though the often-paired soles declare a kind of fealty to iconographic standards, they also describe something else, especially in the way that they turn up as either bendy, even rubbery plasticity-demonstrations or plank-like, weighty death emblems. It is not only that shapes in Guston's paintings must assert their demarcation as unities and their propensity for repetition. They also assert a characterological variation, a connotative range that exceeds formal questions of what shape *is* and asks instead what shape *does*. In other words, when we see the shoe-sole shapes bend with a Chaplinesque rubberiness and then straighten out, plank-like, into morbid weights, we should ask not only about how they signify (these homonyms for "souls" pun about Guston's dread of his own mortality). For what they do, as shapes, is to draw us into a set of questions about how history can be communicated, both as an ongoing set of conditions in the present and a sense that those conditions perpetuate past trauma.

It is history itself—unfolding as a brutal repetition or continuation of earlier devastations, but unfolding as such for a viewer whose experience is insistently internalized—that Guston is picturing in his return to figuration and that he signifies with his formal shape experimentation.

Tragicomedy and Myth

Those identical, U-shaped shoe soles, surging up to meet the viewer staring at the "ancient wall" made of bricks and hairy legs, are metonyms for mass extinction. In this they join groups of other signifiers that we find over and over in the last half decade of Guston's painting: the floating, pneumatic heads already identified in paintings like *Yellow Light*, *Cabal* (1977), *Deluge III*, and *Group in Sea* (both 1979); the same grouping of legs and soles in works like *Pit*, *Wharf*, *Monument*, *The Door*, *Green Rug*, and *Room* (all 1976), and 1977's *The Street*; coats, often with soles pinned to their architecture, such as we've seen in *The Coat* but also *Back View* (1977). To this list we might also add cacophonous pileups of heterogeneous items, as if gathered from across a lexicon of "common objects" made just for this purpose: U-shaped soles transformed into horseshoes with heavy blocks of sinking iron on each end are joined by a cigarette smoking away near a paintbrush in its cellar in *Tomb* (1978). Or the similarly chaotic *Plain* (1979), like *The Street* a kind of war painting. These are not merely signs for mechanized death; they set the stage for a kind of painting in which the vaguely comic "space" to which we have become accustomed is turned to look at the deluge—to quote one title he reuses several times—of history.

In Guston's late painting, the sense of the comic—both the "funniness" of some of the shapes themselves and the comics-like space in which we find these shapes—mobilizes as a response to his present. We cannot enter these spaces as if we were individuals akin to the figures who might turn up in another painter's scene setting: this is not a performative painting that speaks to the medium's world-making capacities, let alone a narrative or figural one.[59] Instead what we find is a space that is rather abjectly given over to a kind of gallows humor, one in which apparent figures float or sink, single themselves out or array manically. It almost doesn't matter. They are so often reduced to graphic building blocks (such as the pneumatic, ballooning circle of the bloated head or the bisected oval of the multiplied shoe sole) that, whether they turn up in multitudes or as single icons, we stop seeing them as figures. This doesn't mean that we forget the figural, which is obviously there, but that we alter our relationship to it.

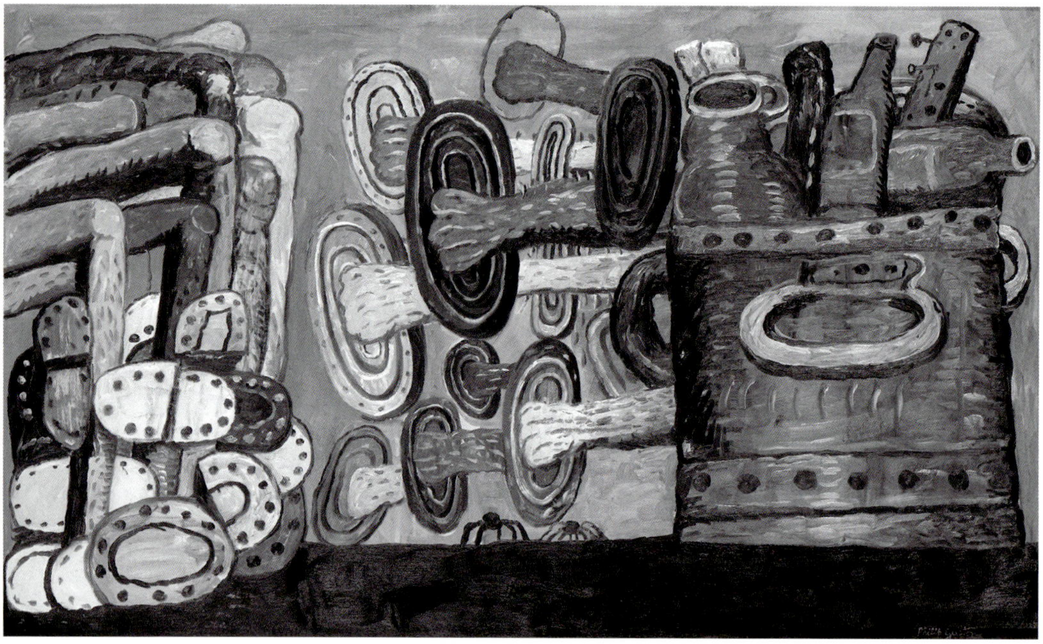

Philip Guston, *The Street*, 1977. Oil on canvas, 69 × 110¾ in. (175.3 × 281.3 cm). The Metropolitan Museum of Art, purchase, Lila Acheson Wallace and Mr. and Mrs. Andrew Saul gifts, gift of George A. Hern, by exchange, and Arthur Hoppock Heam Fund, 1983. Image © The Metropolitan Museum of Art. Image source: Art Resource, New York. © The Estate of Philip Guston, courtesy Hauser and Wirth.

The philosopher and Heidegger scholar and translator Alfred Hofstadter, writing in 1967, called the tragicomic "concern in depth," pointing to the kind of special concern that develops when an author (he was primarily concerned with dramatists) can only treat a tragic problem with a sense of the comic: "If the world seems to be thoroughly absurd, the only possible reaction left is to laugh at it. . . . Indeed, we may well suspect that the new tenant is himself the humorist who, carefully choosing his place of immolation and carefully regulating the actions of the furniture movers . . . finally settles into position, with hat and bouquet, calling for lights out, preparing in this thorough way for his amazing flight into ontological space."[60] As much as this final phrase rings familiar to those looking at Guston's overwhelming preoccupation with mortality in his paintings from 1976 until his death, the tragicomic is in evidence throughout his paintings of that final decade and is perhaps strongest in those works from 1969 until 1975. For that is not only when Guston "returns to figuration" but when he starts painting history, *before* he turns to the more existential and apocalyptic anywhere scenes of his last years. KKK hoods populate emptied cityscapes and painter's studios or mingle with shoe soles, boots, and pointing fingers in paintings like *Scared Stiff*, *Flatlands*, *Dawn*, and *A Day's Work* (all 1970). Between emblematic reminders of events like the shooting at Kent State (the stiff legs ending in strangely turned shoe soles in *Dawn*) and a trove of references to the 1930s, Guston is producing a form of history painting that both sets up the figural within that genre and dismantles it.[61]

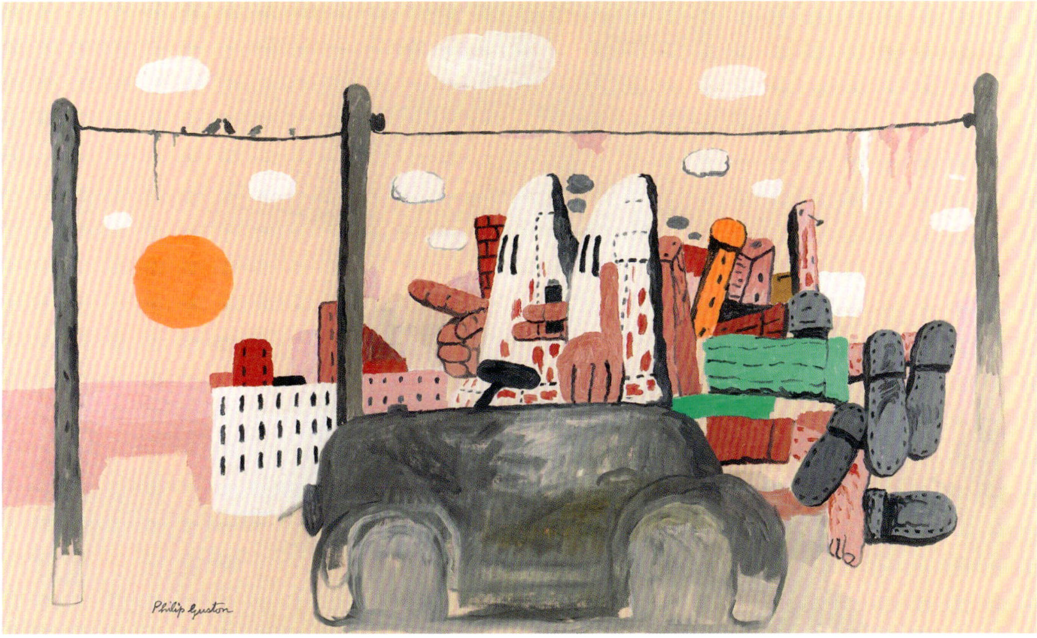

Philip Guston, *Dawn*, 1970. Oil on canvas, 67¼ × 108 in. (170.8 × 274.3 cm). Glenstone Museum, Potomac, Maryland. © The Estate of Philip Guston, courtesy Hauser and Wirth.

The question here is not whether these are figures but in what sense they fight the "recognizability" of their shapes as signs. Backgrounds empty out because we are zooming in on the critical information, as if in a single comics panel extracted from its sequence.[62] Comics here lend a sense of the "existential dilemma" on which comics and cartoons rely, endlessly submitting their characters to repeated assaults, forever-returning death scenes.[63] Extracted from panel-to-panel sequences, these paintings toy with what "comic concern" would mean: in *Dawn*, two erect hoods angle attentively forward, following one's giant red pointer finger. With an overflow of corpse legs and shoes sticking out of the back of their fading jalopy, they recall nothing so much as a couple of homicidal village idiots venturing into deindustrialized hinterlands. Can such figures be funny? They evoke the funnies, but only insofar as it is "their pathos [that] founds their comicality."[64] The tragicomic is never actually funny or even comic: it leverages concern and determines that the dynamic between the tragic and the comic suspends both, gravely.[65]

Classically, tragicomedy has been understood as a form that arises when the tragic is no longer adequate. Or, more precisely, when "we," a collective subject position that can be articulated within some notion of presentness, no longer can identify with the lofty and even godlike or at any rate mythic cohesiveness of tragic heroes. For some, tragicomedy is a narrative designation that depends on the difference between action and the potential for action.[66] For others, including the philosopher Alenka

Zupančič, it is an essentially modern and postmodern genre developed "in recognition of the fact" that the tragic does not survive its own repetition intact. The more we understand the tragic in Zupančič's terms, as drowned in a historical repetition in which the immiserating conditions of the present show us that it is but a "mask that cannot survive its own repetition," the less we can pretend to address it as if we were full subjects, able at least to face the objects of our perception with what we deem "reason."[67] That is when the comic enters: "This point has been systematically made in literature on comedy, and is splendidly epitomized by Horace Walpole's remark: 'This world is a comedy to those that think, a tragedy to those that feel.'"[68] All of us in that moment are denuded of this "full" subjectivity, of indeed the subjecthood that was once marked by an audience member's ability to recognize in the tragic hero a kind of emblem of human tragedy. The tragicomic, in other words, is about our shared, universal incapacity to view the present as such, as if we were over and over again at the dawn of history; instead it is a sense that the pseudocomic takes over now, in this round.

The distinction between present conditions of existence and those that heralded "the subject" is foundational to our moment.[69] The challenge to understanding Guston's tragicomedy lies in confronting the universalism that seems to underpin it. Such a Clarkian "we" (or its corollary "our," as in "All of *us* are denuded . . . *our* shared, universal incapacity") seems to demand a universalist subject, or at least one that reaches a plural form readily. But what I am designating is not that which is shared universally among subjects but that which can be imputed to a singular, even individuated viewer in 1970 or 1976 or today. Engaged in the act of looking, viewers are addressed by the ways Guston's shapes claim something beyond their semiotic content, something that reaches—albeit dramatically, to show us its failure—to show us "what is," but instead bears for us the mechanisms for totalization. The empty, ballooning head uses its emptiness to leach from its figurality; the sinking shoe sole uses its weight to not only complicate the sign (now a gravestone as well as a shoe sole) but to indicate the shape's own capacity, qua shape. To give a head or a sole a subfigural range of qualities is to expose shape's ability to totalize and overwhelm a representational system. At the same time, that shape speaks to us not in the language of the figural, but in the self-consciously "anti-painterly."

Shape's ability to take over from the complexity of a figure means gathering into itself all the nonworldly aspects that form can convey: the pipelike emptiness of these limbs, their diagrammatic cylindricality, their bloodied finish. Zupančič, describing the key character Sosie in Molière's *Amphitryon*, writes of how "Sosie's ego [is] taken not as an imaginary unity of his personality but as his unary trait, as the one and only characteristic of Sosie."[70] It is not merely the leg shapes' emptiness (weight) or cylindricality (volume) or bloodied finish (surface texture) but the totaling of these qualities into something bigger, overwhelming even the signifier (an image of legs). This is totalization at work, making shape do a lot of work aggregating what all these apparently *other* characteristics contribute. In other words, Wölfflin's "anti-painterly" closed forms do not merely rely on their graphic line, but rather that "consistently defined line still has something corporeal about the way it grasps things."[71] Making shapes gain a figurally informed but postfigural, graphic but corporeal Gestalt (or totalization) in his paintings is what Guston discovered, I think, as an outcome of his work's tragicomic perspective, first experimented with in those "common objects" paintings. Having a "main feature" or "principle oddity" is the key to comic characterhood, as not only Zupančič but Walter Benjamin writes, also describing Molière's comedy, in which "character develops . . . like a sun, in the brilliance of its single trait, which allows no other to remain visible in its proximity."[72] The "exclusive character trait" is the result of a comic accumulation or, as Zupančič puts it, "The comic character could be defined precisely as an enjoying incarnation of some unary trait. It is a unary trait walking around."[73] Shapes are that trait: the condensation of a complex structure into what appears as an uninterruptible whole, denying any fragmentariness. In Guston's painting, that gathering together or condensation is almost trippily oriented toward the comical. He evokes comics and their zoomed-in panels, cartoons and their death drive antics. But he pushes that comical envelope toward us with the acknowledgment that it is empty, a signifier *of* the comic rather than its instantiation. Instead, it serves as a recognition that "the repetition of tragic events deprives the latter of their aura and transforms them into something common, unexceptional. A thing can be terrible and devastating in its repetition (the repetition does not necessarily take that away), but it is no longer tragic, and this, we could say, constitutes a supreme tragedy of modernity."[74]

The KKK hoods in Guston's paintings become no less pathetic once we recognize that these shapes, with their stitched plates and rigid conicality, are also aluminum nose cones, the likes of which we still find littering yards near Guston's Woodstock home. These cones that have none of the drape of fabric, that feature unlikely stitching, help us to imagine a type of history painting that does not rely on figuration to do its job. In that form of history painting, referents can populate the image, but it is the way that the shapes take over from those acts of reference that allows us to perceive them, *shape wholes*, as totalizing fictions. Shapes gather together more than reference when they bring the impossibility of a ballooning head or a sole that sinks or springs to or from the bottom of the canvas: when they tether and totalize into themselves sometimes fantastical suggestions, like a flowering nail. Yet they call on us, or on a sense of the "intuition" we can each name as "our own," in order to see these totalizing fictions. Even as deeply as one can sense oneself to be a subject, formed by history and seemingly immovable structures, the sense of interiority, of being not altogether explained by the subject's overdetermination or totalization, persists.

Amy Sillman / Recent Work

Dear Jackie,

I guess you didn't know this but me and Abstraction broke up!!!! Last summer!!!! Well, I mean, I've been feeling like kind of confused for a long time, like years. I'm friends with all of A's friends and stuff, and I think A's really cool and I totally learned a lot from A—but you know what? I don't want to say anything bad about A, but I have to totally move on with my life. I started to really feel like A's been holding me back and even like kind of manipulative. I mean, when I moved to NYC it was kind of incredible to get to know A . . . but you know what? I am super worried that when you get really to the core of things, A is just super conceited and can't talk to me. I feel really bad saying this but i kind of wonder sometimes if A is just dead inside. I don't know, maybe A is like a meal ticket for me. I mean, I get invited to a lot of shows and things because of A, but when I'm there, A just kind of talks to other people. Like I don't feel A can really concentrate on one person at a time—A always addresses the whole room, if you know what I mean. I mean, it's not like Representation even knows I exist either. I feel like when I come into the room, R is like all glassy and actually really conservative; it's a weird feeling, too.

AMY SILLMAN, 2009

This comic sendup of a painterly dilemma "between" Abstraction and Representation, each presented as a deeply flawed, would-be friend or girlfriend, gives us Amy Sillman's relation to that old dichotomy, circa 2009. It takes the form of an internal monologue turned into a kind of epistolary set piece, "Jackie" being the artist Jackie Saccoccio, whose survey sent to twelve painters in 2009 occasioned Sillman's response. Perhaps ironically (because it is easy to hear Sillman's voice talking to herself even as she "responds" to Saccoccio), the question at the heart of this internal monologue is the notion of a communicative painting, painting that could "talk to me" or "concentrate on one person at a time." Communication here is delivering a sense of private address, much like the pseudoletter Sillman has written. Painting incapable of such communication is deemed to be "dead inside." On the one hand, dominating this passage is an idea of interiority, of an "inside" that could be either dead or open to communication. It is both what Sillman is talking about and, in this little ruminative monologue, illustrating. On the other, we have a question of publicness, "the room" Sillman pictures herself entering, hoping to be addressed. Publicness and interiority—the inside of both the room and that person deemed to be not "dead inside"—are in dialogue, and the question of painting's communicativeness is at the center. Painting, in Sillman's work and this set piece, both projects the possibility of being spoken to and complicates the grounds on which we imagine that to be taking place.

Interiority—the notion of a psychic refuge within each of us, however overdetermined—serves as a repository of selfhood in the collective imagination. Even those theories of the subject that appear to eliminate the idea of an interior unique to each of us do not displace or dismantle the notion of interiority, regardless of how they reframe it. Like Freud's notion of the unconscious or Marx's theory of alienation, they simply reiterate a framework in which psychic interiority is structured *from beyond*, by exterior structures that subject us. These still, like more naive notions of psychic interiority, depend on a notion of the interior.[1] If the idea of interiority has not only survived but somehow thrived despite the impact of "the subject" on our ways of thinking our selves, what can painting, a medium tied to very specific spatial and historical configurations long associated with "the bourgeois interior," do for those ideas?[2] And more specifically, what can a painting like Sillman's, which frequently announces its interest in psychology, do for the ways that shape and interiority interact?[3]

One of the ways interiority has recently been reframed is as a battle between emotion and affect, between the subject whose feelings "belong" to her, and the affect that remains somewhat formless, either generalized across a population or indistinct to those of us in its grip. Brian Massumi, for example, argues that while emotion is a "subjective content, the sociolinguistic fixing of the quality of an experience"—which he describes as "personal" but I would further describe as "interior"—affect is an intensity "disconnected from meaningful sequencing, from narration."[4] Two strong issues are at play, at least insofar as shape is concerned. One is the way that emotion gets qualified as distinct and formed, whereas affect is described as "unformed and unstructured."[5] That is crucial when we are considering shape, which seems to pose as the antithesis of the "unformed and unstructured." In other words, shape appears to rhyme with emotion and its claims on the distinct and formed, resulting from its "socio-linguistic fixing." But when an affect can be described, it too has to emerge and cohere as some *thing*, even if it resists a level of utter distinctness: Would we call that coherence a shape? The second issue at play in the distinction between affect and emotion is that affect, in our discourse, has gained access to the historical present, while emotion is treated as if it could be contained as nonpublic, interior, ahistorical. Lauren Berlant: "Affect is a metapsychological category spanning what's internal and external to subjectivity. But it is more than that too. . . . Affect's saturation of form can communicate the conditions under which a historical moment appears as a visceral moment."[6] It is through "affect's saturation of form" that one can, as Berlant did, discover new genres "of crisis." While she was particularly riveted by the coherence of those forms as "female complaint" or "cruel optimism," I want to press on the prior distinction, by which the private or interior feeling—emotion as "subjective content," as Massumi puts it—is set into contrast with publicness.[7] Can a person who "comes into the room," as Sillman describes, find a mode of painting that addresses her, intimately—and doesn't just "address the whole room"? Or, if we can sense ourselves at the center of a painting's address, is it because we sense ourselves to be communicated to, uniquely? What subjective relations to others does a painting or installation of paintings permit, whether it addresses us one by one, intimately, or collectively? Is it possible to do both, to address a multitude intimately? Finally, what do we make of the distinction between the room as an interior space and our individuated interiors, as analogous spaces of address? These are the paradoxes that are instilled in the most proprietary of art mediums, painting. Even as Sillman extends that medium through printmaking and installation (as well as video and poetry in works and exhibits that I do not discuss here), she uses painting and its histories and conventions to profoundly pressure the distinction between private and public, interior and exterior.

While I was finishing revisions to this book, Sillman curated an exhibit that opened with the newly renovated galleries of the Museum of Modern Art in New York. Entitled *The Shape of Shape*, it brought together seventy-two works by seventy-one authors in a variety of media, including floor sculpture, photography, painting, and her own floor-to-ceiling wall painting in a crimson wash. That mural covered a white partial wall positioned in the middle of an open gallery, so that one could see it while approaching and while taking in the entire room and its tight concatenation of art works. The gallery was lined with shelves at different heights on which works could sit, sometimes leaning against the walls on which other works hung. Thus was a wildly, intensely varied group of works brought into close proximity and a web of unexpected relationships. Photographed shapes entered conversations with molded ones, painted-on shapes came into confrontation with shaped canvases, and drawings on paper dialogued with painted wood. Many works, like Sillman's own crimson wall painting, begged the question of how we perceive the boundaries of a shape. Frequently, shapes repeated within a given work, and viewers were left with a question about whether the identity of a shape is wrapped up in its singularity or whether it can exist as that duplication, in the relation or negative space between them.

Sillman's wall painting, with its small, lower ovaline shape meeting a much larger, vertical one, also recalled those paintings that helped Jules Olitski become the center of a mid-century US debate about shape. Specifically, her crimson wall painting asked about the "inclosing shape of the painting"—meaning, the shape of the usually rectangular or square stretched canvas—and its relation to the viewer. Borrowing from the "all-over" format that Olitski refined in mid-1960s paintings of bouncing, nested, and otherwise interacting shapes, Sillman's mural

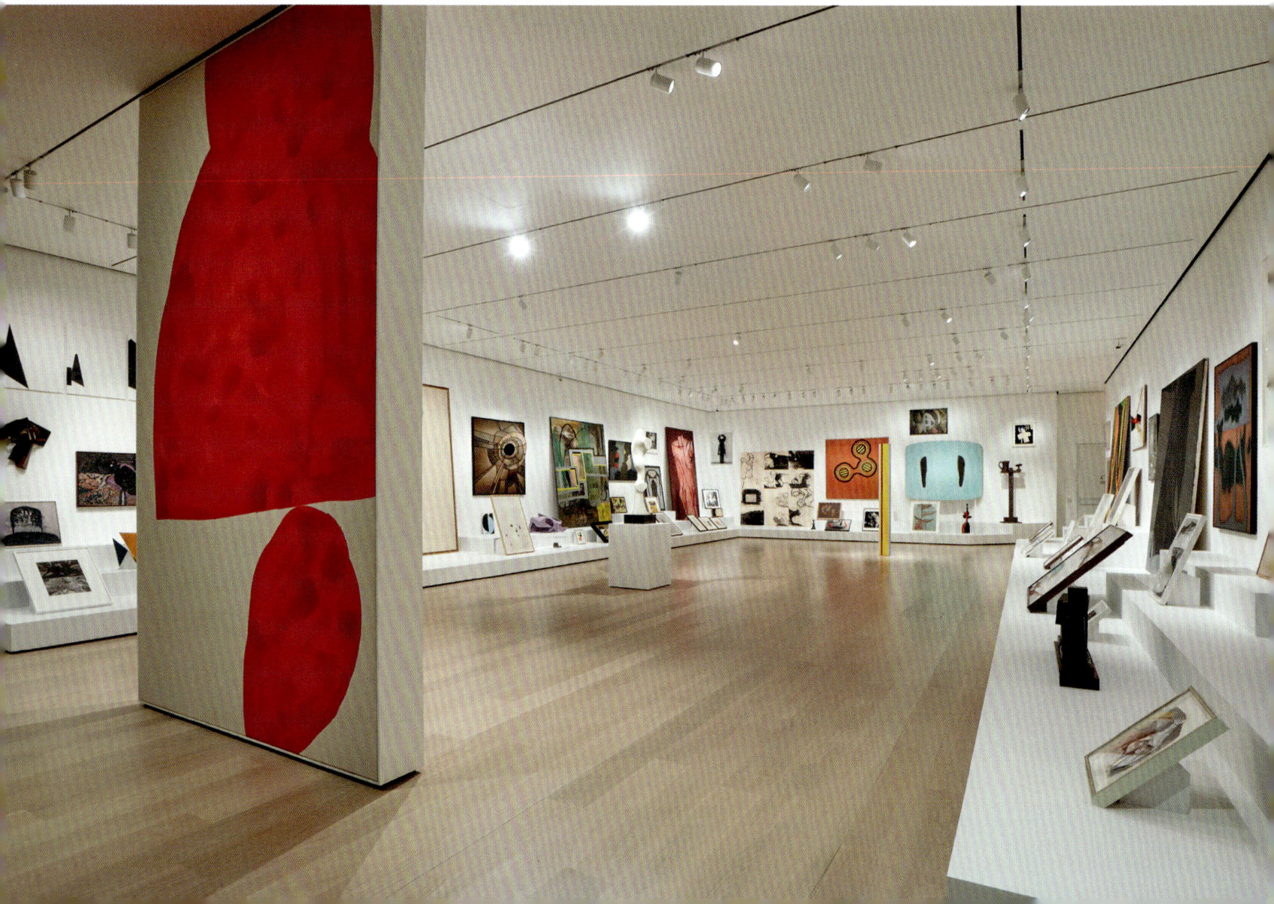

Amy Sillman, installation view of the exhibition Artist's Choice: Amy Sillman; *The Shape of Shape*, October 21, 2019–October 4, 2020. Photo: Heidi Bohnenkamp. The Museum of Modern Art, New York. Digital image © The Museum of Modern Art / licensed by SCALA / Art Resource, New York.

asked direct questions about the relation of shape to the grounds against which shapes are painted. By transferring its ground to the wall, it proposes that ground as one that possibly extends into the viewer's space. That space shared between the viewer(s) and painting is the first difference between Sillman's shape painting and Guston's. Whether it can be a psychologically ("emotionally" or "affectively") charged space, or whether it merely remains a more neutrally defined room space can give voice to a set of questions that reframes Sillman's debate about her inamoratas A and R.

One of Sillman's painting teachers, Elizabeth Murray, was a key figure in the 1980s confluence of Neo-Expressionism and late modernism. In that decade, Murray's complex structures built from multiple shaped canvases, splashy colors, and brushy, interruptive forms confronted Ellsworth Kelly's chromatically restrained, simple-shaped canvases. Similar confrontations erupted across painting more broadly: where Gerhard Richter turned to the gestural brushstroke in what appeared to be a self-conscious revision of earlier tenets tying painting inextricably to photography, Agnes Martin's ability to make even a grid feel immediate, intimate, and urgent transformed into an insistence on the horizontal plane of drawing *and* its modes of resisting the view's so-called horizons.[8] But the confrontation between two different visions of shape, between the layers of shape upon shape—painted, carved, bisected, whole—in Murray's *Her Story* (1984) and the bichromatic simplicity of Kelly's *Green Curve with White Panel* (1989) tells a story that cuts through some of this complexity. Murray's "Neo-Expressionism" is as indebted to the ordered crowding of shapes inside her dynamic composition as to the gestural brushstroke and its immediacy. Kelly's sparser arrangement calls our attention to the ambiguous relation between those qualities like gravity and buoyancy, the diagonality of movement as opposed to static, hieratic verticality, which I claimed, earlier, that Guston needed paint to convey. In Kelly's *Green Curve with White Panel*, it is not paint on canvas but the canvases themselves, chromatically differentiated, doing the work of asking how shape conveys its "meaning," or a possible range of meaning (levels of buoyancy; potentialities of motion). Murray's composition does not merely substitute oil on canvas to create the same range. It is rather that her layering of shapes replaces this notion of a painterly lexicon within another framework, that which ties the problem of the totalized shape to its opposite—dispersal, fragmentation—and to the problem of painterly process. When we see a painted shape like the teal circle painted on a yellow ground in *Her Story*'s upper right and we contrast that with the wholeness of several bright blue triangular shapes nearby, we get a sense of where *Her Story* is going. The question of painterly composition and

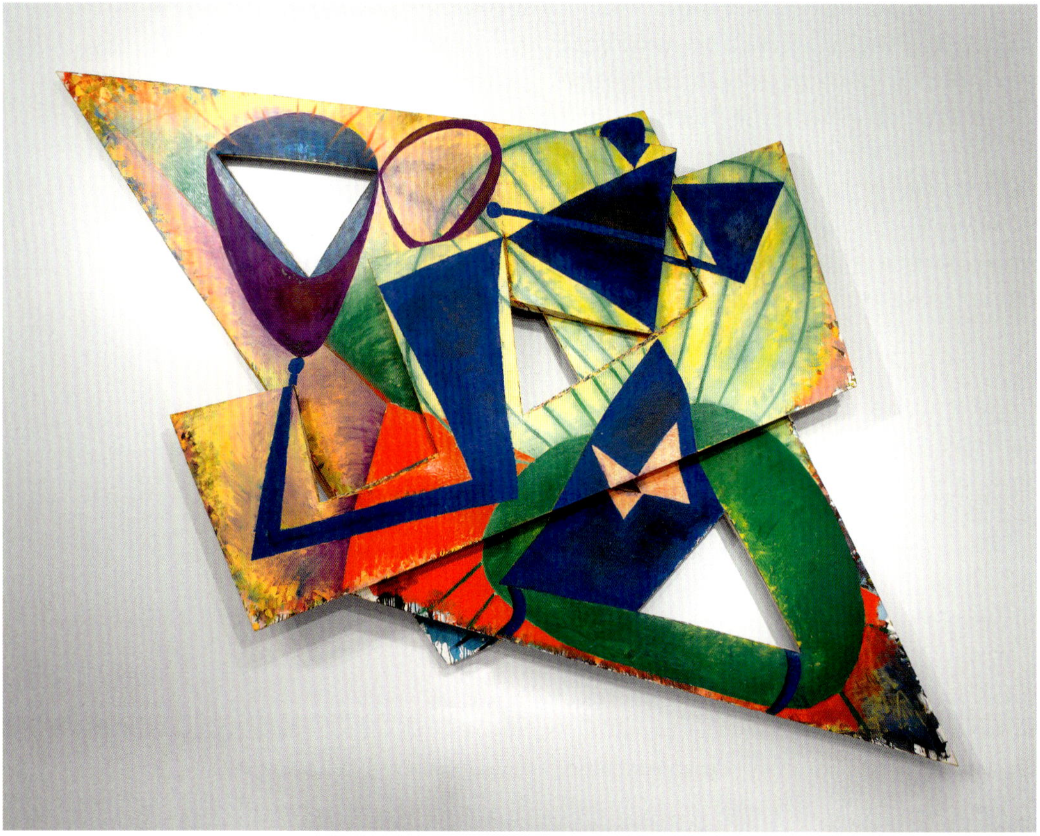

Elizabeth Murray, *Her Story*, 1984. Oil on canvas, 105 × 132 in. (266.7 × 52 cm). © 2021 The Murray-Holman Family Trust / Artists Rights Society, New York.

its traditions of pitting separate elements against each other to create a balance of weights, colors, textures, etc., is here upended. Compositional "balance" devolves into a map of procedures like cutting and superimposing that ultimately deprive shapehood of its claims on the totalizing or singular.

Gesture and shapes in paintings are only part of the lexicon that became identified, in the course of the 1980s, with new forms of Expressionism that then and since have been linked to painting's markets, national styles, and cultural hegemonies. Critiques of both historical Expressionism and Neo-Expressionism describe how psychic interiority is smuggled into hegemonic modes of subjectivation: Benjamin Buchloh's often-quoted essay "Figures of Authority, Ciphers of Regression" lays out an opposition between modernism (that which is "revealed" in the artwork as "fissures, voids, irresolvable contradictions, irreconcilable particularizations, pure heterogeneity") and what he calls "the historicist image: that of synthesis, of the illusory creation of a unity and totality which conceals its historical determination and conditioned particularity."[9] Modernism, in this

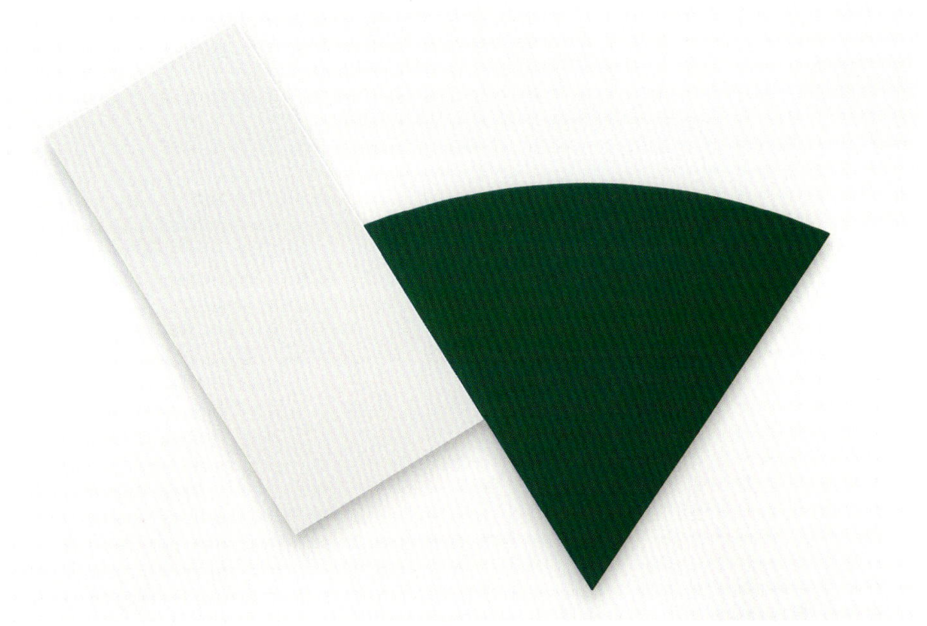

Ellsworth Kelly, *Green Curve with White Panel*, 1989. Oil on canvas, two joined panels, 90 × 125 in. (228.6 × 317.5 cm). © Ellsworth Kelly Foundation, courtesy Matthew Marks Gallery.

logic, is an art of aporia, whereas "historicism" is the myth of totality that easily lends itself to hegemony and worse. Expressionism, building on such totalities, is a tool of dominant and dominating cultural forces, which readily develop fascist tendencies. As Hal Foster would assert as early as 1985, not only is Expressionism a language like any other, built on rhetoric—in other words, conventions, syntax, learned associations.[10] And not only is it as such that it builds toward essentialisms (of national identity and gender, for example).[11] Rather, there is no such thing as an "immediacy" to Expressionism in painting that isn't already translated by a claim to subjectivity that turns out to be empty. Such claims are post facto, part of the language's development, rather than evidence of preexisting subjectivities. By extension: any Expressionism that wants immediacy would have to confront the manner in which its own lexicon is already a set of tropes and conventions used to leverage the idea of a self. Indeed, a set of arguments has surfaced more recently across several fields to point out that, as Rei Terada puts it, "expression is the dominant trope of thought about emotion. . . . The claim that emotion requires a subject—thus we can see we're subjects, since we have emotions—creates the illusion of subjectivity rather than showing evidence of it."[12]

Over the first decade of the twenty-first century, Sillman's work exploited Gustonian approaches to shape painting. She referenced his iconography (light bulbs, bulbous and stocky heads, pointing fingers), but more importantly, she played with the model of closed shapes that

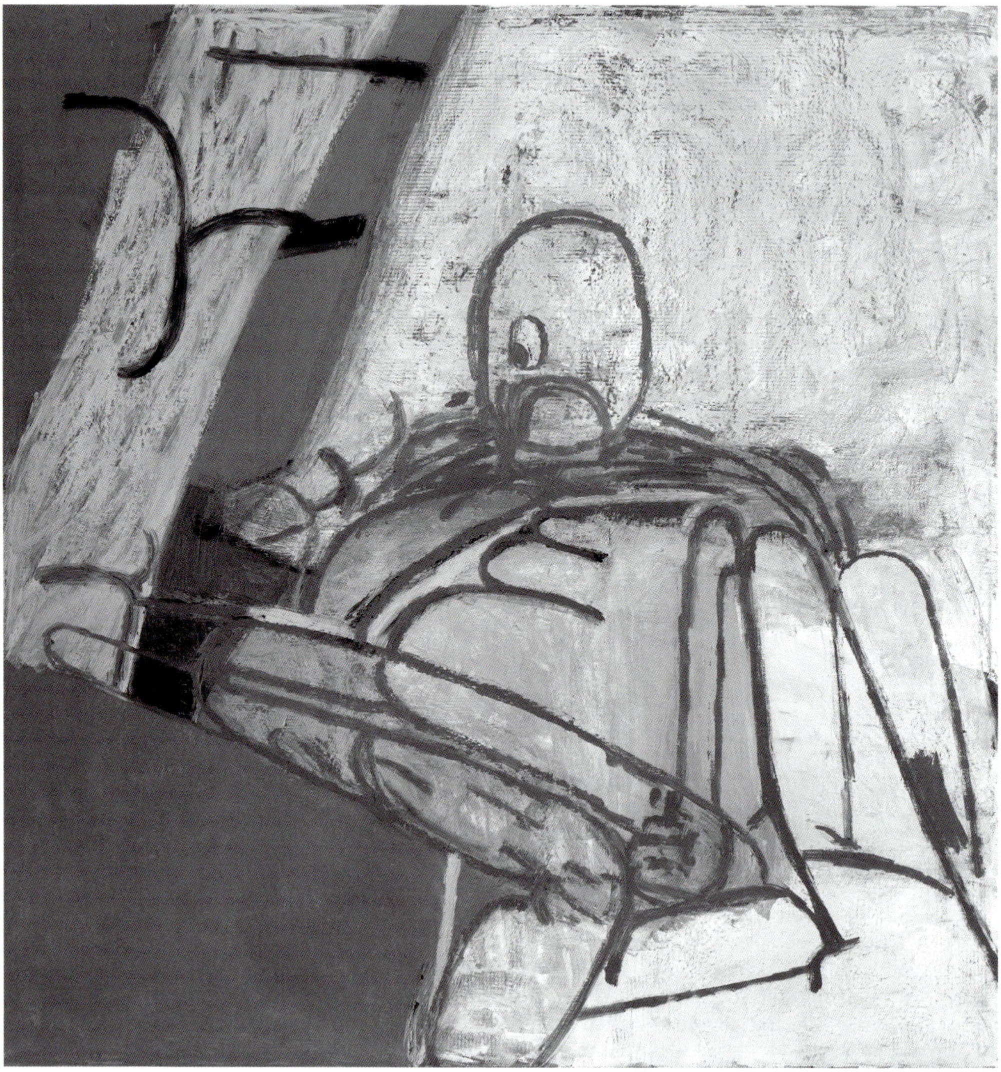

Amy Sillman, *Fatso*, 2009. Oil on canvas, 90½ × 84½ in. (230 × 214.6 cm). Photo: Bernd Borchardt. © Amy Sillman.

he brought to the table in the 1970s.[13] In the second half of the aughts, her skinny, drawn-outlined shapes—the breasty, leggy figures of *Them* (2006) or the disdainfully held sack of *The Plumbing* (2006)—and her close examinations of bodily part objects were placed into less and less explicitly "expressive" painterly spaces. Take, for example, the rolls/fingers and unhappy expression of *Fatso* (2009). These lines are not "filled in," let alone given a sense of dimensionality or weight, but instead drawn with paint, relying on outline and barely shaded fields exclusively; they are also sometimes repeated, brushily, as if these strong green paint strokes were part of a sketch. Gone are shape's characterological, totalizing developments through weight and gravity, texture and color, that we found

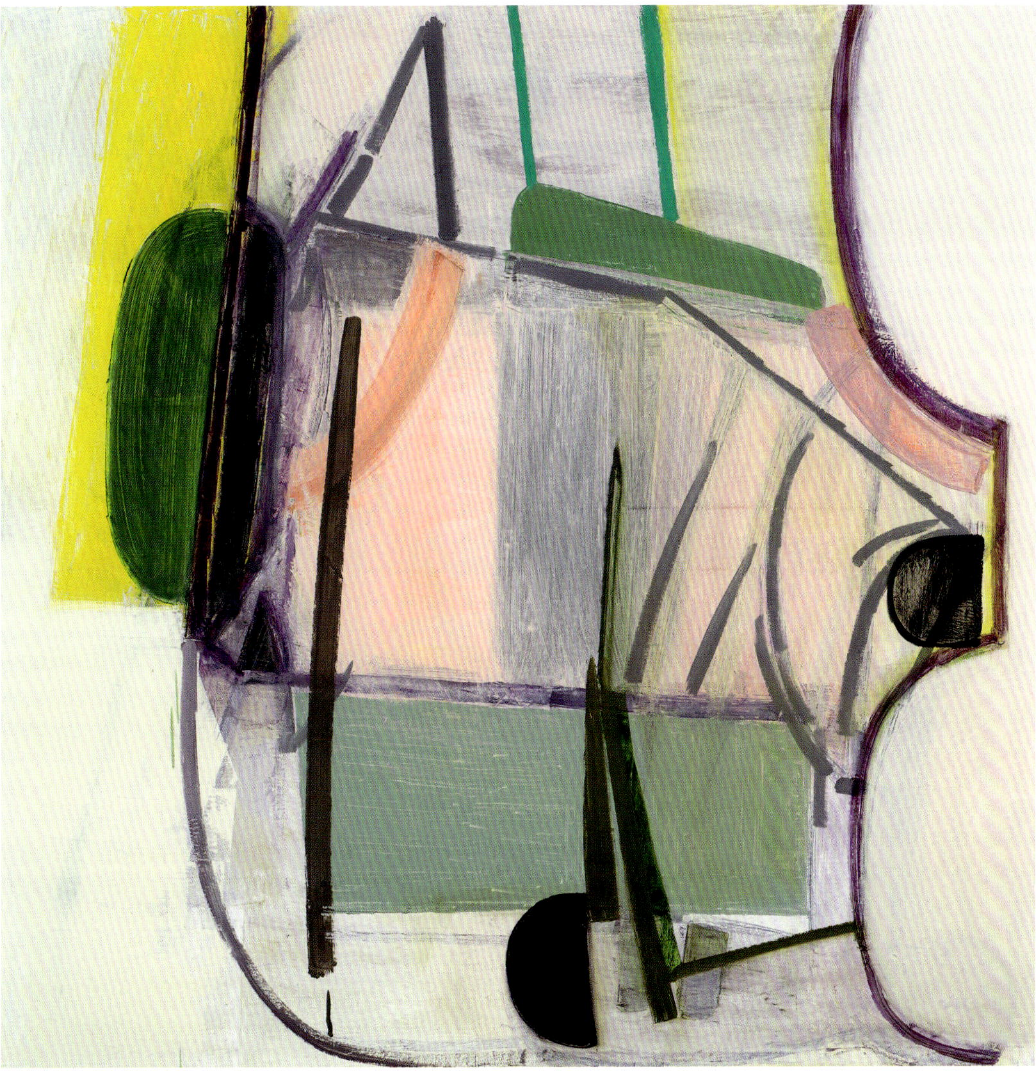

Amy Sillman, *Untitled*, 2010–11. Oil on canvas, 51 × 49 in. (129.5 × 124.5 cm). Photo: John Berens. © Amy Sillman.

in Guston's paintings. Instead we find shape approaching *drawn* "expressivity." Then look at *Untitled* (2010–11), where black, gray, dark green and dark purple lines do not encircle or reveal closed shapes but a kind of echoing concatenation. The cartooned body is still in play, with suggested eyeballs and nipples and breasty curves wanting us to rotate the canvas or figure out a "point of view." But the sense of an expressive subject seems to have left the picture.

Yet expressivity remained a key arena for Sillman to explore in the decade to come, during which she turned to a set of questions about process and product. In 2010, Sillman began putting her shape lexicon through experiments in collage and printmaking. These experiments allow her investigation of painterly processes to become something both systematic *and* invested in what such systematization does to painting's address of the viewer's interiority. This might seem like an incursion on the so-called Expressionism of her earlier work, or even on the communicativeness that I have been arguing is shape's domain. But this recent work offers a deeper investigation into what "Expressionisms" use as their languages and what they presume about the self either express*ing* or being expressed *to*. By importing systems of collage and printmaking into her painting, Sillman undoes some of the fundamental claims against Expressionism and its "Neo-" returns as aesthetics of false totalities. After all, the most maligned of the "historicist images" that Buchloh described were "'concealed collages' in painting"—in other words, paintings that incorporated juxtapositions of images *as if* they were collaged together, and as if such juxtapositions were meaningful.[14] Many of Sillman's recent works use actual collage—and on top of that, printmaking procedures (sometimes incorporating digital modes of printing) that continually alienate the "final" image from other layers that are encrusted into the work. Thus the question of a unity or totality, and whether it conceals or reveals the condition of being both historically determined and experienced *as* particularity, becomes crucial once again, albeit on different grounds.

How can Expressionism, conceived as a rhetoric, meet the demands of a subject who wants to express to herself (or be expressed to) an affective life that at least appears both innate and real, sui generis, her own and unique? Conversely, how can she express that affective life as communal, shared? Expressionisms, rather than merely enacting a hypocrisy about the subject, can be seen inversely to show us an apparently persistent desire for (or assumption of) uniqueness: they *bear witness to the demand* that we "express," using modes that are inevitably both shared and prescribed. Bypassing charges against Expressionisms, Sillman's work finds a way to allow that externality that is borne in sharing and prescription to surface within her painting as system. "System" here means the patterns of production that become present and highly palpable in her adoption of collage and printmaking; they are something we can see as well as something she puts into place in her working process. Moreover, her work focuses our attention on the point at which a system becomes a structure—that is, a set of differences able to generate meaning (like language itself). That is how her work points to an idea of interiority even as it investigates how that interiority would relate to the processes of painting, printmaking, and drawing, and their means of approaching structure (i.e., meaning production). Her painting provides a way to think about how a mark can appear to be "one's own" while also fitting into the systems of collage and reproduction that expand the scope of her work, incorporating that which might have once been seen as external to the canvas as such. For collage, like reproduction, points to externality itself; it points to the place where the cutout has gone or come from (or the infinitude of copies). In Sillman's work, these systems that refer us to an "out there" are also conveying, through their use of shape, the singular "me" that a paint stroke or a shape's totality seem to index. It is that interplay we see in Sillman's treatment of Expressionism, leading toward a new awareness of how totality and unity, fragmentation and externality, might function in a present that can only be shared.

A Shape That Stands Up and Listens (2012)

> She makes them by drawing on large sheets of paper, cutting shapes out of the drawings, and then pasting either the shape or the whole piece of paper with the shape cut out of it onto other drawings the same size. The drawings are predominantly black, white, and gray, although some have red calligraphic marks in pencil or crayon, sinuous lines that border on doodles. The cutout shapes look like the shadows of Henry Moore sculptures, voluptuous forms that evoke ceramic vessels and the human form. Thick, emphatic, hand-drawn lines of black watercolor ink traverse the tops of the collages, both gliding over and being obscured by patches of pasted paper.
>
> These lines do a lot of work. . . . Every once in a while the black lines form a representational image—here a vase of flowers, there an eye, here a window, there a sofa. But even as they do this, they retain their identity as marks, swipes, and drags of the brush, plays of thick and thin, exercises in movement across the page. In other words, even though they are figurative, they are also trenchantly abstract.
>
> Observing this gave me one of those big "Aha!" moments; the dichotomy between figuration and abstraction is untenable. All representation is abstract and all abstraction, no matter how rigorous, is funneled through the language and habits of mind that are representation.
>
> HELEN MOLESWORTH, 2013

Here, Molesworth is discussing works that form the series entitled *A Shape That Stands Up and Listens* (2012), after a line in Jayne Anne Phillips's novel *Lark and Termite*.[15] These collage-drawing-paintings in gouache, ink, chalk, and pencil on paper are dominated by a palette of blacks, grays, and whites; into this narrow spectrum so familiar from the medium of drawing are imported a chorus of pinks, lavenders, acid greens and mustards, electric orange and red, as well as an array of surfaces and textures that result from various forms of drawing and painting. We see close cross-hatching by one or more colored pencils; stains of watery paint; straight lines that seem as if they could only result from the use of

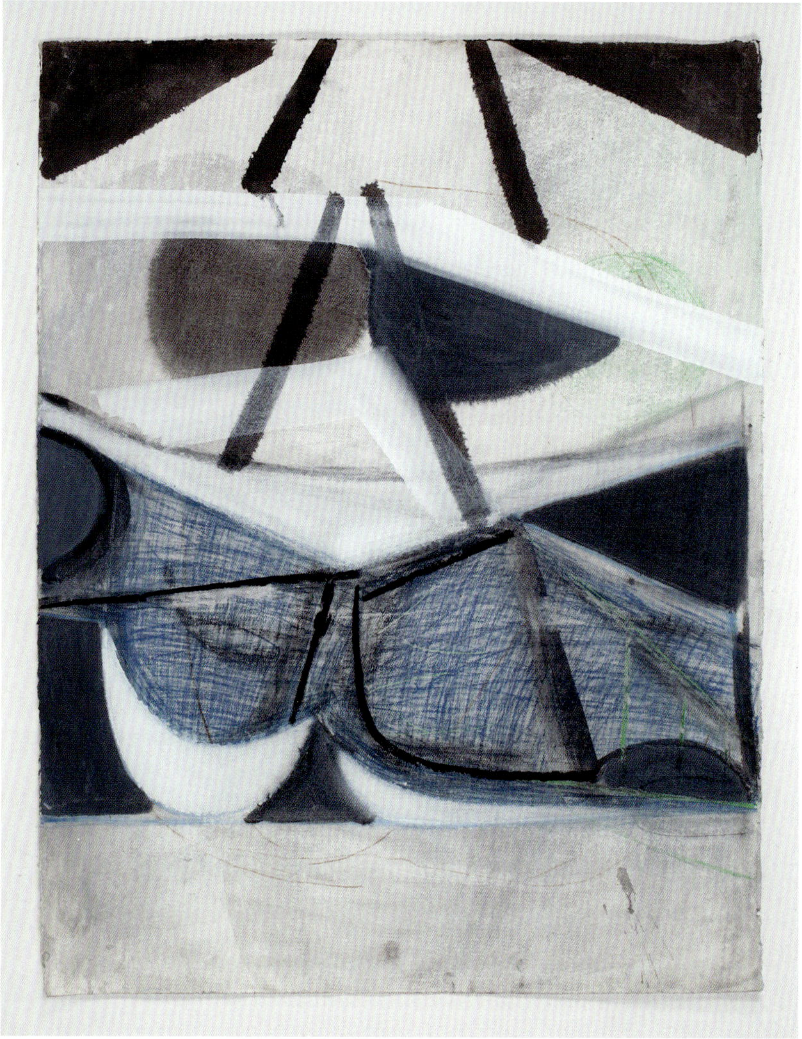

Amy Sillman, *A Shape That Stands Up and Listens #8*, 2012. Ink, gouache, pencil, chalk, and charcoal on paper, 30 × 22½ in. (76.2 × 57.2 cm). Photo: John Berens. © Amy Sillman.

a ruler. These works are internally heterogeneous, and also impossible to see all at once; this series of dozens of works is never shown as a totality.

In one work, *#8*, two thickened, angled lines appear to be the exact reproductions of two other angled lines just above, foreshadowing the use of digital printing that will evolve from this series in the coming decade. But each of the four lines of paint (and even a fifth, in the shadowy area below) bleeds differently. If they repeat the same angles and thereby refer to reproducibility and mobility, they keep intact their separate identities as hand-drawn or hand-painted lines. Even when the works of *A Shape That Stands Up and Listens* are collages—when we can see the cutout of a shape either layered on top of others, or providing a negative space in these works on paper—they are all emphatically involved in the ways that drawing and

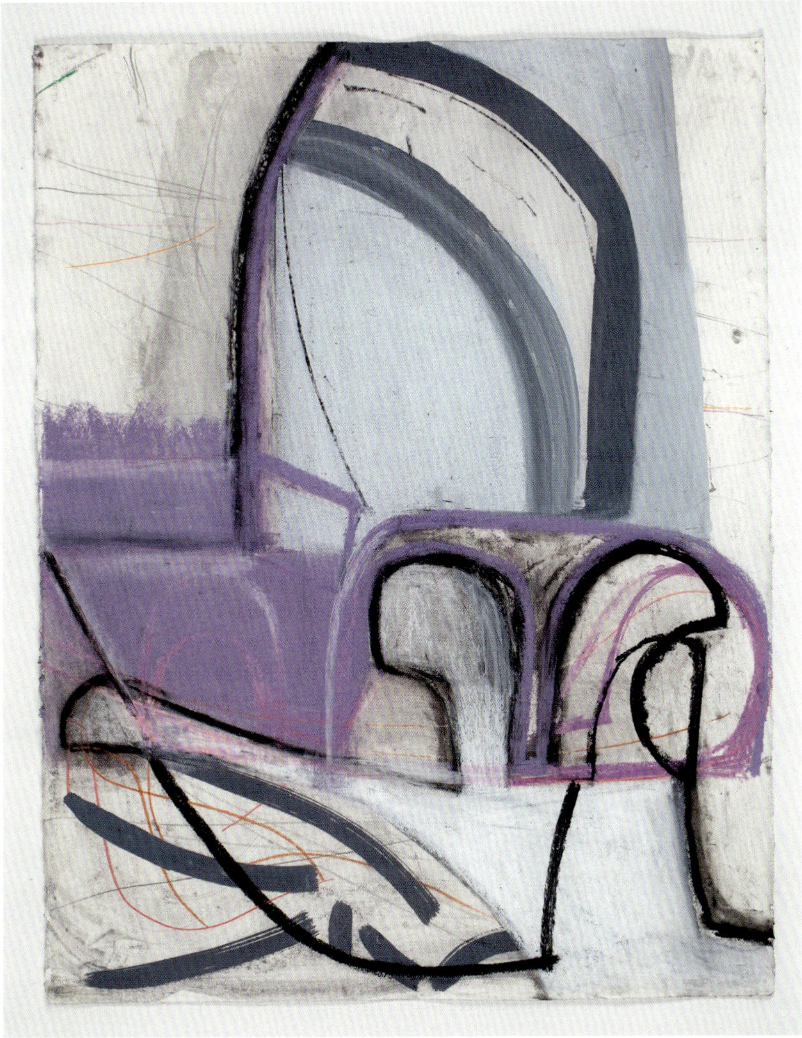

Amy Sillman, *A Shape That Stands Up and Listens #10*, 2012. Ink, gouache, pencil, chalk, and charcoal on paper, 30 × 22½ in. (76.2 × 57.2 cm). Photo: John Berens. © Amy Sillman.

painting hold onto the “singular” line, the visible brushstroke. (See the gray lines at the bottom of *#10*—single strokes of unmodulated color—or the feathery violet rectangle folding over them.) This series is the earliest sign that Sillman's work will address shape's mutability and transferability, its transformation into process, system, and structure. But *A Shape that Stands Up and Listens* also holds on, almost aggressively, to the ways that nonreproduced singular lines, washes, and strokes do their own work amid the effects of mobility and permutability. In other words, shape is seen as *both* structure and gesture, repetition and immediacy: a shape doing two things at once, as the series' title suggests.

A Shape That Stands Up and Listens eventually becomes the basis of Sillman's ongoing investigation of how it might be possible to merge printmaking and painting as ways of underlining how shape might produce a new set of possibilities for viewing. By taking painting apart through the processes and effects of printmaking, Sillman starts wrecking painting's alleged specialness based on its claims to the unique and the singular. But this isn't because of a binary contending that printmaking aligns itself with the multiple and painting with the singular. It is by breaking up how shape presents itself as a kind of sign whose totalizing capacities would correspond to the subject's wholeness that Sillman demonstrates painting's potential to resolve (by fragmenting) our claims on the singular and the unique. In other words: *A* shape that stands up and listens is both not a whole bunch of shapes and not *the* shape. It makes the inverse of a claim to singularity: its claim is to being one of many. The desires it expresses, the listenings this shape performs, are communal.

As Molesworth explains, *A Shape That Stands Up and Listens* is a series of works on paper (most are around 30 × 22½ inches) made by first creating drawings, then cutting shapes from within those drawings, and then either using those shapes or the leftover cutouts—the negatives of the shapes—to paste onto other drawings. The series' title calls out shapes as being at its center. But so is the medium of collage, itself shape dependent: what collage's cutting and pasting moves between pieces of paper is always shapes. Sometimes, in *A Shape*, the shapes don't shift, at least not across the material planes: plenty of the works are not collages. Yet each work in the series (that I have seen) manages to convey a sense of the multiplicity of collage, its implication of shiftiness or movement, of presence and absence. Sometimes the works do this by performing symmetry, so that a shape might appear to be doubled even on one piece of paper. This happens multiple times in *#8*, which works on symmetries, with crosshatched denim-blue shapes on the bottom half doubling one another along a vertical axis as do the pairs of black angled lines above them. Its symmetries always remain imperfect; the works are interested in performing or alluding to symmetry rather than executing an impeccable version of it. Such symmetries (perhaps more than their ideal cousins) describe repetition and "presence and absence" without necessarily manifesting them as collage, as things multiplied, taken away, or replaced: one side is describing what the other side "redoes," closely. Then, sometimes the works do transfer one shape or set of shapes to another surface via collage or its imitation. *#11* boasts an interior parallelogram lined up with its bottom edge, with green at the upper left corner, which interrupts another set of shapes on top of which it seems to be laid. When (as here) the collage is "actual," it is also pictorial, reenacting the collage system on each plane. In all these ways, Sillman's shapes are emphatically mobile

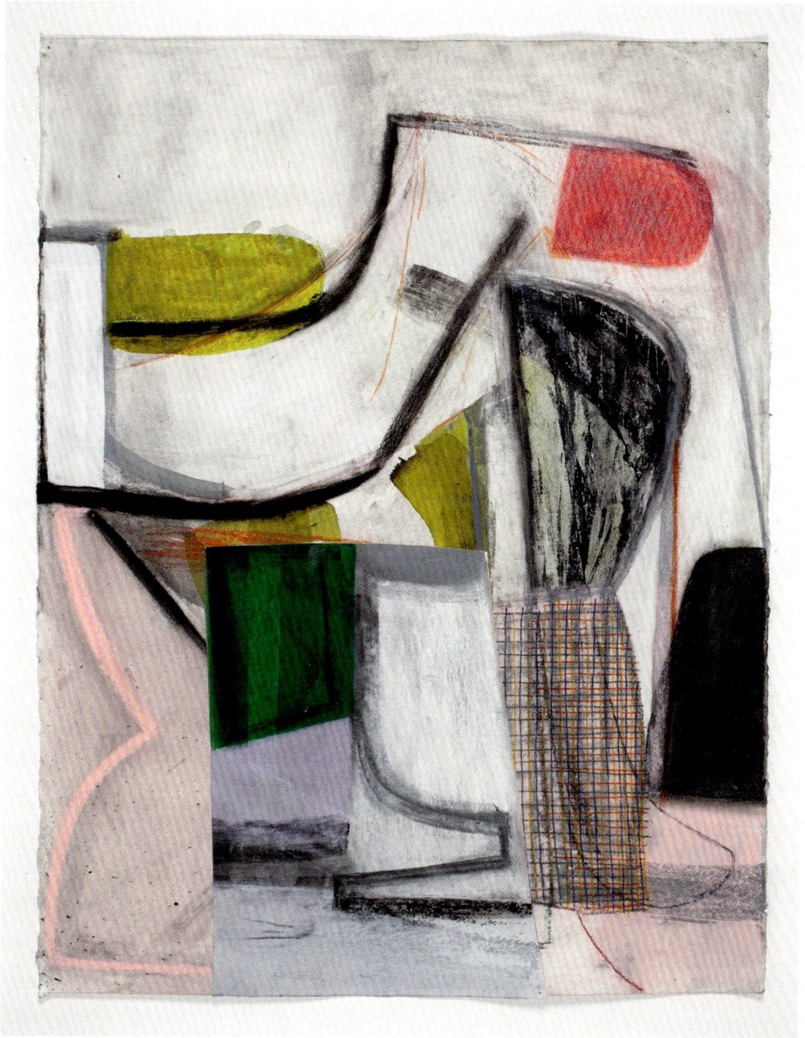

Amy Sillman, *A Shape That Stands Up and Listens #11*, 2012. Ink, gouache, pencil, chalk, and charcoal on paper, 30 × 22½ in. (76.2 × 57.2 cm). Photo: John Berens. © Amy Sillman.

and modular. They articulate shapes' inborn potential to shift across and recombine either on one surface or across multiple works. They make that shiftiness a *part of* shape.

At the same time, the multiple shapes that proliferate across the works have, seemingly, *all* the characteristics: some are curved, some are straight, others are phallic, brute, delicate, bulbous, breasty, flattened, handlike, trellisy, and so on. They are textured and nontextured, in generations of different colors (including black and white), in stained or brushed-on paint; they are painted, drawn, cutout, and pasted on. Sometimes they gesture toward some of the totalizing, unary qualities of Guston's shapes; for example, the netting-like cross-hatching of two generously globular bra shapes in *#8* have a quasi-figural energy that the watery brown and blue orbs above them do not. Or the alert, amaranth tip of a cartoonish shape poking rightward in *#11*; it holds together as "a shape" not simply because it continues a heavy black outline but because the reddish tip speaks to what might be comic readiness or reactivity. Sillman, having closely observed Guston and others, knows about the comic potential of shape as well as its characterological depths: the ways it can pull that comicality across a canvas. If many of her earlier works—like *Fatso*—bring up that comicality, these works occasionally recall that capacity but bury it in another set of procedures and questions about what shape does.

In the use or suggestion of replication and symmetry that unfold across *A Shape That Stands Up and Listens*, Sillman enters her shapes into the register of ways that abstraction allows shapes to bounce around, to perform all kinds of compositional and anticompositional functions that seem to reject representation, narrativity, and the figure. This is accomplished especially insofar as Sillman's shapes, as described, depend on repetition, absence, and arbitrariness. The shapes of *A Shape That Stands Up and Listens* are thus interested in the structures that produce meaning through the alternation of positive and negative, through repetition and layering, while seeming to abandon interest in "meaning" or communicativeness. Like Wittgenstein's triangles that flip from suggesting one thing to another, pine cone to mountain, or even flipping between one kind of weightedness to another (heavy/light), Sillman's shapes in this series both glance at their capacity to signify and remain fundamentally untethered to any singular meaning. Even the possibility of a shape's claim to signification is in question.

At the same time, as soon as we start studying the series, we can start to sense the properties of "scenes." That is not accidental: The notion of a scene is part of the series' lore. In an interview Sillman explains to the artist Rebecca Quaytman that the series grew from an assignment she'd presented to herself: to draw, quickly, from memory, every room in which she had experienced shame.

> AS: These collages are interiors, they are based on rooms. The assignment was to draw a room as fast as I could, a room in which I remembered feeling shame.
> RQ: What do you mean by assignment?
> AS: The assignment to myself. The starting point was shame. I had to remember a feeling that I couldn't get rid of, which quickly became a room. And they were all based on palpable—
> RQ: (*yelling*) Ah!
> AS: —memories of feeling embarrassed.

RQ: Are those beds? (*laughter*)

AS: Yes, many of them are.[16]

While shame is, for some theorists, the "meta-affect" demonstrating how affect theory works, here I am less interested in that meta level than in the mere way that such an affect enables the subfigural to operate—at least in the work's process.[17] If references to beds and other figures haunt *A Shape That Stands Up and Listens*, that is both because of the concept of an expressive author and because signs persist in this series as such—as a group of works nonsequentially drawing each other, and the space in between them, into the way they redefine shape.

First of all, as the works' individual numbered titles remind us, *A Shape* places its shapes into the context of an entire series. The series sends shapes from one piece of paper to another, or in its use of doubling and symmetry, implies such sending. In each work the shapes generate new sets of echoes, proliferations, or isolations on each piece of paper. Secondly, even while the shapes' mobility enables a kind of abstraction across the series, in any given work they are often allusive, subfigural. One sees, like Quaytman, beds or other signs of domestic interiors; *#10* seems to imagine an armchair, deconstructed, just as others, like *#57*, seem to show a figure lying on a bed with two pillows, with a dresser and perhaps a chair nearby, signified by very primitive shapes that then recur, fragmented, in another piece (*#48*'s smaller bed with pillows). Here, the collage system is working against its tendency toward pure self-reflexivity, as Rosalind Krauss once defined it: "For it is collage that raises the investigation of the impersonal workings of pictorial form, begun in analytic cubism, onto another level: the *impersonal* operations of language that are the subject of collage."[18] Sillman modifies this course of operations, so that what collage continually implies in *A Shape That Stands Up and Listens* is another scene or site—perhaps that highly personalized scene or site from which "this piece" came. Rather than language, it is the offsite (the place from whence a shape or memory has come) that is at stake.

It is not always a figural scene, but the general scene of "elsewhere" implied by externality that is in all of *A Shape*'s duplications and symmetries, repetitions and reversals. It points to how collage is *always* implicating another site, not merely the structural, "*impersonal* operations of language." Even those works that show no sign of cutting and pasting participate in a suggestion of mobility and permutability. Sillman's shapes insist on this, loading *A Shape* with allusiveness and suggestiveness merely by pointing to how an "elsewhere" defines the structuring power of the collage system. It is not only the highly personal sense of a scene that happened elsewhere that *A Shape* describes, once we learn about its origins. It is the structural or "*impersonal*" itself that is the subject of these works.

By accentuating their own adherence to structure—that way that a system of repetition produces meaning by merely generating presence here (of a shape) and absence there (as a cutout)—Sillman's series escapes becoming "expressionistic," in the conventional sense of the term. But even as her shapes mitigate shape's totalizing capacities, they also allow the structuring, meaning-producing capacity of reference to enter and perhaps cleave their own "abstraction." By merely working off-sitedness into the structuring of the work, by intervening on the concept of experience and its transposition into two dimensions, Sillman has made works that look anew at how thinking of the "operations of language" as "structural, *impersonal*" might deprive us of understanding how structure is affecting.[19] If shapes here derive some of their strength from the offsite, the effect of their own perambulatory, mobile capacities, then they demonstrate how the structure that generates meaning out of presence and absence is itself affecting.

Ultimately, *A Shape That Stands Up and Listens* is where what we might have thought were shape's claims to immediacy or expressivity are interrupted by a new form of distance, even a way of naming or thinking about reflexivity. Shape, in these works, becomes a means for understanding how something (shape, its signifying capacity that nonetheless does not rely on a stable referent or signification) can be both an effect of structure and its ability to affect. To recall Massumi's distinction between emotion as "subjective content," both fixed and personal, as opposed to affect, as intensity "disconnected from meaningful sequencing, from narration": it would appear to be the latter that is in play in Sillman's shapes. They do not go so far as to express anything as formed as an emotion, or even shame—an affect or the meta-affect—as per Sillman's assignment to herself.[20] But they do reflect an intensity "disconnected from meaningful sequence, from narration." That is part of how they start to carve a path for shapes that does not require the kind of narration or even tropological accumulation that figuration imposes. In migrating from one plane to another, or in effecting their own repetition and modularity, shapes in *A Shape That Stands Up and Listens* defer to the structuring effects of language or process. But they also hold on to their own affective potential—to what can still "reach out" to an as-yet undefined sense of interiority, even defined within the system of affect as one of relays and rebounds, storage and receptors.[21] *A Shape That Stands Up and Listens* concentrates this doubleness, producing both affecting shapes and a way to understand the distancing work that structure does.

Mostly Drawing (2018)

The first three works that greeted visitors entering *Mostly Drawing*, her first gallery exhibit at her new New York gallery, Barbara Gladstone, exhibited a kind of busyness that fans of Sillman's telegraphic shapes drawn in paint on canvas will find surprising. Three works announce two things. The first is the chromatic through lines of the show: a range of orangey-peach to lemon-yellows. The second is the presence of milky washes, either cut out into strips laid over other silkscreened and "real" brushstrokes or simply laid over *other* layers of paint and silkscreen, with new layers painted or printed on top. These two features are in a constant push and pull in the pictures that make up *Mostly Drawing*: one might add to that two-way dynamic Sillman's eponymous process, drawing (in paint), which happens all across these multilayered works. Shape resurfaces, in various forms and modes, plenty: the scissored shapes of those milky cutouts; the strong, thick black lines, either on top of or half washed out by other layers; and shapes made by brushstrokes that have been reproduced, like inverted Lichtenstein brushstroke paintings.[22] Rather than painting the shape of the brushstroke, as Lichtenstein did, Sillman collages the magnified brushstroke as a shape unto itself, and rather than competing with drawing's lines, such shapes often *are* the drawing.

Amy Sillman, installation view, entrance to *Mostly Drawing*, 2018. Courtesy the artist and Gladstone Gallery. Photo: David N. Regen. © Amy Sillman.

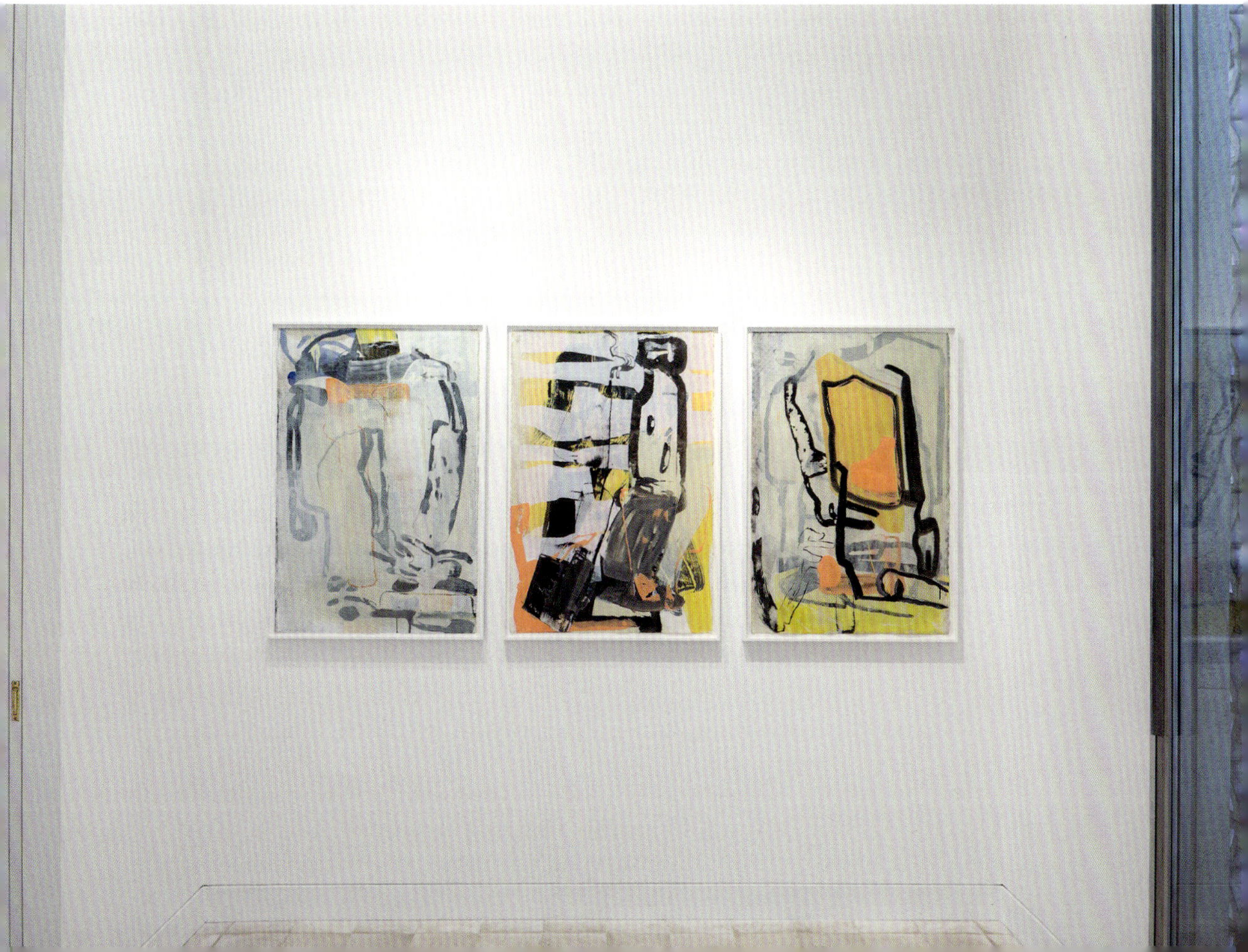

That which once gave Sillman's shapes brevity, sometimes leaning into the tragicomic or even the burlesque, is still here, conveyed in the merest figural ideas—the droop of a line, the knobbiness of a curve—that still make up much of her painterly lexicon. Such repeated suggestions of bodily shapes turn up in *Mostly Drawing* in the work done by thick black lines, which ultimately also give us a worried-looking face that keeps reappearing, sometimes atop shoulders and breasts. That face made of thick black strokes that keep declaring themselves like a refrain, a ghost, even a signature of authorly presence, ends the show, staring back hard at the viewer, or perhaps at the other works that have led to her position (she's next to a doorframe, looking back at a long line of works). There at the end, on the top floor of Gladstone's uptown New York City gallery, we can see some repetitions more clearly than anywhere else: the same face, or parts of it, three works away from the end of one wall's hanging. Just to the right of that twin of the downstairs entryway series, another repetition, this time of two comically close-together eyes, one in black, and to the left, one in dark grayish blue, raising the question whether Sillman has digitally printed parts of her paintings in different colors.

But these figural or shapely refrains fight against layers of milky washes that layer collage and silkscreen into one another, repeating both processes over and over in the same work. The shapes, in other words, fight against processes that fragment them. Collage and silkscreen and digital printing are laid into one another, often keeping lines from becoming whole shapes. Twenty-nine out of the thirty works on paper lining the walls in this exhibit have identical measurements—$40\frac{1}{8} \times 26$ inches. The remaining work, *XL-18-1*, measuring 60 × 40 inches, sits above a mantel, one of few remaining architectural details testifying to the domestic framework in this converted townhouse designed in 1956 by Edward Durell Stone.[23] As one moves through two floors of works, always hung with the same couple of inches between them, one sees works that are virulently formless, especially in their agglomeration. Each uses cascading layers from repeated processes to both differentiate and dedifferentiate across sharp and blurry contrasts. We can only imagine the earliest, bottommost layers; too many layers since have obscured all but their edges. And this buried sequence, repeated again and again, also mostly rebuts narration or sequencing—aside from that last piece and its face. Throughout, Sillman has developed a system that involves drawing in paint, silkscreening, printing, and collage—and then she's repeated steps in these processes so many times that no one can tell which layer is painted and which is reproduced. You can see *that* there are recurring shapes but you can only rarely pinpoint *where* they recur. *This* might be a repetition of *that*, but there are too many layers in the way: one can't be

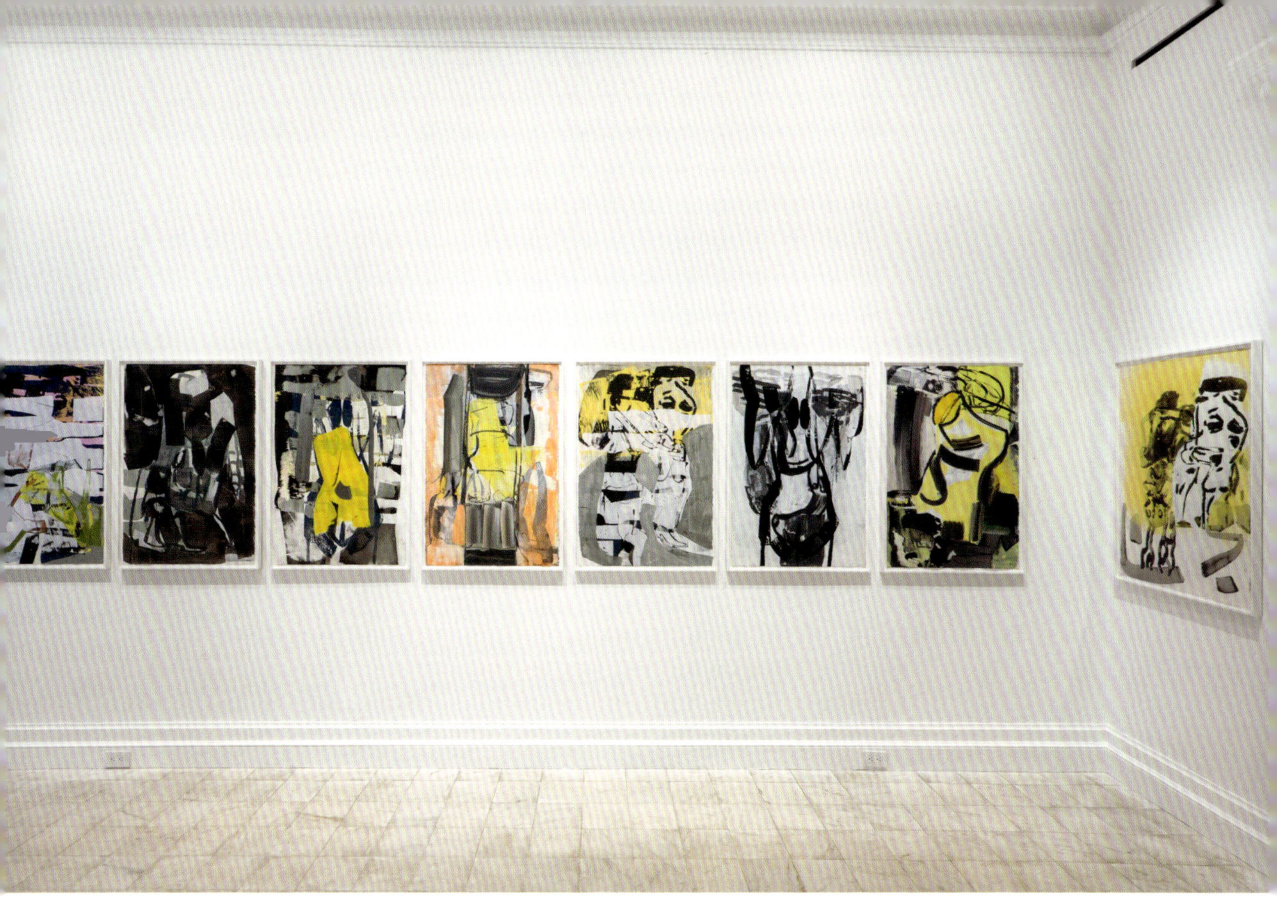

Amy Sillman, installation view, last room of *Mostly Drawing*, 2018. Courtesy the artist and Gladstone Gallery. Photo: David N. Regen. © Amy Sillman.

sure. The shapes have become information hidden in a version of formlessness that makes them only sometimes recognizable as shapes.

"Formlessness," as Hal Foster explained in 1983, "does not dissolve convention or suspend mediation; as the expressionist trope for feeling, it is a rhetorical form too."[24] This was part of Foster's study of Expressionist (and Neo-Expressionist) claims of immediacy and expressivity. He focused particularly on how immediacy claims both emotionality and the kind of subject who would be able (according to legends of German Expressionism) to both convey and receive emotional states through brushstrokes or indeed "formlessness." Brushstrokes emanate by virtue of an artist's "inner necessity," as Kandinsky put it, and communicate by virtue of abstraction's leveling powers.[25] The brushstroke functions as the emblematic "trope for feeling" through its shape, speed, and perhaps "organicism," as well as the chromatic intensity it can deliver.[26] In *Mostly Drawing*, the relation between those two—the brushstroke, presented in black or in color, as "real" or reproduced, and the formless, created by so many layers of milky washes, cutouts, and chromatic interventions—is central. In attacks on and defenses of Expressionism, brushstroke and formlessness are allied. But here, in *Mostly Drawing*, formlessness and the brushstroke enter a peculiar dynamic, cleaved and yet united by repetition and reproduction. Formlessness creates a kind of abyss against which the thick black brushstroke claims its identity, but that brushstroke is itself reproduced continually within seas of formlessness. Are the two in competition to dominate their decompositions, or in concert?

If we look more closely still, we find that formlessness in *Mostly Drawing* is created out of brushstrokes treated across a range of processes. In *SK42* the feathery fine lines of brushstrokes are reproduced at least twice: in the top right corner, in a navy-and-peach combination, and in the top left corner, in lemony yellow and a darker orange. Almost buried—on top of the navy blue and peach, and a bright pink underneath them—is that worried, anxious figure. But a whitish cutout stripping laterally across the entire piece almost masks her entirely, even if it too is interrupted by an olive-green dab in the bottom left and also, confusingly, a kind of green and lemon-yellow—and gray and blue—confiscation of that whitish strip's authority. Which is the top layer, and which gets to claim the "immediacy" of the brushstroke? Which is the "formless" underlayer? It doesn't really matter: this "formlessness" created through processes that include silkscreening, collage, and digital printing seems to have little to do with the kind of immediacy claimed by expression, except perhaps as part of a gestural buildup one recognizes as participating in the codes of Expressionisms.

Conventionally, brushstrokes can compose shapes and sometimes supplement them. This doubleness allows the painted shapes to give us a sense of the "referent" entering the picture *and* allows the brushstroke, or its concert with shape, to gain independence from that "outer reality," even if that independence is sometimes ephemeral. Take Emil Nolde's 1915 *The Burial*, with its blue-robed swaths laid over Christ's green-gold skin etched with pain. This skillful recycling of a highly familiar repertoire—classical gestures, mythic-religious-spiritual scene, anguished witnesses—produces the "reality" of the "coded, realist outer world": that of Christ's body rescued. But what makes it "Expressionist" is its "inner world," conveyed in a manner departing from Nolde's early modern forebears: loose brushwork revealing elegant but also clawlike finger rakes; red brushstrokes that are more like gashes in the painted surface. In other words, the "shapes" here are both fingers and what they become when the brushstroke takes over, making fingers more like prongs, or making small red cuts more like apertures in the painted surface. If these strokes are where the "outer" reality of the composition gives way to "inner" truth, per Expressionist credo, then they are also where Expressionism indexes the role of that familiar interior/exterior spatiality through which we think we know the self.[27] Sillman's approach, however, makes the brushstroke into a question

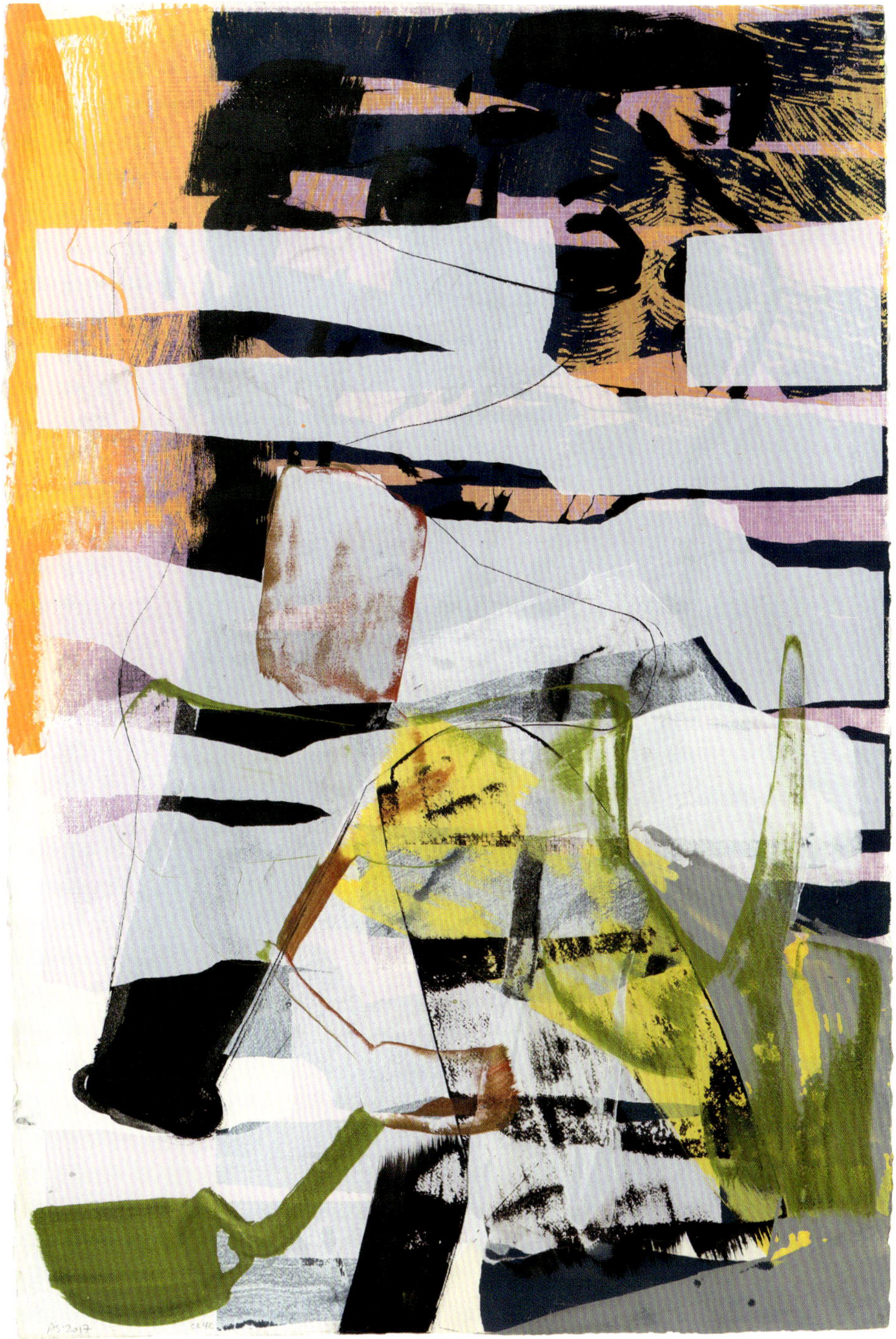

Amy Sillman, *SK42*, 2017. Acrylic, ink, and silkscreen on paper, 40 × 26 in. (101.6 × 66 cm). Photo: John Berens. © Amy Sillman.

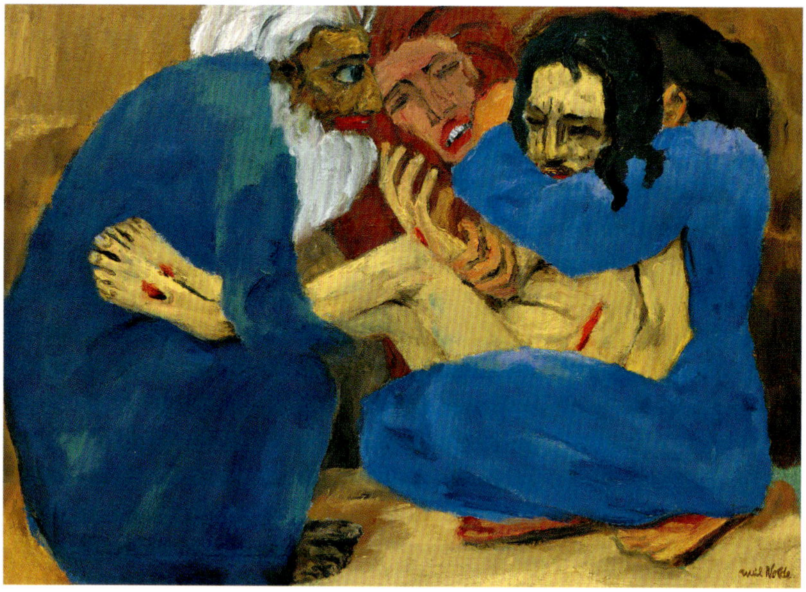

Emil Nolde, *The Burial*, 1915. Oil on canvas, 34 × 46 in. (86.5 × 117 cm). © Nolde Stiftung Seebüll.

of process that denies that spatial metaphor its supremacy and substitutes for it a different relation between the codedness that is painting and the "immediacy" that supposedly marks the emotional or inner self.

The notion that "formlessness is a rhetorical form too" has its antecedents in Adorno's condemnation of American jazz. Perceiving the respect of "basic rhythmic structures" alongside "the vibrato which causes a tone which is rigid and objective to tremble as if on its own," Adorno rejects the pretense by which jazz "ascribes [to such trembling] subjective emotions."[28] In other words, if Expressionism is a language, it cannot simply refer us back to a "self as originary": it has to emerge from the rhetorical powers built up through repetition and difference, just as jazz's "practices of syncopation and improvisation [are mere] pseudo-spontaneity and illusory self-expression, contained as they are within a metrically conventional, banal architecture."[29] Thus we encounter the central paradox of Expressionism in painting: even if the painter were to want to claim she "feels" the internal truths of emotion, she finds they require the same kind of code as "outer appearances," "reality."[30] That codedness that allows us to think of painting as being a structure like language means that emotions and "reality" are not only communicated in the same ways but can only be communicated insofar as they are not "internal" to any self but indeed part of a set of quasi-universal codes.

Thus does the paradox of Expressionism get us straight to the paradox of the subject, who asserts the uniqueness of her experience via her "own" feelings, but in fact registers those feelings—that hurt, that anomie, that joy, etc.—as part of a punishingly scripted and delimited range. For Terada, the question of expression and its relation to emotion begins with

> the relatively uncontroversial observation that expression is the dominant trope of thought about emotion. The ideology of emotion diagrams emotion as something lifted from a depth to a surface. . . . The claim that emotion requires a subject—thus we can see we're subjects, since we have emotions—creates the illusion of subjectivity rather than showing evidence of it. This sleight of mind, in which "expression" serves as the distracting handkerchief, strikes me as self-serving. It is this relatively large complex of circularity, naturalization, and inversion to which I refer as the *expressive hypothesis*. To object to the expressive hypothesis or any other mechanism of the ideology of emotion is not to discredit emotion, but to extricate it from expedient mythologies.[31]

Slightly before Terada, in a parallel effort, Foster called what she describes as an "expressive hypothesis" an "expressive fallacy." Neither, however, lingers over that which is interesting to me here: the analogy between the depth-reliant "trope of thought about emotion," which allows Terada to picture it as something "lifted from a depth to a surface," coinciding with articulations of depth and surface in Abstract Expressionism and Color Field or "all-over" painting.[32] Such metaphorical language, ascribing depth and surface to both emotion and painting, is at play in works well known for their address of the "scriptedness" of our communications, whether taken at the level of the sign (Jasper Johns) or its mass-cultural and sociopolitical troping (Sherrie Levine, Cindy Sherman, Barbara Kruger, etc.). But how does that question of scriptedness and the play across surface and depth unravel when we look to *Mostly Drawing*'s concatenations?

Whereas affect is often used, conceptually, to "deprivilege interiority, depth, containment, and recovery," its usefulness is indeed, as affect theorists and critics maintain, to retain a concept of the subject as acted upon—as opposed to emoting, communicating, etc.[33] "'Affect' thus invokes force more than transmission, a force that does not have to move from subject to object but may fold back, rebound, recursively amplify."[34] But when we understand that an aesthetic work can *possibly* "produce in us" an emotion (or record that emotion as produced "in" another) but *definitely* signify the inscriptive nature of emotion—drawing out the ways that emotion can be "recognized" as a sign in a painting—then the notion that the subject only relates "to" an object, as opposed to *as an object*, begins to falter. Relearning, noticing, recognizing the inscriptive nature of the emotions or interior states that the one might have thought was one's own, "one" becomes an object of reflection—not merely an effect of structure or an obdurate whole.

This is the kind of subject who knows herself to be in the room, looking out, as implied by the way Sillman's works ribbon around Gladstone's uptown gallery. The works produce their places for the viewer, but what they continually "express" is, to begin with, their own structuration, the systematic manner of their production. The viewer who walks through *Mostly Drawing*, however, finds not only a reiteration of that systematicity and structuration but its relentless entanglement with formlessness, the replacement of "expressive" gesturality with *excessive* gesturality.[35] Psychic or "interior" life is being remapped so that interior life is made up not of pure, isolated things—*this* fury making *that* brushstroke. Rather, it re-creates itself continually in the image of a process become systematic, just as shapes not only enter but illustrate a system of cutouts and transfers, a sense that our interior lives are both shaped by external forces and demand that we see them as a superseding of the internal/external divide. Thus does the notion of an emotional interior become reliant on both expression and "Expressionisms," and even on that level of formlessness inside Expressionisms that allows the busyness and complications of the works in *Mostly Drawing* to do more than gesture *at* Expressionist formlessness. They erect it as their premise and devolve from there, exploring the push and pull between the preformed and the spontaneous, the idea of an irrupting flow of paint and its embeddedness in a shape cut out and reproduced, transferred and interlaid with so many other shapes. The identical size of nearly all the exhibited works confirm one's sense of a uniform basis or framework for understanding the repetitions and permutations in *Mostly Drawing*. It also reinforces the exhibit's ambiance of codedness, the sense that we are looking at structure not "as itself" but as overflow, excess, something that gets remapped and reused precisely *because* it exceeds its own bounds.

It is inside just such a regimen that Sillman's shapes turn out finally to be not at all unary. Often no more a magnified paint stroke or cutout given its shape by the layers of paint that set it off as such, these are shapes generated out of complexly layered compositions that are themselves made of monochrome swaths digitally printed and painted atop other such layers. Each layer erases another and forms its own layer to be-erased; the same can be said of the shapes entailed in each of these layers. In other words, what we see in *Mostly Drawing* are not many "organic" shapes—though the occasional whole shape turns up, sometimes as an opaque layer of paint, sometimes in outline—but shape as a process of accumulation, redistribution, and excision that forms the basis of something else. The thick black painted lines are not merely in competition with formlessness, but drawn into its own excavation *as* formlessness: they too are reproduced, redistributed, reinserted by processes that keep erecting themselves as the maps, the schemas of production. The work of mediation (*All those layers! All the processes!*) that painting and drawing *are* is thereby rendered as a structure or indeed a "language," albeit one that marshals an intensity and almost exaggerated immediacy without telling us about any particular emotion or indeed any particular thing.

Mostly Drawing composes a picture of structure as complexity and oversaturation, of its contrast with singleness and unariness—rather than as decipherable structure. Structure, in other words, is shown not as a result, not diagrammatically, but all at once, as the fury that is displacement and excess, the longing produced by the vicarious. Whereas Morris Louis's rivulets or washes, poured across giant canvases, "retain the full saturation and intensity of the colors," Sillman's *Mostly Drawing* shows us process as shapes that have already been made and then decomposed, "overprocessed," as it were, just like those milky washes and reproduced colors.[36] In seeing that structure is itself what we see, and yet sensing the immediacy, the gesturality of her "Expressionism," we understand that inscription is already required by emotion, that the latter lives in its inscription, not in a "postmodern," supplementary way, but because supplementarity is its own makeup. In these pictures' reordering of cause and effect, we see emotion not borne out as painting or even drawing, but preexisting as hypercoded formlessness. What we see in this reversal is that emotion *wants* codedness, and that inside that codedness we recognize the nature of emotionality *to* ourselves.

Interiority here is not a place that painting reaches "into" with a gesture; it is an array of shapes thrown into a process that fragments, redistributes, and obscures those shapes, making them fight their own "unariness." Inside this degree of processing is a story that is both about our interior lives and a way for us to understand how we think of structure not only overdetermining those inner lives but allowing for their thickening. "Interiority" is shifted out of its spatializing—even bourgeois domesticating—metaphor to become a question of process, of starts and stops, of endpoints that become middle and start points. This has an implication for how we think of shapes and our "selves": not as matching correlates in a Gestaltist universe, nor merely as fragmented subjects. The rhetoric of emotionality reminds us that our own interior lives are also built on the sedimented. It is reproduced not as a demand that we see "into" but as an arraying process that allows us to see all the lateral complexity, the paradoxes that arrive from the all-at-onceness of emotions (or emotionality) that present as if singular but exist in fragmentation, reduplication, and repitition. We may be driven to see *as if* emotions occurred one at a time and could be expressed as such; and this drive is itself worth paying attention to. As is the other side of the coin, that such a drive toward inscription—toward sign-making logics—also thrives within our affective lives. This is where shape both returns and reveals itself as not dependent on the unary, the singular, the possibility of wholeness or even its overcoming of the figure, but on decomposition. If unary shape pulls other painterly elements together to totalize, then decomposition as shape gives us shape as key to an interior life dependent on inscription and its mapping. Shape tells us that we are ourselves at the "center" of that mapping even as it resists decoding.

Coda: History Painting

In a show at the Camden Arts Center in 2018–19, opening in the autumn following the spring of *Mostly Drawing*'s installation, Sillman installed a ribbon of works, a sequence of twelve double-sided drawings, each sixty by forty inches, from a wire crossing the London art institute's massive second-floor, street-facing gallery. The work as a whole was called "Dub Stamp," and each individual panel's side was given a name identifying it with its verso (e.g., *Dub Stamp, 1A*, and *Dub Stamp, 1A back*). Across one side staggered a figure, pooling into a kind of vomit that could become limb-like or part of that figure's new, crouching shape. On the other side of the line, the figure resurfaced intermittently, but less linearly, as if she was being tuned in and out through a kind of overwhelming visual static. Here, interior life asserted itself as a form of history painting and as a map of inscription. What to do with the individual pictured, whose downslide into despair felt so intimately familiar—and with a sense of the group id she evoked, perhaps confirmed by the work's crisscrossing installation? The inalienable backdrop to *Dub Stamp*'s crawl was the end of a decade in which burgeoning authoritarianism seemed to be the flip side of an expressed, explicit emotionality and desire on the part of *many*. If it was hard not to make that connection—hard not to assume that the historical present mattered to *Dub Stamp*—was it merely because the work's figural reference stood out, as an emblem of plenty-recognizable despair?

Shape, I've argued, directs us toward painting's draw on the emotional and the interior by letting its own totalizing capacities overwhelm the referential (in Guston) or argue with its decomposing, formless "other" (in Sillman), finding a new definition of the interior in that argument. When shape is pitted against the figural, as we see in Guston's multipli-

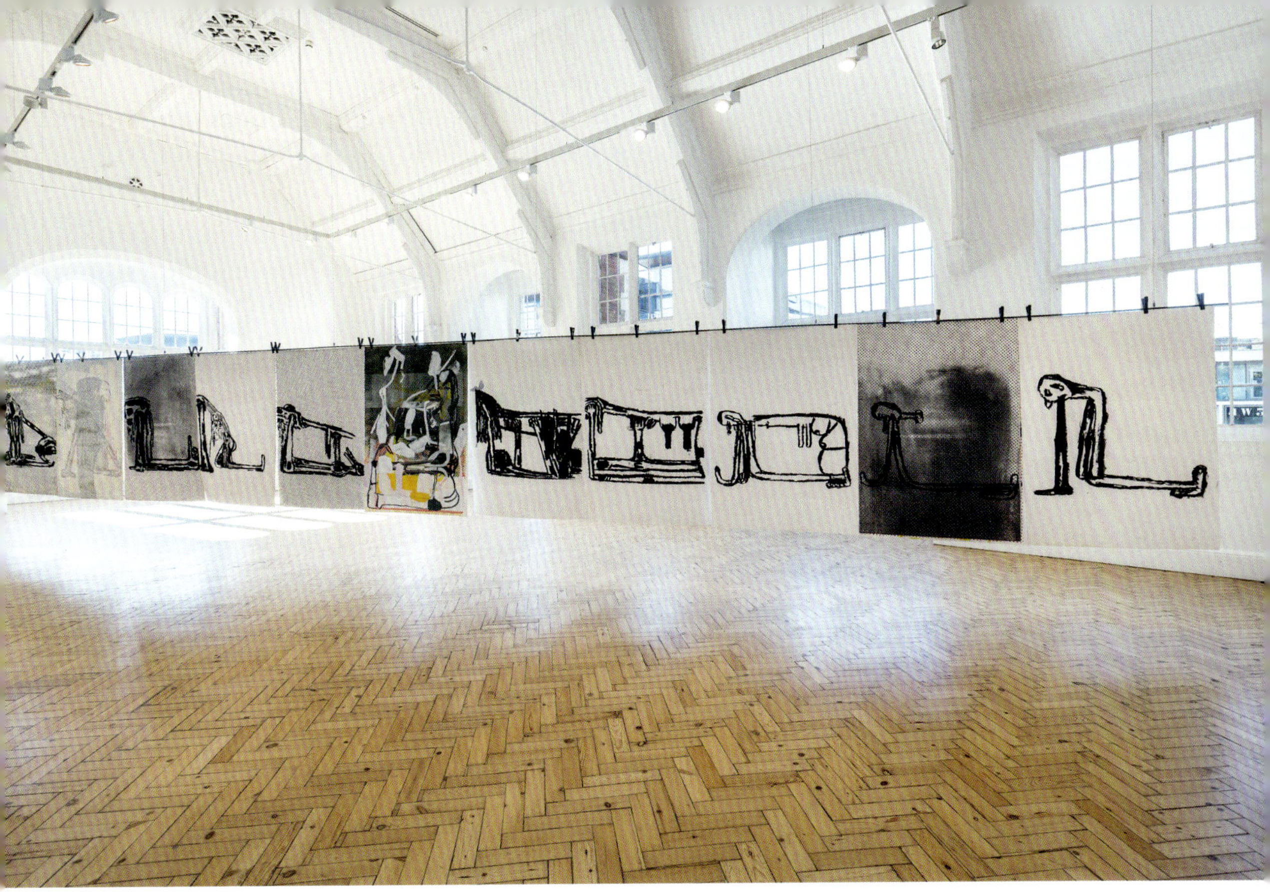

catory canvases, or the way that he lets a tubular pipe-shape take over from a leg, or a cone take over from a hood, it shows itself reaching *in* to us, bathetically stretching past the recognizability of a tube as limb to work on the linkage of expressivity and history. That is where Guston finds the too "easily recognizable to be so intolerable in a painting." With Sillman's recent work, the emphasis has been on spreading out—across a series too long to take in at once, across a ribbon of works lining a room, with no start or end point or, in *Dub Stamp*, from beginning to end of a cartoonish sequence, reminding us of how animation both builds up figures and dissolves their boundaries.

Amy Sillman, installation view of *Dub Stamp*, 2018. Acrylic, ink, and silkscreen on paper. Photo: Damian Griffiths. Image © Camden Arts Centre. © Amy Sillman.

That this kind of spread should occur as twenty-first-century subjects wrestle with questions of uniqueness and group identity, self-securing "emotionality" and a dawning realization that certain affects and "affectless" feelings are spreading across populations as surely as rage and righteousness, seems right. We—each one another, separated from each other by an individuating sense that something or someone is speaking to "me"—might be able to recompose a sense of self in the face of these spreads, but that selfhood might be improved if it unfixed itself from a proprietary sense of "one's *own* feelings." History is always happening to "me," and indeed always, also, to others. Proprietariness demands that we marshal all the tools for dissolution that can be found—and painting, as the art most affectedly associated with the bourgeois interior, is ready for use.

II

Character

> By means of which critical discourse will I be able to grasp that which "character" can neither cover nor contain nor designate? and yet, who bears a first name and who becomes?
>
> . . . How is one to describe, circumscribe this subject-plus-one that explodes structures and ruins social and affective economy? No designation can connect Nobody. This subject is any other—and all those that precede it and those it anticipates.
>
> HÉLÈNE CIXOUS, 1974

> So we come to think that we "have" selves as we have heads. But the very idea that we have or are "a self," that human agency is essentially defined as "the self," is a linguistic reflection of our modern understanding and the radical reflexivity it involves. Being deeply embedded in this understanding, we cannot but reach for this language; but it was not always so.
>
> CHARLES TAYLOR, 1989

> Entrances and exits make characters.
>
> YVONNE RAINER, 2015

In her remarkable essay "The Character of 'Character,'" Hélène Cixous vehemently attacks the conventions of character, arguing that most literary characters merely reinforce the existing social order.[1] The "ideology underlying this fetishization of 'character' is that of an 'I' who is a *whole* subject . . . conscious, knowable," and we know where that story goes: toward discussions of the subject's fragmentation and the impossibility of self-presence.[2] In her article, Cixous isolates those rare instances in which the text refuses to close down around a character, refuses to make it cohere as a "*whole* subject," instead allowing the character to disrupt the text itself. In other words, she is interested in characterhood as opposed to subjecthood, where the latter is understood as obeisant, formed by the structures of the state, language, gender, and more, and always manifesting to itself as whole.

I want to shift the question of character here to moving-image works. Flowing from the framework of the "figure" in the last section, character becomes that onscreen apparition intended as an image foil to our bodies, placed before the screen and taking in its colors and sounds, editing cuts and camera positions. According to the strictures of suture theory, the onscreen character indeed functions as a fixing device, "suturing" us to the screen and therefore the structures named above. But characters can be more than formal and narrative devices and mechanisms of suture. They can allow the film, like a literary text, to "refuse to close down around a character, refuse to make it cohere as a "*whole* subject." It is that potential for characters that interests me.

Fifteen years after Cixous's fiery essay, Charles Taylor's tome *Sources of the Self* emerged, dedicated to understanding selfhood historically and philosophically. Taylor's notion of selfhood draws a sharp distinction from subjecthood as defined by psychoanalysts and poststructuralists. In his own words, the term "self" designates "the ensemble of (largely unarticulated) understandings of what it is to be a human agent: the senses of inwardness, freedom, individuality, and being embedded in nature which are at home in the modern West."[3] Despite his reliance on an antediluvian notion of the "modern West," Taylor remains important because his book points to one crucial premise proffered by both the psychoanalytic and the poststructuralist (as well as Wittgensteinian) camps: that the self is only accessible through the language that it uses, becoming a recursive problem.[4] How do we know anything about the self except through language—and how, thereby, do we know anything about the self that isn't ultimately *about* language, its structures, and its relation to structure? How do we access the self in a way that doesn't merely tell us about language? Yet language is not the only frame of accessibility to self that we encounter. Works of art have a particular ability to underscore that fact, even when they use language as well. A painting might feel intimate to a viewer, and the viewer might feel herself "accessed" in a way that has nothing to do with language. Part of painting's magical, hypercapitalized aura rests precisely on this promise to the self.

Much art that uses language—fiction or poetry, drama or film, song, paintings, and sculptures that take up the impulse to narrate or voice (think Jenny Holzer)—evokes the same kind of promise, directed at our "inner" selves. Some uses poetic or truthful or provocative phrases, piercing both the "autonomy" of the visual artwork *and* the reader-viewer's sensibility. But art that centers on narration and language, and especially art that streams toward characterhood, can track a similar "piercing" through uses of language that are far from transparent, and that even—as the works I discuss here do—fold the effects of sound, color, and other aspects into its reinvention of characters and their relations to language. If Taylor's question about how we know anything about the self that isn't ultimately about language were answered through an artwork that renounces the transparency and immediacy of language, instead filtering it through plasticity, materiality, and corporeality, we would have a different kind of answer than one that can be delivered by a philosophical treatise.

When I interviewed Yvonne Rainer in the late summer of 2015, she claimed that to "make an entrance" is to start making a character.[5] If the performer is already in place when the audience enters the performance space—moving or talking or performing some combination thereof—then you lose the frame of characterhood. But as soon as you present a performer as coming onstage, you engage that frame. To me, Rainer's experimentation with the category of characterhood is vital to her trajectory as a choreographer, filmmaker, and art thinker. It constituted one of the major challenges to dance and art more broadly as she formulated them in her famous 1966 text "A Quasi Survey of Some 'Minimalist' Tendencies in the Quantitatively Minimal Dance Activity Midst the Plethora, or an Analysis of *Trio A*."[6] In the graph accompanying that text, "character" appears as one of the aspects to "eliminate or minimize" in "Dance": its corollary, under "Objects"—a rubric devised to help clarify the relations between dance and "Minimalist" tendencies in sculpture and painting—is "figure reference." Character, like figuration, was then perceived as a hangover from art that sought to please the spectator or flatter his gaze. Even more importantly: for Rainer, to reduce characterhood was to develop the dancer as a "neutral doer," diminishing the frameworks of skill, narrative, and phrasing. Instead, as her own work demonstrated, dance could become more involved in the transitional and workmanlike aspects of movement pure and simple. In eliminating aspects of character, dance's movements would become more "objectlike," discrete rather than supportive of a theatricalized illusion. If you walk into a space and the performers are already there, warming up or talking among themselves, then the movement that follows has a better chance of being perceived as movement pure and simple rather than as part of a conventionally theatrical artifice.

Here too is where I pick up characterhood: as an aspect of the framing device of aesthetic experience that two filmmakers, James Coleman and Steven McQueen, have sought to examine and undermine. The hero of Steve McQueen's *Shame* (2011), Brandon, is a character, full stop, just as the film, which had a full theatrical release, is a "real" movie, intended for mass audiences. It was a major step in the star-making force of McQueen's multiproject collaboration with Michael Fassbender, who had starred as Bobby Sands in McQueen's *Hunger* (2008) and would go on to play the key

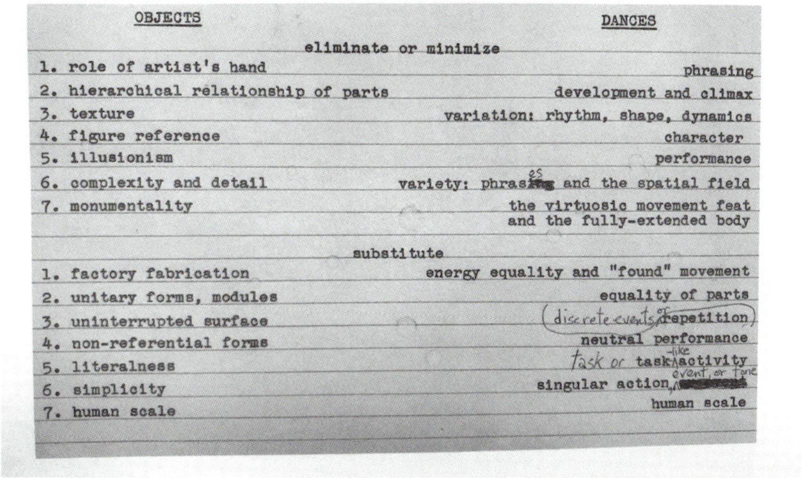

OBJECTS	DANCES
eliminate or minimize	
1. role of artist's hand	phrasing
2. hierarchical relationship of parts	development and climax
3. texture	variation: rhythm, shape, dynamics
4. figure reference	character
5. illusionism	performance
6. complexity and detail	variety: phrases and the spatial field
7. monumentality	the virtuosic movement feat and the fully-extended body
substitute	
1. factory fabrication	energy equality and "found" movement
2. unitary forms, modules	equality of parts
3. uninterrupted surface	(discrete events or repetition)
4. non-referential forms	neutral performance
5. literalness	task or task-like activity
6. simplicity	singular action, event, or tone [redacted]
7. human scale	human scale

Yvonne Rainer, original manuscript for "A Quasi Survey of Some 'Minimalist' Tendencies in the Quantitatively Minimal Dance Activity Midst the Plethora, or an Analysis of *Trio A*," 1966.

role of Edwin Epps, plantation owner and slaveholder, in the filmmaker's Oscar-winning *Twelve Years a Slave* (2013). Possibly, the nature and duration of their collaboration helps us to see the importance of character (and performance) to McQueen's larger artistic project. But Fassbender is not the only major movie star to collaborate with an artist-director: Isaac Julien's 2003 *Baltimore*, starring Melvin Van Peebles and Vanessa Myrie, like his 2010 *Ten Thousand Waves*, starring Maggie Cheung and Zhao Tao, are two other examples of works made with major actors for museum installation. Yet it is James Coleman's *Retake with Evidence* (2007) that will serve as the first work examined here. Built around a performance by Harvey Keitel—and expressly building off his star power—the forty-five-minute work was shot on film, transferred to video, and debuted as a video installation inside a space built specially for the work at Documenta 12. *Retake with Evidence* is not a "movie" like *Shame*, but its work on and with characterhood, and specifically the ur-character Oedipus, makes it an ideal starting point for this discussion.

Character both offers a seductively easy analogy to us, as audience members, and is one of the most fertile grounds for disruption in the work of art. Yet it is a category almost absent from the ways we discuss the representations of selfhood in visual art. We talk about bodies and figures, portraits and gazes; we refuse characterhood, which carries with it the taint of the literary arts and the fulsomeness of language. But let's try to invert this problem, asking instead what characterhood can tell us about the terms by which art presents us with analogies to our selves. Let's even invite the conversation about how language, bringing the obstacle of recursivity to understanding selfhood, functions in this dynamic. After all, for centuries characters have brought the literary tropes of narrative and myth into pictorial art. By recognizing characterhood as a strong category in visual art, we might even see how its reliance on language and narrativity infuses the way we look at bodies and figures in art.[7] Moreover, we might be able to think about the category of character as broadened by the possibilities that visual art brings to it as a kind of compensation or return gift for that which characters have brought to the museal arts from their natural home in cinema, theater, and fiction.

In particular, art might deepen what inward-turning or even silent characters do to the category of characterhood. A character that refuses the expressivity of dialogue or action, or that contains her story within her self, might become a richer site to explore what characterhood offers the self. In the following discussion, I reconsider silence, or the refusal to speak, as a refusal of the kind of relationality that has become the new standard of both art and virtuous life. In our silence, the conversations we have in our heads are potential sites for understanding our selves and our historical emplacement, outside the dialogical framework that has been naturalized as *the* site of encounter with others. With this in mind, we could re-ask Taylor's question: What might these relations to language—those that have us talking to ourselves or not talking at all—offer the self? What conditions applied in a work of art can translate into ideas about how we live as selves?

First, let's linger for a moment on the exclusion of characterhood from the study of visual art—and how peculiar it is. Consider the many artworks since Andy Warhol's *Screen Tests* and Cindy Sherman's *Untitled Film Stills* that have confronted contemporary audiences with the extreme porosity of our conceptions of selfhood and "interiority" vis-à-vis the cultures of film and celebrity. Or we could consider Kara Walker's archetypal silhouettes—always predicated on the possibility, even withheld, of narrative, always evoking the protocinematic as foundational spectacle—or Ryan Trecartin's video mazes of "micropersonae" that play with the hypertexts and forms of celebrity unique to the age of the iPhone.[8] These works of art suggest that on one level, character is being *refused*; after all, these works are not strictly narrative. But the descriptive capacities of their media—including drawing, makeup, scenery, costume, voice, and line—confront the boundary between the intimate and the impersonal in ways that suggest the specificity of characterhood (as opposed to the generality of "the figure"). They evoke narrativity in order to allow that specificity to take root, even if they dead-end narrative as a linear, unspooling progression.

Meanwhile, a range of works of art that do include what we conventionally call characters prove more often than not to present *not*-characters. The individual personae in Melanie Gilligan's teleseries

Popular Unrest (2010–), for example, are overshadowed by the panorama of a near, dystopic future and by the series' irony. The same is true of other works that ape commercial film or television, like Stan Douglas's *The Secret Agent* (2015), and those that more thoroughly dismantle it, such as Douglas Gordon's *24 Hour Psycho* (1993) or Candice Breitz's many works involving Hollywood actors. The introductions of their pseudocharacters serve to invert "our" investment in characterhood, the psychic pull of the character as it has been conventionally understood.[9] As works of art that often mimic or alter the actual material of other cultural forms, they embed their characters in frameworks that are as invested in signifying the possibilities of mimesis, appropriation, and citation as they are in representing selves.

When we push past postmodernist mandates, we are able to uncover what precisely those thinkers that mattered most to the formulation of postmodernism—such as Roland Barthes or Fredric Jameson—made of the intertwining of narrative and interiority in visual art. Describing Edvard Munch's 1893 painting *The Scream*, Jameson writes:

> Munch's painting stands as a complex reflection of a complicated situation: it shows us that expression requires the category of the individual monad, but it also shows us the heavy price to be paid for that precondition, dramatizing the unhappy paradox that when you constitute your individual subjectivity as a self-sufficient field and a closed realm in its own right, you thereby also shut yourself off from everything else and condemn yourself to the windless solitude of the monad, buried alive and condemned to a prison-cell without egress.[10]

This somewhat doctrinaire reading of the painting, which essentially argues for a binary between the expressive, individuated self and the collective—a problem I return to in the last section of this book—also refuses to see the subject of Munch's painting as anything other than a figure for the universal subject. Might it be possible to see that Munch's title, *The Scream*, refers us, as Jameson himself writes earlier in the essay, to the "failure" of the painting's "gestural content" to release "the sonorous, the cry, the raw vibrations of the human throat"?[11] In that case we would return the difficulty that Munch's character seems to be undergoing—a scream that can be mouthed but not heard, a question of how indeed we "access" the self through both language and its other, a raw or silenced cry—to whether there is anything to say, via art, about individual subjectivity (let alone its relation to collective suffering). Munch's painting then reveals the problem of *how to address* that "experience of atrocious solitude and anxiety which the scream was itself to 'express.'" Solitude and speechlessness are redounded to the subject without the moralism of a doctrine that argues that to "shut yourself off from everything else and condemn yourself to the windless solitude" is your bad choice.

For Taylor, it is impossible to talk about the self without recourse to language. Is it similarly impossible to talk about characters without talking about the material conditions through which we perceive them? Or to anticipate, imagine, "identify with," judge, dislike, or abandon interest in them? In the works of Coleman and McQueen, those material conditions become expressly part of the work, not merely the background. The material conditions are how we understand ourselves seeing and hearing the characters before us. These characters lose some of their "figural" distinction from the background: we see them as so much conditioned on that background, and on our own conditions of viewing, that we cannot perceive them as if they were simply figures set against that background. Their strangeness to us is contingent on their backgrounds made strange, and on the ways we experience the "apparatus" of filmmaking. Film's apparatus links such aspects as the shot-by-shot progression of a film, the darkened cinema, a character's point of view, and the film's apparently omniscient viewpoint.[12] In the 1960s, theorists made the connection between this cinematic point of view and its reinforcement of the ideologically interpellated and reproduced subject.[13] In so doing, apparatus theory largely displaced more conventional conceptions of characters. (Of course, the category of character has returned to film studies in new form since.)[14] In other words, around the same time that Rainer was altering the DNA of dance and entering the field of filmmaking, film studies was shifting from a lexicon that could simply address characters as such to considering them as epiphenomena and extensions of the construction of the subject.

Similarly, in theater studies, what had been called quite self-consciously the "death of character" fueled the expansion of performance theory. Though residues of interest in characterhood and selfhood persist, what had once been the apotheosis of a characterological "whole"—that character presented on the stage—became the ground for complex performances and stagings that refused such holism outright.[15] In works by such important theater collectives as the Wooster Group and La Mama or solo ventures by Richard Foreman or Eve Ensler, character is most often a vehicle for disruption. As with Bertolt Brecht and his colleagues, conventions in 1980s experimental theater enabled alternate routings of audience relations to the actors onstage, often for revolutionary or at least resistant conceptions of self and collective. Even the very fact of individuation on which the character (and actor) relies provides a ground for such radical critiques.

That is to say that if we are to take up characterhood today, we cannot ignore the conventions of those media or their apparatuses. Just as artists like Douglas, Sherman, Gilligan, and Trecartin demonstrate, the apparatus is part and parcel of how we consider characters today. This echoes Raymond Williams's contention regarding a "tragic society . . . [in which] tragedy has, if you will, broken out of its frame." When the frame is both disappearing and the object of investigation, as it has been throughout modernism and its "posts," what becomes of those selves that are presented to us onscreen and onstage?[16] If tragedy's heroes are something like the epicenter of narrative theory and its grounding in classical drama, what becomes of their resurfacing within frames that show us the continuity of the characters' experiences with our own or with those of our tragic society? The works of McQueen and Coleman treat both the frames around their protagonists and those that we feel as our own, as spectators. The ways we experience our own shell-like exteriors are ways that their films establish then perforate a kind of monadic separateness, both sensorial and reflexive, on the part of the audience members. These shells are at the core of these works. They are key to how the artists reimagine both the category of the character and its apparently easy analogy to the selfhood of the spectator. And, as we will see, they are key to how we can understand characterhood as a useful concept with which to upset the narratives of universalism underpinning Jameson's critique.

The hero of Coleman's *Retake with Evidence* is in some ways the title character for Western modernity: Oedipus, or some version of Oedipus. The Oedipus "character" or indeed the Oedipus paradigm, as elaborated by Freud and others, aggregates all that is patriarchal, doomed, and blind, serving as an emblem of vulnerable political and military power as well as familial tragedy. Coleman's version frames *Oedipus at Kolonnus*, that part of Sophocles's cycle that "divides its attention between the king and the place" and, not coincidentally, rides on the already-confirmed fact of Oedipus's guilt.[17] But Coleman's film is not the document of a performance of *Oedipus at Kolonnus*. In it we see Keitel's performance, which is not at all a straight performance of a character, rhyme with scenery and uses of the camera that similarly diverge from the "straight." We audiences are pulled into a soliloquy that forces us to consider our own position vis-à-vis the onscreen character's interior monologue. That pull makes it impossible to see the film as mere critique, an exercise in reflexivity. For to listen to a soliloquy (or watch it onscreen or onstage) is to admit a character's "show quality," their exerted pull on one's attention and psyche. Of all of the theatrical or cinematic tricks that reveal the showmanship of the camera or stage, the soliloquy also gives us the most immediate means of understanding that threshold between the exterior and the internal. It speaks *to* interiority. But it does so seemingly without differentiation, exerting on each of us in the audience *the same* conditions for our spectatorship. The soliloquy says: each of you audience members is inside this character's head, or else the character is speaking aloud, to herself. Either way, the distinction between your shell and theirs is no longer a finite, objective fact. It is at play and spread over the audience. As is the category of character, separate from the performer or indeed the mere figural apparition onstage. The one who speaks to herself has an interiority to talk *about*: we are left merely *feeling* ours.

Oedipus's guilt—the incredible twist to his family romance—is also a supposedly generalizable guilt. "Oedipus's story serves as the myth not only of Western personal identity but also of Western cultural identity," writes Charles Segal.[18] If the maxim "Know thyself" as Apollo articulated it at Delphi is a kind of obsession underpinning Greek tragedy, it is also a remonstrance, at least in a twenty-first-century film version. Even as the soliloquy becomes a device for understanding what is "his" and what is "mine" as I watch and listen to Keitel's performance, I am aware that Sophocles's and Coleman's works are writing a story about "Western" claims on the universal.

Meanwhile, McQueen's tragic hero is defined by the film's eponym, "shame." As such, Brandon, his protagonist, epitomizes an affect or condition that Giorgio Agamben describes as "truly something like the hidden structure of all subjectivity and consciousness" in the post–World War II or post–Abu Ghraib present.[19] Shame is not only a special affect—an affect that for some is the key, meta-affect, showing us how affects work (as mentioned in the last chapter). As an affect, it is a different species from guilt, a mere "emotion": moreover, as Eve Sedgwick describes, it is, developmentally, "often considered the affect that most defines the space wherein a sense of self will develop," for it is that which "attaches to and sharpens the sense of what one is."[20] Shame, which Brandon, as the title character of a film called *Shame*, seems to "characterize" (literally, to render or make as character), may be what makes Brandon a kind of update to Oedipus's more classical "guilt."

Instead of letting us as audience members simply "identify with" these subjects of guilt or shame, however, in both works we are treated to a set of formal inventions that interrupt the conventional apparatus on which classical drama theory (and classical Hollywood film) has predicated audiences' identification or projection. Rather than straightforwardly identifying with the subject as one who is both patriarch and homeless (as in *Oedipus at Kolonnus*), or one who is a white male sex addict, barely able to control his drives, we are given characters that exemplify these states of being *and* thwart our ready identification, even as we hear and watch their thoughts. Watching Coleman's work, we are thrown into a series of analytical mazes filtering both our relation to the actor/character onscreen and our positions as his audiences. Watching McQueen's *Shame*, we are the ones shot through by chromatic and sonic effects, making us crucially aware of our own sensory, bodily selves, and even the terms of that proprietary relationship we have with our bodies. If *Shame* is in a sense parlaying the cringe-inducing, reflexive, whole-body torment of shame as an affect, the film also defies the kind of easy relationality assumed by the classical conventions that allow us to "project onto" or identify with characters.

In *Retake with Evidence*, Keitel performs a soliloquy. He is framed by multilayered scenery that, like the actor's performance, forces us to consider the shell around the actor speaking. The soliloquy form demands we consider whether the onstage or onscreen speaker is speaking words behind a fourth wall. Are we being spoken to? On what terms are "we" present to the speaker? This question parallels that of Oedipus's guilt: On what terms does he stand for us, or for the rules of exclusion on which an "us" can be conceived? And then in contrast, shame might be a highly individuating affect, one that makes us feel the edges of our own individual, private horror/selfhood. But does that self not encompass a sense of the without, the outside to "me," now also *ours*?

We can, in other words, see these characters as aesthetic objects that combat the urge to see characters as mere screens for our projection. Like Rainer's efforts to decharacterify her dancers' performances in order to make them less theatrical, less illusionistic, the characters of Coleman and McQueen become more objectlike while also fighting the terms on which we encounter them as objects. As they open up the category of the character, encumbering it with work *on* the terms on which we encounter characters, we see them refusing any onscreen framework of encounter that would be open-ended and intersubjective. Keitel's character soliloquizes; Fassbender's Brandon refuses to speak to others, to "open up," to "account for" himself. In this way these works fight a recent tendency within art to prize intersubjective communication—and indeed intersubjectivity itself. Relationality and intersubjectivity are replaced in these works by characters that are removed from the kinds of dialoguing, relational frameworks that invoke or indeed instantiate the social.[21]

Certain instrumentalizing and often patriarchal versions of aesthetic experience that depend on dialogue often privilege the aesthetic consumer and risk degrading "the Other"—sometimes ignoring or masking the manner in which that aesthetic consumer, like any subject, comes to know *herself* through encountering the work.[22] Returning to one of the oldest tricks in the dramatic playbook—the soliloquy—in my analysis of Coleman's film, I emphasize a kind of character that we meet very much as an object, even a shell that we come to perceive through the actor's performance and the film's staging. By also emphasizing the kind of character who would reject speech altogether—McQueen's protagonist in *Shame*, who refuses language as much as he can—I explore the means that film has to engage the aesthetic subject solitarily accessing a world either invented or real. These present an alternative way that we, as audiences, come to know what others imagine or think—a way that does not introject us within dialogues or indeed intersubjectivity as it is classically formulated.

My point, here, is to return to the conditions of a solitary, individuated encounter with the world that is the fundament to much daily, constant experience. Critical to this project are the continual internal dialogues one has with oneself—whether alone or surrounded—and the reclaiming of a right *not* to explain oneself, *not* to "account for" oneself. Self-accounting is a crucial part of the claim made to exert the primacy and criticality of encounters with others, as I will examine. Here, I am arguing for a self that hears and is engaged with a kind of continual, reflexive, often digressive and ruminative self-accounting—but one that repudiates the social or even ethical requirement to make that account public, social, intersubjective, or even audible.

James Coleman

Retake with Evidence

Retake with Evidence was shot on 35 mm film, digitalized to HD video, and has been shown in several different editions.[1] It was originally installed as a massive, floor-to-ceiling projection at Documenta 12, in 2007. No seating was provided to these first audiences, so they sprawled, lounging and lolling on the floor beneath the video. Other viewers, in a kind of antechamber to the room showing the work "itself," could watch those audience members through a window that blocked sound but showed the work—and its sprawled audience—as one image. But that distinction between one group of audience members and another was to be only one of many frames that *Retake with Evidence* would put in place.

The forty-six-minute video shows a massively magnified image of Harvey Keitel moving around a set while speaking. Keitel, the celebrated Method actor known for his work as pimp, bad cop, mobster, and Judas in films such as *Taxi Driver*, *Bad Lieutenant*, *Mean Streets*, and *The Last Temptation of Christ*, looks in *Retake with Evidence* like an ordinary guy, maybe on a day off from work; scruffy in his sweats and stubble, every bit of aging and camera-unreadiness amplified by the scaled-up image. Keitel is not in costume, in other words, or makeup—or rather, not in a costume or disguise matching the grandiosity of the scenery across which he wanders, which places broken, evidently fake columns and Greek ruins against a black-and-white photo and a neutral soundstage.

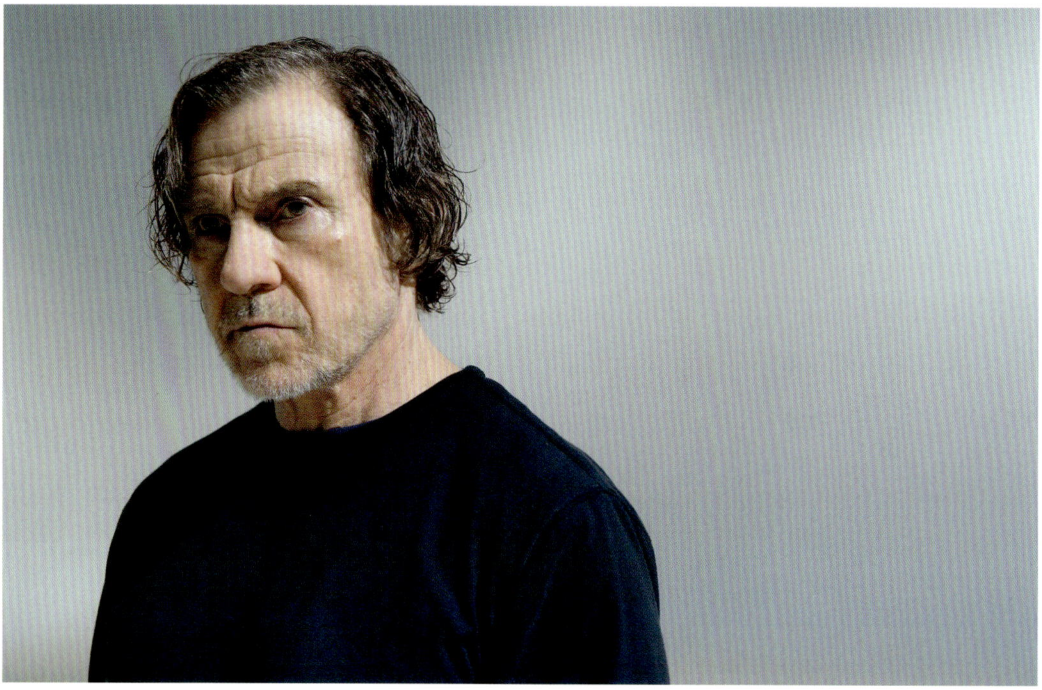

James Coleman, *Retake with Evidence*, 2007. Video projection, performed by Harvey Keitel. 35 mm film in 4:3 ratio digitized to HD video. Courtesy of the artist and the Marian Goodman Gallery. © James Coleman.

The spectacle of this Hollywood megastar lording it over the audiences prostrate beneath him irritated some of the work's first critics and produced an emblem of what they didn't like in that edition of Documenta and its "ahistorical formalisms."[2] A few imagined that the "histrionic" or "spectacular" image of Keitel might in fact be a kind of meditation on theater, the photographic image, and Coleman's own mythos.[3] Indeed, Coleman is best known for his "slide works" that since the 1970s have coordinated slide projectors with audio tapes, using pseudofilmic linear and looped successions of images in ways that reflect on the conditions of live performance, photographic reproduction, and ultimately questions of thought, speech, vision, self, and otherness. One of his best-known and most frequently exhibited works, *Box (ahhareturnabout)*, from 1977, invites audiences into a room thumping with a diastolic beat that mimics a heartbeat. At the same time, flashes of the famous 1927 boxing match between Jack Dempsey and Gene Tunney appear in all their grainy, black-and-white documentary brilliance. Grunts, the thrum of Tunney's heartbeat and breath, and barely audible murmurs and groans suggest that we are "inside" the blood rush of the underdog who was forced to win a second fight in order to defend a title he had already won.[4] The ramifications of this conceit include its analogy to questions of Irish independence, a major theme—as is colonialism writ large—in Coleman's work. Others of his slide works are silent, dilating instead the time of the image: *Ligne de foi* (1991) superimposes two photographs, taken from two slightly different angles, of a 1991 *tableau vivant* reenactment of a Currier and Ives print of the American Civil War's Battle of Bull Run (1861). That print was built on painterly codes of anamorphosis and perspective that the double projection resurfaces. Coleman often uses such twinned systems of reproduction (painting and photography, photographic and audio recording) to ensnare the viewer in a relation to history—here, that of "Civil War America" or indeed Irish independence struggles. This approach threads that historical reflection through complex ways of positioning the spectator's own body. In every case, the spectator's body is embedded in history in a manner that operates critically on History itself.

Throughout his works for stage and screen, it is impossible to miss Coleman's interest in characters. In his works, characters are not a mere formal conceit but key to his mode of production. His collaborations with actors began with the two anonymous actors hired via newspaper advertisement to make *Clara and Dario* (1975) and intensified with his long-standing collaboration with the French actress Olwen Fouéré from the late 1970s through the mid-1990s. Hiring Keitel to make *Retake* only ups the ante of an established practice. Both the star's recognizability and the stylistic charge that accompanies that—his public persona as a highly expressive Method actor and a macho alpha male—participate in the project. But in a sense Keitel's celebrity only accentuates further how Coleman steadfastly denaturalizes and defamiliarizes the category of

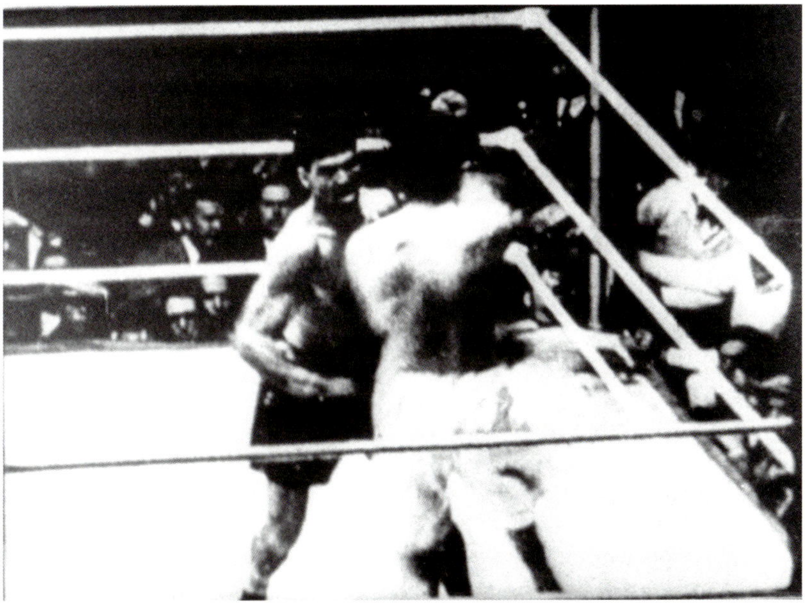

James Coleman, *Box (ahhareturnabout)*, 1977. 8 mm film transferred to 16 mm. Black-and-white audio. Courtesy of the artist and the Marian Goodman Gallery. © James Coleman.

character. Characters, denoted through costume and makeup inside the vaguely narrative scenes that his slide works present, are really vehicles for conceptual questions made palpable by techniques of defamiliarization. For example: *Lapsus Exposure* (1992–94) invites the viewer to try to sort out who is who among a few groups of musicians who array themselves across a sound stage in different configurations and postures in each slide in a sequence. Their conversations, private thoughts, and a potential omniscient narration are elliptically intercut in the audio track; we usually cannot tell who we are hearing or to whom a pronoun refers, or if we think we can tell, that sense of semicertainty is eventually reversed. When we are not even sure of the identity of a character, we cannot be sure of her status *as* character. *Lapsus Exposure* also leads us to ponder the manner in which our own thoughts—or those of the characters we pretend to be learning—are composed of ellipses and palimpsests and characterized by parataxis. That is the liminal zone in which Coleman normally presents his "characters": as figures shifting across screens and into and out of registers of audibility and legibility, but also into and out of their positions as separable and distinct, marked individuals within a text and within our consciousness.

The work that I focus on here features a sole character and, unusually for Coleman, only one performer. Throughout *Retake with Evidence*, the camera focuses on Keitel with limpid precision, but he appears to have wandered onto a set that is like a maquette for something that will be performed or staged differently, at another moment. We are treated to shots that show us the floor and the set as belonging to two different registers. Keitel, the white floor, and distant gray walls are all shot on color film, but the objects shown to be on that soundstage are a massive black-and-white photographic screen—changing the scale of set to actor—and a series of pillars and broken statues that seem to be remaking the scene depicted in that photograph. (Eventually, different shots will include other black-and-white photographs—more familiar ones—as well.) Just as strikingly, Keitel's mode of speaking seems to be, like soliloquys themselves, a test of the "show qualities" of theater or film. From his first words—"Why are you here?"—we are aware that we are watching a stagy, recursive performance. If Oedipus, as kingly protagonist, is perhaps overly familiar, he is also standing here for an entire civilizational order, pictured on the photographic screen. The set serves as more than a character, as is often claimed in film reviews; it is a complex of semiotic systems that in turn clues us to the stakes and the meaning of the performance we are watching.

The set's biggest and most important element is that long, curved screen, on which is printed an enlarged black-and-white photograph

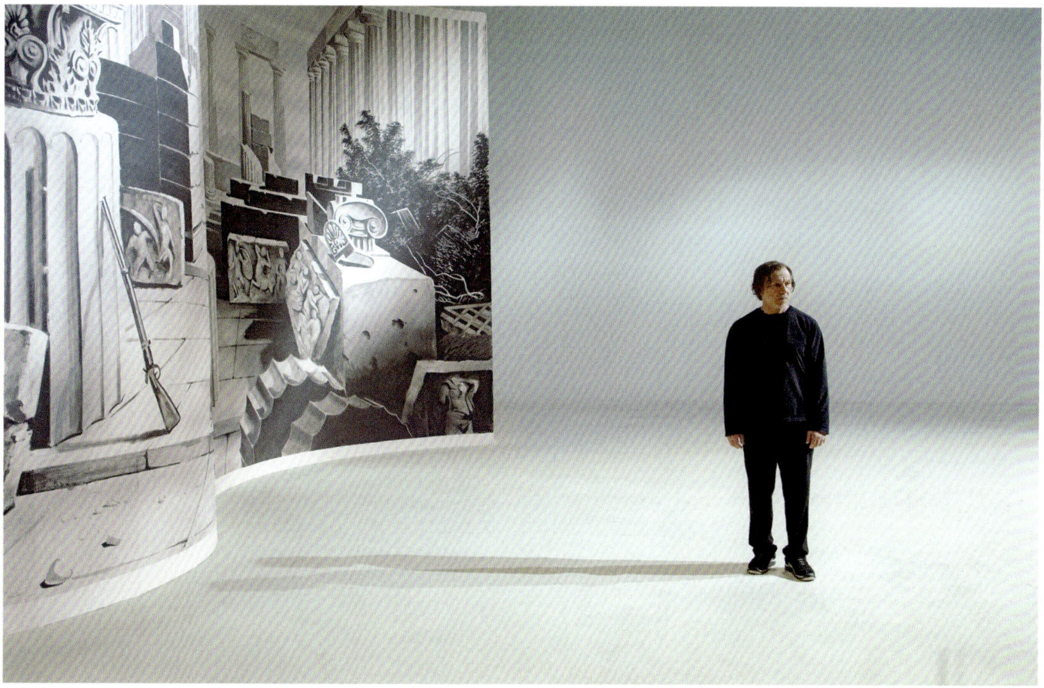

James Coleman, *Retake with Evidence*, 2007. Video projection, performed by Harvey Keitel. 35 mm film in 4:3 ratio digitized to HD video. Courtesy of the artist and the Marian Goodman Gallery. © James Coleman.

of a dreamlike scene of what could have been, perhaps in the late nineteenth or early twentieth centuries, an excavation site somewhere in the classical world. A rifle leans against a massive column, and the rest of the screen shows a Romantic view of a veranda-like plateau surrounded by pillars, with overgrown shrubs and tumbling fragments of friezes and remnants of capitals. In the far distance of the photograph a row of pillars disappears into a sky and distant landscape. As a photograph, it has an unreal depth of image; the rifle in the forefront is pictured with gleaming precision, while the background disappears into an almost painterly, diffused grain. It is as if the viewer's gaze were being explicitly focused on the violence that constitutes an archaeological dig and its Romantic scene-setting. We often see the screen at an angle, so that its curves are fully visible, its status as screen indisputable. Like the actor wearing his street clothes, the screen indexes both the second-order performance we are watching—not a king, but someone playing a king; not a kingdom but the photograph of the excavation of one—and the layers of violence it takes to reach this second order. We are seeing, in other words, residue of an actual historical situation underpinning the myth of representation: that of the colonial or imperial scene, represented in all its durability.[5] But we are also seeing it as representation, the photograph looking deeply unreal, romanticized, mythical in itself.

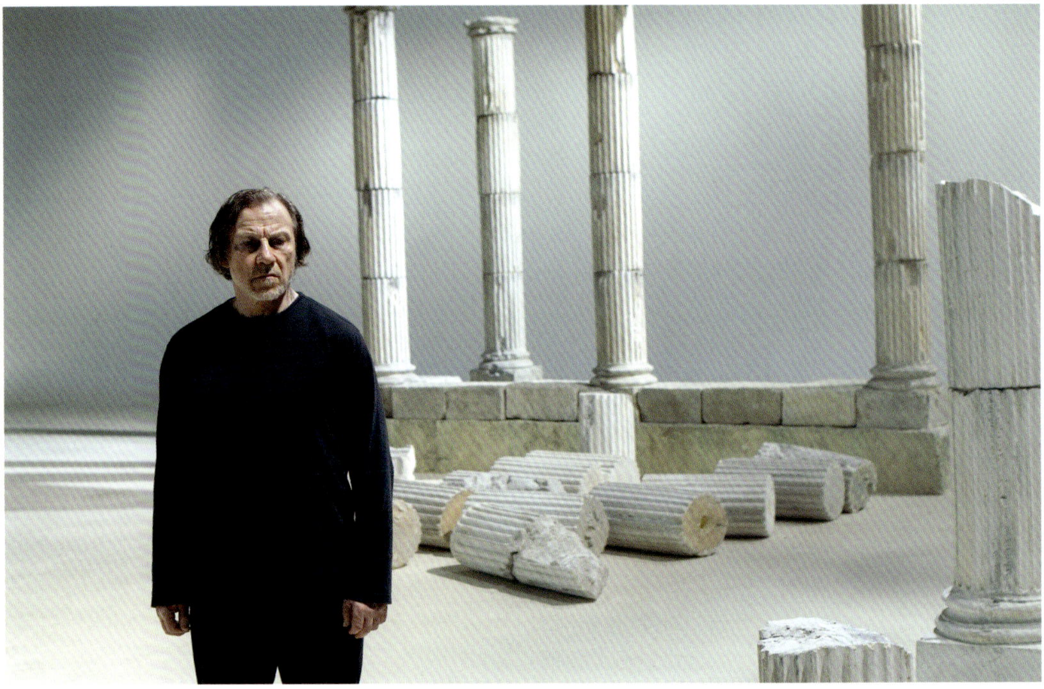

James Coleman, *Retake with Evidence*, 2007. Video projection, performed by Harvey Keitel. 35 mm film in 4:3 ratio digitized to HD video. Courtesy of the artist and the Marian Goodman Gallery. © James Coleman.

Around the bends of the screen are rows and fragments of actual pillars and statues—actual because three-dimensional, but also evidently plaster replicas, not the "originals." At one point, Keitel will come to a photograph, indelibly familiar though hard to place, of a mass grave. Thus do we become aware of an explicit set of references to the patterns of colonial theft, pillage, and appropriation—and the durability of colonialism in contemporary wars—that have made ancient texts a part of contemporary civilization. These are what has also allowed contemporary civilization to name the terms of its own "modernity." Various parts of Coleman's set underscore both the cost of the supposedly universalist establishment of Euro-American laws (such as the carceral logics of justice and retribution) and norms (for example, against incest, of patriarchy), as well as their correlates: the supposedly universal psychic laws and norms (e.g., the Oedipal complex) that trace back to the ancient Greeks and to Sophocles's works in particular.[6] Coleman's title highlights this connection by playing on Freud's lines about what he called "the Greek legend": "The work of the Athenian dramatist exhibits the way in which the long-past deed of Oedipus is gradually brought to light by an investigation ingeniously protracted and fanned into life by ever fresh relays of evidence."[7] These "relays of evidence" have been transformed into "retakes" through the work's relentless exposition of its own status as film recording as well as the ways it demarcates its spaces and sole character. These spaces and this character belong to both dramatic history and that which is not stage, not theater, not film.

The retakes of *Retakes with Evidence* are also literal. The film accentuates the length of its takes by ending them with slow dissolves. These dissolves are vital to how the film is structured as a series of acts and takes, with the camera in a new position relative to the actor with each "retake." Thus does the film accentuate or double the nested representational frames that make up its physical scenery. The fragments of plaster pillars, like the black-and-white screen, are all set on a monochromatic, cool gray soundstage whose walls and floors are visible and whose lighting, unlike that of the grainy black-and-white photo, is hypervivid. Unearthly, dreamlike qualities fasten to the shifts between these concertedly evident takes. This drawn-out version of shot-to-shot and scene-to-scene editing in turn points to how, inside each take, physical borders within the set are marked, and vice versa, how those physical borders within the set reiterate the framing of the film as a whole.

If King Lear and others lurk among the referents of Keitel's performance and any contemporary reception of Sophocles's Oedipus cycle, these ghosts also underscore that chasm that opens up between the text that Keitel pronounces and any notion of a unified text at its base. First, every critic writing about *Retake with Evidence* seems to have believed that they have seen an Oedipus character, but unlike the majority of the lines Sophocles gave to Oedipus, there are no proper nouns among the lines Keitel pronounces, none of the actual names that he uses (in particular in *Oedipus at Kolonnus*) to give his words weight with his various onstage counterparts (from the Chorus of Old Men to Antigone and Theseus). Indeed, I have not been able to find any of the lines I've scribbled down during multiple viewings of *Retake* among the various translations of Sophocles's cycle I've collected. I did find, through simple Google searches, that some of those lines turned up inside texts by a range of authors, from Simone Weil to Cervantes. Secondly, the character's lines are ordered without any sense of chronology: despite the marked transitions between "scenes," there is no sense of narrative development as Keitel speaks. Instead there is only an aura of a developing, enveloping "Oedipus"—a deposed king, a remorseful patriarch, a colossus written not only into one play but across a dramatic canon if not the world stage. Thus does the character before us in *Retake* speak to the manner in which ideas of civilizational continuity themselves authorize an imperial relation to texts as well as other objects, bodies, and beings. Traces of conquest, like those that are part of the Oedipus story, are scattered around the set: they are also the text itself.

Scene Setting

It is not just any Oedipus, however, but *Oedipus at Kolonnus* that is at stake in *Retake with Evidence*. That is the last part of the trilogy, in which the hero is blind and penitent, ancient and homeless. In this part of the cycle the former king is meant to share a sense of importance with the setting itself, as indeed the title suggests.[8] The opening scenes of *Oedipus at Kolonnus* are set on the edge of a sacred grove that Oedipus greets eagerly once it is explained to him where he is (though he is being warned he should leave); this is the place that was mentioned almost as an afterthought when Apollo, long before, delivered his horrific, disbelieved curse.[9] The Grove of the Eumenides (or Furies) is where one is supposed to receive grace, the transformation from exile to hero. (Even though Aeschylus had cast the terrifying Furies as relentless avengers in *The Eumenides*, their sacred grove is where justice and mercy supposedly merge.) As the classicist John Gould explains: "Nowhere else in Greek tragedy does the primitively mysterious power of boundaries and thresholds, the 'extraterritoriality' of the sacred make itself felt."[10] The power of this place is that it is a nonplace, a zone of extraterritorial terror avoided by mere mortals, a zone between worlds. It is also the sign for "a kind of interdependence of man and place."[11]

In *Retake*, this extraterritorial zone is marked by an alignment between the array of photographic and sculptural semiotic systems that surround Keitel and his performance. Just as the set is not a scenery made in the service of "the verisimilitude of perception, and the very sense that this filmed world could be known independently," Keitel is not playing a character as such.[12] Throughout *Retake* Keitel articulates his lines, as Manuela Ammer has pointed out, with "finely wrought Shakespearean diction." (His native New York City accent is utterly missing.)[13] He is playing a king, quite obviously—maybe Oedipus, maybe Lear, maybe all of the kingly tragic heroes wrapped together. But he is also not "in character." Ammer describes Keitel as delivering a performance of a "state of 'post-performance,' that is, performing his role(s) and at the same time pondering the meaning of his actions and of the words he speaks."[14] Not in character, Keitel is, however, acting: as a result, Ammer observes, we "become aware of a language that is 'spatial,' almost sculptural. . . . The archaic English effectively works as a filter that makes it impossible to forget language's physicality, its bodily provenance and delivery."[15] Keitel's "post-performance" performance comes to hold, for Ammer, a consonance between the words articulated and the setting around which the actor wanders, and a difference between the way the character is being *not* performed and the body of the actor performing.

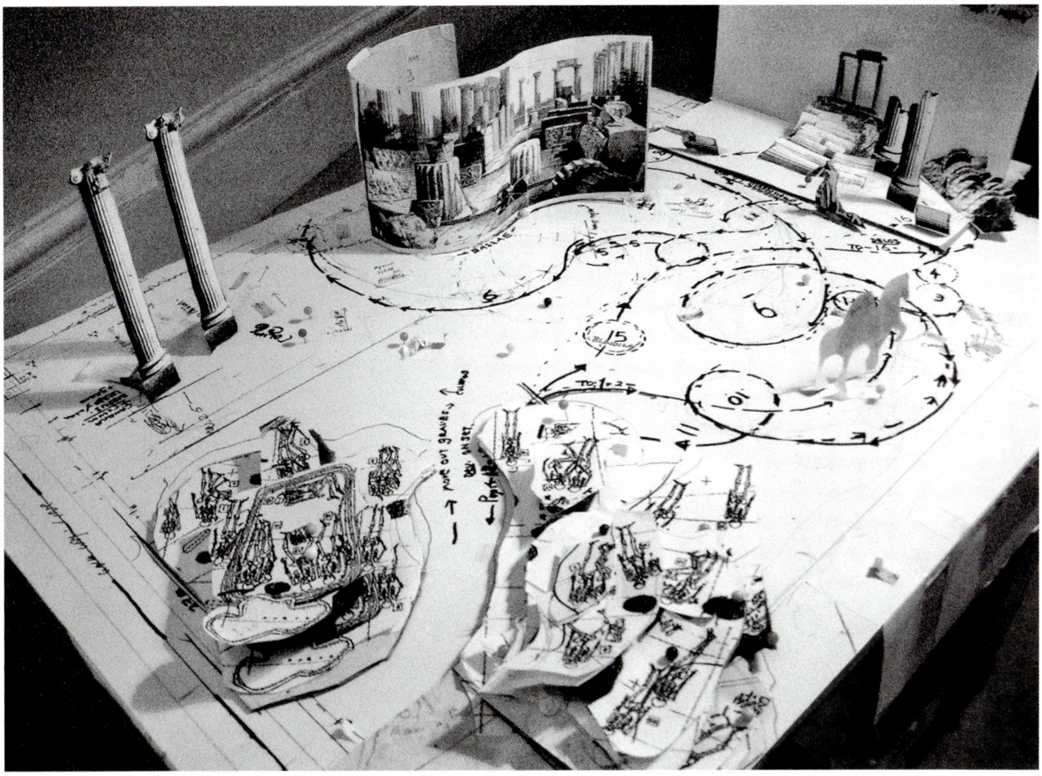

James Coleman, *Retake with Evidence*, 2007. Model for production set. Courtesy of the artist and the Marian Goodman Gallery. © James Coleman.

In the aftermath of *Retake*'s debut, Coleman released photographs of a maquette for the work: a small paper sculpture showing, with inked arrows, the trajectory of Keitel's physical movements throughout the film's "retakes."[16] When performers want to practice or indeed learn the ways that their words or movements will interact with space—the physical coordinates of a stage or set—they do the labor called "marking." While marking, they speak lines or perform moves in order to see or adjust when and where they will be in the course of a performance. Marking is about the performer's body learning its place as a conjunction of language, movement, timing, and space. It is an element of rehearsal or practice in which the actor does not need to perform the text or enact it as an illusion.[17] Marking is essentially a performed spatialization of the script, whether that script is linguistic or choreographic. It is partly mnemonic, partly prescriptive, partly about the body learning its place inside the character or role, and partly about the relation between words or movements and the spaces that hold them.

While marking, Keitel is visibly considering the words he is enunciating: while marking, he is also shaping them, letting their plasticity take up space. He is speaking them in the diction of an actor—not "his" (natural) speech, but one that proffers his words' connection to the set as set. Keitel is inventing a diction that materializes his words, alongside the set's components, showing them to be incapable of totalizing immanent meaning within any given enunciation.[18] As he speaks, he seems to look into an inner space; he is not simply playing a blind character but enacting a relation to speech, to spoken language, that blindness could exert.[19] It would be extremely difficult to signal the materiality of language in a performance, but Keitel, under Coleman's direction, comes very close. Pronouncing words in an actorly manner, as if to signal both "acting" and the legions of "important" dramatic roles that have descended from the great Greek tragedies, he is both speaker and metaspeaker. His words must operate simultaneously within one term defining a register and its opposite: blindness and materiality, deterritorialization and territoriality. He must appear and sound like one who cannot see "material" but who senses the materiality—the nonimmanence—of his words; he must convey both his own eviction from his homeland, indeed from the registers of territoriality as we know it, and his consciousness of a colonial civilization as ruin. His words must indicate the strangeness of a setting meant to perform Sophocles's Kolonnus even as the components of that (unseen, to him) set stress their importance as quasi-objects (photographic signs, remnants of the sculptural process of molding, etc.). They must both couple a sense of place and time inside the durability and absolute sitedness of the colonial time-space and uncouple them inside the dark nonspace of theater and the vastness of imperial history.

Even before his soliloquy gets into its main themes—of ruination, massacre, and monumental loss; of remorse and shame before his witnesses and before the end of life—we are confronted with the critical question: Who are *we*? The first line, "Why are you here?," is immediately followed by another, "What is the meaning of this gathering?"—which gives us a better sense of who the "you" is that he is addressing. It is collectives, referring perhaps simultaneously to the collectivity of audiences (and their echo in Athenian democracy) as well as to the *khora*, in this case the Chorus of Old Men, who in the opening scenes of *Oedipus at Kolonnus* sweep the stage to warn Oedipus away from the dangerous Furies. The *khora*'s voice belongs to a collective character that stops short of being a stand-in for the public but instead leverages "a public language of moral generalization and ritualized expressions of communal sentiment."[20] That collectivity's perspective "reaches beyond the human limitations of any single character," to remind us of the importance of broader perspectives ("the forces of nature outside the city, of the gods and their cults and oracles," etc.).[21] Thus, "What is the meaning of this gathering?" is addressed to a collective with a very specific voice, open to persuasion and dialogue. The *khora* is the other that one speaks to, and yet it is other *to us*—even the Athenian audience's "us"—as well.

Oedipus is primarily interested in Oedipus, so it is not surprising that his address to this strangely construed group of others turns back instantly to himself. Almost as soon as he claims, "I am here to address your sufferings," he stipulates: "Let it not be said that *under my rule* we were raised to fall" (emphasis added). His narcissism is as totalizing as his self-damning guilt: "If I relinquish may I be judged the vilest of mankind." As he ruminates about what he is to do, he can't stop thinking about what he has done. He ruminates about an "I" who is a doer, incessantly produced before the gaze of an Other that can only be imagined, neither seen nor engaged with. It is a very short circuit of One with whom he engages, ultimately. And indeed, if that is the nature of a soliloquy, then this one, structured around the question of an awaited judgment even after the revelation of his identity has been made, is especially acute: "I should not have come here. . . . To a childless father was I born a son." There is no way out. And yet, as he recognizes, even his internalized horror at his own self makes him an untrustworthy witness: "Accusations snare and trap my mind." In other words, even when the theme of the self being judged by others expands to the frame of the state—"There . . . the governance of this state . . . a crime unwitnessed"—he acknowledges the handicap to his role as witness/judge. "As if I had been present then. Therefore will I speak as if a stranger to the present and to the deed." Incapable of properly witnessing his own deeds, he must acknowledge that even in the trial in his own mind, he is incapacitated. Finally, the last line of the film—"Oblivion is sorrow's greatest comfort"—speaks directly to a state of consciousness to be fervently wished for: one in which this waiting, the endlessly deferred trial or exposure to others that has become an endless trial by one's self, would finally end.

In *Retake*, there are two ways that Oedipus's monologue is spoken in a manner distinct from conventional performances. First, Keitel's performance is more of a marking, less of a performance, revealing the concreteness of his words. As objects inside the marking, these words show Keitel portraying an amalgam of Oedipus and his successors (like Lear), as well as himself, Keitel, a man of our moment, a man living in "the Oedipus complex" in his own right. The amalgam Oedipus/Keitel is both the subject "Oedipus"—recognizable as a paradigmatic Western male subject—and a kind of intervening on that subject, a materialization that both hardens and blurs its boundaries. Secondly, because of the ways that Keitel rolls his words around as if to accentuate their plasticity and rhyme them with the assertive strangeness of his setting, they interrupt the vehicularity of conventional characters. Rather than a character presented to hold our projections and identifications, we have a character letting us into his mind by virtue of his words and then showing us how those words are continuous with a setting that is utterly material, even plastic. It is an uncanny form of encounter that almost masks its status as encounter. That might in fact be what the antechamber or waiting room in its first installation, at Documenta, was for: to underline the fact of the audiences' relation to the huge, kingly image of Keitel's face and body as the point of the piece.

Speaking to Oneself

Encounters with others are foundational to our political, ethical, and social lives. That is where we live out our subjecthood and negotiate our differences with others. It is also that dimension of shared public life that both Judith Butler and Adriana Cavarero deem central to the self, insofar as the self is constituted in self-narration or self-accounting. (This is signaled readily by the titles of two of their books, *Giving an Account of Oneself* and *Relating Narratives*, which accent the transitive verbs *giving* and *relating*.) Cavarero cites Oedipus as a "figure" of a "theorem" reversing the direction of self-accounting: "Autobiography does not properly respond to the question 'who am I?' Rather, it is the biographical tale of my story, told by another, which responds to this question."[22] But overall the positing of that other to whom one *would* account for oneself is the singular move upon whose central importance both she and Butler agree. Their works on selfhood are not particularly interested in the finer points of how dialogue unfolds: they are fixated instead on the scene of encounter that Hannah Arendt describes, in which the listening others are a stable and unyielding fixture to the unfolding self.[23] "As Arendt explains, 'a unique being is such only in the relation, and the context, of a plurality of others, which, likewise unique themselves, are distinguished reciprocally—the *one from the other*.'"[24] But at what point do I determine that these others, "unique themselves," are there for my story, or conversely, that their stories decenter me? What is the purpose of their presence to my story, if my story is to remain "mine," its central purpose to attest to *a self*? Aesthetic encounters, I suggest, offer a means to explore these questions while also allowing us to reconsider how our notions of selfhood rely upon these dialogic frameworks.

This problem eventually came to haunt the works of relational aesthetics that had come to dominate the world of international exhibitions like Documenta at the time of *Retake*'s debut. And despite the years that have passed, during which those works have inevitably passed from the center of an ever-churning art market's appetites, we have not yet created a thoughtform for how to move past the condition of relationality generally—let alone with respect to self- or subjecthood. That is why my intervention, leveraging characterhood, is centered on two examples in which relationality is conducted through a necessarily passive audience (in the sense that spectating does not admit the kind of engagement that relational practices invite). By focusing in this example on the soliloquy, I am attempting to negotiate a path that acknowledges the Cavarerian "narrative" or Butlerian "account" without demanding the Other who is always already problematically entwined with the requirement to "relate." I am tying the decidedly aesthetic form of the soliloquy to the apparently ethical injunction to relate—to dialogue—with others as a means of claiming selfhood.

But what is such self-accounting or self-narration made of? What are its conditions? Butler discusses the manner in which the subject is an "effect of discourse" in Foucault's early work, and then moves on to his work on "the self," explaining that "to make oneself in such a way that one exposes those limits ["of the historical scheme of things, the epistemological and ontological horizon within which subjects come to be at all"] is precisely to engage in an aesthetics of the self that maintains a critical relation to existing norms."[25] The self that is so created maintains an "opacity of the subject [that] may be a consequence of its being conceived as a relational being, one whose early and primary relations are not always available to conscious knowledge."[26] If that is the case, Oedipus once he reaches Kolonnus is an obvious example of a self with an account to give: having realized that his "early and primary relations" were devastatingly unavailable to conscious knowledge, understanding how completely they have subjected him, he is ready to acknowledge and even maintain that core opacity. That is perhaps what he is talking about when he describes his own capacities as a witness to his self with such ambivalence and anxiety. It is not his origin story that is a mystery to him anymore but that core opacity that is a consequence of his relations to others.

And yet making a work about selfhood is not as simple as putting a man onscreen who complains he might not be the best witness to his own self. Hamlet's famous "To be or not to be" soliloquy presents Hamlet as a character whose selfhood develops through *our understanding of our relation* to the character onstage. A two-step process that is not simply "relationality," nor even listening and watching, but a sensing of the distinction between the conditions of his accounting and the conditions of our reception: this is what Coleman's complex direction of Keitel/Oedipus's soliloquy delivers. It focuses not on a mere border between our selves, as might be understood in a dialogue or indeed an Arendtian encounter. Instead it focuses on the double conditions—for "his" speech, already complicated by the divide between the present-day actor and explicitly second-order staging and the "character" or indeed paradigm "Oedipus"—and ours, both listening to and watching him as if he were "present," and realizing the uncanny mode of encounter into which we have been placed, where we can see the plastic materiality of his words as continuous with his setting. Let's compare this to another unusual but somewhat more literal filmic soliloquy. In the 1948 film version of *Hamlet*, directed by and starring Laurence Olivier, we are visually brought into Hamlet's skull as he is about to start his soliloquy. As the camera nears Olivier's head, the film images push through an image of a skull to show both an image of brains and then brain waves. Imitating the waves crashing on Denmark's shores, these abstracted waves form, dissolve, and reform the same cloudy, tenebrous images. This brief passage becomes a perfect illustration of the ambiguity of an ordinary soliloquy. It makes explicit the audience's uncertain relation to the character speaking that is itself a function of an aesthetic invention, the fourth wall, now reconfigured within film's spectacular, quasi-magical editing capacities. Whereas Olivier's Hamlet presents this as a transitional state, Coleman conceives it as a permanent state, lasting for the duration of the entire work. It is not an effect of a single speech but a condition of our relation to the character onscreen and perhaps, by extension, to any other self we might encounter.

Soliloquys force us to remember that language exists not merely in the *inter* of intersubjectivity, in the interstices of social life and the orders it requires and produces. Too easily, we forget that monologues are not reserved for theater alone—or at least, that their productiveness need not be considered just an aesthetic convention. Speaking to our own selves might be one of the most highly underrated experiences—outside classical philosophy, in which it is a major thoughtform. Denis Diderot (theater and art critic extraordinaire) describes his habit of going home "sad and chagrined" after an evening out, to talk to himself in his *cabinet*. He writes: "I question myself and I ask myself . . . What's wrong with you? Are you in a mood? . . . Yes. . . . Have you misbehaved? . . . No. . . . I press myself, I tear from myself the truth."[27] He presents this scenario as one that repeats nightly, and though he cites "the truth" as a potential object of this exercise, both neurosis and self-soothing are more obviously in play. The comfort offered by one's "*cabinet*"—literally, a private room or even antechamber; metaphorically, one's own mind and ability to talk to oneself, a refuge postexposure, postsociality—rules Diderot's text. Distantly, we understand the exercise to be universal.

Theater's built-in sociality privileges the soliloquy as a test of its own "show quality." As we are suspended in a sense of not knowing whether "in fact" (i.e., in the conceit of the play) the character is speaking or whether we are in a state of diegetic suspension, having penetrated her mind, paradoxically it is that ambiguity that confirms the effectivity of the fourth wall. But works of theater and cinema can also show us the edges of the self speaking in ways that dialogue or narration mask, and this is what Coleman has focused our attention upon. From the manner in which the actor performs a soliloquy to the ways their words interact with "real" objects—sets, props, costumes, and even qualities of light, sound, and color—the soliloquy can produce questions about language's materiality, its relation to objects around the speaker. These interactions are key, for they show us the interdependence of speech acts with their settings. Or, perhaps just as pointedly, the cleavage between them that might rob those acts of their effectiveness. Pointing to such interactions allows the aesthetic work to disturb signals of normality. If we were to be cautioned regarding our "dispossession of the future and of time," we would want to be alerted to the manner in which even the languages we use and the places in which we find ourselves coordinate our own imminent and immanent processes of dispossession.[28]

A soliloquy is a perfect test site for the privileged scene of self-accounting, a place where one tells about oneself. In Cavarero's *Relating Narratives*, we confront the impasse between the constructedness of the aesthetic encounter and the immanence of the "life-story" to the self: "Life-stories never have an author. Biographies or autobiographies result from an existence that belongs to the world, in the relational and contextual form of self-exposure to others."[29] One's existence in the world is a form of "relational . . . self-exposure," but as Cavarero argues, the essence of selfhood lies in one's narratability. Not whether or how or when or why one will narrate one's story, but the mere knowing "that I have a story and that I consist in this story—even when I do not pause to recount it to myself": that is what is key for her.[30] In other words, the narrative models the form of selfhood in which one "exposes" oneself "to others"; that urge to tell who we are *is* our selfhood, and *also* our relation to the work of literature. Relationality cuts toward the work of narration just as it cuts toward the other.

Cavarero, like Butler, relies heavily on Arendt's work. For Arendt, the very question of the self is tied up in the "'web' of human relationships," and for her it is the *scene* in which individuals encounter one another, especially through speech, that is key.[31] In other words, self-exposure in these philosophical accounts engages language, but each of these philosopher-critics is also enraptured by the visual component in the encounter between two selves. For Arendt, the fundament of the social world is the reciprocal "Who are you?" that is engaged in an encounter she asks us to visualize.[32] Likening the public realm to a table (separating the bodies that must come together) or a séance (such that the table might "vanish from their midst," so that two people would "be entirely unrelated to each other by anything tangible"), she insists not only on the physical, embodied nature of public intersubjectivity, but its representability.[33] Here, in our examination of *Retake with Evidence*, it is the inverse: I am mainly interested in the already-visual encounter that seeks to tell us about the self, for which the invisible barriers between me as a spectator and the speaker drive the scripted, artificial nature of a nonencounter. *Retake*, as an artificial nonencounter at whose core is the question of what motivates and circumscribes my relation to a speaker, delivers that very framework as its code.

That code is both linguistic and visual, sonic and representational. But the broad category might be more capacious than just works about characters who talk to themselves—or even, as in the next chapter, merely refuse to talk to others. My interest in characters as vehicles for thinking about selfhood ultimately is invested in the debt we owe to the authored, aesthetic encounter. I'm arguing that aesthetic encounters can become a way to rethink the dialogical nature of ethics and to restart a conversation about the self—a self no less political for being in conversation firstly with herself. Indeed, if, as Butler suggests, the "making of the self" is an engagement of an "aesthetics of the self that maintains a critical relation to existing norms," here I am focusing on works whose critical relation is *to* the existing norm of social relationality. I am conserving the idea of self-making as an aesthetic project, but pointing out that one of the norms can be that equation between self-making and self-accounting. The norm has here been introjected into the project of accounting to shift its "aesthetics," in which aesthetics are understood as the very basis of the process of self-making.

The move that *Retake with Evidence* provides is not a simple decentering of dialogue. "We," in the sense of an audience, are present to Keitel/Oedipus only in his imaginings, not as a "real" stage audience, let alone a *khora*, a participant in the scripted work. The encounters the film presents are with Others that exist only in his head, where "his head" does not belong to a pure character, but marks a territory somewhere between the actor and the character, between Keitel and Oedipus. "We" are similarly ambiguous, ranging between those who sit in art institutions like Documenta to those whose sufferings are mental representations to him or whose judgments he fears. These versions of "us" are after all what enable the actor-king to encounter himself as fundamentally split, and by extension, to present himself as an internal imago, a character to himself. This allows us to ask ourselves whether the scenery we see presented with so many seams is not the scenery of his inner landscape, made up of mere signs *pretending* to be things. Suffering would then be only distantly implicated in the obviously fake plaster pillars and "marbles" that rematerialize a scene of colonial archaeology so patently romanticized that the photo dissolves into grain. But in Coleman's film suffering comes rearing back in the photograph of the mass grave that provides one hard point of connection between our world and his. A photograph that is unplaceable—that looks as much like Sarajevo as Rwanda—replaces the "we" that could be conveniently distant from the actor-king's performance right inside its seamed set. The king's relentless tussle with his own guilt testifies that "others" have thus far failed to decenter his position in his own internal monologue. But in the moment in which we see that photograph, we are identified with those already-abstracted others. It is both their deaths and our irrelevance to his internal monologue that we witness.

Mikhail Bakhtin is often hailed as a hero of the dialogical. But when Bakhtin famously describes the moments of intersubjective speech—speech between two or more subjects—as a struggle between the aims of the speaker and the "conceptual horizon of the listener," he importantly asserts that the "phenomenon of internal dialogization . . . can become such a crucial force for creating form . . . only where dialogic reverberations do not sound in the semantic heights of discourse (as happens in the rhetorical genres) but penetrate the deep strata of discourse, dialogize language itself and the world view a particular language has."[34] Oedipus's speech exemplifies "the semantic heights of discourse . . . the rhetorical genres." It also presents "the world view a particular language has." That language and its world view is not, in *Retake*, the ancient Greek of Sophocles's original, but its English translation into a lineage of iconic, homeless, or deposed kings (including Lear), rendered in kingly/actorly diction. The semantic heights of discourse happen to unite, in this speech, with the "deep strata of discourse." In Keitel's specially constructed performance, however, this language or deep strata is also testimony to the "phenomenon of internal dialogization," the rivenness of the one speaking by the mere fact of speech and internality or interiority. Keitel/Oedipus's understanding of others extends not even to a single proper name, a single identifiable individual. What is striking about this is how completely the phenomenon of internal dialogization sets up the category of character as one enabling a reflection on how our own internal monologues operate.

Perhaps the scene allowing Keitel/Oedipus to come onto the site of mass graves, presented as an iconic but unplaceable image, is the cornerstone of *Retake*'s diegesis (such as it is). Finally, the scenery is not simply a vacuumed-empty soundstage featuring a Romantic image of dig and ruin, marble and gun. Here are the human others reduced to their merest representational figment, one that Keitel/Oedipus seems to know of, even if, blind, he cannot see them. Here the other is a past-and-present other, sacrificed to a specific historical moment that both recognizes suffering (the dead) and anonymizes it (the mass). The "other" that is instrumentalized in Cavarero's imagined encounter to produce a listening horizon for the self is here represented as a part of the scenery, another black-and-white photograph. Perhaps that level of anonymizing representation is part of the way an internal monologue conditions its language, its "access to the self." It presents the self not with the particulars of others but with their massing and unparticularity, or—same thing, seen otherwise—their monumental, even fetishistic specularity. "Others" are hedged into a function much like the *khora* even in one's own internal monologue: perhaps reasonable, possibly forgiving, but ultimately as abstracted as any other projection.

"I Don't Want to Be the Character. I Want to Watch the Character."[35]

Coleman is often treated as an utterly sui generis artist. Trained—for a time—in Milan's Brera Academy of Fine Arts in the mid-1960s, when Arte Povera was overtaking the Italian art scene, he showed films, drawings, slide works, and even such complex audiovisual installations as *Box (ahhareturnabout)* throughout the 1970s. Countering Conceptualism's Minimalist aesthetic, he went past the ways that artists like Dan Graham, Vito Acconci, or Bruce Nauman were at that time using performance and audience engagement to question the inherence of a person's presence, behavior, words, or, indeed, thought. Directing actors, providing both scripts and opportunities for improvisation, playing off archaic artistic conventions like the portrait or the narrative, his approach makes theirs look as if they subscribe to hegemonic and outdated binaries between the apparent immanence of performance or direct experience and photography and sculpture. Coleman instead insists on the representational quality of all of these modalities. His work foretells the manner in which the Conceptualist machinery was adopted by the Pictures Generation, moving toward acknowledgment of the "constructedness" of representation. It is only in that context that he might appear less sui generis. But where he remains utterly so is in his works' redirection of the question of constructedness back to the conditions of our inner dialogues, our own perception. His works give art a position at a liminal juncture, where the fact of constructedness is present even in our inner conversations, and those conversations are remade as the work's unabashed spectacle.

Constructedness becomes not an aspect of the social world and its means of forming us collectively, as subjects, but something located within the "deep strata of discourse," where "language itself and the world view a particular language has" persist, even in their internal manifestations, the means language has of making world pictures in our head.

What even a work as early as *Box (ahhareturnabout)* does is reroute the manner in which we have been thinking about art as addressing the social world through public settings. Instead, the social world is shown to reside inside a colonial foundation that is both material (the physical world) and psychic (the epiphenomenal counterpart to that physical world). Indeed, the fold between those two "worlds," as if they were ever separate, is the zone that Coleman's works inhabit, so that no reach into our interior consciousness—by the play of voices, for example, or the dangling tease of narrative—can ever be extricated from the spoils of a colonial civilization. *Box (ahhareturnabout)* is the classic demonstration of this, giving us the "interior monologue"—mostly breaths and grunted fragments of speech—of boxer Gene Tunney as he is forced to try to win a second match in order to "retain" his title. The fact that the title was already his, like a freedom supposedly already won, was irrelevant both in his lived moment and in the historical reality (forcing him to "repeat, or one might say reiterate, what he already was").[36] That doubling—a status for the self that has to be continually retrieved in the historical present regardless of the alleged gains of history, and the fact that experiencing *Box (ahhareturnabout)* we are both "inside" Tunney's self and fully cognizant of its historical exemplarity—is what is so unique to Coleman's art. He returns to this set, or possibility, of doublings as if it were the scene of a crime, compulsively reminding us of its existence.

So many of Coleman's works refine this juncture that if we were to claim them for the category of "characterhood," we would want to expand what that category can hold. Take, for example, *The Ploughman's Party* (1979–80), an audiovisual work made up of a taped narration and a sculpture in forged iron onto which a slide of the same sculpture is projected, giving it an extratranscendent and ethereal appearance.[37] The sculpture, with gold and silver paint and blue neon edging, married with its digital reprojection, is shaped after the Irish "Starry Plough," a symbol of a free Ireland based on the shape of the constellation Ursa Major (what Americans call the Big Dipper) that also borrows the shape of the plough as a symbol of Irish farm labor.[38] Installed on the ceiling of a room in "Without the Walls," curated by Dorothy Walker for the Institute of Contemporary Art in 1980 as part of the festival "A Sense of Ireland: London Festival of Irish Art," the visual motif was matched to an accompanying audio component, which consisted in a bilingual (French/English) narration, in which a male voice describes getting ready for a party. The internal monologue—this time cleaved by bilingualism—is "full of puns and double-meanings and repeats itself in a continuous cycle," the sound of the French according especially with the gilded motifs of the room, covered from floor to ceiling in white felt.[39]

As in *Retake with Evidence* or *Box (ahhareturnabout)*, the use of an internal monologue incites us to understand the presence of a character, however abstracted it might be. But even more graphically than *Retake*, *Ploughman's Party* materializes the bedrock of colonial European civilization as one that is both setting and psyche, physical and epiphenomenal: the thing itself and its quality as mental activity. Bilingualism is an acute form of the epiphenomenal replay of the colonial system, particularly enhanced by general recognition of how deeply language structures the brain. To speak—especially to oneself—in two languages is to align oneself in two cultures. When they are *both* the languages of the colonial powers, one exercises doubleness without even admitting the *other* other (the one who's been colonized, the remainder to one's doubled identity/language; let's say, in this particular grouping: the Irish, the Algerian). That is the framework of *Ploughman's Party*, made more explicit even than in *Retake*, where the substitution of an internal monologue for a dialogue is made so spectacular. In *Ploughman's Party*, the absence of a recognizable character like Oedipus should not distract us from the mechanisms of identification and projection that Coleman is mapping out on his ceiling sculpture. Characterhood is here both enacted by the vocal narration and diagrammed in the room, where those stars said to direct human movement might allow us to renew how we think of it.

To rethink how we situate "accounting for" within our selves and within the concrete, material conditions of our existence is to ask for more than most internal monologues can achieve. The boundary of an internal monologue, as Keitel/Oedipus demonstrates, is one's own consciousness, however much one's guilt or shame irrupts within it. But the impulse that Coleman urges us toward is not that blindness that Oedipus actualizes and that Keitel performs so masterfully. It is instead toward the setting of our own internal monologues. *Ploughman's Party, Box (ahhareturnabout)*, and *Retake with Evidence* make clear how utterly that setting is a function of the colonial regimes of representation, meaning it is ours as well as the narrator's, the boxer's, and the king's.

The "world" in which Arendt imagined the self's encounter with an other is as striated as that which she eventually characterized as belonging to the origins of totalitarianism, where the "homeless" shatter "the façade of Europe's political systems."[40] But to imagine that our most important dialogues are with others is to sell short the manner in which one is always one's first interlocutor. Those conversations with oneself conveniently let in only as much of the world as one can stand at a given moment: like the curved screens, they render a world in black-and-white, romantically at that. But in a world cheating us of the ideal conditions imagined for such dialogues, one shifts into internal monologue without even noticing. That was indeed a world that, presciently, Sophocles presumed, setting his deposed king into a garden of Furies, with no one else for his hero to speak to. If an awareness of what others would say to him was nearly unbearable, the king had the good fortune of not being able to see where he was, either. That might have finished him off—but that is indeed where the twenty-first century picks him up.

Steve McQueen

Shame

Like *Retake with Evidence*, *Shame* mobilizes the differences between video installation practices and the conceit of character as we encounter it in feature films. It too shows its director working the distinction between artist-auteur and auteur-director, and mobilizing not just professional actors but a particular male actor whose performance is at the very center of the work. And just as *Retake with Evidence* tangles with the relations to identity, statehood, and extraterritoriality, McQueen's *Shame* reflects on what we might consider a parallel and overlapping complex: one sparked by sex panics and the kinds of globalized neoliberal nonspaces that they induce and reflect—from the internet to "the dark net," across campuses, workplaces, and ever-growing stages of politics and government.[1] But at the center of *Shame*'s sex panic framework is a character both more conventionally presented—without the peculiar kind of performance Keitel delivers in *Retake*—and who impertinently, albeit subtly, runs against the grain of conventional characterhood. Characterhood and self-expression are considered complements, as Cixous points out: the "enunciatory 'I' *expresses himself* [*sic*] in the text, just as the world is represented complementarily in the text in a form equivalent to pictorial representation."[2] What of those whose authors have allowed them to fall silent, whose characterhood, as expressed in actions, for example, are mitigated by diminished speech? Whose "I" in the text is perhaps interrupted, in turn "exploding" structures and "ruining social and affective economy," as Cixous hopes?[3] What kinds of expressions can we find not only in their silences, but in the other means through which we come to identify them as characters—which is to say, as both "others" to ourselves and forms of being separate from that which we know as "real" selves?

There are plenty of characters who resist speaking or use few words. Like most of them, the protagonist of *Shame* isn't actually silent; he just speaks very little, and never about himself, or about the questions—about sex—that make up his alleged central problem. Such characters of few words have at times been seen as ideals of characterhood. Aristotle famously valued characters who are figured more through their actions and choices than through the register of language and self-reflection. But here there is more at stake. I am particularly interested in McQueen's protagonist because of his refusal to self-narrate. As such, he joins other "characters" in McQueen's work; for example, Bobby Sands, the protagonist of *Hunger*, the first feature film McQueen released, three years before *Shame*. Sands used not only his hunger strike but his silence as a mode of protesting English rule in Ireland as well as Margaret Thatcher's nonrecognition of political prisoners as such. Like Gene Tunney (and indeed the Irish subject of English rule generally), Sands was a character who had to re-earn his "title," his legitimate status.

Fassbender's Brandon echoes his performance as Sands: these are two caged or silenced bodies whose characterhood models a failure/refusal to speak or move. Both make this refusal a way of living (and in Sands's case, dying as well), even if Brandon's takes place within a far more comfortable, bourgeois existence. We find a similar matrix of refusal across many of McQueen's works for museum and gallery spaces, where it sometimes takes place within an excess, troping or absence of verbiage. *Western Deep* (2002) shows South African miners descending into a mine shaft and undergoing routine exercises. Its method of "showing" this to us emphasizes our own entrapment. We go, the camera suggests, "with" them, undergoing flashes of bright light and sounds so abrupt that one is warned about epileptic seizures before entering to watch the work. Their routinized movements are a form of imprisonment that is hard to miss—or bear. *Girls, Tricky* (2012) shows the British record producer and rapper Tricky inside a recording cage as he works on his song "Girls"; the camera encircles him, but he is caught inside, his underexposed head jerking in obscuring darkness to enraged lyrics. *End Credits* (2012) is an hours-long scroll through thousands of pages of the FBI's files on Paul Robeson, the Black American singer, actor, and activist blacklisted in the 1950s. As the pages shed a blindingly white light across the installation space, a soundtrack of frighteningly "neutral" voices reads a portion of the massive file. Like the fast-scrolling pages, their voices testify to the relentlessness of Robeson's surveillance, a kind of caging that is as real as any other. On a formal level, *End Credits*, *Girls*, *Tricky*, and *Western Deep*, like many other McQueen works, replace a literal cage with one made of sounds, light, and camera movement; the same, as we will see, transpires in *Shame*.

One more telling counterexample is *Illuminer* (2001), based on the body of the director himself, whom we first perceive as sound. Before we can see him in the video, we hear his breathing as he fidgets with the camera whose lens we are apparently looking through. He adjusts the focus, allowing more and then less light in. We are looking at a corporate-style hotel room, lit by a television screen at the foot of the bed, where the camera is also stationed. We immediately know there is a television in the room by the bluish tint it casts over the bed, flattening the image; the television's flickering glow is not enough to give objects in the room dimension or volume, at least not at the camera settings McQueen is using. Quickly he stops adjusting his lens and lies down, and *Illuminer* begins a second time. That prologue introduces us to the ways that color and sound are going to rhyme to create the rest of the piece. Now we are watching the body of a fifteen-minute video of the artist's body, illuminated only by the television screen, recorded by the camera that we know he set up for us, sounded by the ambient noise of the hotel room.

McQueen's body is being "scored" by a program on Navy SEALS in Afghanistan: the voiceover, rambling almost indecipherably (in an urgent French voice that is clearly a dubbed voiceover of an original American narration), narrates a story about a unit, their "brotherhood," their training. The flickering image that we never see is not only the only source of light; it is the trace of an invisible or implied image accompanying the soundtrack that is all that we hear. Thus, McQueen's Black body on white hotel sheets is illumined by the shifting light of a television screen, as well as a set of convergent associations: Black men and the militarized US state, Black men and violence, Black men and 9/11. At the same time, the digital image that illuminates also fails in the face of McQueen's Blackness. Echoing generations of analog film that were keyed to white skins, the combination of skin color and light source occasionally drops his body from graphic clarity.[4] The specular setup that allowed us to see from the artist-auteur's viewpoint (in the first seconds of the video) is both disrupted and technologically enabled by social and political reality. The encaging is not literal, in other words, but occurring on every other plane and, notably, not to just any figure, but to the author's. What we cannot miss is how the language of others—indeed, a military and propaganda apparatus that targets Black bodies as eagerly as it absorbs them—

"speaks" McQueen's silent body, forming it and in that sense formally enclosing it.

Shame's Brandon lives alone and works at a corporate job in Manhattan. His sister Sissy (Carey Mulligan) wants to stay with him while she gets back on her feet after what seems to have been a bad breakup. We first encounter her through his answering machine, during a long opening sequence filled with flashbacks and flash-forwards. In that first, long sequence, her words, "Pick up, pick up," echo through his sterile, empty apartment as he gets ready one morning after an encounter with a sex worker. Then, as the film begins a second time, after the extended opening credits set to Harry Escott's soaring score, Sissy arrives, unannounced, and Brandon agrees to let her cohabitate with him while she gets on her feet. Meanwhile, he remains very busy pursuing sex whenever he can. Sissy has a Manhattan singing gig, and Brandon brings his boss, David (James Badge Hale) to the nightclub; Sissy then brings David home for a night, sparking a fight between the siblings. Brandon briefly dates a coworker, Marianne (Nicole Beharie), and when their second date ends in a bout of erectile dysfunction staged in a hotel room overlooking the West Side piers, the film's climax arrives. Brandon, mutely furious, orders Marianne out of the room and goes out for a long night of anonymous sex, seen as a sequence of flashbacks and flash-forwards taking place in a bar, a gay bathhouse, and a sex worker's bed. In the meantime, Sissy, who has tried repeatedly to reach Brandon on his phone, tries to kill herself. Finally, at some point after daybreak, he emerges from his long night onto the subway and listens to the voicemails he's ignored. Hearing Sissy's desperate messages, Brandon panics and runs to his apartment, where he finds her bleeding and unconscious. She survives, and he breaks down—again, on the West Side piers.[5]

Brandon fails many standards of characterhood according to the conventions of classical film. His (literal) point of view is sacrificed throughout the film: rarely does the camera grant us a viewpoint that could be identified as his. This editing choice echoes the film's erasure of Brandon's enunciatory or linguistic point of view: despite Sissy's many entreaties, he never explains himself, and indeed never reveals much of anything about himself. (Marianne, his date, extracts a brief glimpse into his childhood, but that opening shuts down almost as quickly when their budding relationship flatlines in the hotel room.) The question for this chapter is not how or whether we get "to know" this protagonist despite such erasures, but what kinds of new borders are generated between his onscreen body or bodily presence and our bodies, our viewpoints. The soliloquy is no longer the privileged modality through which we can negotiate these borders, or even experience them as quasi-literal.

Moreover, because of how *Shame* is made, without those point-of-view shots but with marked use of color filters and occasional disruptions in the auditory track, our relation to the protagonist as character is shifted. So we can ask: If Brandon's characterhood is *not* made specularly, through point-of-view shots, then how does *Shame* generate it? If, in the absence of stories he refuses to tell and the point of view the director won't share with the audience, Brandon takes contour in other ways, what is the nature of those contours, and their reflection on this thing we call a character?

In most regards, *Shame* delivers an experience of characterhood that is more conventional than *Retake with Evidence*—it is a narrative film made for theatrical release, with conventional acting and sets. But it features at its core a character whose very refusal to talk is radically different from *Retake*'s positioning of Keitel/Oedipus as a profoundly conflicted speaker, knowable largely through his words, mode of enunciation, and relation to a set explicitly shown as such. Brandon is known to us on one level by what he does in the film's diegesis. But given the peculiarities of the film's editing technique, we cannot identify with a sense of his "inner" self as a deepening of his ocular, mobile perspective, as a function of filmic suture, or by his speech and actions. Instead we come to encounter him as an *it*—in other words, not "knowing him"—through effects of color and sound. There is a crucial distinction to be made here. It is not that *his* inner life is made up of sounds and colors but that *our* means of accessing that life are auditory and chromatic. And it isn't that what we perceive is only what art historians would call "local color," the colors of things, or what film historians and critics would call ambient sound (though there are those things as well). What McQueen relies on additionally is the coloring of the entire frame, and an auditory track that works similarly, so that what we hear and the way we hear it intervenes on film's naturalizing apparatus. That is how McQueen makes his audiences' sense of our own sensory boundaries suddenly at stake in the film, mattering to the question of what happens when one—*an other* one, who is not oneself—refuses to speak.

What transpires is then not simply the construction of an interiority or characterological depth through chroma and sound but a modification of our relationship to characterhood as a convention. In place of a character's presumed interiority and the means that film conventionally allows us to engage with that interiority, we gain a sudden awareness of our bodily, phenomenological container as it relates to that body or container as we see and hear it onscreen and in the cinema. That distinction—between our bodily containers and his—is what *Shame* gives us in the place of the protagonist's interiority. In fact, it is Brandon's very particularity, his uniqueness, and his claim to an interior life that come into question with particular acuteness in certain moments of *Shame*, with dividends for how we think about characterhood and selfhood and their coexistence. As we will see, the colonial-hegemonic framework through which the figure of the author is addressed in *Illuminer* becomes a different kind of stage for the character Brandon. If Blackness is required on the level of both physical embodiment and discursive conditioning for the subject "McQueen" to appear to us in *Illuminer*, then how does the psychosocial framework of "sex addiction" create the condition in which Brandon's refusal to speak is a legible, perhaps even political response to the mandate to self-account?

Chroma and Sound

Shame is a complicated film, at least if you like it. Otherwise, it's easily dismissed; even its title stokes charges of righteous moralization and rank psychologism, and much of the storyline cooperates.[6] It is advertised as a film about sex addiction—a topic that spawned several independent films around the moment of *Shame*'s 2011 release.[7] And with a barely-there plot and melodramatic climax, it does little to interrupt a sense that this quasi-tragic hero is a fairly unlikable casualty of a digital, corporate age that takes little interest in the lives of others. The film's chromatic palette rhymes with this hyper-judgmental, "clinical" idea of looking at, rather than with, its primary subject. In the first shot, in fact, we stare down at Fassbender's body arranged on blue sheets as he reciprocates, staring back up at the ceiling (or at us), unblinking. Even then the film declares a very narrow chromatic range. That bloodless range—from the powerful, Christlike, swathing blue of those bedsheets to the cloudless, sunless white-gray New York City skies that populate its daytime scenes, to the corporate gray blues preferred by computer software companies and dressing Fassbender's body—does little to argue for Brandon's humanity.

But as he stares up at the camera and we stare down at him, we hear a distant alarm coming gradually into our audial range, which then flips into the ticking of a metronome. The dailiness with which Brandon wakes up to himself, the soundtrack suggests at that moment, is as uninterruptible as an alarm or a metronome. One sound—the alarm—offers itself as diegetic and the other—the metronome—as metaphoric. Even that slender metaphoric offering, like the blue of his sheets, is less powerful than the way in which sound becomes a focus, like chroma, one that leads us both "into" Brandon's experience and into our own, as

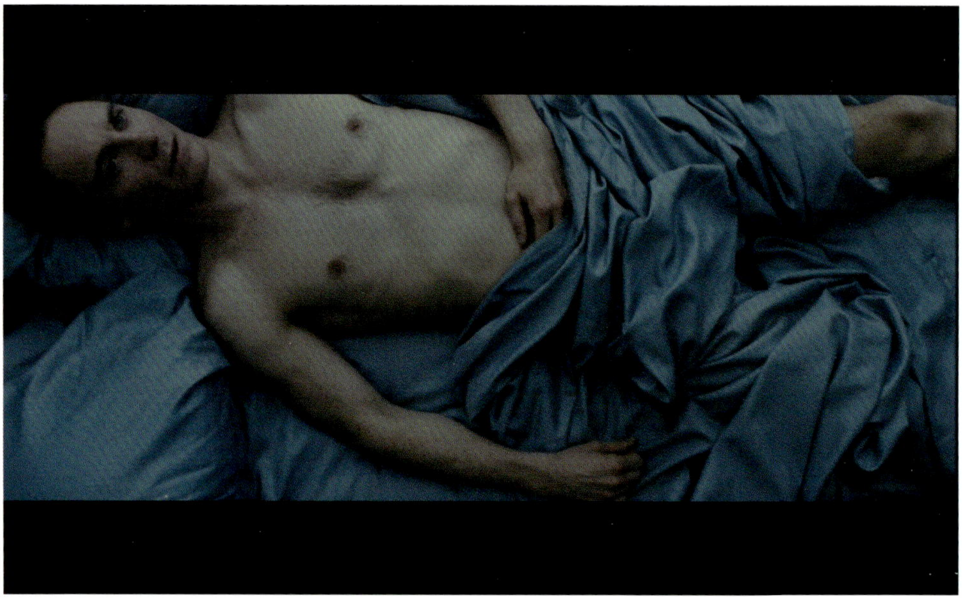

Steve McQueen, *Shame*, 2011 (Michael Fassbender).

listeners suddenly made aware of our experience of a sound that transforms as it nears our bodies.

In their theory of suture, Jean-Pierre Oudart and Daniel Dayan describe the ways in which audiences are sewn into the fabric of a film. Our positions as subjects are confirmed by its diegesis, the world of its stories and characters, as well as its shot-by-shot editing system and indeed, the apparatus as a whole (involving sound, the darkened auditorium, etc.). This seamless "stitching into" has a remainder: as one shot replaces another in the edited film we watch, a figure of silent authority stalks the process of our "suturing." In his famous "The Tutor-Code of Classical Cinema," published the same year as Cixous's essay, Dayan explains that the tight sequencing of shots in classical cinema offers a point of view that, though naturalized as "ours," belongs instead to a kind of ghost haunting the film.[8] Through that perspective, established in each shot but most subtly and effectively in the editing of shot *after* shot, we seem to enter the spaces of the film. The mechanism of our suture connects viewers to a film's plot and characters. Even more importantly, Dayan and Oudart and other "suture theorists" claim, it sews us into the cinema's naturalizing capacities, its development as an ideological apparatus that in turn helps to develop and reproduce us as ideological subjects.

In that first shot of the film, taken from directly above his bed, Brandon is a *gisante*, a *tableau vivant*, a coyly covered body and a blank gaze. His torso barely moves, so that we are only gradually aware of his breath, which will come to play an important audial role. His eye twitches at ten seconds, then not again for another twenty. The length of the shot and its unmoving object is not only impressive but crucial in allowing a local color—the color of the sheets, a colored object that has also, in this case, become the "ground" of the image—to set the tone for the majority of the rest of the film. Most of the rest of the film is shot with a filter that unites Brandon's minimalist apartment with the anonymously corporate enfilade of office spaces in which he works, the blue shirts and gray pants of his daily uniform, and the Microsoft Blue of his potently connected laptop and work desktop (which are confiscated in an early scene, suggesting that his corporate overlords might know about his porn addiction). This gray-blue corporate haze tells us one thing: that everywhere in this life, nothing is specific; everything is generalized. What matters is not where we are at a given moment but how such blandly neutral, corporate-minimalist elegance shields its attendants from expression and deconcealment.

The blue-gray chromatic and lighting schema of the majority of the film adopts what Gilles Deleuze saw in Josef von Sternberg's use of white: "that which circumscribes a space corresponding to the luminous," or, per Goethe, "between transparency and white opacity . . . an infinite number of degrees of cloudiness [*trouble*]."[9] Blue-gray light thus offers not only ambiance but also metaphor and structure, allowing the introduction of a further "veil or net which is superimposed, and gives it a . . . shallow depth."[10] In *Shame*, a metaphor for this filtering is lent not by veils, nets, or curtains but by the room-dividing office windows and laptop screens into which Brandon pours his gaze. (It's through just such a room-dividing window that Brandon watches his office crush, Marianne, and it's in the many laptop screens both implied and seen in the course of *Shame* that almost all the sex in the world seems to reside.) But when these chromatic unities break, we are either plunged into darkness surrounding those warmly lit faces and bodies—Sissy's, as she sings, or Brandon's on his date with Marianne—or into the luridly red, orange, and peach-toned sequence of flash-forwards and flashbacks making up the film's climax. The strategy of allowing figures to come into vision in contrast with surrounding darkness is older than the camera by centuries; such lighting is familiar from Old Master painting, even if *Shame* seems to be referring rather to classic Hollywood cinema. These strikingly lit scenes make a concerted contrast with cloudy blue-gray-white light that deprives the rest of the movie of any kind of specific light source.

For Deleuze, expressionist "chiaroscuro" interrupts the "infinite number of degrees of cloudiness" he calls *trouble*, and that's the kind of distinction that frames Brandon's date with Marianne and especially

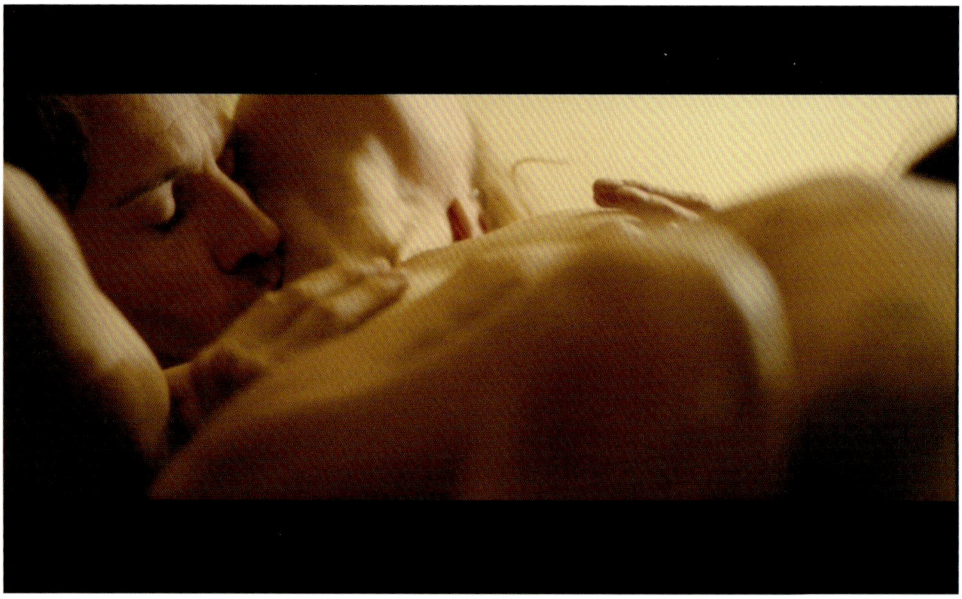

Steve McQueen, *Shame*, 2011 (Michael Fassbender, Deedee Lux).

Sissy's singing solo, as it fills out the (extra-wide) horizontal ratio of the screen. These scenes are dark and dramatically lit, heightened, climactic night scenes that interrupt the aquarium atmosphere of Brandon's sex-addled routines. Suddenly we are inside what feels like a wildly expressionistic three dimensionality, a vivid form of life that doesn't normally light up the aquarium. Whether he is gazing into the wall of Manhattan windows à la *Rear Window*, in one of the film's very few over-the-shoulder shots, or walking down the street with Marianne after a seemingly successful dinner date, Brandon's nighttime New York City is dark but lit just enough to make it exciting and full of possibility. Still, daytime New York is where the pervasive light and glass dividers keep things cloudy, where the real *trouble*—sexy on its own terms—resides.

A third kind of light interrupts this binary and springs Brandon, as it were, from his double life. When he is suddenly bathed in peachy-orange red light during the film's long climactic sequence, the formal difference in the status of color is striking. We transition immediately from chiaroscuro night into a sexcapade shot through a filter (or made to seem that way, in postproduction). This peachy-orange red light is a different beast, from its very first moments: from the moment that he has been beaten up by the boyfriend of a woman he's hit on in a bar, Brandon begins a journey into a night whose chromatic differentiation from the diegetic only gets more intense as he goes deeper "underground." First, the camera follows him into a gay bathhouse swathed in red light—actually lit by

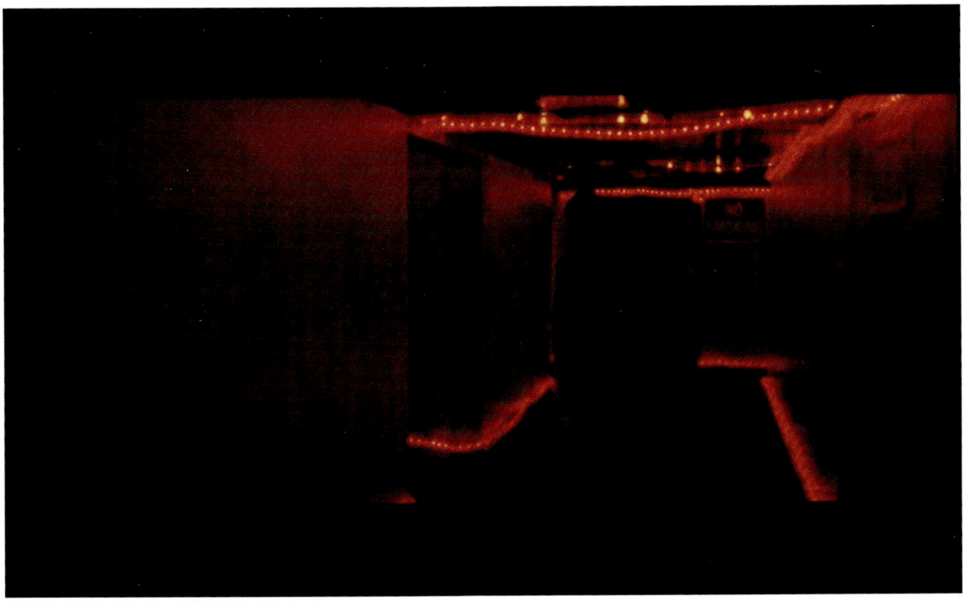

Steve McQueen, *Shame*, 2011 (Michael Fassbender).

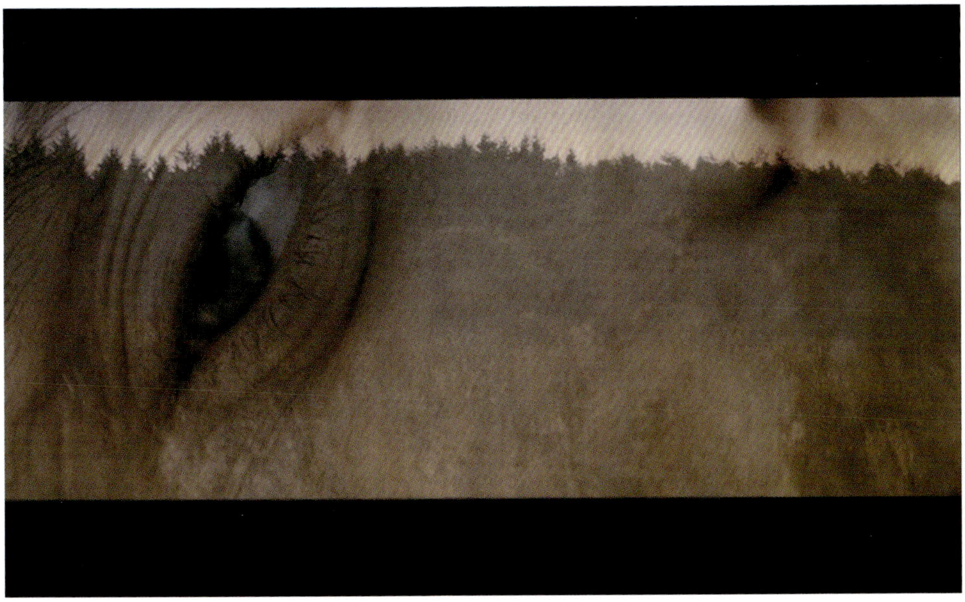

Steve McQueen, *Hunger*, 2008 (Michael Fassbender).

the permeability of our auditory experience: What is it made of; how does it work?[15] How is it *mine*? *Is* it "mine"?

The second time we hear Bach in this manner is after Brandon's all-nighter, as he takes the subway back home. A subway stoppage reminds him of Sissy and the messages he knew she was leaving while he turned off his phone in order to better enjoy his night. As the montage intercutting the subway ride with the flashbacks to the long night winds down, fear rushes in. The Prelude and Fugue no. 16 in G minor is the party crasher, finally prompting Brandon to listen to Sissy's messages and repeatedly try calling her back, to no avail. It is in that state that he breaks into a run, again, this time not away from the sounds of her lovemaking in his apartment (the first time we heard Bach in an extradiegetic way), but toward her expiring body in the same location. As he waits for the elevator, heaving and shifting from foot to foot, we are back to hearing his jagged runner's breath. As the camera closes in on him, anxiety transfigures his face. We watch his expression grow into that look of agony that we just saw, minutes before, as he climaxed during a threesome. As he wrestles his jangling keys into his apartment door, the fugue overtakes the rest of the soundtrack, blocking out even his own breath. By the time he sees Sissy's bloody body and cradles it on the floor, screaming, we hear nothing but Bach: any expletives are silenced, there is no more ambient sound. In other words, marking this extraordinarily "melodramatic" climax is a shot in which one of these sound transitions—nondiegetic Bach entering our hearing and cutting out all ambient sound—accompanies a chromatic implosion: a red-spattered white bathroom means that the colors of the night, of his secretive and desperate "other life" have intruded onto his pristinely controlled white-gray apartment.

Sex Panics: Tragedies or Melodramas?

Seeing Brandon as "isolated in soul-sickness against an indifferent city," James Quandt argues that nothing in this "passion play to gladden Michelle Bachmann's heart" can recoup *Shame*.[16] His review oscillates between defining *Shame* as a tragedy (a "passion play") and as a melodrama, characterized by its "moralizing coda" and "bathetic Barber-like lamentation." This ambiguity, as it seems to me, rides precisely on those late moments in the film when its narrative is finally trounced by the formal unities I have been describing. For Quandt is particularly irritated by the precise chromatic and sonic interruptions that I have focused on. He notes both chroma and sound—the sequence in the bathhouse is "luridly lit in Hades red and sordid strobe lights"—and decries McQueen's deployment of "Glenn Gould's lugubrious second recording of the *Goldberg Variations* over both a showy long tracking shot of Brandon jogging at night and the film's histrionic denouement." Might it then be fair to assume that even if this acute critic is indisposed to submit to the very moments that this drama unfolds its most spectacular effects, they are nonetheless part of what he sees overdetermining *Shame*'s genre-bending hyperbole? What genres can *Shame* be seen to bend—and to what effect?

For Blair Hoxby, the defining characteristic of tragedy is its use of pathos. This is true by virtue of "the end of the genre: to effect through pity and fear the catharsis of such emotions" and because of the way tragedy is defined, for Hoxby, by its historical concessions to the spectacular, or what he names as the operatic.[17] Those concessions include music and song, costuming and sets. The leveraging of *pathos* to become the central criterion for tragedy upsets the distinction between theatrical performances and the idealist framework, in which "theatrical performance is tied to *the very appearances that must be dissolved before tragic insight can be generated*" (emphasis added).[18] In other words, Hoxby's contention is that tragedy's spectacle must be *so* elaborate, in order to "generate tragic insight," that it actually must end in order for that insight to actualize. After all, he reminds us, "the heroes of tragedy *did* sing in the Greek theater"; thus, "the representation of *pathos* might be [the tragedian's] essential task."[19]

What is pathos? It is the genre's mimetic and performative side, the *showing* of suffering. "Because the whole weight of the ancient rhetorical tradition maintained that the best way to move the passions of an audience was to exhibit those passions," then to think of passion as pathos, as *representation*, was to reconcile the effects seen onstage with "the soul's *passive suffering* of the strong movements of spirits and fluids in the body when the mind formed some judgment that an object promised good or evil."[20] In other words, pathos is not action but the scene of what it does to a body rendered passive, perhaps even sculptural, plastic. It is only as such effortful, visible accentuation of suffering so acute that it renders the body passive that pathos insists on a reciprocity between the scene of suffering and the movement of passions within the audience. Ultimately it names the concern for that movement as both inherent *in* representation and in the "soul's passive suffering."

It is those scenes of suffering that Hoxby deems more critical to tragedy than the "divorce between moral freedom and natural necessity" that preoccupies idealist thinkers.[21] (He is, as he states, methodologically devoted to "surface reading," in which one departs from such preoccupations and their service to the hermeneutics of suspicion.) And indeed it would seem as if *Shame* also participates in any definition of tragedy that is at least as invested in pathos as it is in the conflict between free will and destiny. After all, while such a conflict is perhaps supposed by *Shame*'s presentation of sex addiction, there is little evidence that McQueen is truly invested in contemporary discourses of addiction, which seek to discount moralizing discourses of individual will in the name of medical illness. Does anyone care whether Brandon has a will? Does this film, concerned so utterly with the play of surfaces, light, shadow, color, and sound, care about such idealist "depths"? Rather, it is the *display* of suffering that we witness again and again: for example, as Brandon climaxes and stares out past the camera in an agonized, Christlike way, or as he takes up another Christlike pose, cradling his sister on his bathroom's blood-spattered floor. Moreover, it is the quasi-operatic aspect of McQueen's film that makes its tragic aspect come alive. Those moments when color and sound, the crystalline notes of Gould's Preludes or Mulligan's voice, and the flooding of the image—and the audience's sensoria—with chroma present a version of tragedy that aims at "spellbinding" the film's audiences.

And it is that turn toward the sensory that might enable us "not only . . . to rewrite a chapter in the history of human subjectivity, [but also] . . . to reimagine our own."[22] Reimagination not only encompasses the belatedness of the subject but the embodied—and aesthetically nurtured—condition of imagination itself. If we are, as reimaginers, to draw on our senses, they will by necessity become *projective*, both casting back over past historical chapters and presenting ideations of a future. If, as the critic Dai Jinhua writes, "only a nonteleological future vision can free history and time from the custody of power and violence," then indeed, "only the imagination and promise of an alternative future allow historical and present suffering to emerge and speak."[23] Pathos projects past the idea of moral conflict and into nonteleological past and future scenes in order to recognize and develop a sensory awareness of "historical and present suffering."

Yet, as Hoxby himself knows, the very tragedies that interest him are those that "idealists declassified as 'escape melodramas.'"[24] This line between tragedy and melodrama is not only a genre distinction but, for some, a political one.[25] In her reading of *Antigone*, Bonnie Honig finds that Sophocles's play can be reread as a melodrama. In fact, she calls into question the classed and gendered distinctions between the two genres and the ahistoricism of such distinctions as they are levied on fifth-century Athenian theater. Her reclassification takes place in the service of an argument that "lamentation (no less than reason!) is itself an essentially contested and politicized practice," thereby challenging the binary that

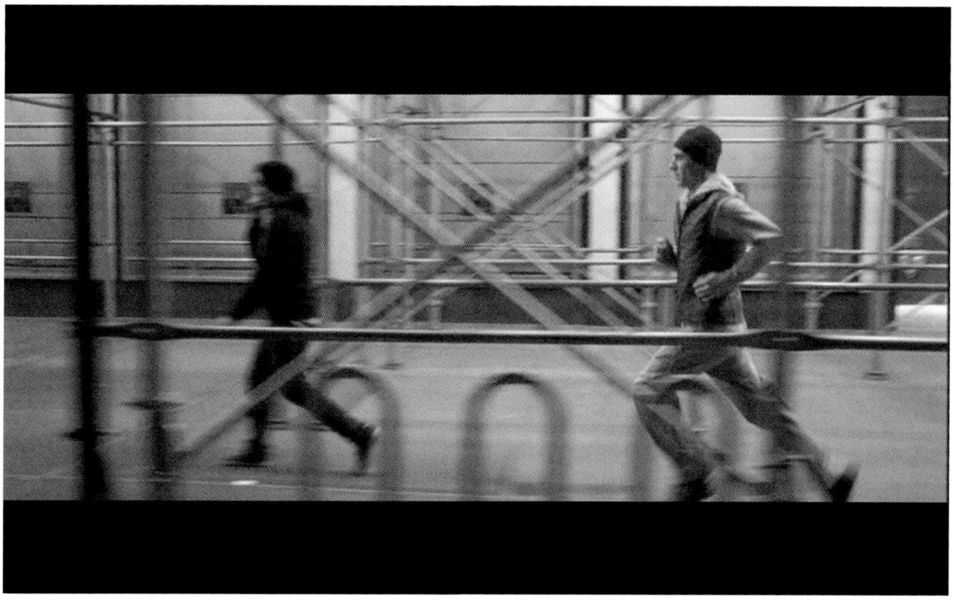

Steve McQueen, *Shame*, 2011 (Michael Fassbender).

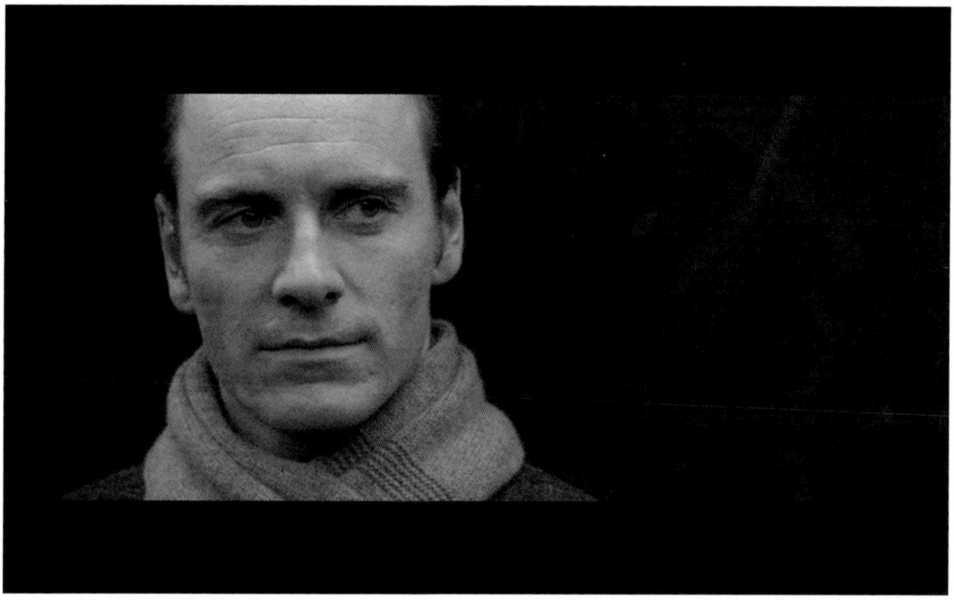

Steve McQueen, *Hunger*, 2008 (Michael Fassbender).

other critics maintain between "conflicts and coalitions rather than . . . suffering and solitude."[26] In other words, tragedy for Honig is ultimately bound up with self-other dynamics as a means of exploring the self and social life. But melodramas—in the sense that *Antigone* can be read as a melodrama—lend political power to the form of the lamentation, which for Honig is bound up with the differentiation of the private and the public, for it is suffused with the politics of solitary suffering. For Honig, melodrama, particularly of the filmic variety (she cites Rainer Werner Fassbinder) is defined in terms of its "emphasis on isolation, paranoia, affect, and suspicion."[27]

It is Brandon as such an isolated hero, fully ensconced in structures of "paranoia, affect and suspicion," that makes him a melodramatic hero. Moreover, we can see Brandon's silence or refusal to speak, particularly as it arrives as a kind of plastic image of suffering (pathos), functioning as a form of lament. In place of an articulated lament, or even an *Oedipus at Kolonnus*–style soliloquy, Brandon is presented as a character whose lament we must intuit or even "hear" in other ways. Those other ways are the chromatic and sonic unities and interruptions I have been describing. That they also compose the spectacle of his pathos, which happens to be the way that we see him as a tragic hero, is the way we see *Shame* as both tragedy and melodrama. His body, convulsed into the same poses as Christ's, is not only a visual object—a "character," as we normally perceive it—but a model for our own plastic, shell-like sensoria, our experience of the film piercing our vision and hearing alike. We *see* Brandon as an object of pathos, including the ways the film lavishes attention on his body as the privileged site of "vivid displays" not limited to suffering, and as certainly as bound up with resistance or lack thereof to "the bodily passions."[28] But where we might expect to encounter Honig's version of a "lamentation," we encounter instead the ridge of our own experience of the film, as a means of knowing its central, meaning-giving character. It is not that *Shame* needs its reflexivity to count as a critical film, for I think its politics exceed the negative dialectics of critique (hence its "failures" as Quandt counts them). Rather, what it does is to give us a way to understand that our experience is directly bound up with our expectations of "entering" or identifying with characters as they are conventionally presented to us, as singular monads with stories to tell. And it gives us an alternative: a way to rethink our own silences, perhaps to replace them within a political framework like Honig's: as laments, albeit "expressed" otherwise.

When we are re-placed "inside" Brandon's body in the two scenes in which we watch him run, we are taken phonographically "inside" Brandon. Driving our attention toward a highly formal musical composition—and even a familiar recorded performance of it—is one way to persuade us not that we are "inside" Brandon but that we are inside insideness. Interiority is, however unknowable to us, at stake; the magnified phonographic close-up of Gould's performance, its note-by-note minimalism, is heightening our attention to it.[29] *Shame*, with its rare point-of-view shots, is not interested in getting us to see *from* Brandon's "point of view," let alone "identify" with him or the filmic apparatus. It is instead interested in getting us to feel and think about interiority. In these interludes we sense our own oneness, the boundaries of the body hearing, an experience that is unusual not only in film but in everyday life. We sense our selves seeing; we understand the chromatic unities of the film by seeing them alternate and also turn into chromatic "baths" that exclude us (their light does not shine on us). When we see color as just such an object—as light itself, become material—it, like the sound piercing our own bodily shells, forces us to think about our perceptual apparatus. When we see and hear these moments that McQueen's film floods and bathes but also demonstrates its own limits that perhaps even erect a narratological system, it becomes not only part of an aesthetic experience but also part of how that experience gets us to think about our own ideas about interiority. Brandon's silence and the modes of connection to him that we are given instead of words become ours only through these interruptive passages in the film, producing a kind of equivalent to a lament. We become aware not only of our own bodies and their permeability but also of the film's mechanisms of interruption. As in Sophocles's tragedies, we as audience members are called on to recognize our own interruptions of his story.[30] But it is the braiding of what is interruption and what is being interrupted, what is ours and what is his, that provide the stakes of the film: not the mere "reflexivity" engaged in this awareness.

On Not Giving an Account

Providing an "account of oneself" to another, or even *as if* to another, is seen by Butler and Cavarero as the ideal framework for understanding one's "singularity."[31] Exposure requires linguistic effort. This is unfortunate for Brandon, who is relentless in his self-protection against Sissy's repeated urgings that he account for himself. She demands that he expose his inner workings by talking about himself, and he refuses and ignores her demands. In one scene toward the very end of the film—immediately preceding the long, sordid, orange night—Brandon and Sissy are watching cartoons on television. Throughout *Shame*, the two characters hardly ever face each other, and this is no exception. This time, the camera only lets us stare at the backs of their heads; our only view of them "talking to each other" takes place when they turn to give us their profiles. Most of their scenes involve similarly disjointed positions for the conversing characters. For example, at the end of their first morning together, Sissy sits on a countertop, facing the camera, and Brandon moves around the kitchen; soon after, when they take the subway together, we watch their conversation, two heads in parallel, from behind. This convoluted manner of showing us a conversation has the advantage of avoiding the shot-reverse-shot format through which most dialogues are filmed. It also draws pictorialized negative attention to the kind of face-to-face accounting that Arendt—and Cavarero and Butler—conceive, even when they dismiss the listener (the "other") as unnecessary.[32]

Unsurprisingly, perhaps, the question they address while watching cartoons is about responsibility. Brandon claims Sissy is not his "responsibility." She counters that he is her brother; they are all that each of them has; ergo, they are responsible for one another.[33] In fact, this scene begins when Sissy, entering the apartment, restates her first lines in the movie, which we heard first on playback on his answering machine. "Pick up"—which she once said to her brother's machine and now says to David's, leaving him a message for what sounds like the umpteenth time—serves as a nice reminder that Sissy's main function in the film is to beg someone to respond, to "pick up" the thread of the conversation she is always presenting. But Brandon instead starts his part of the conversation with an accusation (as Mickey Mouse cartoons play in the background), regarding David—his boss—whom he accuses Sissy of wanting, maybe needing: "He's not going to screw you again. You left him a message, didn't you? Can't help yourself. It's disgusting." Sissy responds: "Why are you so fucking angry?" Eventually, Sissy apologizes, to which Brandon replies: "You're always sorry," and we hear, faintly, the metronome tick that started the movie. As she repeats herself—"At least *I say* I'm sorry"—they truly get into it.

Sissy asks for a dialogue and Brandon responds by claiming that dialogue—and even relationality—is a trap. The form of being other that he wants is to be left alone. Not to be taken care of or dragged into self-accounting. The two fall into silence, and the sounds of TV animation take over the scene; the sense that we are being proffered characters as such, drawings with no life inside them, is overwhelming. The fraternal order that implies coevalness—that Sissy claims she alone lives up to—is indeed the framework that has become normative for us, beyond the film. It is the framework of what we call dialogue. Brandon rejects coeval responsibility ("I'm responsible for myself"—meaning, apparently, he has an apartment and a job). He also rejects the notion that the conversation that's required is one of give and take. Instead, Brandon suggests "not talking . . . just listening, or thinking, for a change." He redirects the question of how to handle the self-other dynamic from conversation to reflection. In rejecting the primary relation of co-responsibility—the kind that comes from recognizing an other as one's initiator into what is already one's primordial state of social *belonging*—he is not rejecting the other per se, but rather that simple injunction to talk as a way of confirming one's place in a pregiven order. His answer to the claims of responsibility and coeval sociality as epitomized by the sibling order is the antidote he offers to talking itself: silence, "thinking."

If the sibling order is one way to formalize the framework of "giving an account of oneself" and the encounters it implies, *Shame* is an ideal counterpart to the patriarchies of Oedipus and those that smuggle in the argument that to be a self, one must give an account of oneself to another. For as we know, that argument does not necessarily account for the way the other is instrumentalized in such a scene of accounting, nor does it truly answer the Nietzschean concern for the moralism inherent in the requirement to "give account."[34] Of course, silence can be multifaceted, and can even index the kind of guilt that is precisely what dramas like *Oedipus* or *Antigone* are built to explore—and that *Shame*, with its interruptive aesthetics proffering a means of resistance to simpler narratives of moral guilt, explores on its own terms. Where *Retake* reminded us of the Oedipal response to guilt, *Shame* answers, to shame: don't let me even talk, even to myself: no soliloquys here. Give me the freedom to be silent.

III

Role

> The face of this character is a fixed mask. We shall have her wear an eye shade to reveal her inner and outer appearance. . . . She must function with a face of stone and at the same time reveal her characteristic dissembling. (Slide projection during *Inner Appearances*, 1972)

The above is a paraphrase, extracted from a description of a film workshop conducted by Sergei Eisenstein. . . . If the unmoving human facial exterior gave up neither interpretation nor meaning, thus belying human interiority—"the idea of an interiority always leads to the idea of a transcendence," wrote Robbe-Grillet—then the "inner and outer appearance" of a performer could be nudged toward a *semblance* of coherence and sense by very minimal means indeed.

YVONNE RAINER, 2006

We have taken a lot of time collectively to experience the material's genesis as well as its transformations, which happen so quickly, so that the deviations from the original elemental phrase are as important as the basis. This also means that we don't regard the material as too precious; it's flexible and constantly liable to change, which is, for me, a very interesting experience.

CHRYSA PARKINSON, 2013

The choreography will write itself until the end. And when we begin to perform it, the movements will become more individuated, because we will have more nuances of interpretation that will build a stronger relation to the dance material.

CYNTHIA LOEMIJ, 2013

Museums are in the midst of cultivating and colonizing dance. They use dance to continue expanding the field of visual art and to "enliven" their spaces, which now compete with the animated and self-transforming spaces of tiny screens. With the entry of dance into museums, one hears and imagines arguments about how the museal institution might be weaponizing liveness against those virtual and infinite screen depths just as it once competed with cinemas. But that just begs the question: What is really interesting about "liveness" when it is what is all around us anyway? Is it liveness or dance's peculiar mixture of liveness and form—in the sense of a pre-given form—that makes it compelling?

In this final section I examine the formalization that dance offers: its means of amalgamating the human body to abstract form that I think provides dance's defining seduction. This idea of formalization is defined through my argument rather than as one of its premises. For now, let us call it—provisionally and incompletely—the capacity of movement to *not* signify even while granting a sense of separability and individuation to dancers and hence to dance. Often, gesture or other semiotic ideas about movement will return to that movement, even as processes of anonymization *and* individuation manifest in a dancer's presence before an audience. Whereas Erving Goffman maps out the ways that social roles set up subjects to behave in accordance with social functions, the dance role—as I'm defining it, from a post-postmodern dance perspective—builds on the absence of social cues, patterns, and norms.[1] As we will see, however, the idea that dance's movements can simply "not signify" becomes an increasingly blurry line, particularly as certain dancers and choreographers use individual styles—specific modes of movement, a dancer's strength, quickness or sinuosity, or even body types, hair styles, skin colors, ages, etc.—that cannot help but tinge even the most "neutral" mode of performance with an aspect of character or narrativity. Nonetheless, this morass of ambiguity that attends to human bodies makes clear to me that there are specific notions of selfhood that can be teased out in ways particular to dance, both to its performance and to its choreography.

The way that a dancer steps into a choreography, and in so doing, takes on what we refer to as a part or a role in a dance, is central to how selfhood can be teased out from dance's formalism, its claims to purposeless abstraction, and ultimately, its relation to other arts that also claim to leverage abstraction to address the spectator.[2] How a dancer occupies a choreography or, conversely, makes it "her own," defining a proprietary relation between the dance and her self, makes dance different from much performance art while generating a formal analogy to theater.[3] It also makes dance's roles peculiarly more continuous with roles as they are defined in the culture generally—for example, as when one names or enacts "the role of the mother" or that of the student or mentor.[4] Roles provide a means of naming the individual's place among others, without asserting that "I have always been such." Roles, as I am defining them, are both formalizations—means by which a body occupies form or maps out its implications for others or the environment into which one has entered—and generalizations, means by which *others* can enter a given role.[5] Roles, in both social life and in dance, are intrinsically about movement; one steps into or out of a role. One can become a mother, but one has not always been a mother; one will not be a student from birth to death in the way one might occupy a single class or racialized identity one's entire life.[6] Roles enable us to enter into relationships with one another in manners that are not dependent on or defined by either subjecting histories or our particular stories: they exist without or outside those stories.

Within dance, roles allow a choreography to be transmitted from one dancer to another across time, as a choreographic work is taught to new dancers or generations. A dancer's role is what is transmissible of the choreography as "hers," to become another's.[7] Property relations always entail structures of transmission and exchange: roles are that which mark such relations as internal to both the performer *and* the work, and also demonstrate the nature of that internalized relationship as a vehicle for transience, transformation, and flux. A role only belongs to a dancer insofar as it *also* belongs (or can belong) to others, across generations or even longer time spans. In addition to erecting this unusual form of property relations, roles also allow the mapping of *this* dancer's set of movements to join *that* dancer's set of movements to others' in the *same* space and time. Roles designate the distinctiveness between different performers and their movement schemes. *This* role belongs to *this one*, dancing onstage now, insofar as it does not belong to *that other one*, sharing the stage with "this one." Put otherwise, dance uses the role to execute choreographies as enterprises for making and showing collectives both diachronic and synchronic. As a means of separation, the role defines one dancer's movements and onstage patterns or trajectories as distinct from others'. This work of distinction and separation signals both the formal status of choreography as a score and the continual manner of *differing* among dancers who are participating in a planned and therefore formalized, durative performance. The degree of difference between this role and that one, between two almost identical parts onstage danced in unison by different dancers, could be great or small. Thus roles show difference as well as likeness and even replicability.

Perhaps it is no accident that roles are underscored in contemporary dance as it migrates increasingly into a set of spaces such as art museums, since the role is a historical artifact of how dance became a theatrical art form. Both roles themselves and the ways that they differentiate between the singular and the multiple—the ways that they work, fanning out individuals across space and time—are aspects of performance that we can trace to the classical Greek origins of the Western dramatic tradition, well before dance separated from theater. Before Sophocles's tragedies, as the nineteenth century German drama theorist Gustav Freytag notes, "Speeches of individuals were introduced between the dithyrambs and choruses," which were in turn "enlarged to an action."[8] Such individuals' speeches became what Freytag calls "pathos scenes" as part of the effort to make theater affectively compelling for the audience; their development was congruent with but not motivated by the narrative sequences that were also beginning to evolve.[9] These pathos scenes, in which are "comprised the touching effects of the tragedy," were "poetic observations upon one's own condition, supplications to the gods," comparable to monologues and at the root of what would become action and narrative. In other words, to simply identify roles as a structure *echoing* the cast of dramatic characters, a kind of post facto formalization, is to overlook roles' development from a formalization of pathos—an appeal to the audience that had not yet become a function of narrative development or the characters' instrumentalization in the service of other objectives.[10] As that formalization of pathos predates the development of the soliloquy, in terms of origin stories we are delving past the format of speech as a privileged expression of the self.

Dance, however, is not a simple artifact of drama and its evolving structures. Instead, according to dance historian and theorist Susan Leigh Foster, Western dance attained its status as an "autonomous art form" in the course of the eighteenth century, when dancers took to the stage as singular performers.[11] These performers represented the subject on three levels simultaneously. They enacted a physical ideal for the rising bourgeois class, conveying a combination of health, aristocratic bearing, and eroticism. Some dances took the form of narratives—however simple—so that dancers presented characters fulsomely conveyed through a language of pantomimic gesture. On a third level, the performer herself often led an offstage life full of intrigue and sexual possibility, making her into a kind of early celebrity for new types of audiences. By the end of the eighteenth century, dance had released from opera a new character system uniting these three levels. Dependent not on "opera ballet's masks, costumes, and interlocked choreographic patterns" but on a new kind of performer, dance—or *dancers*—allowed "the desirable [to become] wrapped instead within a personality."[12] Dance's uncoupling from opera and plays thus required that its performers attain a degree of individuation, one that would be parlayed off the stage as well as in the success of their execution of various characters. Ultimately it was these historical dancers who were each responsible for generating their own styles onstage—not choreographers' or directors'. Dancing not only mimetically but rhetorically, with virtuosity and individuality, their performance "styles," in concert with their offstage lives—filled with "affairs in the worlds of art and real estate"—gave dancers apparently replete, self-made identities that in turn fed the way that dance pictured the self onstage.[13]

reentered postmodern dance. This is not new: even as eighteenth-century dancers mimed correct manners or idealized emotions, their movements did not index "real" purpose or aim; these were not necessarily the movements of *characters* onstage, whose curtsies or other gestures advanced the narrative, the goal of character development, etc. Rather, these dancers were defining nonpurposive movement, using movement, gesture, abstraction, and characterhood to index both their own selves and others', beyond the stage.

If the body onstage implicates some terms of selfhood, we as dance's audiences know that we never actually know *that* dancing self—the dancer onstage or in our midst. What we know is that there is a difference between the dancer's self and her dance. This is as true of story ballets as it is of modern and postmodern dance. What they share in common is the role performed as an "inner actualization" of the dance, as a choreographed form.[15] It is not that the story ballet's character needs "development" and that that development takes place through dance, though that might also be the case. Neither character development nor the balletomane's fascination with specific dancers' abilities accounts for the continuing popularity of Western dance. Rather, dance provides an opportunity for the body to be other than a pure signifier and to move in ways that may be "a volume of traces in displacement"—in other words, signification building forever, rather than to an endgame.[16] Dance provides an experience of the dancing (or "danced") body both hiding and revealing: the duration of dance allows us to take in that suspension, to live inside it, as it were.

Yet this complex of ideas about the role points to a gaping question about what we mean by "abstraction" in dance. What does it mean to us to see bodies move "as they are supposed to," with what Erin Manning calls technicity or "the dephasing of technique . . . a craft . . . how the field of techniques touches its potential"?[17] Technicity lends to dance the chance to see a body and apparently a subject enter form as something "abstract" in the sense that it need not *imitate* selfhood in the manner of characters, figures, or other representational forms, or build to an "endgame"-style signifying practice. It nonetheless, I argue, makes a claim on selfhood. If selfhood has been claimed by philosophers like Cavarero and Butler to lie in the "account [one] gives of oneself," then the nonverbal work dancers undertake, which nonetheless involves acts of transmission (between generations of dancers, or from one dancer to the next in a given moment), amounts to not merely the *absence* of accounting. Roles, being about transmission, circulation, and exchange over time, also demonstrate the interdependence of each one, *other to* another, at a given time.[18] They are mostly wordless alternatives to instances of self-accounting or other "relational aesthetics" described in the previous section. Roles, as a mode of transmitting and exchanging form—as opposed to accounts, "content"—show us something about how we ourselves circulate. Those modes of circulation skip the kinds of intense dynamics that are inherent in subject positions and perhaps in "relating narratives"; they are formal and abstract, but it is as such that they redirect us to the ways we might think about *social* roles outside the norms and expectations that such roles confer or hold out. For example, being a student or a parent might seem to be one of the most overdetermined social positions. But insofar as it represents a space that we transfer into and out of—perhaps multiple times a day; certainly, over a lifetime—it can also indicate a kind of vehicular emptiness, a formalism that itself marks our own circulability. Perhaps dance roles, indicating the very spaciousness through which "they are *not* associated with a function, *not* tied to attitudes, or *not* associated with norms or social positions," could be precisely the way we reimagine ourselves, a way we understand ourselves to be circulating despite the baggage we carry, as our selves?[19]

The ballet *Giselle*, from 1841, provides a useful framework for considering the relation between the role and the story. Its first half introduces a cast of characters through set pieces, and its second half demonstrates that these characters are nothing but excuses for dance that might kill the characters off (or, as often happens in the strange landscape of Romantic literature, theater, and ballet: alter the terms of their deaths). In a ballet like *Giselle*, the wildness of dance, its difference from the ordering of gesture and semiotic meaning, are used to evacuate characterhood. That is, even as *Giselle* holds up and depends on gesture, narrative, and characterhood, it defuses the ways that dance can be seen to rely on those fundamentally theatrical or operatic structures. The protagonists and the ensemble do dance the melodrama of the broken heart: they even dance a battle over the lovers' souls. Yet we see that the ballet's characters are also a mere mechanism to enable the dance of the second half, where the choreography intensifies and the dance restarts, this time *for real*. *Giselle* develops narrative suspension in order to demonstrate that dance is itself about the suspension of identity.

But such story ballets (for many follow *Giselle*'s format: *The Nutcracker* is a particularly famous example) provide only one declension of rolehood in dance. In some modern ballets, we find that a given role is often elaborated as highly specific to a certain type of movement. That is, as one dancer dances a particular *kind* of movement that is different from what another dancer dances, a kind of spectral characterhood emerges. This is particularly strong in a ballet like 1967's *Jewels*, known as George Balanchine's first "abstract" ballet, in which each dancer dances a role identified by the name of a gemstone, which is in turn associated with a nation (Russia, France, America) deemed critical to ballet's evolution. Because *Jewels* has no narrative or character development, the roles depend for their definition and differentiation on qualities of movement; for example, on different levels of "attack" or sinuosity, and on differentiated national vernacular dance traditions. Roles, across *Jewels*, provide the framework or structure that allows the dance to unfold; in this way, roles provide the same mechanism as *Giselle*'s narrative (or something like the idea of a story in *One Thousand and One Nights*). Roles, insofar as we see them as purely formal devices, can deny the linearity of character development and narrative, even while providing legible frameworks (of symmetry and repetition, for example, aligning a sequence of pas de deux or solos). But *Jewels* also allows us to see roles differentiating according to movements that cohere as one role or another, as not substitutable for each other, while still not violating codes of abstraction or nonnarrativity.

How does dance, as an art that is particularly "abstract" even though it is built on human bodies, enable us to understand selfhood through differentiation as exemplified by roles? What does this differentiation in turn imply for how we consider abstraction in relation to selfhood? Are the two—the differentiation between selves that is always being performed by real bodies in the here and now and the abstraction of the dance form—separable? And finally: What are the dividends of these questions for the frameworks of individuation and collectivity at the basis of the role as a structure? Roles condense dance's means of presenting something separate from "character"—that is, roles show the ways that dance shapes nonpurposive movement into something that cannot be fully disentangled from the individuated body dancing it. This is the work that dance's roles do to individuate and formalize selfhood.[20] Like character, dance points us toward the narrative and artifice of theater.[21] But it refuses the "content" that character demands or allows the viewer to project. A dance role, even in a story ballet, fundamentally serves the project of distinguishing dancers from one another, in the same way that dance built itself up, historically and institutionally.

In that sense, the role, in producing separateness and unity, is analogous to shape. Consider Lauren Berlant's description of acting: "Acting, like many forms of engagement with convention, requires the subject to sublimate her being into another's *shape* while nonpsychotically having a personality to snap back to when the intersubjective moment is over"[22] (emphasis added). Dance is like acting insofar as the dancer must retain a subjective shape that is not her own while onstage—and then "snap back" into her own "shape . . . when the intersubjective moment is over." That part of its relation to role is what dance shares with acting. In other ways, however, dance's roles differ from both theater's roles and from shape. Theater truly does rely on the *inter-* in Berlant's "intersubjective"—even, as discussed, in moments that a single actor onstage is speaking (the *inter-* is then traduced by the audience). As soon as one has language, one has the sense of communicable content that is at the basis of intersubjectivity, however crossed its signals can become. But dance allows for "a subjective shape" that cannot be pinned down to a subject, whether it is construed as the dancer's own or a character's. The *shape* that the dancer's movement develops, as a unity, is a *role*, and as such it does not map onto a subject position or a subjectivity. It is foremost a device for getting the dancer onstage in her place and time relative to the space and music (or silence) around her, and by extension, allowing another dancer to perform the same choreography at another space and time.

Role, for me, enables us to understand the abstractness or formalization of difference between selves. One dancer is always *not* dancing the same role as the one beside her; but ensemble dancing, as discussed below, works on how the edges between dancers' roles can speak to the edges of selfhood, of our understanding of how replication and substitution work in relation to roles for *us*. When we look at how dance re-presents the self, it visually reminds us of that sublimation—of what is sacrificed or missing in "another's shape" as it is presented to us—without the entrails of characterhood. Dance's roles, in the modern and postmodern era, usually expunge what characterhood brings to that object that is "another's shape," though some works (again, I think of Bel or Lemon) invite characterhood back in. Indeed, most essentially, a role is simply a container, a formal relationship to both the other dancers onstage and those that come before and after *this* dancer, to dance the same role. In institutional terms, roles are also the regulative framework that much of dance's experimentation with movement, with music, and even with characterhood has left intact.

And yet this "pure" formalism is not unhinged from history. Melodrama, in this scenario, becomes not a device or genre permitting the ecstatic unification of audience affect with easy cultural codes, as it might appear to those associating the genre with a reductive view of soap operas and the mass-audience pleasures of Hollywood film. Instead it provides a key way for us to understand the motivation behind the pleasures that the role offers to audiences who understand that we too not only "play" roles but, entering and leaving them, find ourselves composed of the traces they leave behind, the ways *they* shape *us*. Douglas Sirk's melodramas are often based on the rigid ways that familial roles box characters in. Children inherit the disdain of the parents whose legacy they also covet: spouses bear and then discover their ignorance of their partners' behaviors. The films also exploit hard, glassy surfaces, such as the framed portrait to which Dorothy Malone dances in *Written on the Wind* or the magical windows and shadows of windows in Rock Hudson's place in *All That Heaven Allows*. That allows Sirk's cinematography to emphasize how glass, mirrors, transparency, and reflectiveness set up boomeranging visual vectors between different characters but also "against" the edges of the character as an inherited shape. This formal mechanism generates a sense of the map inextricably binding characters to one another through their ordained roles. That is how the *inter-* in Sirk's melodramas function, both on the characterological level and a formal level making a fairly clear mid-century argument about the desperate straits familial roles can land us in.

Yvonne Rainer has become a monumental figure in contemporary dance and art since the era of Judson Dance Theater. That group's improvisational experiments extend beyond even her best-known work, *Trio A* (1966), which has been cast as paradigm shifting in its "seamless flow of everyday movement like toe tapping, walking, and kneeling."[23] That movement lexicon, along with strictures against the dancer looking at the audience, helped incorporate Rainer's choreography into a tight narrative of modern and postmodern art that valorizes the "objective" world of the everyday over the hyper-"subjective" world of a dance formerly characterized by theatricality, though recent works by Elise Archias and Carrie Lambert-Beatty have truly complicated that reductive account.[24] Nonetheless, notions of characterhood, expressiveness, and virtuosity were the explicit targets of attack in Rainer's early writings, including her "Quasi Survey of Some 'Minimalist' Tendencies in the Quantitatively Minimal Dance Activity Midst the Plethora, or an Analysis of *Trio A*."[25] In that manifesto, as discussed in the previous section, Rainer zeroed in on the problem of character, producing it as a negative term alongside "phrasing" and virtuosity—relics of ballet and its hangover in modern dance. In her work in the Grand Union and Judson Dance Theater, she experimented with improvisation and role playing, speech and movement, instructions and audience response. But just as her move to filmmaking in 1972 allowed characterhood to become an explicit question, we can see its overtones—characters' theatricality—in her early dances.

Rainer's early works were often highly, even hilariously "melodramatic" in the most familiar sense: for example, the final part of *Three Seascapes* (1961–62) entails a woman having a "screaming fit downstage right in a pile of white gauze and black overcoat."[26] Works like *Ordinary Dance* (1962) or *At My Body's House* (1964) enabled the dancer either to speak her "autobiography" or to merely breathe (electronically amplifying that breathing). For dance to become Rainer's medium, it had to claim the dancer's body as *not* a vehicle for virtuosic performance—and hence, a vehicle for the audience's sublimated desire and the dancer's mode of masking "herself." And yet that body brought melodrama—perhaps specifically but not always exclusively of the female subject—onstage. Hence, the taint of a kind of characterhood, in this case attending to the gendered body, can be as subtle as that screaming fit or as explicit as a spoken autobiography; only later in the 1960s would it be more fully eradicated from her dance. But then, in her first feature-length film, *Lives of Performers*, Rainer moved toward characters *and*, as if the two were inextricable, toward the genre of melodrama. In other words, precisely that which she had sought to eliminate from dance became not only the basis of her filmmaking—a filmmaking that would over years denature and disclose the terms of melodrama—but her departure point from dance. That very departure point, for me, reveals an undercurrent in her work that has become all the more striking since her return to choreography in 2002. I pick up that recent set of developments with the 2015 work *The Concept of Dust, or How do you look when there's nothing left to move?* If that work's subtitle plays on the choreographer's aging body and on the question of the look, the audience's gaze, that was so precisely addressed in that earlier phase of her choreography, it also reframes such questions within a temporality that places us within "the concept of dust." Just as our dust—our future selves—is joined to the planet like the debris of a sunken ship, dance enables a framework of roles like the social ones that connects us with past and future occupiers of those roles.

But this section begins with a dancer-choreographer who is even more evidently committed to melodrama in dance. Anne Teresa De Keersmaeker trained as a young dancer at Mudra, the international school associated with the Ballet of the Twentieth Century that was directed by Maurice Béjart, who also served as choreographer in residence at Brussels's opera house, De Munt / La Monnaie, a post that De Keersmaeker would eventually occupy herself (from 1992 to 2007).[27] She made her early works, such as *Fase: Four Movements to the Music of Steve Reich* (1982) and *Rosas danst Rosas* (1983), immediately after returning from a year studying at the Tisch School at New York University. According to sources including De Keersmaeker herself, these early dances were built out of her direct encounter with "analytic postmodern dance"—the works of Lucinda Childs, Trisha Brown, Rainer, and others—in New York.[28] Yet De Keersmaeker's legacy is in many ways overdetermined by the classical ways that European avant-garde dance still links itself to opera houses and theaters. Others of her "influences," as important as these New York choreographers, include Pina Bausch and William Forsythe, both of whom embrace not only theatricality but institutional conditions for spectacle. Indeed, one link between the main body of work of De Keersmaeker's examined here and that of Rainer's is that they have been performed inside museums. Though Rainer's *The Concept of Dust* was not made for a museum, it was staged in one, while De Keersmaeker's *Work/Travail/Arbeid* (2015) is the restaging of another work, *Vortex Temporum* (2013), made for theatrical performance. The ties that both Rainer and De Keersmaeker construct between the objecthood of the dance performance, underscored by the transfer of their works into museums, and the conventions for seeing dance are critical to the implicit ties that I am setting up between the two choreographer-performers.

To return to where this introduction began, liveness is not only something we associate with the self as a living thing but also something that at times has held emancipatory potential for art. Modernist instruments such as the aleatory or the polysemic, the "refusal of fixed meanings," failed Rainer as a "self," according to her memoir. It was those failures that inspired her own work, particularly her decades-long abandonment of dance for cinema. Yet she has qualified them as aesthetic failures, failures of art to produce a set of responses appropriate not just to the emotional work of living but to the political demand of making aesthetic work. Such modernist tactics that could lead the spectator into a "refusal to differentiate events," a "risk of trapping the spectator in a chain of unlimited interchangeability," would, for Rainer, inevitably wrap back around to the sense of self:

> In the next several years I would grapple with the challenge of representing and fictionalizing the inferno of my own passions. . . . The terms, or formal conditions, of my new world of "emotional facts" would at first also remain tied to the disjunctive and aleatory procedures which had laid claim to my earliest development as an artist via the ideas of John Cage and Robert Rauschenberg. On the one hand, this mindset can be characterized as a refusal of narrative and fixed meanings and a deep distrust of the "telling" and shaping strategies of fiction and history. On another, it can be seen as a refusal to differentiate events, thus running the risk of trapping the spectator in a chain of unlimited interchangeability.[29]

Such "interchangeability" was too impersonal and *hence* apolitical for Rainer. Her disenchantment is not only about herself, her personal frustrations, but about a dawning realization that the politics of selfhood would require something more from art.

Anne Teresa De Keersmaeker

Work/Travail/Arbeid

Vortex Temporum and *Work/Travail/Arbeid* are two works that stem from one choreography. Both are set to a 1996 score entitled *Vortex Temporum* by the composer Gérard Grisey. The dance *Vortex Temporum* is performed in black-box theaters, on stages stripped of all forms of set design, and features dancers from De Keersmaeker's troupe, Rosas, as well as musicians from the Brussels-based group Ictus. *Work/Travail/Arbeid* is performed in museum spaces: I'll be discussing its original staging, in Brussels's center for contemporary art, Wiels, in the spring of 2015. (It has since been restaged at the Tate Modern, the Centre Pompidou, the Museum of Modern Art in New York, Mudam in Luxembourg City, and the Volksbühne in Berlin.) For *Work*, the dancers wear light-colored costumes—white, khaki, or taupe pants and shirts, sometimes with a pink undershirt or contrasting belt—and brightly colored or dark sneakers. The musicians wear individuated costumes (identical in every performance) that suggest they have walked into the performance space in their street clothes. By contrast, for *Vortex Temporum* the dancers wear black pants and shirts, as do the musicians. In both stagings, musicians not only perform alongside dancers, but their movements around the shared spaces (whether stage or museum gallery) are as choreographed as the dancers'.

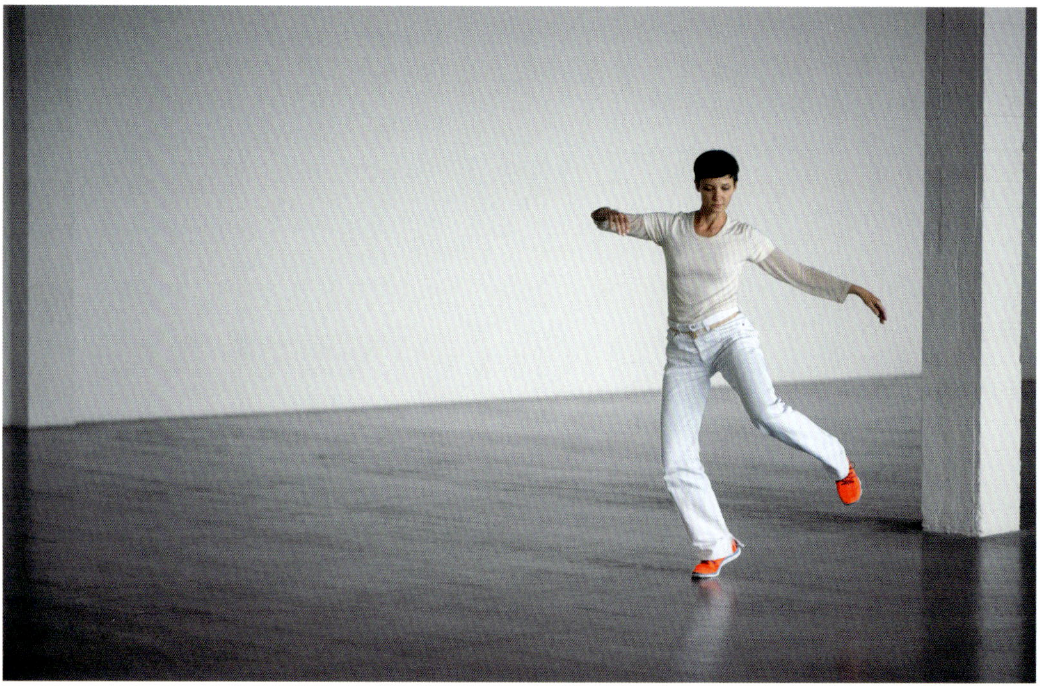

Anne Teresa de Keersmaeker, *Work/Travail/Arbeid*, 2015 (Marie Goudot), Wiels Contemporary Art Centre, Brussels. Photo: Anne van Aerschot. © Anne van Aerschot.

The black-costumed, stripped-back staging of *Vortex* matches the graveness of Grisey's score, its dirgelike first movement and quickening, anxious climax, as well as the composer's interest in drawing both microcosmic and planetary scales of perception into musical experience. *Vortex* announces itself as a somber, even austere dance, while *Work/Travail/Arbeid*, staged so as to enable audiences (including small children) to mix and wander among the dancers, can appear light-hearted and playful. Whereas *Vortex* concentrates on the plasticity of the stage space—at several points the dancers run and turn together, suggesting a shared point of orientation and a churning or roiling "vortex"—*Work*, though it performs the same movements and shapes, uses these vortices to invade the often beautifully lit space of museums and investigate the novelty of those spontaneous effects that emerge from having audiences wander amid performers.[1]

Both dances work, melodramatically, on multiple levels. Both capitalize on Grisey's intensely affecting score, the "orgy of feeling" it churns up, especially at its climaxes, when dancers walk, then run, then run faster in shared, concentric rings.[2] The two works' shared choreography insists on melodrama's "expressive code . . . characterized by a dynamic use of spatial and musical categories"—rather than its literary or theatrical conventions.[3] But the most important way that both dances enact melodrama has less to do with affect or formal codes than with the ways

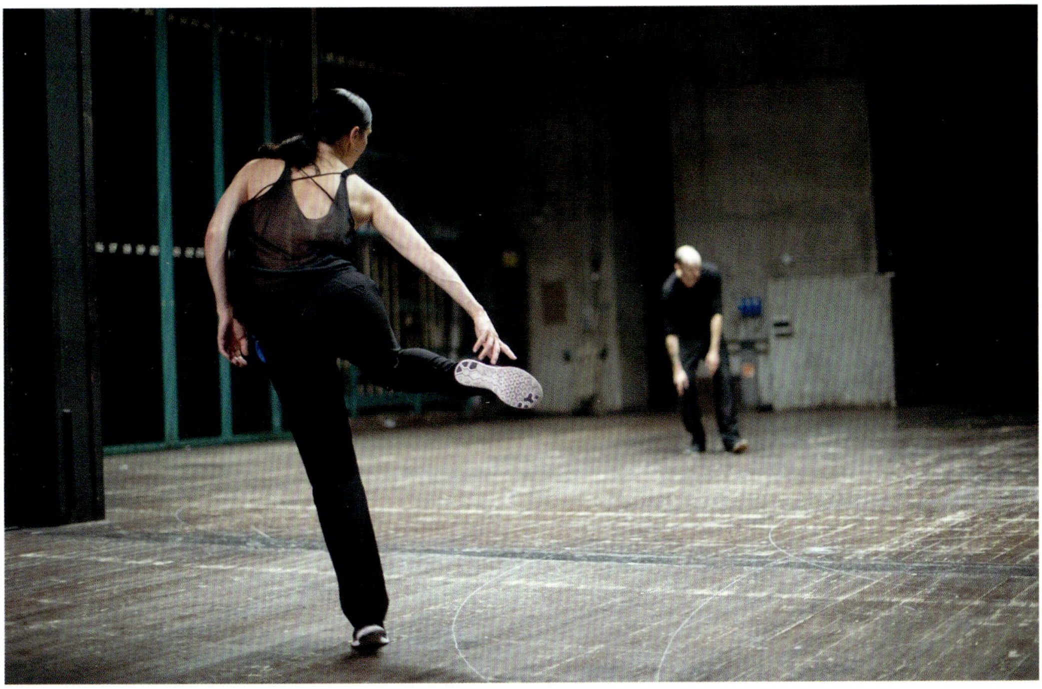

Anne Teresa de Keersmaeker, *Vortex Temporum*, 2013 (Cynthia Loemij, Carlos Garbin). Photo: Anne van Aerschot. © Anne van Aerschot.

that the dancers themselves present a kind of monadary, a pageant of differentiated entities that slowly unfolds in the course of the dance and our experience of it. These are entities lacking either narrative implications or indeed "characterhood," and despite the spectrum of differences among the dancers as performers, the differences between these roles appear to have little to do with the dancers. We gradually understand that each dancer's role correlates to something *beyond her*—and thus that each dancer is identified with a role that is her own, but not "her self." This will be underscored by the arrival, midway through each performance, of a second set of dancers performing the same roles. Seeing these dancers dancing their "own" and "each other's" roles shifts the ways we understand the self in her navigation of others.

Work/Travail/Arbeid begins with the members of De Keersmaeker's troupe, Rosas, drawing chalk circles on the floor using preset points and string.[4] Audience members are invited to wander through the space and stand, sit, or play anywhere—even directly in the way of the moving dancers and musicians. The circles mark out a kind of spatiality unique to the work, a performative adjustment to the unspoken understanding that the space of a dance work performed in a museum is predetermined by the squared-off walls of each gallery.[5] It is not that the dancers merely dance within those circles, though at times they will run along them. Rather, those circles represent, albeit complexly, the individuated space

Anne Teresa de Keersmaeker, installation view of the exhibition Anne Teresa de Keersmaeker: *Work/Travail/Arbeid*, March 29, 2017–April 2, 2017. Photo: Julieta Cervantes. The Museum of Modern Art, New York. Digital Image © The Museum of Modern Art / licensed by SCALA / Art Resource, New York.

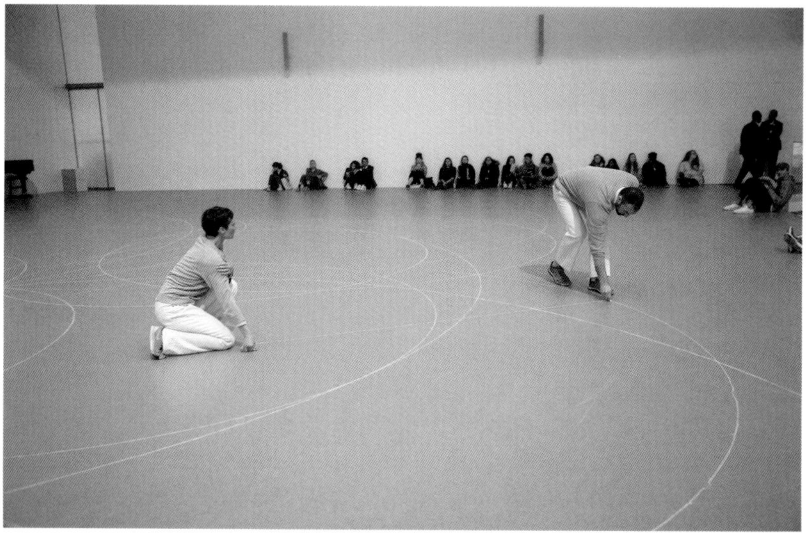

Anne Teresa de Keersmaeker, drawing of a floor pattern with names of the dancers assigned to pentagon circles for *Work/Travail/Arbeid*, 2015.

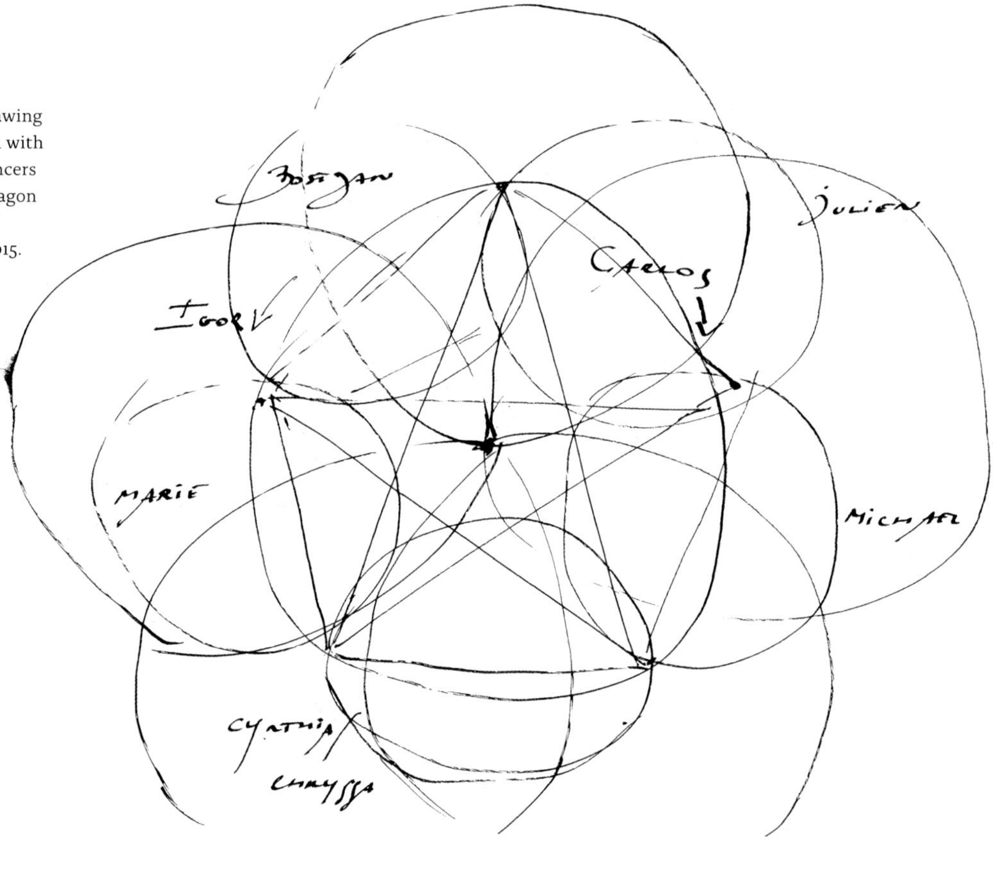

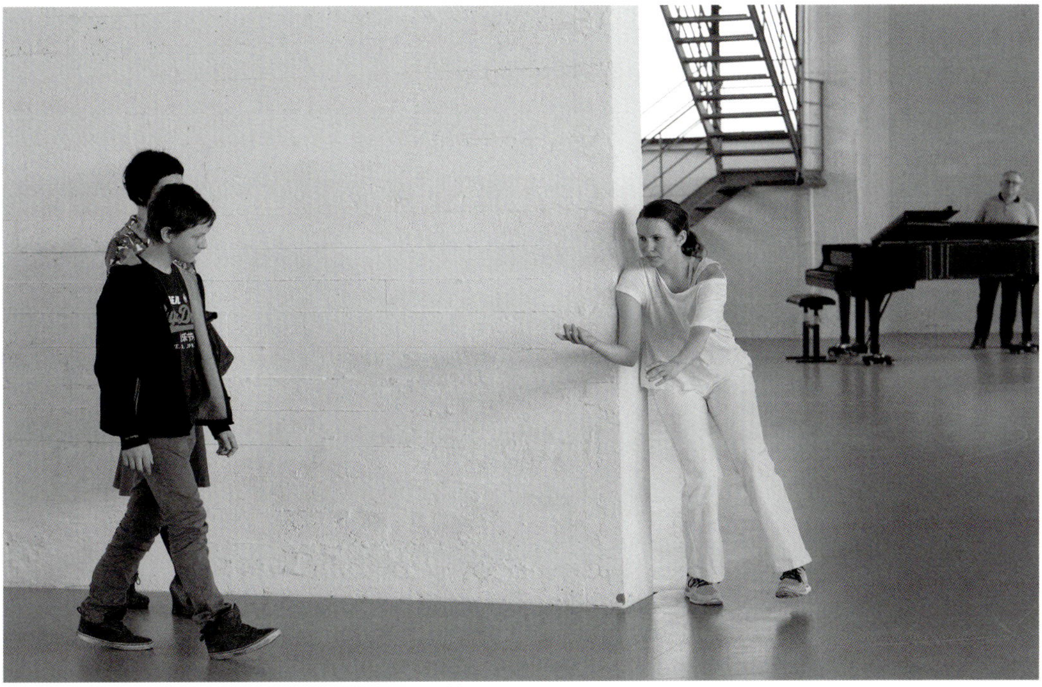

Anne Teresa De Keersmaeker, *Work/Travail/Arbeid*, 2015 (Bryana Fritz), Wiels Contemporary Art Centre, Brussels. Photo: Anne van Aerschot. © Anne van Aerschot.

occupied by each dancer. Each places herself, at the second start of the dance, at the center of her own "magic cube," that three-dimensional container that De Keersmaeker derives from the magic square, itself a recurring motif in her work.[6] With different body positions assigned to the different points on the cube, the dancers' movements are dictated by a sequence of numbers that in turn dictate which direction and which movement or position is next. (At different points in the work, these numbers are spoken aloud, conveying to the audiences the verbalized instructions allowing dancers to tell one another what to do.) The magic cubes thus form portable, invisible envelopes around each dancer, carving up the space each shares with other dancers, with musicians, and with audience members.

This geometrization fed the working process of the choreography. De Keersmaeker often relies on certain individual members of her company to originate dance phrases. For example, the dancer Michaël Pomero originated the basic or "elemental" phrase that all roles in *Vortex* share. The single elemental phrase "which originates in the movements of the sternum and develops in directions pointing into space," shared by all dancers, is at first performed in relation to the same points of each dancer's magic cube. Each dancer's cube is placed at a different point in interlocking rings.[7] The movements making up the elemental phrase are simple; some installations of *Work* include not only large photographs but a video in which Pomero breaks down that "elemental" phrase, as if to teach it to audience members. The simplicity of that phrase is striking at first. It begins with leans, walks, a look over the shoulder: means of indicating points in space, and even setting up a map of vectors, arrows that the bodies will continually reiterate. During performances of *Work*, audiences can situate themselves close enough to a dancer to see exactly where their eyes are looking, noting that what might appear to be a void is instead a kind of invisible envelope that the dancer can see but we cannot. Eventually, in its installation in Wiels's two adjoining rooms, the dance tips from one room into the other. But even that threshold is not crossed all at once, but by a series of ventures up to the threshold; only gradually do the dancers pour into the second room.

Partway through each hour, the members of a second cast of dancers arrive. In *Vortex*, they simply enter from the sides of the stage, as in any other dance work; in *Work*, they arrive to first sit on the sidelines and watch, amid the audience members. Only after a period of ten minutes do they perhaps remove an article of clothing (a sweater, for example, that has helped to keep them warm), take their places on the floor, and join the dance. This second dancer, shadowing a member of the first cast, introduces a slight counterpoint, a wedge between the dancer and her role. She starts off dancing near the first dancer, whose movements she performs in exactly the same way but facing a slight—perhaps ten- or fifteen-degree—angle away from the first. Not only is the invisible envelope of the first dancer "reiterated," as it were, by this new arrival, but its plasticity is re-marked. The angled degree of difference, a kind of spatialized, directional wedge between the two dancers, both shows us the significance of their spatial orientation and the sense that the space is being molded through movement.

By that point in the dance we might have already gleaned that each dancer's role or part correlates to one of the musicians—or, more precisely, to a musician, their instrument, that instrument's score, and even the position of the instrument in the performance space. In the original first cast, Carlos Garbin "plays" the piano (Jean-Luc Plouvier); Marie Goudot plays the clarinet (Dirk Descheemaeker); Boštjan Antončič plays the violin (Igor Semenoff); Julien Monty plays the viola (Jeroen Robbrecht); Michaël Pomero plays the cello (Geert De Bièvre); and Cynthia Loemij plays the flute (Chryssi Dimitriou). Each dancer "dancing" her or his musical referent is therefore not only explicitly dancing the project of individuation but mapping that project onto a set of referents and making that vector of referentiality into the piece. The second cast both underscores the project of individuation and disrupts it: If *this* one dances *this* role—for example, that of "the clarinet"—what does it mean

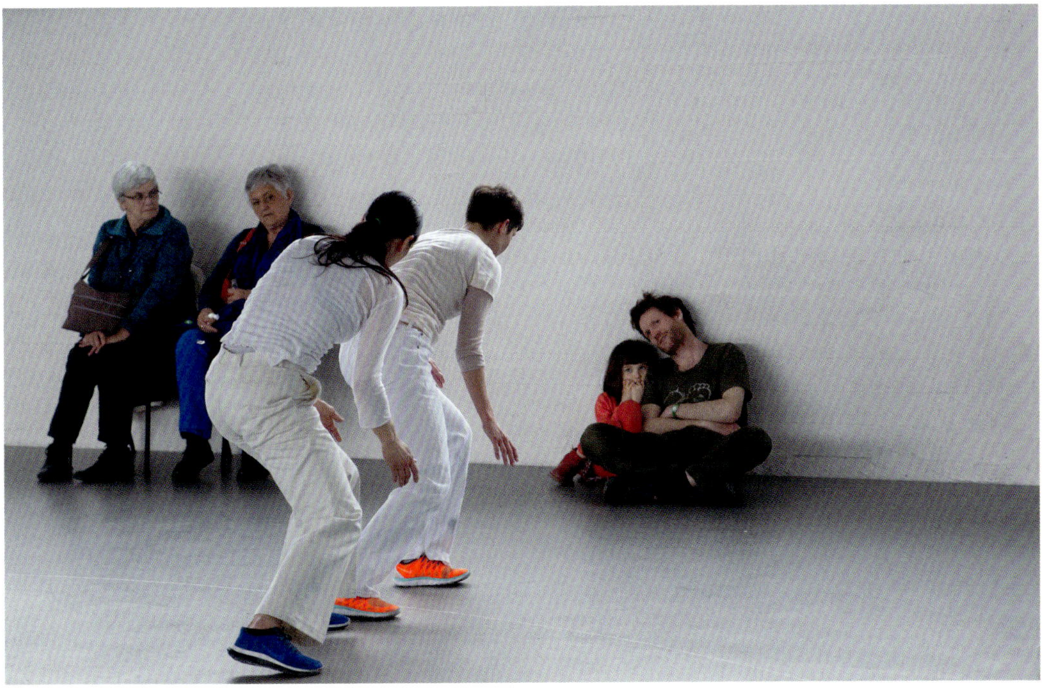

Anne Teresa de Keersmaeker, *Work/Travail/Arbeid*, 2015 (Cynthia Loemij, Marie Goudot), Wiels Contemporary Art Centre, Brussels. Photo: Anne van Aerschot. © Anne van Aerschot.

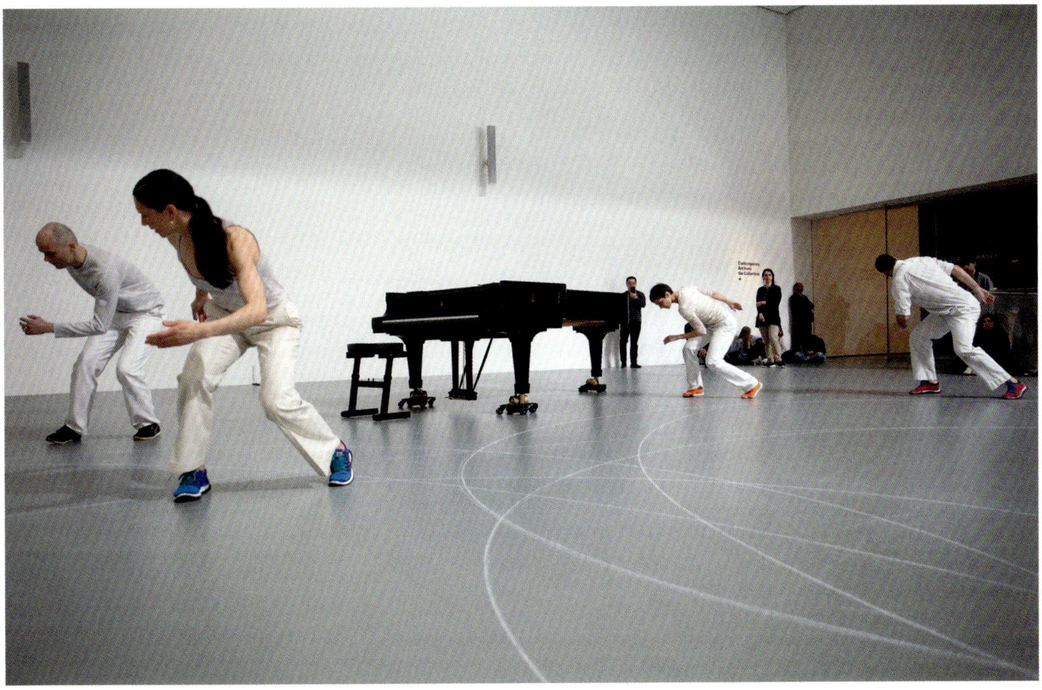

Anne Teresa de Keersmaeker, installation view of the exhibition Anne Teresa de Keersmaeker: *Work/Travail/Arbeid*, March 29, 2017–April 2, 2017 (Carlos Garbin, Cynthia Loemij, Marie Goudot, Boštjan Antončič). Photo: Julieta Cervantes. The Museum of Modern Art, New York. Digital image © The Museum of Modern Art / licensed by SCALA / Art Resource, New York.

to have another, from the second cast, *also* dance "the clarinet"? What is the difference between *this* one dancing a role and *that* one dancing "the same" role? What impact does this role, which therefore *splits* halfway through every hour of *Work/Travail/Arbeid* (or halfway through each performance of *Vortex Temporum*) have on the idea that every dancer dances *her* role? These dances are not mere showcases for the question of *how* a dancer dances her role; they are far from the conventional ballets that made stars out of how so-and-so danced Swanilda or Giselle.[8] They move into the "what" of the role; how a choreographer conceives the project of roles themselves is what the works are about. *Vortex* and *Work* thus address the way that roles can become the vehicle through which dance can address individuation and deindividuation.[9]

What De Keersmaeker accomplishes in pairing each dancer with a musician is not merely to make problems of individuation perceptible but to allow them to unfold as experimentation with how a dancer "owns" her role. That proprietary relation is established in the first movement and disrupted by the arrival of a second cast in *Vortex* and *Work*. Moreover, the relations between dancers and musicians are not limited to such acts of reference but are also spatialized. From the start, musicians occupy and move around the space, playing music but also traveling spatial trajectories as carefully choreographed as the dancers'. When the dancers turn, together, the musicians do as well, facing their own points on their own magic cubes. At times they turn while playing, at other times while silently accompanying their fellow musicians; when the dancers walk and then run their roiling vortices, at the climax, the musicians do not run but they do walk, then turn, exactly echoing the directions the dancers are facing. At various points in *Vortex* they leave the stage, and in *Work*, the galleries. De Keersmaeker's choreography thereby replaces one of the conductor's key functions—to indicate when a musician's part enters the music. (In fact, in these performances the musicians play the first two movements of Grisey's composition without a conductor; he only enters for the last movement.)

These physicalized entrances and exits re-mark episodes in the composition in which Grisey develops his spectralist approach.[10] Though Grisey disowns the label that he shares with Tristan Murail, the other great Parisian "spectralist" composer, he also subscribes to "a central belief that music is ultimately sound evolving in time" in ways that enable composers to "use the available knowledge in the fields of acoustics and psychoacoustics within their music. . . . Sounds and musical colors (timbres) can be sculpted in time to produce musical effects."[11] Indeed, the use of instruments to produce sounds well outside the ordinary spectrum of

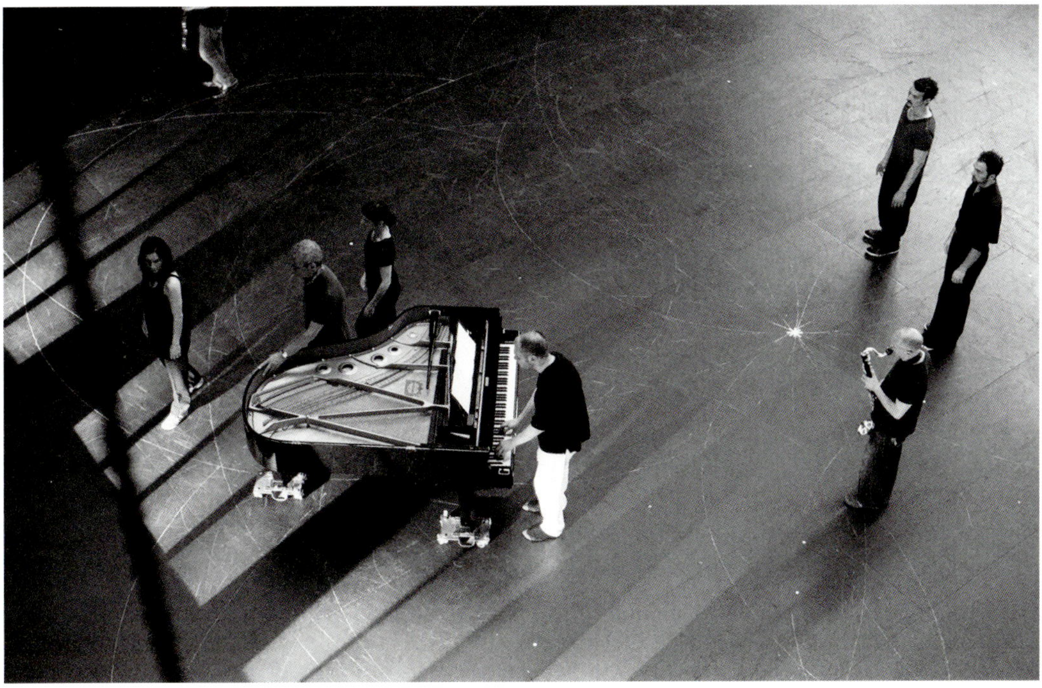

Anne Teresa de Keersmaeker, *Vortex Temporum*, 2013 (Cynthia Loemij, Georges-Elie Octors, Marie Goudot, Jean-Luc Plouvier, Michaël Pomero, Boštjan Antončič, Dirk Descheemaeker). Photo: Anne van Aerschot. © Anne van Aerschot.

notes—harmonic or otherwise—not only draws attention to the spectra of new or "unmusical" sounds but to their location, for these sounds' emergence no longer belongs to a quasi-transcendent (e.g., orchestral) set of harmonies, but often relates specifically to the instrument's material makeup (the horsehair of a bow and the wood of a stringed instrument, for example) and the musician's location. Thus, at the start of *Vortex*'s second movement, each string instrument is bowed so hypergently that at first we barely perceive the sound—and then bowed so hard against the strings that the sound breaks into tiny, acrid increments. What we hear are not only *not notes*, but not recognizably musical tones. Like hearing nothing but an audible breath—or the actually inaudible movement of air as a bow is picked up, or the almost-audible sound of a bow placed on strings—these are sounds that are properly "psychoacoustic" and even intersubjective, as much within the listeners' individuated, spatialized experiences as the score's formal direction.

Eventually, the simple phrases that allow listener-watchers to enter *Vortex Temporum* or *Work/Travail/Arbeid* give way to the more complex work of individuation that Grisey's score enables. As Jean-Luc Plouvier, the pianist with Ictus who consistently performs with Rosas's dancers, explains, regarding the separate instruments' musical scores, the music is gestural, embodied, and physically performative:

> *Vortex Temporum* is a sophisticated work, but it is underpinned by a fairly reduced gestural vocabulary that has to be made clear to the listener-cum-viewer. A perusal of this vocabulary offers a rewarding insight into what a musical "gesture" represents: in some circumstances, the word may be taken quite literally, as a synonym for an "instrumental gesture." Examples are the piano leaps pianists make by crossing their arms and traveling across the keyboard in three moves (low, medium, treble range): run-up, leap, and fall. The sonic outcome is perfectly consistent in this case with the instrumental gesture. However, the musical "gesture" may also be a dynamic "figure," an energetic pathway using the inside of the musician's body (and that of a listener) without any visual equivalent: hence the arpeggios played by the clarinet and flute at the start of the work, a repetitive pattern, abating like a whirling planet moving further out into space, then suddenly reviving to produce a further shock. This "gesture" is almost archetypal in its clarity, as are the aforementioned piano leaps, but it does not get the interpreter's body dancing in an equally demonstrative way.[12]

This distinction between the "instrumental gesture" that is literal and physicalized, such as a pianist crossing his arms as they travel across the keyboard, and the "dynamic 'figure'" that remains invisible, perhaps using "an energetic pathway . . . inside the musician's body," is at the core of how both Grisey and De Keersmaeker conceive not only the individuated parts they compose or choreograph but their relations to space, sound, and time. While each dancer "dances" an instrument in these works, from that point, everything complicates. The dancer who dances the clarinet is not only dancing while the clarinet plays, but also dancing that instrument's qualities, and most of all, the particular aspects of that instrument's timbre, which Grisey expands in the course of his work. "Instruments" are conceived (by both Grisey and consequently De Keersmaeker) as double entities: the capacities of the instrument (wind or string, tonal range, etc.) and the individual instrument's score. To this, De Keersmaeker adds the person of the musician, including where they are located and how they play. Whether one plays with breath, with a bow, with fingers, or even with the entire upper body, whether one plays while standing, stationary, or while walking or turning, these aspects to the questions of musical timbre in turn translate into effects on how De Keersmaeker's dancers dance their assigned instruments.

Timbre is the almost indefinable quality of sound that refers both to sound's origin (in an instrument's physical properties, for example) and to the space in which we encounter it. As ethnomusicologist Cornelia Fales describes it, "Not only does timbre carry the most information about a source and its location . . . but of all parameters of music, it also carries the most information about the environment through which the sound has traveled."[13] Composer and writer Jean-Charles François stipulates that dynamic timbre can "break the fixity of sound objects and . . . elaborate a space without any permanent features."[14] These questions of space are at the core of Grisey's so-called spectralism and its abandonment of the harmonic spectrum (itself a kind of fiction enabled by composers' delicate avoidance of "inharmonic tones" and a means of limiting timbre and hence musical spatiality). Performances of the musical composition *Vortex Temporum* entail modifications to the instruments. For example, four of the piano's notes are tuned a quarter tone lower in order to "fit with the microintervals played on the other instruments." This is aimed at extending the range of sound and at bringing listeners into a spectrum of sound that is both more "natural"—it includes inharmonic tones—and more "technological."[15] The instruments then expand how we hear music not merely as notes along a harmonic spectrum but as positions relative to our consciousness; their timbres have been subtly shifted away from the spectra of notes. With that, our listening positions have been deidealized and respatialized.

In his "temporal vortex," Grisey examines how "sound objects" ("*gestalt sonores*") can become means by which conventionalized, experiential human time can be contracted or expanded.[16] He names the three movements of *Vortex Temporum* after three categories of time: "that of man (time of language and breath), that of whales (spectral time of sleep rhythms), and that of birds or insects (time contracted to the extreme where boundaries are blurred)."[17] In other words, the emphasis in his thinking about temporality is on perception and activity, which in turn evoke questions of scale and duration. Time becomes spatial not only through imagination but in temporal experience, which music indexes or even manipulates. These manipulations become quasi-thematic in contrasting the sinusoidal waves emitted by whales at one edge of perceptible time (that of expansion) with the micromovements of insects and birds at the other edge of time (that of infinitesimal, barely perceptible contraction). Both edges blur the borders of durational time by forcing us to understand time beyond our unmediated perception of it.[18] Animals, or the consideration of durations that are not our (human) own, provide means of thinking about what we hear in a musical time, amplified or expanded by the modification of instruments and their ranges.[19]

As a spectralist composer, Grisey's interest lies in having us hear instrumental sounds that are not only outside the spectrum of tones and notes, but that are part of our environment—even part of an environment we barely hear or rarely listen to.[20] When his music builds on the "time" of

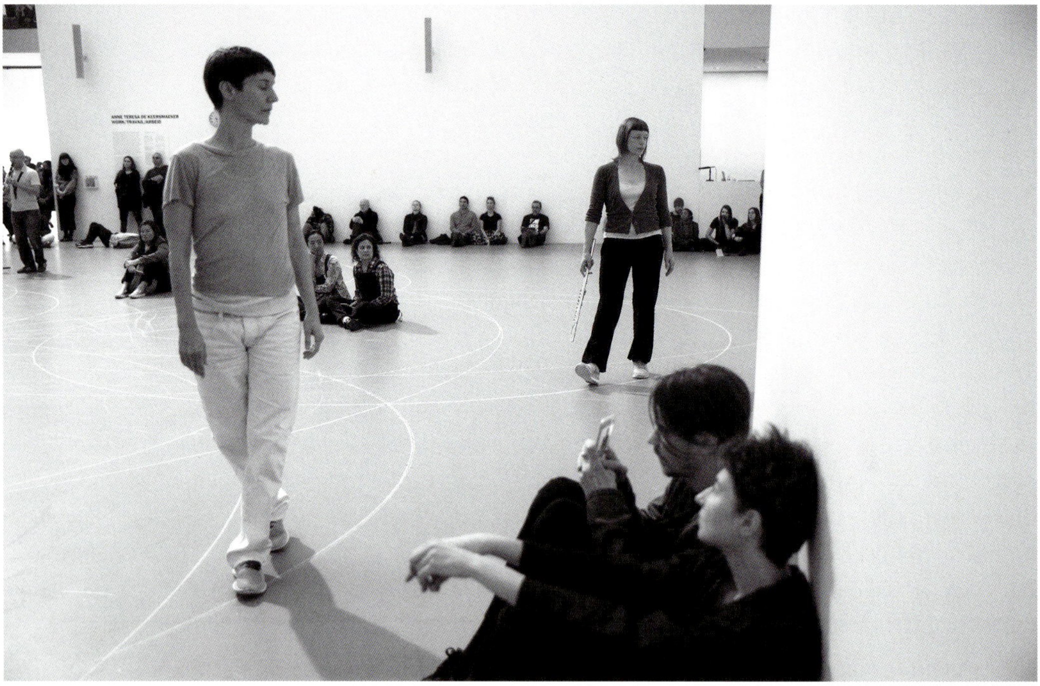

Anne Teresa de Keersmaeker, installation view of the exhibition Anne Teresa de Keersmaeker: *Work/Travail/Arbeid*, March 29, 2017–April 2, 2017 (Marie Goudot, Samantha van Wissen). Photo: Julieta Cervantes. The Museum of Modern Art, New York. Digital image © The Museum of Modern Art / licensed by SCALA / Art Resource, New York.

whales and birds, it refers not to songs and chirps, but to the microintervals to which the listener can tune at various points of *Vortex Temporum*.[21] For sound to result from the question of a "time of" birds and insects or whales, one has to think in terms of how time relates to the musical interval. Even in articulating temporality as sine waves—mathematical curves that describe smooth or repeated oscillations—Grisey takes the twinned questions of experience and perception to their limits as both mathematical abstraction and figural form.[22]

De Keersmaeker's *Vortex Temporum* and *Work/Travail/Arbeid* follow Grisey's composition in claiming time as a primary subject. By taking her dancers through deep abstractions—both graphic and musical—their performances arrive closer to the question of time, almost as a kind of content that might at first seem unexpected. This begins with the careful drawing of circles on the floor at the start of each hour of *Work/Travail/Arbeid* or the same circles visibly marked onto the stage of *Vortex Temporum*'s performances. That marked spatiality then becomes clearly indexed to the music and its approach to temporality, from the squeaking intervals of a bow dragged haltingly across strings to the trajectory that the musicians walk, often circularly, in vortices. Her dancers' magic cubes and floor-drawn circles refer us even more explicitly to the musical composition's thematization of temporality; they are geometric abstractions that increasingly, over the course of a performance, clarify and deepen our sense or perception of time.

Roles mark time: to shift into a role, as a dancer does, is to begin a performance. Same, as I have noted, with dance roles' intergenerational nature, allowing dancers and choreographers to teach works to the next generation or to learn them from previous generations. It is the same in social life, where roles are construed in terms of transitions and transitional processes, "role entries" and "role exits."[23] But while "the experience of a given role identity and role transition plays out against a backdrop of a life cycle" in social-scientific discourse, in *Vortex Temporum* the context is a sense of time expanded by a range of species.[24] That is, the temporality that *Vortex* engages is not a merely human life cycle, or even an intergenerational life cycle. It is a cycle that entails the contraction and expansion of time, as required to perceive the flutter of tiny insect wings or the lowest frequencies of a whale's song. It is, in other words, a temporality that exceeds human perception, that draws on our imagination but also exists beyond time's measures as we conventionally understand them.

And yet time is not the only way we understand these works. Watching *Work*, one is taken by the uncomplicated erotics of proximity. One watches the dancers breathe, their chests sometimes heaving or sweat soaking their shirts; one can stand so close to a dancer as to watch beads of sweat, or the trail of a gold necklace at the nape of a neck.[25] One might cathect similarly to a musician, whose playing can—especially in *Work*, which isolates sometimes only one or two instruments from the ensemble—feel wildly intense. The way that the performers' bodies interrupt the temporal framework indexed by roles is not incidental to the staging of *Work*. Further, it is built into the problematic of the role and, even more, to its melodrama.

Signs and Bodies

In *Vortex Temporum* and *Work/Travail/Arbeid*, the relationship of dancer to instrument/musician/timbre takes place, inconsistently, across a variety of registers. Throughout, care is taken to avoid literalism, or what De Keersmaeker calls "Mickey-Mousing," referring to the ways Disney cartoon characters "draw" the sound of their score by mirroring the length of notes, one movement per note.[26] Thus, for example, the clarinet and flute open Grisey's composition with a sequence of lightning-quick arpeggios, but the dancer whose role corresponds to

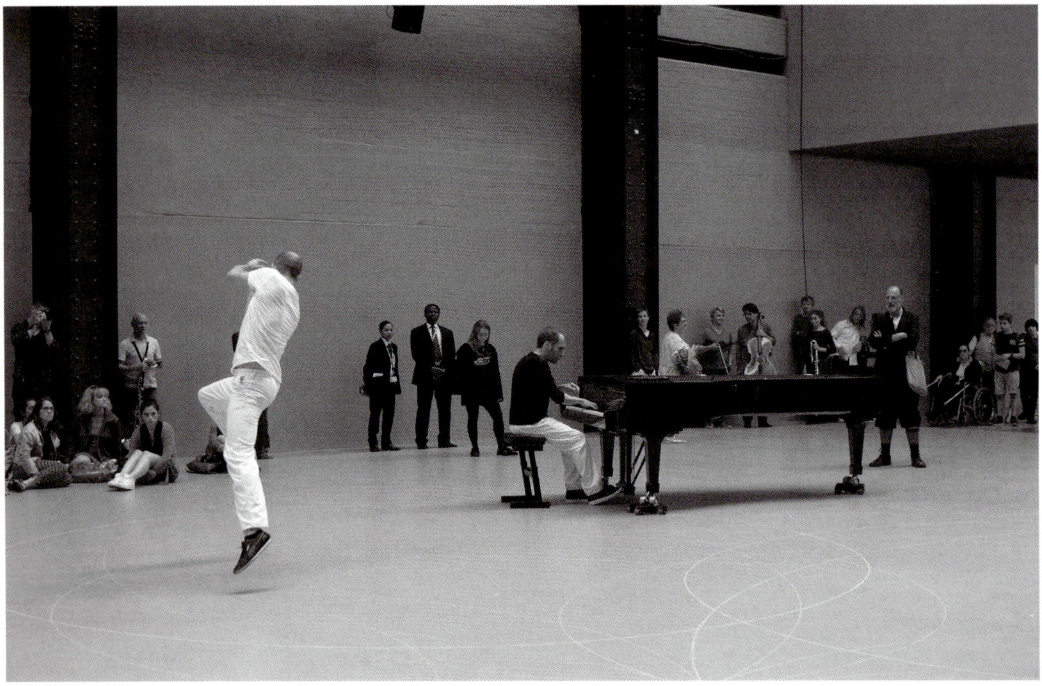

Anne Teresa de Keersmaeker, *Work/Travail/Arbeid*, 2016 (Jean-Luc Plouvier, Carlos Garbin). Tate Modern. Photo: Anne van Aerschot. © Anne van Aerschot.

the flute—De Keersmaeker's longtime collaborator Cynthia Loemij built the role—never shakes or flutters like a physicalized arpeggio, nor does she synchronize her movement with the flute's notes as if she could give literal shape to its sounds. Despite this prohibition on literalism, *Vortex Temporum* has fleeting moments in which a dancer mimics the bowing of strings with her arms or the attenuation of a note in her extension. And there are a few moments in which the dancers coincide dramatically with the musicians. Most powerful among these belong to the piano role: the dancer playing the piano role at one moment not only jumps like the pianist's hands, raised as he hits a dramatic sequence of chords, but even uses the piano to lean on as he jumps, and eventually sits down briefly at the bench and hits the keys themselves, once the pianist has stalked off the stage (or out of the room, in the transposition to museum spaces). But if the spectrum of ways that the dancers relate to their musical instruments generally avoids the literal, the relationship between dancer and instrument/musician nonetheless tightens across the hour-long dance. Sometimes a dancer will simply come into close physical proximity to the instrument she's paired with, perhaps standing behind or facing the same direction as that musician. They'll then turn together—for example: right after their paired solos, the clarinetist, no longer playing, turns on an axis, and so does the dancer paired

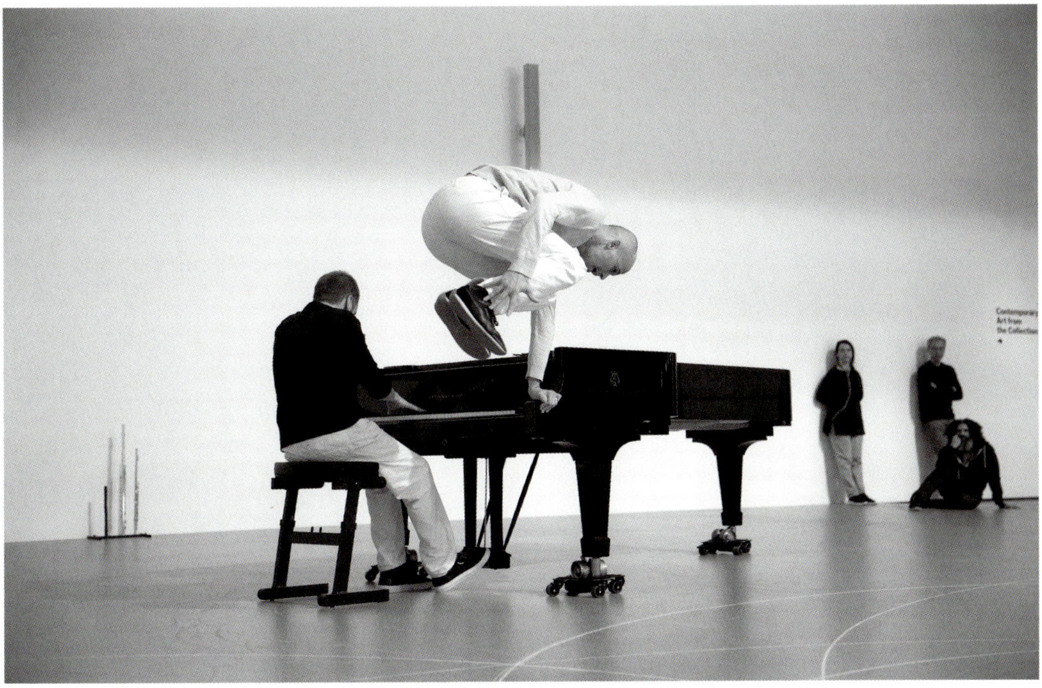

Anne Teresa de Keersmaeker, installation view of the exhibition Anne Teresa de Keersmaeker: *Work/Travail/Arbeid*, March 29, 2017–April 2, 2017 (Jean-Luc Plouvier, Carlos Garbin). Photo: Julieta Cervantes. The Museum of Modern Art, New York. Digital image © The Museum of Modern Art / licensed by SCALA / Art Resource, New York.

with him, a few yards away. Both head in the same direction at the same time. Both then take off, orbiting one another, at times syncing up quite closely. At other times, the dancer will handle the instrument, as when the dancers paired with the piano help to roll it around the stage.

Work/Travail/Arbeid, transposing *Vortex Temporum* from the stage into galleries built for art, adjusts not only to those galleries' spaces but to their hours. The opening hours of Wiels, and eventually the Tate Modern and other museums, offered to De Keersmaeker a way to change the populations of her dance. Every hour the dance would restart, but only sometimes with a full cast. It might be only one dancer and one musician, at least until the second cast enters; or it could be a trio, a quartet, the full cast, and so on.[27] This variation permits a kind of refolding of *Vortex Temporum*'s unfolding of the dancer's role as instrument: the audience in a given hour experiences the version available *then*. As we understand the dancers as participating in a kind of monadary, each signifying not only her instrument but its difference from others, we become more aware of how this "correspondence" that the role enables is dependent on our experience, particular to *this* hour, and even *this* place in the gallery, *our* position, at the moment. The fundamental unfolding is not merely the map of dancer to musician but a temporal unfolding, through our own experience, of the dance as such. Or indeed, the dancer as such, giving us not a peek into "her" interiority or even the depth of "her" role (as a signifier for an instrument), but that role as a kind of pressure on the plane of representation.

"Self," here, frames a notion of individuation that does not correlate the individual to "her" interiority but rather uses another system to disrupt that one. Or rather, if bodies can project a vessel-like conception of how they hold the "interior" of the self, then roles themselves, as alternative vehicular conceptions, disrupt the one-to-one framework through which bodies seem to individuate selves.[28] *Vortex* and *Work*, insisting on the ways that we experience the unfolding of their roles, invert the formal project through which individuation is presented as the natural correlate of interiority. Their dancers dance, each *an other*—but not another interiority, as in characterhood (even the stripped-down "flat" character who presents as another human, just one we know less well). Indeed, what *Vortex* and *Work* demonstrate so forcefully is that we can experience the function of that otherness with all the immediacy and embodied fullness that music, liveness, and the excitement of dance enable—without the assumptions and projections that interiority entails.

But this is not merely about the defeat or death of characterhood. The dancers of *Vortex* and *Work* enact the pressure *entailed* by the vectors and relations of vehicular notions of embodiment: they dance those vectors rather than the dramas of interiority. Moreover, these are not works danced by a single self—ever (as the entry of the second cast reaffirms). The displacement of the work of individuation onto the self only takes place within a network—a monadary—of other selves , both contemporaneous and past/future.

De Keersmaeker's dance produces the plane of representation as a drama in itself: these are highly modernist works in at least that respect. But they also dramatize and heighten this pressure on the plane of representation. These are not works in which mediumistic interest is quietly or dispassionately established. Grisey's score already, in his timbral experimentation with the condensation and dilation of time echoing multiple species' temporalities, uses high drama to frame the question of representation in music. De Keersmaeker's choreography leaves the interspecies plane alone, keeping the audiences' attention on the dancers' bodies and their musical counterparts. But *Vortex* and *Work* are saved from being mere structuralist theses by the ways that we do not observe this critical capacity but experience it, as we do Grisey's score, dramatically—even melodramatically. *Work* and *Vortex* show us how structuration is itself a melodrama. Melodrama—that which we have come to know as the high-stakes, supposedly "feminine" genre through which "excess, sensation, spectacle and affect" produce "the body and the interpersonal domain as the sites in which the socio-political stakes its struggles"—is itself *about* structuration.[29] Even without narrative conventions to dramatize "the interpersonal domain," these dances not only offer melodramatic experience; they show us the manner in which such experience is, at root, about the structure of individuation rather than the drama of interiority.

Individuation and Melodrama

The disruptive movement I have focused on is consistent throughout De Keersmaeker's work on roles. In her earliest works, such as *Rosas danst Rosas* (1984), *Mikrokosmos/Quator No. 4* (1987), and *Ottone, Ottone* (1988), she focuses on how individuation unfolds as distinctly gendered, feminine.[30] In her declensions of musical tropes—like phase shifting in *Fase: Four Movements to the Music of Steve Reich* (1982), polyphony in *The Six Brandenburg Concertos* (2018), or the differentiated vocal lines of *ars subtilior* in *En Atendant* (2010) and *Cesena* (2011)—she shows how roles can be unfolded relative to musical (and hence historical) experiments. In these works, she also attacks the fundamental questions that certain composers define as core questions to music (and often, by extension, to issues such as duration, repetition, difference, and seriality and so on). For example, Reich's meticulous attention to detail and its effects on structure are part of an approach to the experience of music different from the de-emphasis on musical authorship that the aleatory strategies of John Cage have made a hallmark of musical postmodernism.[31] If in constructing his early works Reich allows melody to emerge from repetition, De Keersmaeker is interested, in her accompanying choreography, in the plasticity of that repetition/melody coupling as it can be shown through bodies, lighting, and staging.

Erin Manning is also interested in the work that dance does to "individuate"; she too claims that individuation is a problem or concept immanent to dance. Indeed, it is, provocatively, the problematic of individuation that enables Manning to broaden her framework past the self, past even the human.[32] But Manning is fundamentally interested in the technics of movement as the basis of individuation, whereas I am curious about how the structured nature of the choreographic project, coupled with its varied life as performance, allows the role to fold back on the self and, from there, onto a politics of selfhood that would be different from that of the subject. *Vortex Temporum* and *Work/Travail/Arbeid* force forward the question of how bodies meld with notions of semiotic meaning in order for the work of individuation to take place *as* dance. This, I'll contend, has only to do with the specifics of movement to the degree that that movement is part of a choreographic project addressing itself to the audience's experience. It is not movement "in itself" that I am watching for in my analysis: it is the structure that De Keersmaeker's choreography makes available. With her intense attention to how movement can become referential or signifying, De Keersmaeker presents an ideal test case. On the one hand, avoiding the literalism of gesture or "Mickey-Mousing," she is dedicated to a kind of abstraction in dance that keeps her performers from becoming characterological; on the other hand, tying each dancer's role to an instrument means that the movement signifies in a way that we have yet to formulate.

And yet performance is never simply reference and signification; it is always also the performance of immanence and its own durative, experiential claim on the present. At what point does the semiotic map, the one-to-one between signifier and signified split not only across connotative depths and their genealogies but through experience? This question is both implied and explored in *Vortex Temporum*, which fundamentally turns on the question whether a sound is ever merely the "objective" sound or also its location in space relative to the listener. Put another way: When does a sound split into two sounds? Or, given De Keersmaeker's pairings: When a dancer is dancing within her own space or cell, which is not necessarily aligned with the front of the stage, how does she expand or contract our sense of space? How does a second dancer, doing the same movements but one "cell" over, as it were, further expand or contract space? How do these notions of space that are in fact questions of perception in turn form our understanding of the roles the dancers are playing, as movements and spatial organizations? What, in the end, do these complications to the idiom of the sign do to our sense of the self perceived? What do they do to the question of time that *Vortex Temporum* takes as its putative subject matter?

In this book I am arguing not that dancers function as mere analogs for selves but that the roles they occupy elaborate forms of selfhood that might guide how we consider our selves beyond the category of the subject. I am not saying that performance can get us outside subjecthood or that the immanence that performance figures, or allows us to experience, has anything to do with this self apart from subject. I am positing that it is the very choreographic nature of dance (as opposed to its improvisatory capacities or iterations), and the qualities of permanence or transcending a historical moment or subject that choreography enables, that gives us the key to dance's version of selfhood. In this function that I am calling the role, dance simultaneously draws our attention to the performance that is right in front of us and to the terms of a choreography that has happened elsewhere and that enables this choreography to also happen elsewhere, again, as a performance in another place and time in the past and in the future. That "elsewhere," that sense of being determined from without that we call representation—and that representation shares with the subject—is called into the here and now by dance.

Space and time and their interlinking are critical to how we understand that beyond the here and now as a framework for *this* self that is our self, right now (or the one before us, onstage). Dance's roles are a way of thinking social roles as form. Mothers and daughters, bosses and employees, guests and hosts, students and teachers: these roles that replicate across the social landscape call up an often dehistoricized abstraction as a means to both solidify and render permanent the object—the "role of the mother"—and to situate the subject in relation to it. The subject doesn't cease to be a subject when she enters a role (often, in fact, the role is another opportunity for subjectification). What roles do offer the subject is a kind of mobility that the terms of subjectivity, with its grasping, securing, and determining function, do not. Dance underscores the formalism of the role and in a sense its relation to permanence, a kind of aesthetic "security." But as we see in a dance like De Keersmaeker's, the role opens up both to have a "content" and to dissolve that contenthood in the unfurling, durative experience of the audience; it shows us that the role is experiential, not static and overdetermining. Put otherwise, dance allows us to think of the formality of roles as inhering in our sense of self as developmental and experiential without aligning such formality with systems of social reproduction. De Keersmaeker's dance, mostly uninterested in such systems, keeps the role "abstract" and in so doing, keeps its potential for sensing mobility intact.

In *Work/Travail/Arbeid* and *Vortex Temporum*, we do not witness a dancing body as simply coupled with a signified. *This* dancer with *that* clarinet/clarinetist/clarinet score. The coupling between signifier and signified is an unfolding, not an identity. In fact, the dancing body's relation to "her" signified is not a matter of property or identity but instead—as the music and choreography and their shared qualities make clear—a matter "in excess of the 'objective correlative.'"[33] That is what Peter Brooks, the first postmodern critic to introduce a discourse on melodrama to the field of literary criticism, describes as fundamental to melodrama, in a discussion of Henry James in particular:

> The need for melodrama, on this basis, is the need for a form of statement and dramatization that will make the plane of representation yield the content of the plane of signification. This means in practice a pressure on the surface . . . in order to make surface release the vision of

> the behind. . . . The technique is expressionistic in that surface forms are treated, not for themselves, in their interrelation and as ultimate integers, but as signs of what lies behind them and charges them. Laurence Bedwell has employed the term *expressionism*. . . . Citing Herbert Read, he talks of an expressionism whose "distinguishing feature is pressure and which is founded on the . . . 'desire to exceed the inherent qualities of the medium.'"[34]

I wish to adopt that notion of "expressionism," which might or might not be built out of affect but "whose distinguishing feature is pressure," from Brooks's conceptualization of melodrama. De Keersmaeker's dancers do not dance "affect"—however affecting Grisey's music is—and they do not dance *with* affect. (They are mostly expressionless modern/postmodern dancers in that regard—even if from time to time, as in many of her choreographies, we see passing through their faces expressions, perhaps of joy or concentration or, in *Work*, recognition of another dancer or even an audience member.) They do, however, dance their roles with a very specific form of energy that lets on not only that their role is the correlation to an instrument, but that that correlation is a form of pressuring both the medium of dance and the very notion of a *surface* now called upon to "release the vision of the behind." Roles may populate dance generally, but few choreographers are as involved as De Keersmaeker with this relay between surface and "the behind" that the role deploys.[35]

On the other hand, Grisey's work is undeniably melodramatic, in its moody, eerie beginnings and burning climaxes. It takes us from moments of anxious, sometimes sinister "pre-audibility," to jarringly vivid moments in which we feel almost as if time has come to a sudden halt.[36] He delivers his audiences into "orgies of feeling," in which the orgiastic derives not merely from the crowding of bodies in the audience (and in De Keersmaeker's work, bodies on the stage or in the gallery), but to a feeling of heightened intensity—*shared*.[37] It is difficult to miss the implicit sense that if we are sensing a whale's time, then we are almost de facto "moved," emotionally; the labor of transposing to another species' time—even on the level of imagination—is affecting.[38] And De Keersmaeker's choreography exacerbates this sense of intensification, sometimes almost literally—as when her dancers run, together, in accelerating circles, or when the addition of the second cast crowds the stage or galleries. Even the ways the increasingly demanding choreography of *Vortex* and *Work* pushes at various physiological and spatial limits creates a kind of melodramatic intensification. Without expressing affect, her dancers, like Grisey's music, produce intensification. If this is not an "intensified affect," that is only because, as is often the case in her work, affect is left to the audience to project, while the dancers and musicians push harder and harder with their bodies and instruments.

That is not to say that these dances are not also *melodramatic*. I came to think about roles because of the ways I enjoy Grisey's score—love it, in fact—for its melodramatic (some might say portentous) moodiness. From the start of the second movement of *Vortex Temporum*—as the air starts to fill with the dirgelike, slow, descending chords—the work of the dancer/music coupling becomes particularly powerful, capitalizing on the sense of building suspense, of something hanging over the piece. We are introduced into the work's logic just as its two parts—one semiotic, one affective—become (respectively) explicit and all-powerful. Grisey's composition relates timbre to the new musical experiences of duration that he is offering, which impress upon us a sense of temporalities deanthropomorphized, perceptible especially on nonhuman scales.[39] In other words, even as melodrama shows us how any apparent totalization of "hereness" in dance is also a reference to the *there*, we are thrown back on the most visceral sense of the erotics of watching dance. Curiously, thanks to the nature of Grisey's composition, we reach through the melodramatic nature of his composition a sense of life deanthropomorphized. The "affective" register in which *Vortex* and especially *Work* operate—through the music—becomes a way of understanding this melodrama as far from "character-driven," and indeed, barely interested in the human at all. Innerness may be what we feel, but what we see and understand is a monadary that is entirely involved with a register that exceeds us.

In every performance of *Work/Travail/Arbeid* in which he participates, the pianist Jean-Luc Plouvier stands, slams the piano cover shut, and stomps out of the room. The piano score has just reached a point of no return, where the pianist plays simultaneously at the upper edge of the treble clef and the lowest edge of the bass clef. There are hints of anger to his stomping exit, as De Keersmaeker acknowledges.[40] But Plouvier is not "himself" angry: he repeats the same action at the same moment every time he performs the work. Nor is his exit part of a character-building effort—and not only because conventionally musicians do not play characters. In *Work*, the musicians' physicality helps to make the music itself more visible: spatial as well as durational, figural as well as melodic. The musicians produce—alongside the enhanced timbre of their instruments' sound—a semiotic line, a sense of "the piano" or "the viola," to which the dancers' lines are joined. Plouvier's stomped-out exit designates not that a character or even the music is "angry," but that at this moment, signification is coinciding with representation. The system by which instruments' entrances and exits are highly marked in *Vortex Temporum*—sometimes entering our auditory perception very minutely, with the

Phuon's overture run singles her out, temporarily, even as it produces a mere overture or framing device for the work to come. But it also signals a relationship to the dance's musical accompaniment that has been striking throughout the work that Rainer has made since her return to choreography in 2000.[8]

Much of Rainer's work starts when the lights go up on dancers already onstage, and if in her early days that could be accomplished by allowing the audiences to watch the dancers doing their warm-up, *The Concept of Dust* only continues that tactic.[9] But what is interesting in *The Concept of Dust* is not the way that roles create a kind of vessel that enables her dancers to correspond, one by one, to referents. In fact, this new work is not interested in individuation much at all, regardless of Hoffbauer's costume or Phuon's opening run. Instead, the dance combines its would-be "content"—its meditations on durational time, calendars, and scales of time and their relation to human history—with the possibilities posed by *ensembles*, by dancers dancing either in unison or broken up into smaller groups and solos. How do temporality and the ensemble relate to one another, and how do they relate to the problematic of the role? If De Keersmaeker's attention to the role helps us understand the melodrama of signification as a project in dance—and as a project of unfolding identity—then how does Rainer's interest in the nonindividuated role, its apparent absorption into the ensemble, affect the linked projects of signification and identity?

For sure, melodrama is far from absent in *The Concept of Dust*. The majority of the work's musical soundtrack is supplied by a work by Gavin Bryars, whose echoing, repetitive chords and montaged sound footage evoke not only insistent pastness but a sense of pasts submerged, even lost to oceanic depths. That loss has been campily etched into collective "memory" by one of Hollywood's most famous commercial directors, James Cameron. Bryars's piece, begun in 1969 and revised several times since, is entitled "The Sinking of the Titanic" and uses as a point of departure the notorious "eyewitness" anecdote in which the *Titanic*'s band allegedly played the hymn "Autumn" as the ship sank.[10] Bryars's composition collages echoing performances of the hymn with found vocal recordings and the sounds of radio frequencies being tuned. Music historian Maja Trochimczyk describes it thus:

> The music supposedly played by a band on board while the Titanic was sinking (performed by an ensemble of instrumentalists) is surrounded with musical glosses associated with memories of the survivors, the titles of hymns played by the band, and so forth—transformed, prerecorded sounds heard from various locations in space. The hymn played

at the moment of the sinking undergoes timbral transformations that suggest four stages in its imaginary history: "'as heard in the open air on the deck, as the ship sinks, as it remains stable on the bottom of the ocean, and in a new state in the open air' after the ship's raising."[11]

Indeed, not only do we hear the music cycling through recognizably different "stages," like the movements of a symphony, but Bryars explores the possibility of reaching sonically from the deep past to the present both in the complexly layered textures of his music and in more figural associations that crop up in the collage, including distant, almost inaudible (but discernibly "old-fashioned-sounding") voices and the sound of a radio being tuned.

Melodrama is in other words part of the frame of *The Concept of Dust*—or at least our experience of its oceanic hymnal soundtrack—and so is that other vehicle of narrative immediacy: the character. Very subtly, one finds traces of the dancers doing "themselves"—not exactly the studied "neutral doer" of Rainer's early work, but a stronger form of dancerly style that brushes the edges of characterhood. This trace of characterhood, for one thing, remains uneven across her dancers in *The Concept of Dust*; it does not provide any kind of key to "roles." Hoffbauer, wearing her long hair in a high ponytail like a cheerleader or athlete, performs moves in unison with other dancers but also with a particular, almost winkingly exaggerated "pizzazz." She sometimes seems to dance in a kind of liminal zone in which her individual manner of performing never resolves into a "character" but does not strive for dedifferentiated uniformity with the other dancers either. This is part of a systematic welcoming of individuation among four dancers who perform most of Rainer's recent work. Elise Archias describes the "differences between the four dancers' styles and habits of comportment" as "striking" in the work *Spiraling Down*, from 2008: "Hoffbauer's movement is muscular and reads as passionately deliberate, determined, earnest, not expecting anything she does to be found particularly funny. . . . Catterson dances with the bodily affect of a very tall eight-year-old: confident and amused by the whole context, occasionally impatient to get where she needs to go. "[12] In her note about Rainer's expressions as she filled in for Catterson in one performance, Archias puts a definitive end to the notion of the "neutral doer" that Rainer's early choreography and criticism erected as an ideal: "Rainer . . . looked grounded and happy, agile . . . her lively face often expressed pleasure in what her body was doing, either through an overt, vulnerable joy, or a kind of ironic screw-you-you'll-be-old-someday-too nonchalance."[13] Indeed, the totalizing evacuation of character that marked Rainer's early dance does go missing from the dancers' performances in

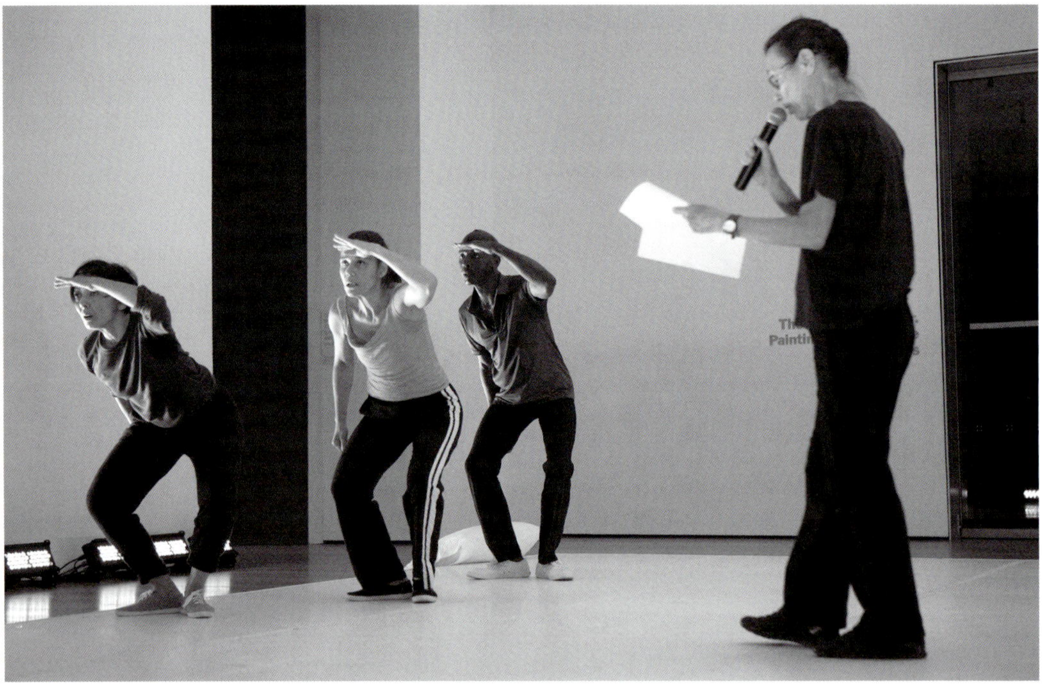

Yvonne Rainer, view of the performance of *The Concept of Dust, or How do you look when there's nothing left to move?*, June 9, 10, 13, 14, 2015 (Emmanuèle Phuon, Patricia Hoffbauer, David Thomson, Yvonne Rainer). The Museum of Modern Art, New York. Photo: Julieta Cervantes. Digital image © The Museum of Modern Art / licensed by SCALA / Art Resource, New York. © Yvonne Rainer.

her recent works. It is as if Rainer had studied the photos of her early work and, seeing the individual performers look so unmistakably different from one another, decided not to try to eradicate such difference, and maybe even to allow it to emerge and develop both in her choreography and in performance.

However, it is not through these subtle signs of selfhood that Rainer's dancers enter their roles in *The Concept of Dust*. The way that Rainer has dancers come into and out of ensemble dancing invites us to consider roles not in terms of their individuating work, as we saw in *Vortex Temporum* and *Work/Travail/Arbeid*, but in terms of how the role relates dancing alone to dancing in ensembles. Even as it constantly changes format (duet and three solos; foursome and solo, etc.), *The Concept of Dust* proposes an idea of the role that both sup ersedes the present ensemble—indexing the way that any choreographic role is a placeholder to be filled by another dancer in another space and time—and investigates the conditions for ensemble dance. In other words, if in De Keersmaeker's works we focused on the role within the monadary—the circuit of roles danced simultaneously onstage or in solos, duets, trios, etc. that becomes particularly perceptible in a museum adaptation—in Rainer's work we focus on how the role portends past and future performances (possibly by this dancer, but possibly not) and at the same time dissolves its individuating work through the ensemble. The role becomes a portal into deindividuation,

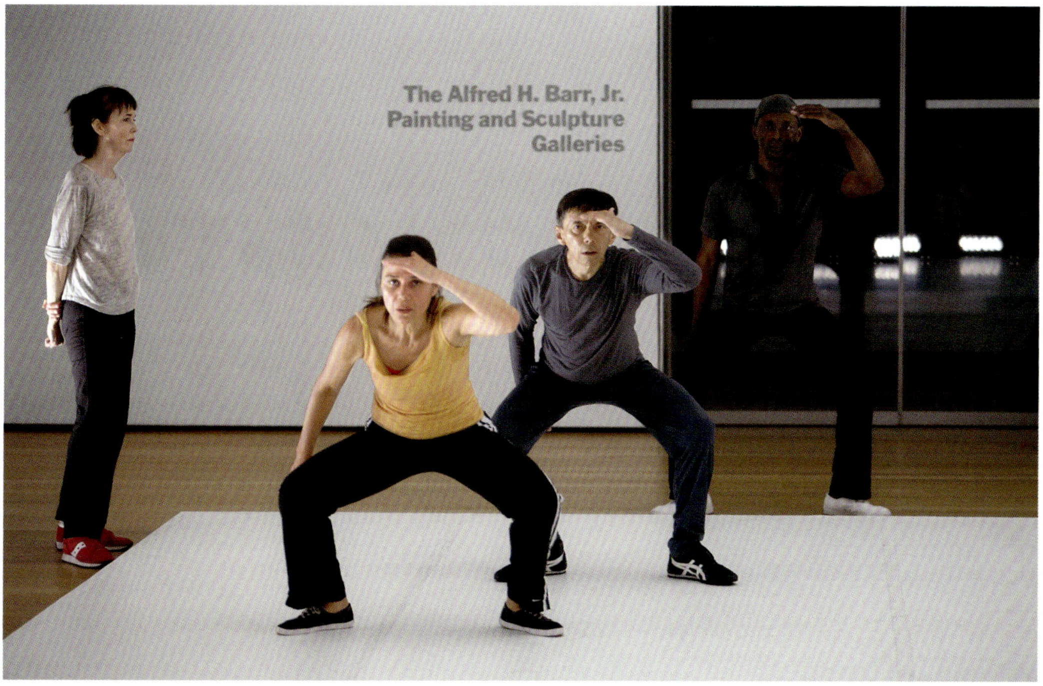

Yvonne Rainer, view of the performance of *The Concept of Dust, or How do you look when there's nothing left to move?*, June 9, 10, 13, 14, 2015 (Pat Catterson, Patricia Hoffbauer, Keith Sabado, David Thomson). The Museum of Modern Art, New York. Photo: Julieta Cervantes. Digital image © The Museum of Modern Art / licensed by SCALA / Art Resource, New York. © Yvonne Rainer.

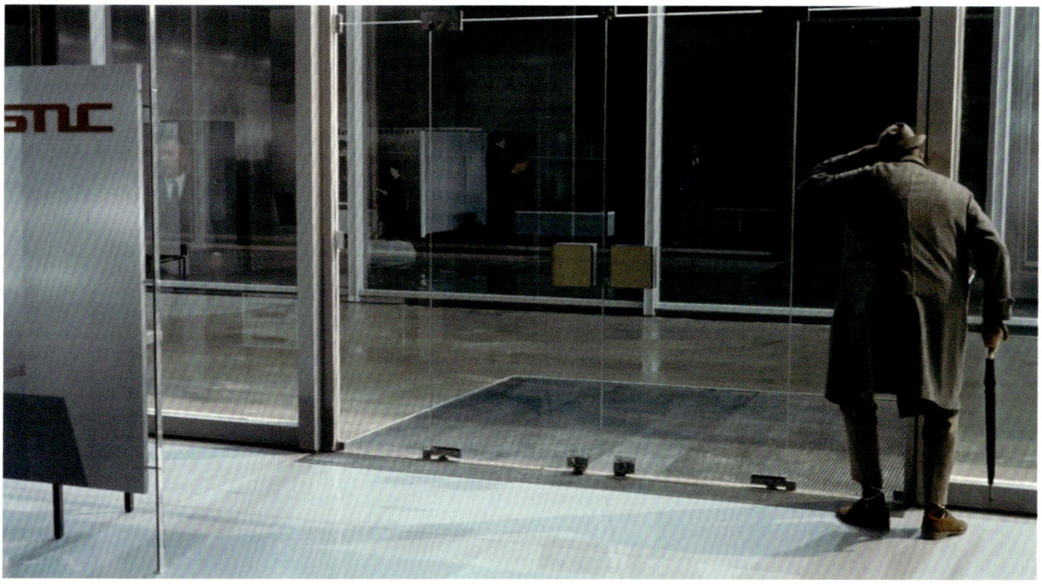

Jacques Tati, *Playtime*, 1967 (Jacques Tati).

not because one dancer "melts" into a group but because the permanence or indeed atemporality of the role pushes the self past the individuating terms of subjecthood. This understanding of roles that Rainer explores rests a great deal on the moody music she's chosen, the texts she and her performers read about time, and even Rousseau's *Sleeping Gypsy*, with its primitivist sense of static "timelessness" and nomadic "gypsy" life. Her work exploits these primitivizing frameworks—or, one might say, the primitivist "underside" to modernism tout court, as necessary as Stravinsky or Rousseau to understanding "the modern." It's through that framework and its ineffable aura that we see her dancers move into and out of groups as they perform the movement she choreographs, which does its own job of evoking and concretizing a timeless register for movement.

Timelessness in movement does not—at all—mean absence of reference. A great number of the dancers' movements are loosely appropriative, and whimsically so: the choreography in *The Concept of Dust* is full of indelibly "character-full" moments that we recognize from (among others) Bugs Bunny, Michael Jackson, and Jacques Tati. One moment we see Jackson's familiar fast wave snap from the music video for "Beat It"; then Bugs Bunny's paws-raised hapless running and bobbing head. My favorite movement set in the dance is borrowed from Tati's periscopic upper-body side-to-side slide—a trademark move from the remarkable extended opening passage in *Playtime*, in which Monsieur Hulot, eager to meet a corporate officer, repeatedly loses his prey in the endlessly expansive set representing modern corporate offices. As he misses and then doggedly reapproaches his prey, waving at what turns out to be his reflection (so that in fact he is losing the target again), Hulot/Tati engages in an endless game of hide-and-seek. The dancers "do" Hulot/Tati as he shades his eyes from refracted glare. But they do so first facing the back of the stage—the depths of MoMA itself, seen through a glass wall—and then later the front, the audience. Each time, we are ourselves sent back (through the halls of MoMA and its versions of endlessly flattened and refractive surfaces) to *Playtime*'s industrial-modernist play of mirrorlike glass.

If Tati's movements recall not only the humor of that now quaint version of modernism, they also index an idea of signification that seems indifferent to the dance. In other words, Rainer is not interested in giving "depth" or content to her dance through these appropriations. But she might be interested in the ways that these appropriations' connotative richness fills up a visual field that adds to the layered, echoing depths in Bryars's score. That would make sense given the texts' emphasis on time and especially scales of time, for if her appropriations have less to do with the particular decades belonging to (or evoked by echoes of) Warner Brothers' animation, Jackson, and Tati, they do give a sense of the storehouse from which dancers cull movement. Moreover, if that storehouse "holds" movement, in a sense, then it also presents a well of work whose continuous surface is punctured, as it were, by the performers' voices reading texts. These voices index us in a shared present; we are invited to join a cultural moment in which these movements can be recognized. On the other hand, and perhaps even more affectingly, the movements themselves are referenced within a long, durable ecology of movement and signs that belongs to the scale of temporality that Bryars's score conveys.

The reading voices thus play off the notion of interiority conventionally indexed by the voice. The voice, as Mladen Dolar writes, "cuts directly into the interior, so much that the very status of the exterior becomes uncertain, and it directly discloses the interior, so much so that the very supposition of an interior depends on the voice."[14] Dolar's formulation appropriately takes place in a kind of visual vacuum, in which the voice is dissociated from a body, let alone the mouth speaking or singing, or another body to which the first body's "interior" would be disclosed. His sense of interiority is abstracted, a kind of mental diagram. But dance is not only visual; its relation to muteness—as we saw above, in our discussion of De Keersmaeker—is less ontological (dance as "drama without words") than it is *melodramatic*. The drama of dance is the drama of disclosure, the unfolding of signs, infected with the drama that inheres in such unfolding. If this is an unfolding that can be danced, made somewhat explicit, as in *Vortex Temporum* and *Work/Travail/Arbeid*, Rainer leans less on that drama of unfolding than De Keersmaeker. Her system of "radical juxtaposition" instead shows us what at first appears as a play of signs as refractive and postmodern as *Playtime*'s glass-paned office building.[15] But the door of possibility that she opens at the same time that dance's project of signification stalls in *The Concept of Dust*'s ricocheting play of signs is linked to both the project of the ensemble and that of the grave, almost posthistorical scale of time that the work evokes as its frame. It is not nihilistically "postmodern" but invested equally in the unmissable melodrama of our present course toward extinction and in the self sensing that drama.

The Concept of Dust alternates between unison dancing—everyone sharing the same movement phrases—and breaking up the group into pairs, trios, and solos. It makes that inconsistency its main strategy by presenting itself, as a dance, as taking place *as* ensemble work, loose and shifting, appropriative and self-contained. For if the literal ensemble is made up of five dancers (or six, including Rainer, who at times joins

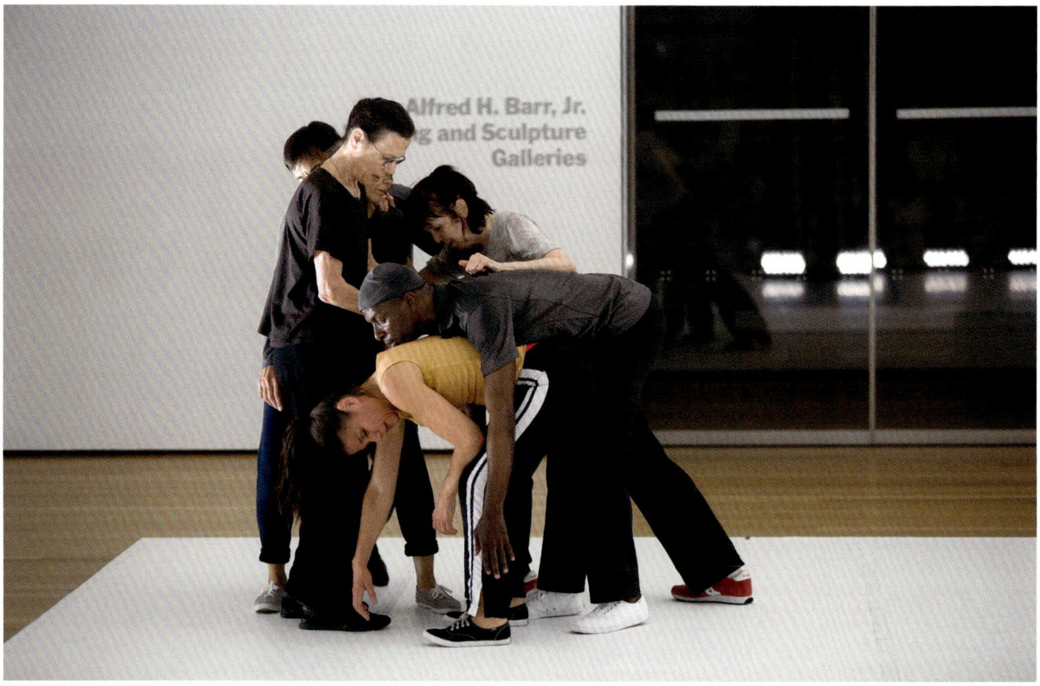

Yvonne Rainer, view of the performance of *The Concept of Dust, or How do you look when there's nothing left to move?*, June 9, 10, 13, 14, 2015 (Yvonne Rainer, Keith Sabado, Patricia Hoffbauer, David Thomson, Pat Catterson). The Museum of Modern Art, New York. Photo: Julieta Cervantes. Digital image © The Museum of Modern Art / licensed by SCALA / Art Resource, New York. © Yvonne Rainer.

her body to the others'), the movements they make, borrowed from Tati, Jackson, and so on, subscribe that group to a larger universe of dancers. The question of the ensemble is both literal (composed of dancing bodies) and figural (composed of the dance that shapes those bodies and composes them into onstage figures). At times Rainer makes such figurality literal, bringing all six bodies—including her own—together to lean into one another, pushing at each other, making shapes that gradually change as one member and then another shift position or even make recognizable shapes of their own. At one point, Rainer's arms cross in an X at her knees, bending over; at another, Hoffbauer raises her arms like the tail of a comma, the period itself the distended, shifting group. Like a shortened and shiftier version of Simone Forti's *Huddle*, these groupings give us an image of the group not only as massed but as figure.[16]

The figuring of the ensemble is part of how Rainer reconceives the work of the role. She has never been interested in the kind of signifying work that De Keersmaeker's dancers do in *Vortex* and *Work*. It's almost difficult to distinguish roles as such in her choreography, especially in a work like *The Concept of Dust* in which the ensembles form, dissipate, and re-form so constantly, as if to mitigate the individuating work that the role accomplishes. But what the work does is to remind us of the extensibility of the role: how it distends the work of the dancer in time. If the role's function is to create a kind of vessel or vehicular function within dance—a sense that this dancer is doing the role (*this* spatiotemporal movement trajectory, different from *that* one)—then it is always, in any performance with more than one dancer, showing this dancer separate from that one. In other words, roles depend on synchrony and on plurality to show their individuating work. In ballet and more historical and conventional "modern" dance—think of Martha Graham—roles extend diachronically: they show this dancer doing a role that another dancer, explicitly, can step into. In a work like *The Concept of Dust*, in which the project of moving in unison is constantly proposed, withdrawn, set apart from the solo bits and pieces that a dancer is doing over here or over there, the project of the role enters into the framework of temporal distension *thematically*—through the back door, as it were.

The split between the dilated time of Bryars's soundtrack and the puncturing superpresence of the voices and their index of interiority at times emerges almost like a narrative crux, a crucible of meaning production in the viewer. For among the bitterly affecting texts read by Rainer are several excerpts from the diaries of Johann Paul Kremer, a physician with the SS whose utterly banal recordings of menus and special concerts belied the nature of the "special actions" at Auschwitz to which he was witness and participant.[17] The nature of time recording indexed by his prosaic diary entries is chillingly inhuman, seemingly utterly separate from "one's own" temporality. Like the description of the Muslim calendar, these diaries remind us of the difficult, unimaginable scale of human history, just as the Titanic and the fossil remind us of the manner in which that human history becomes part of a planetary post-Anthropocene. Both are scales that we consciously understand "through" aesthetic experience insistently scaled to the human: music, dance, and text that remind us not only of our present but what seems at first like an ultrahuman framework of individuation and collectivity.

The Concept of Dust, framed by Bryars's extraordinary music that is itself punctuated by the performers' voices, deploys temporality—and specifically, scales of time—as its explicit subject matter. Muslim calendars, Kremer's diaries, the hedgehog fossil: all of these ways of pointing to time bring us not only to "the concept of dust" (time nearing us to death; time vouching for the dusty afterlives of our bodies) but to the larger framework that dust evokes: of cyclical life-and-death times well beyond our individual bodies and lives ("How do you look when there's nothing left to move"). The notion of a planetary or even supraplanetary time might inscribe *The Concept of Dust* within an ecocritical movement or mood: more immediately, for our purposes, it inscribes the problem of dancing and its project of individuation within a framework for understanding roles quite apart from identity and even subjecthood. As Archias remarks, "It is in her formal assertion of the inseparability of bodies from prescriptive tasks, codes, and rules that we become conscious of another's desire to make sense of the concrete struggles around her."[18] This interpretation of how Rainer exploits what I have called the "storehouse" of movement seems correct to me. But I also want to call attention to the beyond of this immediate, neighborly, historically contained notion of the "concrete struggles around" a specific body and her specific, inalienable identity. What of the concrete struggles (and also joys and other forms of experience) that remain unknown, in the as-yet-to-be-realized concreteness of pasts and futures to be discovered? What of the ensembles that the self can project with other selves, well beyond that desiring "other" right before us?

What happens again and again in *The Concept of Dust* and defines some of its difference from other recent works of Rainer's (*RoS Indexical*, *AG Indexical*, and *Spiraling Down*) is the way that the dancers share a set of movements that belongs equally to all of them (except Phuon's opening jog), and that they perform at different times in unison, in small groups, or solo. That is, the movements themselves are like a bank, a tighter version of that storehouse previously referred to. There can be no "role" as such, except insofar as each dancer dances a specific trajectory of movements—these movements at this time, here, and not then/there. The role is reduced to its purest form, without any sense of signifying "behind" it—regardless of the modicums of personal style that might be evident (e.g., Hoffbauer's perky athleticism) or not. Yet it is through this completely "neutralized" relation of movement to dancer that we see the role come to its most profound effects. The accentuation of the spectrum of time—from the pole of the inconceivable, near timeless work of planets and their degradation (the hedgehog's fossil) to the extremely immediate sense of punctured time (the voices reading, one's sense of the immanence of that planetary degradation), through the continuum of a kind of relentless extensibility (the storehouse of movement)—as the framework through which we see this "neutral" role is the work that roles themselves are assigned.

The subject is always being subjected to position(s): the frameworks of race, gender, sexuality, class (among others) produce us "as such," as ourselves. A subject position is often defined by its very inescapability. But the role offers to us positions that we slide into and out of: the role is fundamentally allied with movement. A role might overlap with a subject position: think of motherhood. Mothers are subject positions just as they are roles; I "become" a mother, perhaps for life but certainly at particular times in a day or the week. My daughter's school calls, and even if I'm in the middle of something at work, I am interpellated as a mother. Though motherhood is far from inescapable, it is undeniably a part of my (inescapable) subjectivation. On the other hand, the very movement in and out of my roles—as mother, as daughter, as employee, as teacher, as host, as guest, as comrade, as friend, as antagonist, as accomplice, as neighbor, as petitioner, as citizen, as expatriate, as tourist, as institution builder, as critic—these roles are what "cross" my subject positions, striating them with movement. They do not necessarily represent agency or even value (I don't choose to be a neighbor; I don't necessarily do a role "well" or in a manner that "contributes" to some overall collective good); they simply allow me to refine who I am both inside my subject position and, as it were, beyond it. Roles are movement.

Individuation and grouphood are not two sides of a coin. Individuation is a key part of our subjectivation, and inescapable. We are also often massed involuntarily into groups (perhaps defined by identity, by law, by social or institutional norms). On the other hand, the ensemble—those groups that Rainer's dancers are dancing into and out of—shows us a kind of massing that is loose and voluntary. Above all, these are groups that become perceptible only insofar as they assemble synchronously: Rainer is showing us these dancers *together*. Just as De Keersmaeker showed us dance that unfolds individuation as a function of our perception, Rainer shows us how the ensemble both arrives as a figure, thereby perceptible, and by extension, how it might unfold beyond our perception. If there is a lesson to learn from *The Concept of Dust*'s insistent return to scales of temporality and the calendrical institutionalization of time, it is the manner in which ensembles form across time, diachronically. Sometimes the ensemble's temporal modality is as barely perceptible to us as the hedgehog is to the fossil discoverers: that perceptibility is what Bryars's score and Rainer's choreography make possible for us, however ephemerally. What the role offers is the solace of knowing that even as we step into and out of a role, we are not merely in this group, *here*, but in one that extends past perceptible durations, one whose temporal magnitude is as flexible as the role itself is based in flux and shift. That combination of ephemerality and durability—with which I move into a category that exceeds and outlasts me—is what the role offers my self.

Acknowledgments

This book was written in many long mornings alone. It was also written over the course of hours spent looking and watching, both alone and in the company of friends, and while preparing seminars and then rethinking things in the light of what had been said in class. Before I can make mention of the many relationships that deepened in that time, I want to first say something about those whose sudden departures also mark this book profoundly. My father, Peter Haidu, who passed away in February 2017, initiated me at an absurdly young age into the delights of graphing texts and thinking like a structuralist. It only took me a lifetime to formulate a reaction! My beloved friend, Douglas Crimp, showed me how to translate into writing the pleasure one feels from looking. Douglas's passing in July 2018 was a second, deep cut. A third loss, of the remarkable collector and friend Herman Daled, felt as if it ended an entire era, both in my own life and more generally. Nothing is the same without these particular beings in the world.

A group of beloved friends read sections of this book at different points and responded both to it and to my own often urgent insecurities. Joel Burges reminded me constantly of the value of a project that was too easy to lose faith in. Darby English set my expectations higher at particularly acute moments and had the grace to see and talk more deeply. Hannah Feldman engaged my text on the molecular and macro levels that are her specialty, but also in conversations and laughter that have helped to sustain me over decades. Anna Rosensweig and Lisa Cerami lent key extradisciplinary insights, bolstered saggy confidence, and walked all over town with me. Kerstin Stakemeier took the level of thought up many notches, as is her habit. And finally, Devin Fore read, encouraged, and housed me during a decade of long weekends. His extraordinary project, written in parallel (but on another level entirely), reminded me of the dialogues that take place between texts and make them worth so much more. Stephanie Schwartz, Magda Szczesniak, Leora Maltz-Leca, Leah Pires—who also masterminded this volume's title—and Yuval Boim were interlocutors and steadfast friends. While the book was in its final stages, Maddie Ullrich was a constant and treasured friend. Benjamin Buchloh's is a voice I hear in my head and with whom I argue still, joyfully and devotedly.

This book is about art and selfhood, and I can't imagine how it could have developed without the insights and friendships of artists themselves. Ulrike Müller and Amy Sillman have been incredible companions in thinking about and looking at work both in their studios and across New York and Europe. I have also learned a great deal from talking, sometimes only briefly, with Anne Teresa De Keersmaeker, Maria Hassabi, Sharon Hayes, Nairy Baghramian, Gregg Bordowitz, James Coleman, and Yvonne Rainer. Samantha van Wissen and especially Cynthia Loemij—who became a wonderful friend and interlocutor over the last few years—made this project even richer with both their dance and their vibrant selves.

This book began as a book on influence. That point of origin provides this volume with an infrastructure that will be at least partially perceptible to readers: there is a set of conversations between artists and generations that subtends it. As I shifted from one project to another, I had the luck of having the most generous and thoughtful editor patiently talking through my ideas as they morphed and resurfaced. Susan Bielstein is not merely an editor but a kind of book whisperer, and I am grateful for her acute eye for detail, her love of dance especially, and her intellectual good sense. Her work makes one a better thinker and writer. Dylan Joseph Montanari and Stephen Twilley made the end process much more than tolerable. To the two reviewers who read the manuscript for the University of Chicago Press with terrific generosity and lucidity, I am deeply indebted. Thank you to Victoria Taormina for her ridiculous know-how and patience throughout the process of getting hold of images and permissions. And to the gifted and dedicated Rio Hartwell, who should indeed have been an art historian: my deepest thanks.

The Clark Art Institute and the American Council of Learned Societies

7 Bollas, *Shadow of the Object*, 63. "The concept of self should refer to the positions or points of view through which we sense, feel, observe and reflect on distinct and separate experiences in our being. One crucial point of view comes through the other who experiences us" (9).

8 Ideally, my account would start at the nonplace that Jacqueline Rose generates in her essay on Melanie Klein's work. For Rose, Klein treats that "unconscious which [the social] sanctions and pursues," focusing on the central role of negation and negativity in order to undo the "account of positive development out of the [psychoanalytic] processes": "What 'Negation' offers is a way of theorizing a subject who comes into being on the back of a repudiation, who exists in direct proportion to what it cannot *let be*." Rose, "Negativity in the Work of Melanie Klein," in *Why War?* (Oxford: Blackwell, 1993), 144, 164, 153.

Drawing an analogy to Stephen Hawking's *A Brief History of Time*, Rose demonstrates how the force of negation as origin of a subject (whether that subject is the universe or the individual) poses a key, existential question for the discourses *about* that subject: "According to the logic of negation, interpretation comes as a stranger from the outside. And let's note too that if Klein makes of the analyst a fool and a fantast, it is from this place that the analyst has to try to speak . . . The question has to be asked: What problems must it pose for an analytic school to situate itself in the place of an infant to whom interpretation is by definition unwelcome and who is fantast and fool?" (170).

9 In fact, both Cavarero, who works on literary texts, and Butler, who works on philosophical texts, do a version of the same. But I am drawing a distinction between their fundamentally philosophical arguments and my own, which remains bounded by the field of art history and its potential to complicate those fields from which it greedily draws.

10 Julia Kristeva, *Powers of Horror: An Essay on Abjection*, trans. Leon S. Roudiez (New York: Columbia University Press, 1982), 3; first published as *Pouvoirs de l'horreur* (Paris: Éditions du Seuil, 1980).

11 See, in particular, Derrida's glosses on Rousseau ("It is toward the praise of silence that the myth of a full presence wrenched from difference and from the violence of the word is then deviated") and Husserl: "These are the words Husserl first uses to *immediately* introduce the following dissociation: 'but not every sign has a "meaning," a "sense" that the sign "expresses."' . . . We have to understand and acquaint ourselves with this structure of substitution or reference so that the heterogeneity between the indicative reference and the expressive reference could then become intelligible, indeed demonstrable—if for no other reason than that their relationship, as Husserl understands it, might become clear to us" (emphasis in original). Derrida, *Of Grammatology*, trans. Gayatri Chakravorty Spivak, corrected ed. (Baltimore: Johns Hopkins University Press, 1997), 140, and *Speech and Phenomena: And Other Essays on Husserl's Theory of Signs*, trans. David B. Allison (Evanston, IL: Northwestern University Press, 1973), 23.

12 "For Merleau-Ponty and, indeed, with Malebranche, it is only by being acted on that any of us come to act at all. And when we do act, we do not precisely overcome the condition of being acted upon. Being touched or handled or addressed as an infant awakes the senses, paving the way for a sentient apprehension of the world. And so, prior to sensing anything at all, I am already in relation not only to one particular other, but to many, to a field of alterity that is not restrictively human." Judith Butler, *Senses of the Subject* (New York: Fordham University Press, 2015), 8.

13 I discuss just such roles in my article "*Rosas*, the Storyless, and Roles," in "Dance and Abstraction," ed. Juliet Bellow and S. Elise Archias, special issue, *Arts* 9, no. 2 (2020): 44. My thanks to the issue editors for their invitation and invaluable feedback.

14 Butler, *Senses of the Subject*, 108–10.

15 Northrop Frye, *Anatomy of Criticism: Four Essays* (Princeton, NJ: Princeton University Press, 1957), 6.

Part I Introduction

1 Sarah Michelson, in performance, *May 2018 /*. Performance Space, New York, April 28, 2018.

2 *May 2018 /* was billed as a "new piece that considers [Michelson's] own history with the organization, the building, and the community from which her work emanates." See https://performancespacenewyork.org/shows/may-2018/, accessed August 19, 2019.

3 Much has been written about the transformation of the Lower East Side, Performance Space's neighborhood. I am thinking here of the transformation of many formerly empty edges of the city from cruising grounds into zones of consumption—artistic and otherwise. See Douglas Crimp, "Action around the Edges," in *Before Pictures* (Brooklyn: Dancing Foxes Press; Chicago: University of Chicago Press, 2016), 146–181.

4 While Brian Massumi considers affect as an "intensity," defined to a large degree by its "strength or duration," I am more interested, for the moment, in the representability of an emotion, one perceptible as such within representation, nameable and therefore part of what he would call a "discursive body": "one with its signifying gestures. Signifying gestures make sense"—that is, they can be decoded to "mean." See Massumi, *Parables for the Virtual: Movement, Affect, Sensation* (Durham, NC: Duke University Press, 2002), 24, 2.

5 "Here subjectivity is represented by the category of intuition. Intuition works as a kind of archiving mechanism for the affects that are expressed in habituated and spontaneous behavior that appears to manage the ongoing present." Lauren Berlant, introduction to *Cruel Optimism* (Durham, NC: Duke University Press, 2011), 17.

6 "From its very beginning art history called upon a theory of representation that would not stop with mere extension (or denotation) but would allow for intension (or connotation). . . . [Art historians] simply took it as a given that it was in the connotative richness and density—that is, the intension—of the aesthetic sign that it lay claim to being art at all. Its intension, we could say, was taken as a record or index of the multiplicity of human meaning or intention; and they equated this capacity for multivalent content with the very capacity to conceive aesthetic signs." Rosalind Krauss, "In the Name of Picasso," *October*, no. 16 (Spring 1981): 9–10.

7 Alenka Zupančič, *The Odd One In: On Comedy* (Cambridge, MA: MIT Press, 2008), 175.

8 Wolfgang Köhler explains in his "Address of the President" at the 67th Annual Convention of the American Psychological Association, in 1959, that Max Wertheimer (the more radical thinker, in Köhler's estimation) "did not ask: How are Gestalt qualities possible when, basically, the perceptual scene consists of separate elements? Rather, he objected to this premise, the thesis that the psychologist's thinking must begin with a consideration of such elements. . . . Perhaps we pay for the subjective clearness of the

customary picture by ignoring all processes, all functional interrelations, which may have operated before there is a perceptual scene and which thus influence the characteristics of this scene." Wolfgang Köhler, "Gestalt Psychology Today," *American Psychologist* 14 (1959): 727.

9 Gestalt theory had its key moment of fascination for art at precisely the moment that structuralism induced questions about the subject as a whole: when artists like Robert Morris wrote about Gestalt, it was in order to differentiate between the "strength of the constant, known shape, the gestalt" that "allows this awareness"—that "this most patently unalterable property—shape—does not remain constant." Robert Morris, "Notes on Sculpture, Part 2," (1966), reprinted in *Minimal Art: A Critical Anthology*, ed. Gregory Battcock (New York: Dutton Signet, 1968), 233. For an excellent text distinguishing Morris's understanding of *Gestaltpsychologie* from his readings in phenomenology, see Anaël Lejeune, "The Subject-Object Problem in 'Aligned with Nazca': On Phenomenological Issues in Robert Morris' Artwork," in *Investigations: The Expanded Field of Writing in the Works of Robert Morris*, ed. Katia Schneller and Noura Wedell, new ed. (Lyon: ENS Éditions, 2015), http://books.openedition.org/enseditions/3784.

10 "If the object, however, through its opposition, settles me within the fragile texture of a desire for meaning, which, as a matter of fact, makes me ceaselessly and infinitely homologous to it, what is *abject*, on the contrary, the jettisoned object, is radically excluded and draws me toward the place where meaning collapses. A certain 'ego' that merged with its master, a superego, has flatly driven it away. It lies outside, beyond the set, and does not seem to agree to the latter's rules of the game. And yet, from its place of banishment, the abject does not cease challenging its master." Kristeva, *Powers of Horror*, 1–2.

11 Judith Butler, introduction to *Bodies That Matter: On the Discursive Limits of Sex* (New York: Routledge, 1993), 8.

12 The slave and "bare life" are the prime (arguably different) exemplars of this logic, the first enabling a haunted afterlife of excluded subjects, the latter entering "a zone of irreducible indistinction" inside the political realm. Giorgio Agamben, *Homo Sacer: Sovereign Power and Bare Life*, trans. Daniel Heller-Roazen (Stanford, CA: Stanford University Press, 1998), 9.

13 This question is taken up by Jared Sexton in relation to the most pertinent and well-developed field of thinking abjection and subjection together, Afro-pessimism. See Jared Sexton, "Ante-Anti-Blackness: Afterthoughts," *Lateral: Journal of the Cultural Studies Association*, no. 1 (2012), https://csalateral.org/section/theory/ante-anti-blackness-afterthoughts-sexton/.

14 Aligning closed form with "linear (graphic, plastic)" style and seeing contours and open form with "painterly" representations that "give appearances a hovering character [in which] form starts playing around; light and shade become an independent element, they seek each other out . . . the whole takes on the appearance of a restlessly swelling, endless movement . . . inexhaustible to visual perception," Wölfflin asserts that "in the system of a classical construction [i.e., "the epitome of closed form"] the individual parts still assert their independence, regardless of how tightly they are tied into the whole." Heinrich Wölfflin, *Principles of Art History: The Problem of the Development of Style in Early Modern Art*, trans. Jonathan Blower (Los Angeles: Getty Research Institute, 2015), 97–101.

15 "The phrase *trait unaire* is Jacques Lacan's translation of a term from Freud's chapter on identification in *Group Psychology and the Analysis of the Ego* (1921). Developing his account of the identification of hysterics with their

love objects, Freud suggests that identification in such cases 'is a partial and extremely limited one and only borrows a single trait [*nur einen einzigen Zug*] from the person who is its object' . . . In Seminar VIII on *Transference* (1960–61) Lacan suggests that in the passage from *Group Psychology* Freud is drawing attention to a primordial act of symbolic identification with the father, 'anterior to the very outline of the Oedipus situation . . . It is starting from this primordial identification that there would arise the desire towards the mother and, from then on, by a reversal, the father would be considered a rival.' The narcissistic, imaginary relationship to the ideal ego 'depends on the possibility of being referred to this primordial symbolic term which can be monoformal, monosemantic, *ein einziger Zug*.'" "Unary Trait," in *Concept and Form: Les Cahiers pour l'Analyse and Contemporary French Thought*, accessed August 16, 2019, http://cahiers.kingston.ac.uk/concepts/unary-trait.html.

16 "Like character, fate, too, can be apprehended only through signs, not in itself. . . . The concept of character will have to be divested of those features that constitute its erroneous connection to that of fate. . . . If the object of psychology is the inner life of man understood empirically, Molière's characters are of no use to it even as means of demonstration. Character develops in them like a sun, in the brilliance of *its single trait*, which allows no other to remain visible in its proximity" (emphasis added). Walter Benjamin, "Fate and Character" (1919), in *Selected Writings*, vol. 1, *1913–1926*, ed. Marcus Bullock and Michael W. Jennings (Cambridge, MA: Belknap Press of Harvard University Press, 2000), 201, 204, 205.

17 Raymond Williams, *Modern Tragedy* (Stanford, CA: Stanford University Press, 1966), 201.

18 "Thus [in revolution] the social fact becomes a structure of feeling. Revolution as such is in a common sense tragedy, a time of chaos and suffering. It is almost inevitable that we should try to go beyond it. I do not rely on what is almost certain to happen: that this tragedy, in its turn, will become epic. However true this may be, it cannot closely move us; only heirs can inherit." Williams, *Modern Tragedy*, 65.

Philip Guston

1 Carter Ratcliff, "Ellsworth Kelly's Tablet 1948–1973," *Art on Paper* 6, no. 6 (July–August 2002): 32.

2 Among the many ways one can distinguish poststructuralist critique from "universalist" concepts, one could point to Gayatri Spivak's concise and colloquial response, in a 1984 roundtable, to a question from Geoffrey Hawthorne (host of a BBC Channel 4 series, *Voices*): "Is there some particular narrative that the French deconstructionists and the English and American followers have in mind? Which they wish to deconstruct?" Spivak responds: "Well, the field is fraught. . . . But it seems to me that the narrative that they are perhaps all of them agreed upon as the object of investigation, is precisely the narrative that you were talking about to begin with, the rationalist narratives of the knowing subject, full of a certain benevolence towards others. . . . In the process, what happens is that such a world is defined, and the norm remains the benevolent originator of rationalist philosophy." Gayatri Chakravorty Spivak, "The Post-Modern Condition: The End of Politics?," in *The Post-Colonial Critic: Interviews, Strategies, Dialogues*, ed. Sarah Harasym (New York: Routledge, 1990), 19.

3 Exhibitions that have begun dismantling these dichotomies range from medium-wide investigations like *Painting 2.0: Expression in the Information Age*

(2015–16) to *Soul of a Nation: Art in the Age of Black Power* (2017–19), which brought together an expanse of work made by Black artists demonstrating the inadequacies of reigning dichotomies between representation/figuration and abstraction to do justice to the demands of identity on our concepts of subjecthood.

4 Robert Slifkin begins his authoritative and excellent volume on Guston's late painting with the absolutely true sentence "If there is one thing that Philip Guston is known for it is his 'return to figuration.'" Robert Slifkin, *Out of Time: Philip Guston and the Refiguration of Postwar American Art* (Berkeley: University of California Press, 2013), 1.

5 Slifkin discusses "badness" in his conclusion to *Out of Time*, 165–83. See also Amy Sillman, "Laura Owens," *Artforum*, April 2018, 174–75, for a discussion of Owens as "a literalist of high-low, peer[ing] eagerly into the bottom of the barrel to see what is usable down there."

6 "Representation here signifies not merely the mimetic depiction of the world or a means of securing political advocacy within democratic or republican institutions. As it is conceived within aesthetic philosophy, representation is an activity that articulates the various spheres of human practice and theory, from the most fundamental acts of perception and reflection to the relation of the subject to the political and the economic, or to the social as a whole." David Lloyd, *Under Representation: The Racial Regimes of Aesthetics* (New York: Fordham University Press, 2019), 7. The present book speculates about what the subject's "relation . . . to the political and the economic, or to the *social as a whole*" (emphasis mine) leaves out, including—as in this chapter—how our ideas of "the whole" itself are suggested or formed by mechanisms like shape.

7 In this sense I am following the lead of Yve-Alain Bois, who contended already in 1990 that "if indeed art can fulfill a political demand it is at its own level, that is, an ideological level, itself stratified." Bois, "Introduction: Resisting Blackmail," in *Painting as Model* (Cambridge, MA: MIT Press, 1990), xxiii.

8 David Román, "Introduction: Tragedy," *Theatre Journal* 54, no. 1, "Tragedy" (March 2002): 2. He is citing Williams, whose relevant text is the chapter "Structures of Feeling," in *Marxism and Literature* (Oxford: Oxford University Press, 1977), 128–35.

9 I retain Williams's lexicon here because I do not find that the discourse on affect has contended with the problem of how subjecthood—with its address of how becoming subject or becoming not-subject are historically determined—differentiates across populations. In other words, affect discourse, understandably, treats affects as universal, while authors like Christina Sharpe and Katherine McKittrick demonstrate how interior life is shaped by the exclusions to full subjecthood (or citizenship) that mark diasporic Black and migrant (and gendered) experience. See Sharpe, *In the Wake: On Blackness and Being* (Durham, NC: Duke University Press), 206, and McKittrick, *Demonic Grounds: Black Women and the Cartographies of Struggle* (Minneapolis: University of Minnesota Press, 2006). That a "structure of feeling" can vary across populations I take as a given, approaching the question of affect/emotion in the following chapter.

10 The "subfigural" is a long tradition within painting. Describing Jan van Goyen's "cloudy skies hanging over narrow strips of land populated by the most ordinary of creatures," Amy Powell writes: "In these skies, the chaos of paint from which he pulled his human, vegetal, and mineral forms is left more or less chaotic. The inchoate origin and antithesis of the image thereby

becomes part of the finished work, keeping alive the question of what there is to see and not to see in his paintings even when they are complete." Amy Knight Powell, "Images (Not) Made by Chance," *Art History* 40, no. 2 (April 2017): 390. My thanks to Christopher Heuer for his suggestion of this term.

11 I take the tropological expansion of the sign within the rather simplistic notion of the figural I am using here echo the manner that Slifkin explains figuration: "Art history's traditional understanding of figurative art and figuration as recognizable imagery or, more specifically, as the presence of the human figure appears narrow when compared with the term's denotation in the discourses of rhetoric and literature. In those discourses figuration entails . . . also the elaboration of a literal or 'proper' meaning by means of analogy (in figures of speech like metaphor and irony). The common denominator is a binary logic in which the figurative statement, whether rhetorical or pictorial, presents a supplementary representation to something beyond or behind itself, creating a semantic disparity that must be bridged by interpretation. . . . The figurative statement requires what the literary critic Paul de Man calls a 'system of relays' in which the chains of semiotic association that relate words to concepts . . . are used to create a powerful and often memorable message. . . . By forging associative chains of reference and analogy, figuration creates a structure of meaning. . . . Simultaneously insisting on a divide between life and art and joining the two realms by associative logic, figuration is structurally incapable of producing the autonomous work of art often held up as an aesthetic ideal in postwar modernist discourse. . . . The Marlborough paintings make meaning by setting up conceptual and temporal correspondences and syntheses and more generally by inciting interpretation and calling attention to their own constructedness and artificiality. In these ways the paintings were decidedly figural—a term I use hereafter in this book to denote the temporal figuration predicated on historical and sequential associations operating in these works." Slifkin, *Out of Time*, 6. In other words, I believe that the linguistic, sensory self to which a painting is addressed—someone whose sensorial capacity (their ability to see that something is weighted or has texture or orients itself in space, etc.) is coupled with a linguistic capacity—does not merely rely on the explicitly constructed sign nor its serial expansion (over "sequential associations," powerful as they are in Guston's late paintings). As his puns and other semiotic jousts clarify, Guston is interested in superseding the sign, and here I am claiming that the use of shape to complicate painting as a semiotic system is what opens it to a different relation to history.

12 "This suspicion, that images are (or can be) made-up 'nothings' and impossible hybrid confabulations, flared up during the image debates of the sixteenth century." Powell, "Images (Not) Made by Chance," 398.

13 See John E. Joseph, "The *Arbre*-Tree Sign: Pictures and Words in Counterpoint in the *Cours de linguistique générale*," *Semiotica*, no. 217 (2017): 147–71.

14 I am aware that here figuration serves as something of a straw man, erecting ideas about iconographic readings that have long been complicated within the history of modern art and art that well precedes the "modern" era. Here, however, my interest is less in displacing other readings than in introducing a conceptualization of shape that gets us into ideas about history, selfhood, and subjecthood in a manner that looks forward, at practices since Guston's (including highly figurative twenty-first-century painting) as well as at ideas of selfhood and subjecthood that are at the center of this project.

15 André Leroi-Gourhan, *Gesture and Speech*, trans. Anna Bostock Berger (Cambridge, MA: October Books / MIT Press, 1993), 196. He explains "mythographic space" further: "Indeed in primitive societies mythologies and multidimensional graphism usually coincide. If I had the courage to use words in their strict sense, I would be tempted to counterbalance 'mythology'—a multidimensional construct based upon the verbal—with 'mythography,' its strict counterpart based upon the manual" (195–96). A manual and graphic "multidimensional construct" of mythological dimensions is what Guston appears to be seeking in his elaboration of shapes that defeat their figurative implications to participate in a parallel (to iconography or figuration) construct.

16 See Scott McCloud, *Understanding Comics* (New York: HarperCollins, 1993), 89–90.

17 Roland Barthes, "Myth Today," in *Mythologies*, trans. Annette Lavers (New York: Farrar, Straus and Giroux, 1990), 115. Tom Gunning has connected Leroi-Gourhan's notion of mythographic space both to questions of writing (and associated logocentrism) and to the temporality of cinematic and protocinematic technologies as they surface in comics. See Tom Gunning, "The Art of Succession: Reading, Writing, and Watching Comics," in "Comics and Media," ed. Hilary Chute and Patrick Jagoda, special issue, *Critical Inquiry* 40, no. 3 (Spring 2014): 36–51.

18 "Myth deprives the object of which it speaks of all History. In it, history evaporates." Barthes, "Myth Today," 151. Barthes repeatedly explains that myth, "hid[ing] nothing," transforms history into nature (129).

19 "For the wrestler's gesture needs no anecdote, no décor, in short no transference in order to appear true." Barthes, "The World of Wrestling," in *Mythologies*, 19. A variety of postwar painting leverages different kinds of "mythographic" space to both evoke history and distance the painter/painting from established modes of history painting: one could signal, as very different poles within this variety, Francis Bacon, George Baselitz, Lee Lozano, and Maria Lassnig..

20 Musa Mayer, "Laughter in the Dark: An Introduction," in *Philip Guston: Nixon Drawings, 1971 & 1975*, ed. Musa Mayer and Sally Radic (New York: Hauser and Wirth, 2017), 5. Mayer explains that her father "was not done with Richard Nixon after the summer of 1971," pointing out resemblances between the Nixon drawings and a number of paintings (including *Alone*, 1971) as well as the further suite of drawings that Guston made when the former president, after his impeachment and presidential pardon, contracted phlebitis (*The Phlebitis Series*, 1975).

21 McCloud, *Understanding Comics*, 70–71.

22 Slifkin relates this to the regularity of the comics strip: "After multiple exposures to the motif, its lone presence can signify for that reader relationships between characters and possibly even universal truths such as the presence of meaningless cruelty in the world." Slifkin, *Out of Time*, 73.

23 Slifkin discusses comics in several parts of his book. In relation to space, he focuses particularly on the aspect of repetition across separate panels, which he reads as part of "the gutters or 'gaps' in Guston's hanging" of the Marlborough show. I will not discuss this aspect of "multiple exposures to the motif," striking as it is, since it is indeed wrapped up in the "referential grounding" of Guston's figures and what Slifkin defines as "the beholder's share," depicting "a decidedly fictional and even phantasmagoric world." Slifkin, *Out of Time*, 73–75. I am interested instead in how comics, given the medium's terseness, allow shapes to do so much of their connotative work.

24 E. H. Gombrich, *Art and Illusion* (Princeton, NJ: Princeton University Press, 1972), 339. Quoted in Slifkin, *Out of Time*, 74. See also David Kunzle's description of how "caricature strips introduced an abstract space that served simply as a container for action," in "The Early Comic Strip: Narrative Strips and Picture Stories in the European Broadsheet from c. 1450," *History of the Comic Strip* (Berkeley: University of California Press, 1973), 1:360–63.

25 Rosalind C. Morris describes how the "terms *figurisme* and *figuriste*" were adopted in the eighteenth century in various efforts aimed at "excessive . . . readings of biblical history and prophecy" to "legitimate political contestation," in a section entitled "The Critique of Modern Mythography: Figurism in Many Forms." I take her use of mythography to refer to a system in which "figural impulses," as she calls them, were marshaled in politically and theologically overdetermined struggles that used the referentiality of the (biblical, scriptural) sign "to subsume the material origins of religion in fetish worship into more flattering allegories of progress." Morris, "Fetishism, Figurism, and Myths," in Rosalind C. Morris and Daniel H. Leonard, *The Returns of Fetishism: Charles de Brosses and the Afterlives of an Idea* (Chicago: University of Chicago Press, 2017), 10–12.

26 For Lloyd, "representation secretes and occludes the founding violence of the state," and when he addresses Marx's *Eighteenth Brumaire of Louis Bonaparte*, he draws out the role of genre: "Theatricality is [the *Brumaire*'s] ubiquitous subtext and Shakespeare, and in particular *Hamlet*, is the mobile ghost in its cellarage. This intertextual relation to Shakespeare's dramas, this alertness to dramatic genre—comedy, tragedy, farce—mimes the historical processes of repetition and reworking in a critically parodic mode. Rather than invoking the stage, in Schillerian fashion, as the institution that represents the eternal and universal image of Man and the exemplarity of political pasts, Marx stages the scene of representation so as to mark the breakdown of the commonsensical logic of self-evidence of the narrative structures." Lloyd, *Under Representation*, 110–11.

27 Bill Berkson, "Pyramid and Shoe: Philip Guston and the Funnies," in *Philip Guston Retrospective* (Fort Worth, TX: Thames and Hudson, Fort Worth Art Association, 2013), 70.

28 Max Wertheimer, "Gestalt Theory," in *Gestalt Theory* 21, no. 3 (November 1999): 181.

29 Wertheimer, "Gestalt Theory," 182; emphasis added.

30 Wertheimer closes his article with a choice set of examples drawn from "nature" and art that betrays his clear preference for discussing the latter.

31 Wertheimer, "Gestalt Theory," 182.

32 Robert Morris, "Notes on Sculpture," *Artforum*, February 1966, 44.

33 Morris, "Notes on Sculpture," 44.

34 Ludwig Wittgenstein, *Philosophical Investigations*, trans. G. E. M. Anscombe (Oxford: Basil Blackwell, 1958), 42.

35 Wittgenstein, *Philosophical Investigations*, 200.

36 Wittgenstein, 200. Here arise questions of the play between signification and abstraction, between "squeezing" one into the other in ways that seem to me to invite precisely the questions of whether and how a "queer form" can appear. Some of the shape painters I admire—Ulrike Müller comes to mind as well as Eisenman—address these questions, often more open-endedly than those who insist on "figuration" more narrowly conceived.

37 See Michael Fried, "Olitski and Shape," *Artforum*, January 1967, 20, and Clement Greenberg, "Introduction to Jules Olitski at the Venice Biennale" (1966), in *The Collected Essays and Criticism*, vol. 4, *Modernism with a Vengeance*,

1957–1969, ed. John O'Brian (Chicago: University of Chicago Press, 1993), 228–30.

38 Greenberg, "Introduction to Jules Olitski," 229.

39 They share much else, of course, including the practice of "illustrating" poetry (in Sillman's case, often using iPhone drawings made into video); the practice of caricature, particularly as a means of political intervention; and an entire lexicon of shape-signifiers, from the light bulb to the pointed finger, that align Sillman's work with her forebear's renegade attitude to the hegemonic possibilities within abstraction.

40 T. J. Clark, *Picasso and Truth: From Cubism to Guernica* (Princeton, NJ: Princeton University Press, 2013), 246–48.

41 Clark, *Picasso and Truth*, 276. The "world" is disclosed in *Guernica* as "not a world in which the enclosing envelope of space is ever transparent or homogeneous, with bodies occurring as finite interruptions in it" (281).

42 See Yve-Alain Bois's masterful treatment of the formalist possibilities opened up by Barnett Newman's "zip" and its negotiation of existential crises both worldly and painterly in "Perceiving Newman," in Bois, *Painting as Model.*

43 In his descriptions of 1921's *Guitar on a Table*—a painting that anticipates *Guernica* in its imitation of collage's pasted-on shapes—Clark writes: "The two terse flag shapes . . . are as salient as shapes can be. They are objects, or maybe part of the same object. But what object precisely? The question is misconceived. . . . The distinctness of the flag shapes could as well be the sign (the stamp) of where exactly things stand—not what they are made of—or the compressed equivalent of their curvature." Clark, *Picasso and Truth*, 34. As I discuss below, there is a direct relation between the "flag shapes" as "compressed equivalent of their curvature" and the semiotic question Clark raises.

44 "Philip Guston's Object: A Conversation with Harold Rosenberg," in *Philip Guston: Collected Writings, Lectures, and Conversations*, ed. Clark Coolidge (Berkeley: University of California Press, 2011), 42. First published in *Philip Guston, Recent Paintings and Drawings*, exh. cat. (New York: Jewish Museum, 1966).

45 I do not mean to elide the important intellectual differences between Giorgio Agamben and Judith Butler's projects but rather to secure for Clark's description of Picasso's history painting a kind of composite identity image for those whose deaths *Guernica* pictures and who I presume are not inscribed in the "we" that names Clark's collectivized viewer-subject. Defining the pressure that thinking about "precarious life" puts on the image, Judith Butler calls for a form of "representation [that] must *show* its failure"; this seems to me to be close to Clark's claim for Picasso's "new style" in *Guernica* (270). Butler, *Precarious Life: The Powers of Mourning and Violence* (London: Verso, 2004), 144.

46 Hannah Arendt, "The Decline of the Nation-State and the End of the Rights of Man," in *The Origins of Totalitarianism* (New York: Harcourt, Brace, 1951), 296.

47 Judith Butler has devoted an entire volume of essays to the "sensible I," ranging from an essay on Descartes in which she asks, "What is the status of the question ["How could I deny that these hands and this body here belong to me?"], such that it can postulate a distinction between the 'I' who asks and the bodily 'me' that it interrogates and so performs grammatically precisely what it seeks to show cannot be performed?" to an essay, "Sartre

on Fanon," that centers on the assertion: "This new man, Sartre writes, begins his life as a man at the end of it; he considers himself as a potential corpse. . . . The destitution of the body is not only an effect of colonialism, where colonialism is understood as something prior, something separate. . . . On the contrary, *the body is the animated, or rather deanimated life of that historical condition, that without which colonization itself cannot exist.*" Butler, *Senses of the Subject* (New York: Fordham University Press, 2015), 25, 189.

48 Dore Ashton, *Yes, but . . . : A Critical Study of Philip Guston* (New York: Viking, 1976), 154–55.

49 See the remarkable website created by the Guston Foundation, at philipguston.org.

50 Harry Cooper treats this question—and transforms it to ask "not 'what thing is it?' but 'what *things* is it?'"—in his essay "Recognizing Guston" in *Philip Guston: A New Alphabet; The Late Transition*, exh. cat. (New Haven, CT: Yale University Art Gallery, 2000), 31.

51 Rudolf Arnheim, *Art and Visual Perception: A Psychology of the Creative Eye; The New Version* (Berkeley: University of California Press, 1976), 57. Here he is citing Julian Hochberg on "simplicity by means of information theory"; see Hochberg, "The Psychophysics of Pictorial Perception," *Audio-Visual Communication Review* 10 (September/October 1962): 22–54, and Hochberg and Edward McAlister, "A Quantitative Approach to Figural 'Goodness,'" *Journal of Experimental Psychology* (1953): 361–64.

52 Arnheim, *Art and Visual Perception*, 67.

53 Arnheim, 5.

54 Heinrich Wölfflin's *Principles of Art History* begins with a distinction between "the linear and the painterly," and asserts that "painterly possibilities open up as soon as the line's role as a marker of borders is depreciated." In contrast, fixed lines, or "strongly articulated edging [that] fixes form to the spot," are the enemy of such movement: I am contending that Guston deliberately employs such "classicizing," antipainterly linearity to introduce both the "badness" of comics and the totalizing effect of "the comic." See Wölfflin, *Principles of Art History: The Problem of the Development of Style in Early Modern Art*, trans. Jonathan Blower (Los Angeles: Getty Research Institute, 2015), 101.

55 Wölfflin, *Principles of Art History*, 104, 102.

56 "The delineation of a figure with a consistently defined line still has something corporeal about the way it grasps things." Wölfflin, 103. This is of course utterly true of Guston's paintings: they too leverage "an appeal to the sense of touch," and if anything, the shift away from depicting things "as we see them" ("Where nature has a curve we might now find an angle") points to the indelicate ways that painting can *demand* touch (103). Guston's relation to hapticity is in that vein: in the commanding, over-the-top intensity by which things bend and float when they should do neither, we are corralled by that counterproposition.

57 Wölfflin, 204.

58 Freud, "Group Psychology and the Analysis of the Ego" (1921), in *Beyond the Pleasure Principle, Group Psychology, and Other Works*, vol. 18 of *The Standard Edition of the Complete Psychological Works of Sigmund Freud*, trans. James Strachey (London: Hogarth Press and Institute of Psychoanalysis, 1955), 106. See also Lacan's description: "You have the unary trait which—filling in the invisible mark the subject receives from the signifier—alienates this subject in the first identification that forms the ego-ideal. . . . This is a retroversion effect by which the subject, at each stage, becomes what he was (to be) [*était*]

before that, and 'he will have been' is only announced in the future perfect tense." Jacques Lacan, *Écrits*, trans. Bruce Fink (New York: W. W. Norton, 2006), 684. See also Wertheimer's gloss on Christian von Ehrenfels's position regarding the *Gestaltqualitäten* in Wertheimer, "Gestalt Theory," and the descriptions of melody, pitch, and tone in Ian Verstegen, *Arnheim, Gestalt, and Art: A Psychological Theory* (Wien: Springer, 2005), 71–82.

59 The majority of the titles of the paintings Bois discusses in "Perceiving Newman"—from *Abraham* to *Onement* to *Horizon Light* to *The Word I* to *Moment*—refer not only to scriptural texts but specifically to the idea of texts that announce the world-making event. The performative dimension of so many biblical utterances—the most obvious is "Let there be light"—signal a linguistic dimension to these nonnarrative paintings. In other words, that space that is painting's own, for Newman, also draws its lineage from texts, and specifically the scriptural urtexts that defy "narrative" dimensions even as they enfold narrative into their claims for performativity. It is in this manner that Newman provides perhaps one of the most interesting counterpoints to Guston's paintings' relations to language. See Bois, "Perceiving Newman," 187–213.

60 Alfred Hofstadter, "The Tragicomic: Concern in Depth," *Journal of Aesthetics and Art Criticism* 24, no. 2 (Winter 1965): 298.

61 See Slifkin's brilliant analysis of how Guston's Marlborough paintings retrieve references from Walker Evans's and Ben Shahn's 1930s photographs (*Out of Time*, 78–83) even as they reignite figuration as a tool against "Apollonian" modernism as well as "the decidedly cool, sometimes blithe engagement of younger artists like Smithson, Oldenburg, and Lichtenstein" (95).

62 See McCloud, *Understanding Comics*, 86–89.

63 Slifkin: "A reader who sees Krazy [of George Herriman's *Krazy Kat*] get hit with a brick for the first time may be slightly confused. The humor, if there is any at all, is only on the level of slapstick violence. But with each successive assault, the reader begins to understand the strange existential dilemma of Krazy." Slifkin, *Out of Time*, 73.

64 Hofstadter, "The Tragicomic," 299. In this passage Hofstadter is describing characters from *The Cherry Orchard*: "Mme. Ranevskaya's squandering of money, Gaev's penchant for candy, his imaginary billiard playing—whose foolish incongruity with the facts of their lives helps to show these characters in their littleness. Through this littleness, their misfortune gets magnified in importance, so that the same value loss that founds their pathos also founds their comicality" (299).

65 "The tragicomic is not such an overarching harmony of the tragic and the comic. In it the two opposites sustain each other, indeed, but only as a tension that points to no possible resolution." (Hofstadter, "The Tragicomic," 301). "To obtain a picture of the tragicomic as a form of concern, it is necessary to see it in its structure as concern. The object of tragicomic concern has a certain importance, and the concerned subject has a certain interest in the object as it is thus qualified" (298).

66 Blair Hoxby, elaborating the term *pathos* that is so essential to (if underexamined within) Hofstadter's analysis, instead reminds us that "tragicomedy has a Renaissance pedigree as a dramatic genre" but points to sixteenth-century definitions in which tragicomedy presents "a serious action performed by illustrious personages, but it does not aim to arouse terror. It is 'tragic' only 'in potentiality,' not 'in action.'" Hoxby, *What Was Tragedy?*

Theory and the Early Modern Canon (Oxford: Oxford University Press, 2015), 13. My gratitude to Anna Rosensweig for pointing me toward Hoxby's book and for her generosity as interlocutor.

67 "The genre of tragicomedy, which has experienced such a significant rise all through modernity (and postmodernity), is . . . a development that takes place within the tragic paradigm. It involves the recognition of the fact that the tragic itself (with all its epic splendor) is ultimately but a mask of the really miserable, a mask that cannot survive its own repetition. . . . What defines it perfectly is the term 'tragedy's comedy.'" Zupančič, *The Odd One In*, 175.

68 Zupančič, 8.

69 To take just two examples: "There are no more workers as such. There are only laboring nomads. . . . They are abandoned subjects, relegated to the role of a 'superfluous humanity. . . . A new form of psychic life is emerging. . . . With little distinction remaining between psychic reflexes and technological reflexes, the human subject becomes fictionalized as 'an entrepreneur of the self.' . . . He is now just one animal among others, lacking an essence of his own to protect or safeguard. There are no longer any limits placed on the modification of his genetic, biological structure." Achille Mbembe, *Critique of Black Reason*, trans. Laurent Dubois (Durham, NC: Duke University Press, 2017), 3–4. "Many of my undergraduate students, some actively involved in the struggle for global justice, stare blankly at my mention of the death of the subject. 'The death of whom?' they ask, demanding clarification. After my initial surprise, I usually find myself trying to explain why the political significance of his death derives precisely from the onto-epistemological irrelevance of his death: the subject may be dead, I tell them, but his ghost—the tools and the raw materials used in his assemblage—remain with us." Denise Ferreira da Silva, *Toward a Global Idea of Race* (Minneapolis: University of Minnesota Press, 2007), xxii–xxiii.

70 Zupančič, *The Odd One In*, 79.

71 Wölfflin, *Principles of Art History*, 103.

72 Walter Benjamin, "Fate and Character" (1919), trans. Edmund Jephcott, in Benjamin, *Selected Writings*, ed. Marcus Bullock and Michael W. Jennings (Cambridge, MA: Belknap Press of Harvard University Press, 2000), 1:205. The notion of "development" here is not the linear one familiar from literary studies but rather a kind of heliographic development, like the instantaneous transformations of photography. Indeed, Benjamin returns to the "sun" metaphor on the next page: "The character trait is . . . the sun of individuality in the colorless (anonymous) sky of man, which casts the shadow of the comic action" (1:206).

73 Zupančič, *The Odd One In*, 66.

74 Zupančič, 175.

Amy Sillman

1 They even entail the spatializing or indeed bourgeois-decorative aspects of the metaphor of interiority. Freud explicitly compares the "system of the unconscious to a large entrance hall, in which the mental impulses jostle one another like separate individuals. Adjoining this entrance hall there is a second, narrower, room—a kind of drawing room—in which consciousness, too, resides. But on the threshold between these two rooms a watchman

performs his function: he examines the different mental impulses, acts as a censor, and will not admit them into the drawing room if they displease him." *The Standard Edition of the Complete Psychological Works of Sigmund Freud*, trans. and ed. James Strachey (London: Hogarth Press, 1953–74), 16:295. See Diana Fuss, *The Sense of an Interior: Four Writers and the Rooms That Shaped Them* (New York: Routledge, 2004), 6.

2 The notion of a "bourgeois interior" will evoke, as it should, the contentious debates about Expressionism begun between Ernst Bloch and Georg Lukács in 1938 and continued in letters exchanged between Theodor Adorno, Walter Benjamin, and Bertolt Brecht. Adorno's viewpoint in particular is discussed below. See Ernst Bloch et al., *Aesthetics and Politics*, ed. Fredric Jameson (London: New Left Books, 1977).

3 Sillman herself not only describes her work as "psychological" but makes the direct connection between psychology and shape: "My work is always psychological, whether I want it to be or not. The shapes that I am interested in looking at and drawing always turn into forms that have some kind of psychological narrative. Even if it's in the sense of a formal predicament, that a shape is at the edge of another, or teetering into a different color, or something is just the wrong color in general. There is some kind of discomfort or complexity that makes the object troubled in a way. The object is endangered, its stability is imperiled in some way; it's tipping over, or you can see through it. Or it is abject. That's the way I read my work." Amy Sillman, "Ugly Feelings: A Dialogue with Amy Sillman and Ian Berry," in Ian Berry and Anne Ellegood, *Amy Sillman: Third Person Singular* (Saratoga Springs, NY: Frances Young Tang Teaching Museum and Art Gallery, 2008), 21.

4 Brian Massumi, "The Autonomy of Affect," in "The Politics of Systems and Environments, part 2," special issue, *Cultural Critique* 31 (Autumn 1995): 85.

5 Massumi, "The Autonomy of Affect," 107n2.

6 Berlant, *Cruel Optimism*, 16.

7 Others, notably Sianne Ngai, have rejected such stringent distinctions between affect and emotion. See Ngai's introduction to *Ugly Feelings* (Cambridge, MA: Harvard University Press, 2005), esp. 21–37.

8 This list of four artists is not meant to delimit Sillman's "roots"—that only refers to Murray's role. On the contrary, Sillman's knowledge of especially painting history puts professional art historians to shame: her encyclopedic but also deeply felt knowledge of artists well past the restrictive canons I am referring to is key to how she thinks, writes, and paints. A leitmotif of our conversations is her shock at what I don't know, and *The Shape of Shape* is also influenced by the broader, vast scope of artists, from Patrick Heron to Paul Feeley, to whom she has redirected my attention. A different project would seek to do them justice.

9 Benjamin H. D. Buchloh, "Figures of Authority, Ciphers of Regression" (1981), in *Formalism and Historicity: Models and Methods in Twentieth-Century Art* (Cambridge, MA: MIT Press, 2015), 152–54. As he explains: "If the modernist work provides the viewer with perceptual clues to all its material, procedural, formal, and ideological qualities as part of its modernist program, which therefore gives the viewer an experience of increased presence and autonomy of the self, then the historicist work pretends to a successful resolution of the modernist dilemma of aesthetic self-negation, particularization, and restriction to detail, through absence, leading to the seductive domination of the viewer by the Other. . . . The reference to Expressionism in contemporary West German art is the natural move to make at a time when the myth of

cultural identity is to be established specifically against the dominance of American art during the entire period of reconstruction. . . . Any art that wants to supplant the dominance of American art through the programmatic return to a national idiom can only be successful on the market if it acknowledges the dominant 'foreign' style" (152–54).

10 Hal Foster, "The Expressive Fallacy," in *Recodings: Art, Spectacle, Cultural Politics* (Port Townsend, WA: Bay Press, 1985), 60.

11 "Expressionism was in many ways an answer to the problem of cultural unity: it drew on Germany's idealist and romantic heritage." Shearer West, *The Visual Arts in Germany, 1890–1937: Utopia and Despair* (New Brunswick, NJ: Rutgers University Press, 2001), 84.

12 Rei Terada, *Feeling in Theory* (Cambridge, MA: Harvard University Press, 2001), 11.

13 Helen Molesworth tracks Sillman's use of color as related to Guston's (the "moody, bruised purples of Philip Guston's abstract paintings"), as well as naming her interest in scale and proportion as "comic." See "Amy Sillman: Look, Touch, Embrace," in *Amy Sillman: One Lump or Two* (Boston: ICA Boston, DelMonico Books / Prestel, 2013), esp. 46–47.

14 With the term "concealed collages," Buchloh is referring to the "painted collages" that Max Ernst found in Magritte and Dalí's works and that would become a standby in "metaphysical painting" between the wars. This system was appropriated in the 1980s by David Salle and Eric Fischl, among others. See Buchloh, "Figures of Authority, Ciphers of Regression," 170n19.

15 Molesworth, "Amy Sillman: Look, Touch, Embrace," 45. In her book, Phillips writes about shape in much the same ways I discuss its enfolding of other elements (weight, texture, color) in Guston's painting, as well as the questions of space, proximity, and scale that become tangible through one's relations—especially desiring, but also forgetting, remembering, etc.—to another: "The flower is the shape so close he sees it still enough to look, blue like that, long and tall, each flared tongue with its own dark eye. Then the shape moves and the flower is too close or too far. The shape becomes its colors but he feels Lark touch it to his face and lips like a weightless velvet scrap." Jayne Anne Phillips, *Lark and Termite* (New York: Alfred A. Knopf, 2009), 63. The full sentence from which Sillman adapts her title reads: "Deep inside his pictures, a shape stands up and listens" (171).

16 See Amy Sillman in conversation with R. H. Quaytman, *Bomb*, no. 125 (Fall 2013), https://bombmagazine.org/articles/amy-sillman/.

17 Describing that metalevel, Silvan Tomkins writes that "shame is the most reflexive of affects" and that "an affect theory is a simplified and powerful summary of a larger set of affect experiences. . . . Shame theory is one such source of great power and generality in activating shame, in alerting the individual to the possibility or imminence of shame in providing standardized strategies for minimizing shame. . . . This is one of the major functions of any negative affect theory—to guide action so that negative affect is not experienced. It is affect acting at a distance. Just as human beings can learn to avoid danger, to shun the flame before one is burnt, so also can they learn to avoid shame or fear before they are seared by the experience of such negative affect." Silvan Tomkins, "Shame—Humiliation and Contempt—Disgust," in *Shame and Its Sisters: A Silvan Tomkins Reader*, ed. Eve Kosofsky Sedgwick and Adam Frank (Durham, NC: Duke University Press, 1995), 136, 165–66.

18 Rosalind E. Krauss, "In the Name of Picasso," in *The Originality of the Avant-*

Garde and Other Modernist Myths (Cambridge, MA: MIT Press, 1996), 39.

19 The key text here is of course Eve Meltzer, *Systems We Have Loved*, which sets the questions of affect, structuralism, and structure into conversation with Conceptualist art made in America at the dawn of structuralism's intervention in US intellectual life. Meltzer argues: "The framing of such works as *Card File* (1962) and the early self-portraits within terms provided by Althusser will first lead me to argue that systems had become for Morris a tool to *manage* or 'administrate,' if you will (as systems are wont to do), the affective experience of the antihumanist subject: Belated, alienated, automated, not fully conscious of itself, but always endeavoring to be so nonetheless. Thus affect is an 'effect' of so many of Morris's hyperbolically, parodically closed systems, each of which wrestles with and 'interprets the predicament' of the subject after antihumanism—the subject that lives in and by the terms of the system." While Meltzer attends to the key claim of belatedness, my argument here concerns the subject's presumptions or experiences of unity and interiority. See Meltzer, *Systems We Have Loved*, 79.

20 Tomkins warns against conflating guilt (an emotion) with shame, defining the latter as the painful intensification of self-consciousness that produces, of shame, "a central motive for human beings." Tomkins, *Shame and Its Sisters*, 141.

21 See Tomkins, "What Are Affects?," in *Shame and Its Sisters*, 33–74.

22 Where Lichtenstein enlarged brushstrokes in 1964–65 as they appeared in a comic book, *The Painting* (printed in the *Strange Suspense Stories* series in October 1964), Sillman reproduces her own brushstrokes.

23 Stone was the primary architect of the 1937 Museum of Modern Art and the 1954 US Embassy in New Delhi among many other significant buildings.

24 Foster, "The Expressive Fallacy," 60.

25 "For them [the original Expressionists] expressionism was an art of 'inner necessity' (Kandinsky) and 'abstraction' (Worringer) that operated by a formula such as this: via abstraction the viewer is compelled by the inner necessity of the artist. Yet this notion of self-expression, which governs the common idea of modern art in general, derives, as Paul de Man noted, from a binary polarity of classical banality in the history of metaphysics: the opposition of subject to object based on the spatial model of an 'inside' to an 'outside' world—with the inside privileged as prior." Foster, "The Expressive Fallacy," 61.

26 "Whenever . . . the apparently organic aspects of the painterly procedure were reinstituted, when the brushwork presented itself as a gesture of symbolic liberation, as the scriptural performance of unconscious forces, this position of expressivity was celebrated by the antimodernist factions as a recovery of the ties between aesthetic, emotional, and sensuous experience against the positivist rationality governing the modernist practice of painting." Buchloh, "The Primary Colors for the Second Time," in *Formalism and Historicity*, 345. An earlier version of the essay was first published in *October*, no. 37 (Summer 1986): 41–52.

27 "We commonly say that an expressionist like Kandinsky 'broke through' representation, when in fact he replaced (or superposed) one form with another—a representation oriented not to reality (the coded, realist outer world, but to expression (the coded, symbolist inner world)." Foster, "The Expressive Fallacy," 60.

28 Theodor W. Adorno, "On Jazz," trans. Jami Owen Daniel, in "Special Issue on Music," *Discourse* 12, no. 1 (Fall–Winter 1989–90), 46. Adorno continues his critique in "Perennial Fashion—Jazz": "The image of the technical world

possesses an ahistorical aspect that enables it to serve as a mythical mirage of eternity . . . Jazz, which knows what it is doing when it allies itself with technique, collaborates in the 'technological veil' through its rigorously repetitive though objectless cultic ritual." Theodor W. Adorno, *Prisms*, trans. Samuel Weber and Sherry Weber (1981; Cambridge, MA: MIT Press, 1986), 125.

29 Miriam Bratu Hansen, *Cinema and Experience: Siegfried Kracauer, Walter Benjamin, and Theodor W. Adorno* (Berkeley: University of California Press, 2012), 242. For a critical reexamination of Adorno's famously problematic, apparently anti-Black response to jazz, see Fumi Okiji, *Jazz as Critique* (Stanford, CA: Stanford University Press, 2018).

30 For Terada, "emotion" is what "entails [the] . . . death of the subject"; emotion "has to be nonsubjective," and "theories of emotion are always poststructuralist theories." Terada, *Feeling in Theory*, 3. Of course Terada has not had the last word either on the relation of emotion to the subject nor indeed on the multiple ways that "affect theory" relates both to the self/subject and to structure and "programs." Sianne Ngai, for example, writes that her "assumption is that affects are *less* formed and structured than emotions, but not lacking form or structure altogether; *less* 'sociolinguistically fixed,' but by no means code-free or meaningless; less organized in response to our interpretations of situations, but by no means entirely devoid of organization or diagnostic powers." See Ngai, *Ugly Feelings*, 27; emphasis in original. Both Terada and Ngai address Lawrence Grossberg's dispute with Fredric Jameson's 1991 *Postmodernism* in *We Gotta Get Out of This Place: Popular Conservatism and Postmodern Culture* (New York: Routledge, 1992), a kind of ground zero for the intersection between Jameson's brand of "historical materialism" and the legacy of poststructuralism in cultural studies that helped to seed the humanistic embrace and eventual—partial—dismissal of "affect studies."

31 Terada, *Feeling in Theory*, 11.

32 The classic formulation of the spatiality of depth-to-surface and its correlations to a conception of the postmodern is to be found in Fredric Jameson's *Postmodernism, or The Cultural Logic of Late Capitalism* (Durham, NC: Duke University Press, 1991), esp. 61–64.

33 Eugenie Brinkema, *The Forms of the Affects* (Durham, NC: Duke University Press, 2014), 24.

34 Brinkema notes that the field of affect studies builds on Foucault's philosophy of the self, itself a fold, as Deleuze (here paraphrased by Brinkema) argues: "Thus, interiority (of thought, as the unthought; as the ground of subjectivity) is brought to the surface, made exterior to constitute a new topography of the subject, the body, and knowledge in the process." And indeed, as she goes on to forcefully explain: "Although Deleuze's appeal to peristaltic movements evokes the clenching waves of the digestive tract, these foldings do not produce or successfully digest anything at all—*all ileus*, they remain in undulation, in the heaving kinetic gesture of perpetual folding." Brinkema, *Forms of the Affects*, 22–23.

35 "For garrulousness, babble, the spasmodic hiccup of repetitious detail, have about them a quality of randomness, disorganization, a lack of system. And LeWitt's outpouring of example, his piling up of instance, is riddled with system, shot through with order." Rosalind Krauss, "LeWitt in Progress," *October*, no. 6 (Autumn 1978): 56.

36 Diana Upright, *Morris Louis: The Complete Paintings* (New York: Harry N. Abrams, 1985), 49–58.

Part II Introduction

1 Hélène Cixous, "The Character of 'Character,'" trans. Keith Cohen, in "Changing Views of Character," special issue, *New Literary History* 5, no. 2 (Winter 1974): 383–402.

2 Cixous, "The Character of 'Character,'" 385.

3 Charles Taylor, *Sources of the Self: The Making of the Modern Identity* (Cambridge, MA: Harvard University Press, 1989), ix.

4 After all, Edward Said's *Orientalism* had been published more than a decade prior, making *Sources* archaic even in its moment, despite the author's pseudo-concessions (e.g., "the modern West among such higher civilizations"). Taylor, *Sources of the Self*, 11.

5 In an interview with the author, August 2015.

6 Written in 1966, first published in *Minimal Art: A Critical Anthology*, ed. Gregory Battcock (New York: Dutton Signet, 1968); republished in Yvonne Rainer, *Yvonne Rainer, Work 1961–73* (Halifax: Press of the Nova Scotia College of Art and Design, 1974), 63–74.

7 John Frow elaborates the distinction between figure and character by drawing on Gilles Deleuze's similar distinction in his discussion of Francis Bacon's paintings: "The Figure is still figurative; it still represents someone." Deleuze, *Francis Bacon: The Logic of Sensation*, trans. Daniel W. Smith (Minneapolis: University of Minnesota Press, 2003), 79. For Frow, whereas "the Figure corresponds to the textual ground of narration, underpinning and preceding it; it would be a pre-mimetic ontological level, not in contradiction with narration or representation but of a different order. . . . Character is a mark made by engraving or impressing. . . . [It is] both figural and figurative: both a figure standing out from a ground and a person-shaped entity which is the subject for narrative action." Frow, *Character and Person* (Oxford: Oxford University Press, 2014), 10, 9.

8 "The video installations of Ryan Trecartin tackle sex, culture, and race; men become women become clowns become micropersonae become mirrors." Jerry Saltz and Rachel Corbett, "How Identity Politics Conquered the Art World," *New York Magazine*, April 18, 2016, https://www.vulture.com/2016/04/identity-politics-that-forever-changed-art.html.

9 "Identification with fictional characters takes place both at the level of the character represented in a text and at the level of an explicit or implicit enunciative distance; Freud's account of the dispersal of ego-identification through the dream serves as a model for the general structure of identification." Frow, preface to *Character and Person*, ix.

10 Jameson, *Postmodernism*, 15.

11 Jameson, 62.

12 This is what Jean-Pierre Oudart calls "the Absent One": "Every filmic field is echoed by an absent field, the place of a character who is put there by the viewer's imaginary, and which we shall call the Absent One." Oudart, "Cinema and Suture," trans. Kari Hanet, *Screen* 18 (Winter 1978): 36. Note the similarity to what Frow describes as "'my padreros,' a word derived from the Athenian legal system where it designates an assistant, but with a later secondary sense of a 'familiar spirit' . . . the 'delegation of what was one's own' to this uncanny double." This "unfigured other, the figured absence, which is at once the negation and the condition of the existence of character" is a strong parallel to apparatus theory's similarly "daemonic" Absent One. Frow, *Character and Person*, 3–4, 47.

13 The key text on the interpellated, reproduced subject and ideology is Louis Althusser, "Ideology and Ideological State Apparatuses: Notes towards an Investigation," in *Lenin and Philosophy and Other Essays*, trans. Ben Brewster (New York: Monthly Review Press: 2001), 85-126.

14 Basing his approach on "certain overlooked theories of 'personhood,'" Murray Smith proposes a "theory of characters" in his *Engaging Characters: Fiction, Emotion, and the Cinema* (Oxford: Clarendon Press, 1995). Smith's approach is close to that of David Bordwell, mentioned below, and explicitly draws on the concepts of "classical cinema" advanced by Bordwell, Janet Staiger, and Kristin Thompson's *Classical Hollywood Cinema: Film Style and Mode of Production to 1960* (New York: Columbia University Press, 1985).

15 See Elinor Fuchs, *The Death of Character: Perspectives on Theater after Modernism* (Bloomington: Indiana University Press, 1996), and, for example, William Storm, *Dramaturgy and Dramatic Character: A Long View* (Cambridge: Cambridge University Press, 2016).

16 Raymond Williams, "Dialogue on Tragedy," *New Left Review* 13/14 (January 1962): 34.

17 John Jones, *On Aristotle and Greek Tragedy* (London: Chatto and Windus, 1962), 214.

18 Charles Segal, *Oedipus Tyrannus: Tragic Heroism and the Limits of Knowledge* (New York: Twayne, 1983), 13.

19 Giorgio Agamben, *Remnants of Auschwitz: The Witness and the Archive*, trans. Daniel Heller-Roazen (New York: Zone Books, 2000), 128. This phrase is quoted in Ruth Leys, *From Guilt to Shame: Auschwitz and After* (Princeton, NJ: Princeton University Press, 2007), 7. Here my approach is not to litigate the different positions represented by Leys and Agamben (nor their periodizing schemas) but to introduce the continuing subject/nonsubject framework of shame under a historical lens, namely that lent by Hannah Arendt to the second half of the twentieth century, in her description of how the "homeless . . . stateless . . . rightless . . . scum of the earth . . . shattered the façade of Europe's political systems and lay bare its hidden frame." Hannah Arendt, "The Decline of the Nation-State and the End of the Rights of Man," in *The Origins of Totalitarianism*, rev. ed. (New York: Harvest, 1976), 267.

20 Eve Kosofsky Sedgwick, *Touching Feeling: Affect, Pedagogy, Performativity* (Durham, NC: Duke University Press), 37.

21 By underlining those works that "remind us of (or indeed instantiate) the social" I am recalling the history of what came to be known as relational aesthetics and was particularly well accounted for by Nicolas Bourriaud and Claire Bishop. See Bourriaud, *Relational Aesthetics*, trans. Simon Pleasance and Fronza Woods, with the participation of Mathieu Copeland (Dijon: Les Presses du reel, 2002), and Bishop, *Artificial Hells: Participatory Art and the Politics of Spectatorship* (London: Verso Books, 2012).

22 Perhaps ironically (given his dedication to dialogue), the best formulation of this conundrum is to be found in Grant H. Kester's work, including *Conversation Pieces: Community and Communication in Modern Art* (Berkeley: University of California Press, 2004).

James Coleman

1 Since seeing its original installation at Documenta 12, I have seen this work at Coleman's retrospective at the Reina Sofia, Madrid (2012), and in a reedited, shortened form at the Museum of Modern Art, where it was shown for the first time in a black-box theater rather in than a conventional exhibition space, on February 13, 2017.

2 "[Coleman's] film *Retake with Evidence* (2007), a grandly installed and even more grandly orated quasi-Shakespearean soliloquy delivered by Harvey Keitel, left many visitors to documenta 12 perplexed and frustrated by the lack of contextual information. Coleman is an artist who expects much of his audience; he insists on the willing participation of the viewer in attempting to unravel meaning where there are often only thickening layers of complication and uncertainty beneath the surface." Jonathan Griffin, "James Coleman," *Frieze*, June 5, 2008, https://www.frieze.com/article/james-coleman. "Bereft of all frames of reference and situated in a 'post-historical' or 'post-apocalyptic' environment, as Agamben (2004) calls it—epitomized by James Coleman's *Retake with Evidence* (2007) in the Neue Galerie, featuring a melancholic Harvey Keitel soliloquizing among the ruins of Western civilization—the crisis provoked by the actual experience of [documenta 12] broke components down into a sequence of isolated utterances, strokes, gestures, moments or even ideas." Anthony Spira, "Infancy, History and Rehabilitation at documenta 12," *Journal of Visual Culture* 7, no. 2 (August 2008): 234.

3 One critic addressing Coleman's 2009 Dublin retrospective wrote, in a positive review: "James Coleman's art is literally histrionic: in other words, attuned to the mechanics and meaning of staged presence, a matter of theatrical projection and perspective on the part of actor and audience alike. . . . Coleman, whose work famously essays a rigorous critique of the photographic image (if not of representation in general) is also apparently not above a certain sly self-mythification." Brian Dillon, "James Coleman," *Frieze*, September 1, 2009, https://www.frieze.com/article/james-coleman-0.

4 In the "long count" match, as it became known, Dempsey stood over Tunney, delaying the referee's count and giving Tunney a few extra seconds to recover. This "extra time" during which Dempsey failed to return to his corner, per the rules, cost Dempsey his title again—having already lost it, the previous year, in a massive upset. Tunney in 1927 was one who "has his status, and yet simultaneously does not. . . . In order to defend his identity as champion he had to repeat, one might say reiterate, what he already is." Dorothea van Hantelmann, "James Coleman's *Box (ahhareturnabout)*," in *James Coleman*, exh. cat. (Dublin: Irish Museum of Modern Art, 2009), 68.

5 "Ultimately, aesthetics naturalizes representation, forging the modern subject's disposition to be represented through an aesthetic pedagogy whose end is the submission of the subject to the State. Above all, representation regulates the distribution of racial identifications along a developmental trajectory." David Lloyd, *Under Representation: The Racial Regimes of Aesthetics* (New York: Fordham University Press, 2019), 7. For a theorization of the "durability" of empire, see Ann Laura Stoler, *Duress: Imperial Durabilities in Our Times* (Durham, NC: Duke University Press, 2016).

6 The framework of tyranny and violence that marks Sophocles's texts is also part of the ongoing dynamic "between" the nations of Western Asia and North American and European imperialism. It was from the "heart of the

Middle East" that the Persians launched the two attacks, in 490 and 480 BCE, on the Athenians, who were first "forced to evacuate Athens and then either complied with the Delphic oracle (making peace with the Persians)." *Two Faces of Oedipus: Sophocles' Oedipus Tyrannus and Seneca's Oedipus*, trans. Frederick Ahl (Ithaca, NY: Cornell University Press, 2008), 86. Meanwhile, crucial thinkers of imperialism and its relations to psychoanalysis have both complicated and refused Freud's "universal" claims, even at the cost of sometimes generating new sociopolitical fetishes, such as Frantz Fanon's claims of the nonexistence of homosexuality in the Antilles. See Fanon, *Black Skin, White Masks*, trans. Charles Lam Markham (New York: Grove Press, 1968), and Ranjanna Khanna, *Dark Continents: Psychoanalysis and Colonialism* (Durham, NC: Duke University Press, 2003).

7 Sigmund Freud, *Introductory Lectures on Psychoanalysis*, trans. and ed. James Strachey (New York: W. W. Norton, 1966), 330.

8 John Jones, *On Aristotle and Greek Tragedy* (London: Chatto and Windus, 1962), 214–18.

9 The stranger who first approaches Oedipus and Antigone, warning them to flee the sacred grove immediately, explains that it takes its name from "the horseman over there—Kolonos . . . we've all taken his name." *Oedipus at Kolonos*, lines 66–67, in *The Oedipus Plays of Sophocles*, trans. Robert Bagg and Mary Bagg (Amherst: University of Massachusetts Press, 2004), 106–7. John Jones cites the lengthy exchange between Oedipus and the Chorus ("village elders of Colonus," sometimes translated as Old Men) as evidence of "a kind of action close-up," and further explains "the title of the play does well to divide attention between the king and Colonus; the local circumstances—the slab of rock, the ledge, the precise distances—matter greatly, religiously." Jones, *On Aristotle and Greek Tragedy*, 219.

10 John Gould, "Hikiteia," *Journal of Hellenic Studies* 93 (1973): 90. This "zone of extraterritoriality" points to the work of Giorgio Agamben, mentioned above. In 2007, when Documenta 12's organizers (led by artistic director Roger Buergel) showed *Retake with Evidence*, art critics everywhere—like many academics and writers in the humanities and even in political theory—were deeply involved with the thinking of Giorgio Agamben, as well as those whom Agamben discusses, primarily Walter Benjamin, Hannah Arendt, and Carl Schmitt, author of the 1922 *Politische Theologie* and thinker of the "structure of exception," whose logic underwrote the Nazi camps. Briefly put, the *homo sacer* that lends one of Agamben's books its name is the "sacred man," "who may be killed and yet not sacrificed. . . . An obscure figure of archaic Roman law, in which [a] human life is included in the juridical order [*ordinamento*] solely in the form of its exclusion (that is, of its capacity to be killed)." Giorgio Agamben, *Homo Sacer: Sovereign Power and Bare Life*, trans. Daniel Heller-Roazen (Stanford, CA: Stanford University Press, 1998), 8. When Oedipus the king is exiled from his homeland, stripped of his citizenship and his eyesight, he enters the category of the excluded, the livers of bare life, and the skirting of the Grove of the Eumenides at the start of *Oedipus at Kolonnus* helps make his dwelling in this "state of exception" clear. But the most politically crucial point that Agamben makes is that this realm of bare life "originally situated at the margins of the political order—gradually begins to coincide with the political realm, and exclusion and inclusion, outside and inside, *bios* and *zoë*, right and fact, enter into a zone of irreducible indistinction." Agamben, *Homo Sacer*, 9.

11 Jones, *On Aristotle and Greek Tragedy*, 219.

12 David Bordwell, *Narration in the Fiction Film* (Madison: University of Wisconsin Press, 1985), 12.

13 That is, conventions of Anglophone drama mean that the Shakespearean diction that we associate with Renaissance drama is also the lingua franca, as it were, for similarly "classical" works such as Sophocles's. Oedipus enters the Western canon on many fronts, but here—in keeping with his decades-long interest in voices and accents, and the audition of such extralinguistic and linguistic elements as the stutter and the sigh—Coleman underlines *actorly* diction in its particularities and specificities. In *Retake*, Keitel's diction ties both the body of the actor to the *socius* witnessing Keitel's performance and the historical body of the Shakespearean actor to the long litany of conventions by which cultures appropriate Greek myth for their own. See, among others, "Whose Culture Is It?," Kwame Anthony Appiah's chapter on cultural appropriation in *Cosmopolitanism: Ethics in a World of Strangers* (New York: W. W. Norton, 2006), 115–35.

14 Manuela Ammer, "Retake with Evidence," *James Coleman*, exh. cat. (Madrid: Museo Nacional Centro de Arte Reina Sofia, 2012), 271.

15 Yet, as she continues, "The delivery of the text is accompanied and interrupted by heavy breathing, audible exhalations, sighs and meditative pauses." Ammer, "Retake with Evidence," 270–71.

16 Coleman is notoriously rigorous about the circumstances by which critics and audiences can access information about his works (including, e.g., photographs, stills or copies—the last of which are completely unavailable). His release of notes or other preparatory files, such as this photograph of the maquette for *Retake*, are very precise and deliberate decisions about the work's framing.

17 In an ordinary rehearsal, one usually performs the piece fully, as if there were an audience: it is a performance that is just not *the* performance. Whether or not he is in costume or on set, "rehearsing" does not explain the nuanced difference between Keitel's version of performance in *Retake* and what would be an actor's conventional performance of the Oedipus character. A dancer marks by doing the movements of the dance often without expending full effort; she might walk the distance of a set of moves across a stage or gesture the moves rather than doing them. An actor will say her lines, but not necessarily in character; what matters is that she (and other actors and/or the director, dramaturg, etc.) understands where she will be when she says a particular line.

18 To argue for the materiality of language is to insert (or insist upon) a differentiating move between the word's claim to immediacy, communicativeness, and self-sameness relative to its "meaning" and the substrate of materiality—the spoken or written sign as such. In other words, it is a rejection of the word or voice as a kind of pure bearer of meaning. This central claim of Jacques Derrida's deconstructive logic threads through (and is performed by) many of his texts.

19 Here Keitel's performance calls up deconstructive thought's meditations on blindness in relation to language and its materiality. One can trace this across Derrida's thought, from his chapter "Meaning as Soliloquy" in his early *Speech and Phenomena* (*La Voix et le Phénomène*, 1967), trans. David Allison (Evanston, IL: Northwestern University Press, 1973), to his *Memoirs of the Blind: The Self-Portrait and Other Ruins*, trans. Pascale-Anne Brault and Michael Naas (Chicago: University of Chicago Press, 1993), which

accompanied an exhibition he organized at the Louvre in 1993. Indeed Coleman's *Retake* can be seen as almost a eulogy to this powerful if flawed intellectual tradition that has mattered profoundly to his own work.

20 Charles Segal notes that the *khora* is not the representative of the dramatist's voice or view but the very index of tragedy as a "public art form." Segal, *Oedipus Tyrannus: Tragic Heroism and the Limits of Knowledge* (New York: Twayne, 1983), 39–40.

21 Note that nineteenth-century drama theorist Gustav Freytag sees a far more formal set of functions—dividing scenes that are themselves symmetrically and carefully structured—assigned to the choral odes: "The different parts of the action were separated by choral songs." Gustav Freytag, *Freytag's Technique of the Drama: An Exposition of Dramatic Composition and Art*, trans. Elias J. MacEwan, 4th ed. (Chicago: Scott, Foresman, 1908), 168. Meanwhile, the relation of "action" to "character," specifically in Aristotle's *Poetics* and in the plays he treats, is of course a subject of debate in criticism. For John Jones, action generates a sense of the character beneath, as it were: "By the erosive flow of action the individual features are carved out, no potent shaping spirit lodges aboriginally behind the face; and thus the Aristotelian stage-figure receives his distinctive qualities." Jones, *On Aristotle and Greek Tragedy*, 38. But Blair Hoxby cites Hegel to represent "the idealists, who assume that the self should, ideally, be absolutely free and sovereign. . . . Whereas neither Aristotle nor his early modern commentators stress the centrality of conflict to tragedy because doing so might suggest that the theater could be an incitement to social disorder, Hegel can make collision a center-piece of his theory of tragedy because he considers contradictions necessary to the advance of human freedom and the revelation of absolute truth through time." Hoxby, *What Was Tragedy? Theory and the Early Modern Canon* (Oxford: Oxford University Press, 2015), 16.

22 She continues: "'Know thyself,' in the case of a self for whom self-knowledge is constitutively precluded, cannot help but become the total self-predisposition to listening to his own biography. In different ways, Ulysses and Oedipus are also figures of this theorem." Adriana Cavarero, *Relating Narratives: Storytelling and Selfhood*, trans. Paul Kottman (London: Routledge, 2000), 45.

23 "For Cavarero, the 'I' encounters . . . the fact of this other as fundamentally exposed, visible, seen, existing in a bodily way and of necessity in a domain of appearance. This exposure that I am constitutes, as it were, my singularity." Judith Butler, *Giving an Account of Oneself* (New York: Fordham University Press, 2005), 33.

24 Cavarero, *Relating Narratives*, 43.

25 Butler, *Giving an Account*, 17. The relevant texts by Foucault include *The Care of the Self*, vol. 3 of *The History of Sexuality*, trans. Robert Hurley (New York: Random House, 1986), and *The Hermeneutics of the Subject: Lectures at the Collège de France, 1981–1982*, ed. Frédéric Gros, trans. Graham Burchell (New York: Picador, 2005).

26 Butler, *Giving an Account*, 20.

27 Denis Diderot, "De la Poésie Dramatique," in *Œuvres complètes de Diderot: Revues sur les éditions originales* (Paris: J. Claye, 1875), 7:320; translation mine.

28 Achille Mbembe, *Critique of Black Reason*, trans. Laurent Dubois (Durham, NC: Duke University Press, 2017), 4–5.

29 Cavarero, *Relating Narratives*, 36.

30 Cavarero, 35.

31 Hannah Arendt, *The Human Condition*, 2nd ed. (Chicago: University of Chicago Press, 1988), 181–84.

32 "In a Levinasian—though perhaps more decidedly Arendtian vein, Adriana Cavarero argues that the question to ask is not 'what' we are, as if the task were simply to fill in the content of our personhood. . . . For her, the very structure of address through which the question is posed gives us a clue to understanding its significance. The question most central to recognition is a direct one, and it is addressed to the other: 'Who are you?' . . . By the 'question of the who' she does not mean the question 'Who did this to whom?' that is, the question of strict moral accountability. Rather, it is a question that affirms that there is another who is not fully known or knowable to me. . . . Cavarero argues that Arendt focuses on a politics of 'the who' in order to establish a relational politics, one in which the exposure and vulnerability of the other makes a primary ethical claim upon me." Butler, *Giving an Account*, 30–31.

33 Arendt, *The Human Condition*, 52–53.

34 M. M. Bakhtin, *The Dialogic Imagination: Four Essays*, ed. Michael Holquist, trans. Caryl Emerson and Michael Holquist (Austin: University of Texas Press, 1981), 284–85.

35 Shirley MacLaine, "Shirley MacLaine on a Different Age of Sexual Harassers in Hollywood," *New York Times Magazine*, November 4, 2019, 17.

36 Hantelmann, "James Coleman's *Box (ahhareturnabout)*," 68.

37 "The neon lighting was inset into a shape cut out of the wall identical to that of the sculpture, which was positioned over it. These two internal faces were painted silver to enhance the ethereal effect." Jean Fisher, "The Ploughman's Party," in *James Coleman* (Reina Sofia exh. cat.), 171n1.

38 In the flag that was adopted by the Irish Citizen Army, a socialist Irish Republican movement from the 1910s later adopted by a variety of Irish political organizations, the part of the plow that reaches into the soil is replaced by a sword.

39 Dorothy Walker, *Without the Walls* (London: ICA, 1980), 21–22, quoted in Fisher, "The Ploughman's Party," 170–71.

40 See note 12 in the introduction to part I of this book.

Steve McQueen

1 Theorization of these spaces is well underway, in particular regarding colleges and universities. See Jennifer Doyle, *Campus Sex, Campus Security* (South Pasadena, CA: Semiotexte, 2015), Joseph Fischel, *Sex and Harm in the Age of Consent* (Minneapolis: University of Minnesota Press, 2016), and Laura Kipnis, *Unwanted Advances: Sexual Paranoia Comes to Campus* (New York: Harper, 2017).

2 "The ideology underlying this fetishization of 'character' is that of an 'I' who is a *whole* subject (that of the 'character' as well as that of the author), conscious, knowable; and the enunciatory 'I' *expresses himself* in the text, just as the world is represented complementarily in the text in a form equivalent to pictorial representation, as a simulacrum." Hélène Cixous, "The Character of 'Character,'" trans. Keith Cohen, in "Changing Views of Character," special issue, *New Literary History* 5, no. 2 (Winter 1974): 385.

3 Cixous, "The Character of 'Character,'" 389.

4 One important aspect of *Illuminer* is the way that film stock has been produced to accurately represent only white skin. Numerous scholarly and popular articles discuss this issue as it has played out in movies made on film stock (unlike *Illuminer*'s digital camera), as do artist's projects including Black Audio Film Collective's *The Last Angel of History* (1995) and Adam Broomberg and Oliver Chanarin's *To Photograph the Details of a Dark Horse in Low Light* (2013).

5 For me, the most hard-to-take part of *Shame* is its relentless focus on the West Side piers as a site of relentlessly straight sex. As we know from the writings of Douglas Crimp among others—and the photographs of Alvin Baltrop about which Douglas wrote—the West Side piers were a key neighborhood for gay male cruising and sex throughout the 1970s and into the 1980s. See Douglas Crimp, "Alvin Baltrop: Pier Photographs, 1975–1986," *Artforum*, February 2008, 262–69, as well as his book chapter "Action Around the Edges," in *Before Pictures* (Brooklyn: Dancing Foxes Press; Chicago: University of Chicago Press, 2016).

6 See James Quandt, "Steve McQueen's *Shame*," *Artforum*, January 2012, 51. https://www.artforum.com/print/201201/steve-mcqueen-s-shame-29809.

7 The romantic comedies *Thanks for Sharing*, *Don Jon*, and *Sleeping with Other People* were released in 2012, 2013, and 2015 respectively, and Lars von Trier's two-volume *Nymphomaniac* (2013) arguably also fills the category. McQueen discussed the film in terms of sex addiction in several interviews. See Jada Yuan, "*Shame* Director Steve McQueen on Sex Addiction in New York City and Michael Fassbender's Full-Frontal Nudity," December 5, 2011, www.vulture.com/2011/12/shame-director-steve-mcqueen-on-sex-addiction-in-new-york-city-and-michael-fassbenders-full-frontal-nudity.html; Marshall Fine, "Director Steve McQueen Discusses *Shame* and Sex Addiction," *Huffington Post*, December 5, 2011, https://www.huffpost.com/entry/director-steve-mcqueen-di_b_1129153. McQueen also claims sex addiction as his film's subject in the conversation with Adrian Searle published in the catalog *Steve McQueen: Works* (Basel and Berlin: Laurenz Foundation / Schaulager Basel / Kehrer Verlag, 2012), 206.

8 Daniel Dayan, "The Tutor-Code of Classical Cinema," in *Movies and Methods: An Anthology*, ed. Bill Nichols (Berkeley: University of California Press, 1976). Dayan's essay was first published in *Film Quarterly* 28, no. 1 (Fall 1974). As mentioned, 1974 also saw the publication of Cixous's *Prénoms de personne* (Paris: Éditions du Seuil, Collection Poétique, 1974).

9 Gilles Deleuze, *Cinema 1: The Movement-Image*, trans. Hugh Tomlinson and Barbara Habberjam (Minneapolis: University of Minnesota Press / Athlone Press, 1986), 93. Deleuze is citing Goethe, *Theory of Colors*, trans. Charles. Eastlake (1840; Cambridge, MA: MIT Press, 1970), 495.

10 Deleuze, *Cinema 1*, 93.

11 Edward Branigan, *Tracking Color in Cinema and Art* (New York: Routledge, 2018), 47–48.

12 Susan Blackmore, *Ten Zen Questions* (Oxford: OneWorld, 2009), 73; quoted in Branigan, *Tracking Color in Cinema and Art*, 47.

13 On the distinctions between tinting and toning, see Joshua Yumibe, *Moving Color: Early Film, Mass Culture, Modernism* (New Brunswick, NJ: Rutgers University Press, 2012).

14 "It was the integration of rapidly developed conventions and rules for shooting and editing dialogue (the use of shot and counter-shot in conjunction with a 'continuous' sound track of speech and dialogue) into a

system of conventions governing the articulation of narrative space and time, together with the degree of 'presence' and psychological individualization provided by the voice, that finally completed the evolution of the sound film." Steve Neale, *Cinema and Technology: Image, Sound, Colour* (Bloomington: Indiana University Press, 1985), 95.

15 It is in that sense a narrowing even past what Michel Chion calls "null extension, when the sonic universe has shrunk to the sounds heard by one single character, possibly including any inner voices he or she hears." Though that might be a conceit of the nightclub scene—that we are hearing what Brandon hears when his sister sings: only her voice, with none of the sounds of the nightclub around her—it strikes me that we are moving past any kind of identification with a character and what is instead at play is what Chion names "contrasts and variations in extension from one scene to another, or even within one and the same scene," pointing to an actual shift in the viewer's relationship to the film, taking us briefly out of the diegesis and into a sense of our own embodied selves. Michel Chion, *Audio-Vision: Sound on Screen*, trans. Claudia Gorbman (New York: Columbia University Press, 1994), 87.

16 Quandt, "Steve McQueen's *Shame*."

17 Blair Hoxby, *What Was Tragedy?*, 9.

18 Hoxby, 55.

19 Hoxby, 55.

20 Hoxby, 9.

21 Hoxby explains the critical function of his "surface reading," in the service of avoiding what Paul Ricoeur diagnosed as a "hermeneutics of suspicion." See Hoxby, 54–55.

22 Hoxby, 56.

23 Dai Jinhua, *After the Post-Cold War: The Future of Chinese History* (Durham, NC: Duke University Press, 2018), 21.

24 Hoxby, *What Was Tragedy?*, 55.

25 See the important, historical feminist literature on melodrama that helped instantiate genre studies within film studies and push the complexity of genre—as I am using it here—past accepted tropes within the film industry: for example, *Imitations of Life: A Reader on Film and Television Melodrama*, ed. Marcia Landy (Detroit, MI: Wayne State University Press, 1991), and the essays of "Phase 4. Spectatorship, Ethnicity, and Melodrama," a section within *Feminism and Film*, ed. E. Ann Kaplan (Oxford: Oxford University Press, 2000), as well as monographs such as Barbara Klinger, *Melodrama and Meaning: History, Culture, and the Films of Douglas Sirk* (Bloomington: Indiana University Press, 1994).

26 Bonnie Honig, *Antigone, Interrupted* (Cambridge: Cambridge University Press, 2013), 194.

27 Honig, *Antigone, Interrupted*, 80.

28 Hoxby, *What Was Tragedy?*, 17–18.

29 The materiality of recordings themselves are underscored in McQueen's films on several occasions. Brandon is an audiophile who defends his record player as aggressively as he defends his own silence; Gould's famous recordings—1955, 1981—contrasted analog and digital recordings as well as two different stages in the pianist's life, which they bracketed. See Anthony Tommasini, "Remastered Glenn Gould in Tempo with the Times," https://www.chicagotribune.com/news/ct-xpm-2002-09-18-0209180046-story.html. See also Alexander Weheliye's argument that "sound gained its materiality in the technological apparatuses and the practices surrounding these devices and in the process

rematerialized the human source." Alexander Weheliye, *Phonographies: Grooves in Sonic Afro-Modernity* (Durham, NC: Duke University Press, 2005), 7.

30 "Sophocles' use of the theatrical device of interruption (what Freud also relies on but refers to, perhaps jokingly, as 'persuasion') calls attention to the costs of the polis' interruption of the heroic form of life: its effort to displace appetite with reason, desire with wants, and bodies with words. This is no rejection of reason but rather a way to highlight its work." Honig, *Antigone, Interrupted*, 29.

31 "For Cavarero, the 'I' encounters . . . the fact of this other as fundamentally exposed, visible, seen, existing in a bodily way and of necessity in a domain of appearance. This exposure that I am constitutes, as it were, my singularity." Butler, *Giving an Account*, 33.

32 There is no real requirement in Adriana Cavarero's philosophy for an actual tête-à-tête: for her, a "narrative" is "related" even in the absence of words—"the other is always a narratable self," just as the subject herself "is not the result of text itself, and neither does it lie in the construction of the story. 'It lies rather in a narrating impulse that is never in 'potentiality' but rather in 'actuality,' even when it refrains from 'producing memories or 'reproducing' past occurrences." Cavarero, *Relating Narratives*, 34–35.

33 In the film, no one ever explains what has become of the rest of their family; the only mention of more family is when Brandon tells Marianne he's Irish but grew up in New Jersey. There is no particular reason we would think, however, that Brandon is telling the truth, as he is hardly truthbound throughout the film, and mostly simply avoidant.

34 Butler is well aware of the Nietzschean argument that the "institution of law compels an originally aggressive human to turn that aggression 'inward,' to craft an inner world composed of a guilty conscience and to vent that aggression against oneself in the name of morality." Butler, *Giving an Account*, 14. My suggestion here is that the function that Nietzsche named guilt is what McQueen—in keeping with the thinkers Leys follows, in both the Arendtian tradition (Agamben) and the psychiatric (Tomkins)—names "shame." While different, perhaps at the level at which they serve the prescriptive demand for dialogue, they are the same.

Part III Introduction

1 See Erving Goffman, introduction to *The Presentation of Self in Everyday Life* (Edinburgh: University of Edinburgh, 1956), 1–9. My thanks to Anna Rosensweig for recommending Goffman at precisely the right juncture in the writing of this book.

2 Simultaneous and related developments in structuralist cinema and Minimalist sculpture, as well as Arte Povera, Neo-Concretism, and other movements in Europe, South America, and beyond leverage specific forms of abstraction to address the subject and self and indeed suggest provocative counterpoints to the following argument. These range from Lygia Clark's propositions that "the house is a body / the body is a house" to Hollis Frampton's *détourned* bildungsroman. See André Lepecki's note on Lygia Clark's *O corpo é a casa* (1969), "Part 1: Affective Geometry, Immanent Acts: Lygia Clark and Performance," August 8, 2017, https://post.moma.org/part-1-affective-geometry-immanent-acts-lygia-clark-and-performance/, and Annette Michelson, "Time out of Mind: Frampton's Circles of Confusion," in *On the Eve*

of the Future: Selected Writings on Film (Cambridge, MA: MIT Press / October Books, 2017), 211–21, first published as the foreword to Hollis Frampton, *Circles of Confusion* (Rochester, NY: Visual Studies Workshop, 1983), 13–21.

3 Here I am thinking of performance artists from the 1970s—Marina Abramović and Carolee Schneeman, for example—for whom the possibilities of reperformance and "flesh as material" enabled different performers to enact the same work, even if that work had (auto-) biographical resonance. To me, younger artists including, for example, Tino Sehgal belong to this lineage even as they introduce the spoken word, improvisation, and other elements expanding the parameters of what we might consider the performer's range: the particularities of a performer's "style" or identity remain distinct and separate from the transmissible, teachable work. A somewhat different lineage, perhaps descending from Yoko Ono to Morgan Bassichis, emphasizes the performer's ability to denote and perform particularity. "Role" is less of an impulse or mechanism in these works that are not designed to be transmitted over generations or reperformed according to a choreography or plan. However, it might be useful to consider how a performer like Bassichis (or My Barbarian or Gregg Bordowitz) plays with the category of the role (including the role of performer, of emcee, of dance or song leader, or rabbi, poet, etc.). These artists perhaps invert some of my claims regarding the "proprietary" nature of one's story and the circulation of stories as a queer, intergenerational project.

4 Georg Simmel articulates this in a 1920 essay: "'Playing a role'—not as dissimulation and deceit, but rather as the flowing of personal life in an outer form that we meet with as something already existing, traced in advance—this belongs to the functions that constitute our actual lives. Such roles may be adequate to our individuality, but it is nevertheless something other than this individuality and its inner and total course. One who is a priest, an officer, a professor, or an office manager behaves in accordance with a prescription that goes beyond an individual life. We not only *do* things to which the exterior fortunes of culture and destiny lead us, but rather we unavoidably portray something that we really *are* not." Simmel, "Toward the Philosophy of the Actor," trans. Philip Lawton (January 10, 2017), https://papers.ssrn.com/sol3/papers.cfm?abstract_id=2897044.

5 In an echo of Yvonne Rainer's brief words on character cited in the last section, Goffman stresses the importance of the individual's behavior as they first enter a social situation. He builds on the experiences of teachers and "attendance in mental institutions" wishing to generate authority for themselves by first showing others "who is boss." Goffman, *Presentation of Self in Everyday Life*, 6.

6 The psychologist Blake Ashforth studies "role transitions," dividing them between "micro"—"the psychological and (if relevant) physical movement between simultaneously held roles. . . . Examples include shifts between one's home and work roles, one's at-work roles of supervisor and subordinate, one's at-home roles of parent and spouse. . . . [These] usually involve frequent and recurring movement both within and between social domains"—and "macro role transitions," defined as the "psychological and (if relevant) physical movement between sequentially held roles," which he tends to define in corporate/career terms (as opposed to, e.g., familial roles, which are also often sequential, if overlapping). See Blake Ashforth, *Role Transitions in Organizational Life: An Identity-Based Perspective* (New York: Routledge, 2012), 7.

7 Simmel defines this as a question of "innerness": "It is necessary to introduce another step: the inner actualization of the play by the actor, the sensual, virtually subjective bringing to life of the objective spiritual content that lies to hand in the published play. . . . Neither what the writer thought nor what the reader imagined is exactly parallel to how the actor understands the role. It is the inner becoming-art, that is, the becoming-theatrical-art of the role as material. " Simmel, "Toward the Philosophy of the Actor," 5.

8 Freytag, *Freytag's Technique of the Drama*, 141.

9 "Well-planned, broadly elaborated sentimental scenes of the performers, sung and spoken, remained in important places of the action an indispensable component part of the tragedy. These pathos-scenes, the renown of the first actor, the centre of brilliance for ancient acting, contain the elements of the lyric situation in a completeness which we can no longer imitate. In them are comprised the touching effects of the tragedy. These long-winded gushings of inner feeling had so great a charm for the audience that to such scenes unity and verisimilitude of action were sacrificed by the weaker poets. . . . There are poetic observations upon one's own condition, supplications to the gods, feeling portrayal of peculiar relations. The first of these may perhaps be compared with the monologues of modern times, although in them the chorus sometimes represents the interested hearer, sometimes the hearer who responds." Freytag, 142.

10 See Blair Hoxby's work on pathos at the core of tragedy, *Theory and the Early Modern Canon* (Oxford: Oxford University Press, 2015).

11 See Susan Leigh Foster, *Choreography and Narrative: Ballet's Staging of Story and Desire* (Bloomington: Indiana University Press, 1996), particularly chapters 1, 2, and 3.

12 Foster, *Choreography and Narrative*, 105.

13 The long attenuation of the star system within ballet is dealt its final blow by the end of the Cold War, which finally ended defections that had made stars like Rudolf Nureyev, Mikhail Baryshnikov, and Alexander Godunov celebrities beyond the world of balletomanes.

14 For a complex and detailed examination of the key development of "attitudes" and *tableaux vivants* that interrupted the dramatization of ballet (as opposed to opera), see Kirsten Gram Holmström, *Monodrama, Attitudes, Tableaux Vivants: Studies on Some Trends of Theatrical Fashion, 1770–1815* (Uppsala: Almqvist & Wiksell, 1967).

15 Simmel, "Toward the Philosophy of the Actor," 5.

16 "The text, in this modern, current sense which we are trying to give this word, is fundamentally to be distinguished from the literary work: it is not an esthetic product, it is a signifying practice. . . . It is not a group of closed signs, endowed with a meaning to be rediscovered, it is a volume of traces in displacement." Roland Barthes, *The Semiotic Challenge*, trans. Richard Howard (Berkeley: University of California Press, 1994), 7.

17 Erin Manning, *Always More Than One: Individuation's Dance* (Durham, NC: Duke University Press, 2013), 33.

18 On the relation of "storylessness" to roles, see my article "*Rosas*, the Storyless, and Roles."

19 B. J. T. Biddle, "Recent Development in Role Theory," *Annual Review of Sociology* 12 (1986): 69.

20 In this framework I am distinguishing my interpretation of abstraction (or "nonpurposive" movement) in dance from that proposed by Elise

Archias, who describes the viewer's experience of Yvonne Rainer's "defensive, withdrawn, almost autistic person in *Trio A*" as "respond[ing] to the diffidence by herself feeling alienated and possibly annoyed or resentful: Why should we engage with her when she does not even seem to care whether we are here? . . . In our resentment is a refusal of the negation inherent in modern conditions—a negation of the richness of embodied communication—that the work mimics. We perceive the symptom of the damage in the performer (her defensiveness) as undesirable in a work of art and perhaps begin to demand artworks that express social desires more clearly and a culture that would support such expression." Elise Archias, *The Concrete Body: Yvonne Rainer, Carolee Schneeman, Vito Acconci* (New Haven, CT: Yale University Press, 2016), 74–75. My position is that we do not see a model for ourselves, as subjects, in the embodied movement before us in Rainer's dance (here Archias is describing Rainer's landmark 1966 dance; I will return to her beautiful and apt descriptions of her post-2000 choreographies in the final chapter). Instead, in her more recent work, from her earlier confrontation with the spectacular seductive nature of performance, which I develop in "*Rosas*, the Storyless, and Roles" (cited above), we recognize the development of roles that in turn illustrate both the monadary framework of roles themselves—and the work used to transition between them as well as their temporal, durative nature—and the capacity of dance as abstract (if quotable, appropriated) movement, to underscore the transitive and open-ended nature of the role. Archias sees figural, expressive form in Rainer's "concrete" movement—the slope of defeated shoulders echoing those of Blacks living in the Jim Crow era—much as Slifkin read tropological figuration in Guston's late paintings. Without requiring that we *not* see such echoes of contemporaneous imagery/behavior, I am insisting that we focus on the elements of abstraction retained despite or alongside those echoes.

21 This return to the dramaturgical definition of the rule holds true in the sociological and psychological discourses on social roles as well (see Biddle's reliance on Simmel). On the other hand, we have works such as George Herbert Mead's *Mind, Self, and Society* (Chicago: University of Chicago Press, 1934), which frequently employs the phrase "take the role of the other" without examining what such an operation means or entails.

22 Lauren Berlant, *The Female Complaint: The Unfinished Business of Sentimentality in American Culture* (Durham, NC: Duke University Press, 2008), 226.

23 See the Museum of Modern Art's website for Yvonne Rainer's *Trio A*, accessed February 5, 2020, https://www.moma.org/learn/moma_learning/yvonne-rainer-trio-a-1978/.

24 See 224n20 and Carrie Lambert-Beatty, *Being Watched: Yvonne Rainer and the 1960s* (Cambridge, MA: MIT Press / October Books, 2008).

25 See 90n6.

26 Rainer, *Yvonne Rainer, Work 1961–73*, 286.

27 For a comprehensive (if brief) overview of the "Flemish dance wave," that puts De Keersmaeker into context among other choreographers including Jan Fabre and Wim Vandekeybus as well as Belgian institutions and the question of Belgian national identity, see Rudi Laermans and Pascal Gielen, "Constructing Identities: The Case of 'The Flemish Dance Wave,'" in *Europe Dancing: Perspectives on Theater, Dance, and Cultural Identity*, ed. Andrée Grau and Stephanie Jordan (London: Routledge, 2000), 12–27.

28 The term is Sally Banes's; see *Terpsichore in Sneakers: Post-Modern Dance*, 2nd ed. (Hanover, NH: Wesleyan University Press), xiv.

29 Yvonne Rainer, *Feelings Are Facts: A Life* (Cambridge, MA: MIT Press, 2006), 390, 398.

Anne Teresa De Keersmaeker

1 "In *Vortex* we often stand in a circle from which we start to dance. This enables everyone to be geometrically and dynamically connected within the same visual field. . . . The geometrical pattern in composing the space entails five circles and one large connecting circle, corresponding to six instruments in the music. In addition, I am investigating the notion of a mobile center, which is the only still point in vortices, and the movements of opening and closing, which correspond to the contraction and expansion of time." Anne Teresa De Keersmaeker, "*Vortex Temporum*, or Choreographing the Sensible of the Music," interview by Bojana Cvejić, in *Vortex Temporum*, ed. Cvejić (Brussels: Wiels, Rosas, and Mercatorfonds, 2015), 14. This volume together with *Essays* (cited below) and two other volumes about *Work/Travail/Arbeid* (also cited below) was published as a boxed set.

2 See Elizabeth R. Anker, *Orgies of Feeling: Melodrama and the Politics of Freedom* (Durham, NC: Duke University Press, 2014), 15. Here I am less interested in the politico-moral framework through which Nietzsche develops the concept of an "orgy of feeling" than his notion of a "great affect [that] explodes suddenly": it is that explosive power that Grisey's score harnesses, along with the notion of music's particularly expiative (for Nietzsche) power. See Friedrich Nietzsche, *On the Genealogy of Morals and Ecce Homo*, trans. Walter Kaufman and R. J. Hollingdale (New York: Vintage, 1989), 139–43.

3 Thomas Elsaesser, "Tales of Sound and Fury: Observations on the Family Melodrama," in *Imitations of Life: A Reader on Film and Television Melodrama*, ed. Marcia Landy (Detroit, MI: Wayne State University Press, 1991), 75. Elsaesser's argument is that the "mise-en-scène" should be given greater priority in judging melodrama than its "intellectual content or story value"; he marshals a spectrum of formal issues, from a director's montage system to visual metaphors to "an acute sense of claustrophobia in décor and locale" to suggest that "the modulation of optical planes and spatial masses which Panofsky rightly identified as a 'dynamisation of space'" finds its natural home in the Hollywood melodrama (74–91).

4 The same pattern is predrawn on the stage on which *Vortex Temporum* is danced. Elena Filipovic explains that "as visitors see the dancers plotting points and arcs, thereby constructing the sole 'scenography' of *Work/Travail/Arbeid* in the form of ephemeral, chalked geometries, they understand that they are witnessing the generation of a clue to the entire piece." In "Vertiginous Force: The Exhibition as Work," in Anne Teresa De Keersmaeker, *Work/Travail/Arbeid*, ed. Filipovic (Brussels: Wiels, Rosas and Mercatorfonds, 2015), 20.

5 At Wiels, the work was performed across two linked galleries, one of which opened into a lobby, and the other containing a door that enabled the dancers to access the performance space from "offstage"; at other sites, including the second-floor atrium of the Museum of Modern Art and the Centre Pompidou, in Paris, architecture provided different constraints.

6 The magic square is a nine-celled grid in which each of the nine integers (1–9) is placed so that the sum of any three cells, whether added horizontally, vertically, or diagonally, is 15. Dating back to ancient China, the magic square has a history with many tributaries, including works of medieval Islamic literature,

mathematics, and Albert Dürer's *Melencholia I* (1514). De Keersmaeker has explained that her use of magic squares enables her to avoid having to make a number of choreographic choices: like other systems she borrows from—for example, Chinese philosophy, medicine, and astrology—it helps generate a skeleton for the movement she devises. In *Vortex Temporum*, the fundamental movement sequence is based on a sequence of turns in which the dancer's body faces each of the nine points of the square in different positions—e.g., a twisted torso, a tilted lean. The magic square is also the basis of the circular pattern generated by the overlapping of these squares drawn in chalk on the floor. See De Keersmaeker, *Work/Travail/Arbeid*, 26–27. Trisha Brown used a similar model to allow spatial coordinates to help define a dancer's movements in her 1975 work *Locus*, in which each of the letters of the alphabet correlates to a point in an imaginary cube, and Brown has choreographed movements "about each point in the series," movements that "move through, touch, look at, jump over" those points, within which the dancer also stays. One of Brown's dancers who performed the piece in the 1970s, Mona Sulzman, wrote a remarkable essay about it entitled "Choice/Form in Trisha Brown's *Locus*: A View from Inside the Cube," *Dance Chronicle* 2, no. 2 (1978). I wrote a piece connecting *Locus* to Sol LeWitt's sculpture and his photographic book *Autobiography*, entitled "'I Inhabit a Cube,'" in *Sol LeWitt: Structures, 1965–2006*, ed. Nicholas Baume (New York: Public Art Fund, 2011), 84–103.

7 Mark Lorimer, in "We Are the Music Played by the Instruments: Interview with Boštjan Antončič, Garlos Garbin, Marie Goudot, Cynthia Loemij, Mark Lorimer, Julien Monty, Chrysa Parkinson, and Michaël Pomero, by Bojana Cvejić," in Cvejić, *Vortex Temporum*, 57. Cynthia Loemij clarifies: "From this phrase, every dancer created their own version, enlarging the same directions in space" (57).

8 "As Swanilda, Patricia McBride seems totally aware of these distinctions [between "the infinite preferability of the living dancer" and "the seductive, yet ultimately threatening, automaton"]; while she charms throughout, her witty impersonation of the automaton is now allowed to move us." Craig Owens, "Politics of Coppélia," in *Beyond Recognition: Representation, Power, and Culture* (Berkeley: University of California Press, 1994), 241.

9 Despite the centrality of Pomero's fundamental sequence, the rest of *Vortex* was composed unusually by dancers working on their individual parts together, sharing the same studio and working simultaneously on their parts. Bojana Cvejić: "Since all of you have already collaborated with De Keersmaeker/Rosas, what's distinctive about this process?" [Carlos] Garbin: In this creation, we are all in together in the studio all the time. In other pieces, we would be working separately and come together at certain moments. A lot of times here, Anne Teresa calls for the changes, the aesthetic decisions that she brings from watching it from the outside." In "We Are the Music Played by the Instruments," 57.

10 According to Julian Anderson, the "use of spectra, whether harmonic or non-harmonic, is only the most superficial feature of the music" of Grisey and Murail. Though Grisey disowned the label, he clarifies: "What is radically different in spectral music is the attitude of the composer faced with the cluster of forces that make up sounds and faced with the time needed for their emergence." See Julian Anderson, "A Provisional History of Spectral Music," *Contemporary Music Review* 19, no. 2 (2000): 7, and Gérard Grisey, "Did You Say Spectral?" trans. Joshua Fineberg, *Contemporary Music Review* 19, no. 3 (2000): 2–3, both cited in Ching-Yi Wang, "Spectral Music and Gérard Grisey's *Vortex Temporum I* and *II*" (PhD diss., University of California, Davis, 2012), 5–6.

11 Joshua Fineberg, "Spectral Music," in *Contemporary Music Review* 19, no. 2 (2000): 2.

12 Jean-Luc Plouvier, "Performing *Vortex*: A Pianist's Firsthand Account," in Cvejić, *Vortex Temporum*, 44.

13 Cornelia Fales, "The Paradox of Timbre," *Ethnomusicology* 46, no. 1 (Winter 2002): 57.

14 Jean-Charles François, "Fixed Timbre, Dynamic Timbre," *Perspectives of New Music* 28, no. 2 (Summer 1990): 112–18.

15 After all, if sound can escape notational systems that have historically limited what we hear to notes and thus "harmonic tones," then measuring sound digitally allows new spectra to emerge, reconfigured according to those digital measurements. Such digital analysis and measurement can take place "in numerical tables of graphically" as "partials of varying frequencies and amplitudes," as Robert Hasegawa explains. See Robert Hasegawa, "Gérard Grisey and the 'Nature' of Harmony," *Music Analysis* 28, no. 2/3 (2009): 349–71.

16 Jean-Luc Hervé, *Dans le vertige de la durée:* Vortex Temporum *de Gérard Grisey* (Paris: L'Harmattan/L'Itinéraire, 2015), 16.

17 "Celui des hommes (temps de langage et de respiration), celui des baleines (temps spectral des rythmes de sommeil) et celui des oiseaux ou des insectes (temps contracté à l'extrême où s'estompent les contours)." *Vortex Temporum* program notes, quoted in Hervé, *Dans le vertige de la durée*, 19.

18 A performance artist who has similarly used animals to confront audiences with the human-centered nature of our perception is Joan Jonas, though her work (and its relation to music) is quite different. See my response to the "Questionnaire on Materialisms," *October*, no. 155 (January 2016): 48–50.

19 For example, "Grisey has the flutist play all four members of the flute family from bass flute to piccolo, the B clarinet [is] tuned a quarter tone lower, and the piano [has] four notes tuned a quarter tone lower to fit with the micro-intervals played on the other instruments." Wang, "Spectral Music and Gérard Grisey's *Vortex Temporum I* and *II*," 70.

20 According to Jonathan Goldman, "Despite the diversity of the productions associated with this current, spectralist composers . . . were interested in microscopic fluctuations of sound, observable through its graphic three-dimensional representation in the form of a spectrogram (a graph which represents frequency on the vertical axis and time on the horizontal, with the relative intensity of the overtones represented with lines of different shades or colors). The spectralists used these representations as the inspiration for their orchestrations, as Hugues Dufourt explained in his seminal essay 'Musique spectrale' (1979), the 'techniques of optical representation of sound . . . allow us to intervene precisely on the details of an acoustic wave and make slight modifications to it.' At the same time, spectralists took their inspiration from techniques of electronic processing of sound, from phase deformation and frequency modulation to the use of filters, resonators, and the like." Jonathan Goldman, "Boulez and the Spectralists between Descartes and Rameau: Who Said What about Whom?" *Perspectives of New Music* 48, no. 2 (Summer 2010): 201.

21 Pierre Schaeffer famously advocated for "reduced listening," a "listening mode that focuses on the traits of the sound itself, independent of its cause and of its meaning." See Michel Chion, *Audio-Vision: Sound on Screen*, ed. and trans. Claudia Gorbman (New York: Columbia University Press, 1994), 29, and Pierre Schaeffer, *Traité des objets musicaux*, rev. ed. (Paris: Éditions du Seuil, 1967).

22 "What a spatial view of musical time—but also what anthropocentrism there is in this image of a man at the venter of time, a listener fixed at the very center of the work to which he is listening! One might say that a truly

Copernican revolution remains to be fought in music." Gérard Grisey, "*Tempus ex Machina*: A Composer's Reflections on Musical Time," *Contemporary Music Review* 2, no. 1 (1987): 242; excerpted in Bojana Cvejić, "Grisey's Views on Musical Time," in Cvejić, *Vortex Temporum*, 35

23 See the collection of papers in Vernon L. Allen van de Vliert and Evert van de Vliert, *Role Transitions: Explorations and Explanations* (New York: Plenum Press, 1984), which includes papers that examine the links between "individual time and historical time." See also chapters 4–8 of Ashforth, *Role Transitions*.

24 Ashforth, 226.

25 De Keersmaeker performed the idea that "my breathing is my dancing" in a seminar at Wiels that crystallized as a work bearing that phrase as its title (and which was made as a collaboration with the flutist Chryssi Dimitriou, one of the musicians in Ictus who regularly performed *Vortex Temporum* and *Work/Travail/Arbeid*; see https://www.rosas.be/en/productions/371-my-breathing-is-my-dancing, accessed March 22, 2019). The fact that *Vortex Temporum* is built from "a single elemental phrase, 'which originates in the movements of the sternum'" relates the dance essentially to the issue of breath as well as that of music. A collaboration similar to her work with Dimitriou, with choreographer/dancer Boris Charmatz and the violinist Amandine Beyer in *Partita 2*, developed from the phrase "my walking is my dancing" during the years she choreographed *Vortex Temporum*. See https://www.rosas.be/en/productions/374-partita-2, accessed March 22, 2019. *Partita 2* provides *Vortex Temporum*'s dramaturgical structure; see Femke Gyselink, "A Few Remarks about the Creation," in Cvejić, *Vortex Temporum*, 64.

26 "Mickey-Mousing" is a common term in dance circles, as Archias points out.

27 "*Vortex*'s original choreography, made to the time of Grisey's composition, is thus expanded in the exhibition space to a nine-hour choreography (nine being an essential structuring number for De Keersmaeker's composition)." Elena Filipovic, "Vertiginous Force / The Exhibition as Work," in Anne Teresa de Keersmaeker, *Essays*, ed. Filipovic (Brussels: Wiels, Rosas and Mercatorfonds, 2015), 19. See also Douglas Crimp's description of the same: "We watch from a safe distance or venture right up close. We stay for the entire hour or leave in the middle, or perhaps we stay for two or three hours at a stretch. If we're really curious or really dedicated or really hooked, we might come when Wiels opens at 11:00, and watch the dancing continuously until it closes at 18:00. We might come back the following day, and again the next. And because the permutations of solos, the various combinations of duets and trios, and the *tutti* add up to more than seven [hours]—more even than the originally projected cycle of nine—and because there is more than one cast, we can come again and again and never see the same thing twice." Douglas Crimp, "Relocating Rosas," in De Keersmaeker, *Essays*, 102.

28 Even as such, the body is always already "confirm[ed] as a metonymic figure for an entire repertoire of human and social arrangements." Hortense Spillers, "Mama's Baby, Papa's Maybe," in *Black, White, and in Color: Essays on American Literature and Culture* (Chicago: University of Chicago Press, 2003), 205.

29 Jacky Bratton, Jim Cook, and Christine Gledhill, introduction to *Melodrama: Stage, Picture, Screen* (London: British Film Institute, 1991), 1.

30 See my article "*Rosas*, the Storyless, and Roles."

31 K. Robert Schwartz, "Steve Reich: Music as a Gradual Process, Part I," in *Perspectives of New Music* 19, no. 1/2 (Autumn, 1980–Summer, 1981): 376.

32 See, for example, her description of "the decision's cut" as "the more than

human force that repositions the field in the event of an occasion taking form: decision is how experience singles itself out as *this* or *that*"; she also describes how two cooks together in the kitchen intuitively move around each other; they are "both dancing the interval of the decisions as they realign [their] cooking bodies." Or her description of a snake "wandering through the desert. . . . Every quick movement—lizard, wind, fly—activates a certain bodying that attends, intensively, to a n environment in the making. A body is in-forming, a bodying more fear than form, taut with a foreboding." Manning, *Always More Than One*, 105, 26.

33 Peter Brooks, *The Melodramatic Imagination: Balzac, Henry James, Melodrama, and the Mode of Excess* (New Haven, CT: Yale University Press, 1976), 171.

34 Brooks, citing Laurence Bedwell Holland, *The Expense of Vision* (Princeton, NJ: Princeton University Press, 1964), 76. See Brooks, *Melodramatic Imagination*, 226n33.

35 For me, a great number of De Keersmaeker's choreographies, from *Rosas danst Rosas* (1983) to *En Atendant* (2010) and of course the works discussed here, attend to this relay. It seems to be both a signature of both her method—amalgamating adjustments made by her dancers as she "finalizes" or stages a choreography—and her conceptual framework, without totalizing either.

36 "If we are to enter the microphonic world of a sound, time needs to be suspended, or, more precisely, we perceive time to stop. Likewise, an unexpected acoustic jolt causes the listener to skate over a portion of time, throwing her violently off course: time can equally speed up and contract." Bojana Cvejić, "Dance in Earnest: On Time and Attention in *Work/Travail/Arbeid*," in De Keersmaeker, *Work/Travail/Arbeid*, 17, 18.

37 "If you start from an intrinsic connection between movement and sensation, the slightest, most literal displacement convokes a qualitative difference, because as directly as it conducts itself it beckons a feeling, and feelings have a way of folding into each other, resonating together, interfering with each other, mutually intensifying, all in unquantifiable ways apt to unfold again in action, often unpredictably. Qualitative difference: immediately the issue is change. Felt and unforeseen." Brian Massumi, *Parables for the Virtual: Movement, Affect, Sensation* (Durham, NC: Duke University Press, 2002), 1. See also Teresa Brennan, *The Transmission of Affect* (Ithaca, NY: Cornell University Press, 2004).

38 Obviously, this labor has an eco-critical component as well, and one might consider the work of Donna Haraway or Joan Jonas (among others) in this regard.

39 "Alors que le premier mouvement était celui du rythme et de la métrique, le deuxième mouvement, dédié à Salvatore Sciarrino, est celui de la durée, durée exprimée conjointement dans le discontinu par le piano et dans le continu par le trio à cordes, la flûte et la clarinette." Hervé, *Dans le vertige de la durée*, 51.

40 In conversation with the author, November 14, 2015.

41 Brooks, *Melodramatic Imagination*, 144.

42 Brooks, 144.

Yvonne Rainer

1 Originally commissioned by (and presented in the frameworks of the J. Paul Getty Museum, the Getty Research Institute, and Performa), *The Concept of Dust* was presented at the MoMA as a work in progress and "East Coast premier," and later presented in other versions and venues. One of its performances at MoMA can be viewed in its entirety, including the long "warmup," at https://www.moma.org/calendar/events/955 (streamed live on June 13, 2015).

2 From the credits on the pamphlet published by MoMA accompanying the performance.

3 See Yvonne Rainer, "The Aching Body in Dance," in *Performing Arts Journal* 106 (2014): 3–6.

4 A tangible sense of performance precedes any beginning of any dance work performed in a museum when it is a punctual (as opposed to day-long) performance. The Museum of Modern Art has perfected this pre-performance "aura" particularly in the works that are performed in their large second floor atrium. Choreographers including Jérôme Bel, Deborah Hay, and Steve Paxton have not only occupied that physical space; the time used by audiences readying themselves for performance, with or without music, becomes part of the work and a meditation on being an audience.

5 Rainer's dancers form a group, which in recent years was colloquially referred to as the Raindears, but was never a formal company; *The Concept of Dust* added two male performers to the all-female Raindears (whose moniker derives from Isadora Duncan's "Isadorables"), Keith Sabado and David Thomson. Of the troupe of "Raindears" enumerated above, Sally Silvers and Emily Coates were absent from the performances of *The Concept of Dust* at MoMA, but Coates performed in other iterations of the work.

6 In that way *The Concept of Dust* is like many of the Judson Dance Theater and Grand Union performances in which Rainer participated decades ago, in Judson Memorial Church and other sites without formal stages. Margaret Hupp Ramsay begins her beautifully detailed account of the experiments of Grand Union—that group that brought together Rainer and Paxton with David Gordon, Trisha Brown, Douglas Dunn, Barbara Dilley, and Nancy Green—thus: "A performance by Grand Union usually began with individual warm-ups by some members of the group. Other members casually joined in, music was put on the phonographs, and the dancers responded by moving and talking, spontaneously connecting and reacting to one another, creating and discovering their text and material as they went along." Margaret Hupp Ramsay, *The Grand Union (1970–1976): An Improvisational Performance Group* (New York: Peter Lang, 1991), 1. The one "entrance" to these performances of *A Concept of Dust* was made by Théodore Rousseau's painting of *The Sleeping Gypsy* (1897), rolled slowly by two art handlers behind the dance floor.

7 For an extended discussion of this point, highlighting how Rainer's dance has belied her own claims of being "anti-music," see Douglas Crimp, "Yvonne Rainer, Muciz Lover," *Grey Room* 22 (Winter 2006): 48–67.

8 Elisa Archias explains how much Rainer's return to dance and choreography in the 2000s is centered in her "appropriat[ion], parody[ing], and pay[ing] homage" to those "who[m] she had reckoned with in the

formation of her own choreographic language." Archias, *Concrete Body: Yvonne Rainer, Carolee Schneeman, Vito Acconci*, 168. We might also consider the specifically *musical* aspect of those modernist dance traditions. Rainer's *A.G. Indexical (with a Little Help from H.M.)* and *RoS Indexical* focus on Balanchine's *Agon* and Nijinsky's *Rite of Spring*, but also on Stravinsky's compositions, their "aura" and reputation, as key to the complex audial accompaniments that Rainer creates.

9 Margaret Ramsay cites David Gordon on Grand Union's tactics for beginning performances: from "walking in the door with the audience and walking out into the space and starting to do something, or nothing. In one of the last performances, I stayed in the dressing rooms for the first twenty minutes of the performance getting into a very elaborate getup." Ramsay, "Interview with Gordon, March 1985," in *The Grand Union*, 115.

10 Andrew Clements, "The Sinking of the Titanic—Review," *Guardian*, April 15, 2012, https://www.theguardian.com/music/2012/apr/15/the-sinking-of-the-titanic-review.

11 Maja Trochimczyk, "From Circles to Nets: On the Signification of Spatial Sound Imagery in New Music," *Computer Music Journal* 25, no. 4 (Winter 2001): 42. She is quoting Keith Potter, "Just the Tip of the Iceberg: Some Aspects of Gavin Bryars' Music," *Contact: A Journal for Contemporary Music*, no. 22 (1981): 4–15.

12 Archias, *Concrete Body*, 178.

13 Archias, 178. "Neutral performance" is what is supposed to substitute for "character" in the graph that Rainer uses to introduce "A Quasi-Survey." She explains: "Dancers have been driven to search for an alternative context that allows for a more matter-of-fact, more concrete, more banal quality of physical being in performance, a context wherein people are engaged in actions and movements making a less spectacular demand on the body and in which skill is hard to locate." Rainer, "Quasi Survey," in *Yvonne Rainer, Work 1961–73*, 65.

14 Mladen Dolar, *A Voice and Nothing More* (London: MIT Press, 2006), 80–81.

15 The term "radical juxtapositions," coined by Susan Sontag to describe Allen Kaprow's Happenings, has been used by Rainer in reference to her own films and the capacity to juxtapose clashing realities—as mass media habitually does. The term has served as the title of a monograph by Shelley Green, *Radical Juxtapositions: The Films of Yvonne Rainer* (Metuchen, NJ: Scarecrow, 1994), and a catalog, *Yvonne Rainer: Radical Juxtapositions, 1961–2002*, ed. Sid Sachs (Philadelphia: Rosenwald-Wolf Gallery, University of the Arts, 2002).

16 Yvonne Rainer met Simone Forti (then married to Rainer's eventual romantic partner Robert Morris) in 1960, when the two of them and Nancy Meehan rented a joint rehearsal space. See Rainer, *Feelings Are Facts*, 190. Adrian Heathfield describes *Huddle* as "simply an embodied communal activity [that] makes a substantive amorphous object or living sculpture. . . . Forti describes *Huddle* as 'an object that doesn't exist in a solid sense, and yet it can be reconstituted at any time.' Six to nine people grasped each other, forming 'a tight mass'; from time to time, participants of the huddle emerged from it, carefully climbed up over the group, and then reintegrated themselves on landing." However, Forti's piece *Huddle* lasts ten minutes and Rainer's communally formed objects last only moments, and Forti's accent on a single member climbing on top of the others is replaced, in Rainer's version, by these more figural moments that

have less to do with climbing onto the group and more to do with giving it a transitory shape. See Adrian Heathfield, "Before Judson & Some Other Things," in *Judson Dance Theater: The Work Is Never Done*, ed. Ana Janevski and Thomas J. Lax (New York: Museum of Modern Art, 2018), 41–42.

17 See Soyoung Yoon, "Where Is That Music Coming From? On Yvonne Rainer's *The Concept of Dust, or How do you look when there's nothing left to move?*" (New York: Museum of Modern Art, 2015), https://www.moma.org/d/pdfs/W1siZiIsIjIwMTUvMTAvMzAva3AxcnFveXE1X3JhaW5lcnlvb24ucGRmIl1d/raineryoon.pdf?sha=fabdccc9ebb195df.

18 Archias, *Concrete Body*, 182.

Index

Page numbers in italics refer to figures

Abstract Expressionism, 19, 81
abstraction, 57, 74, 175; in dance, 152, 224n20; figuration and, 5, 38; gestural, 37–38; leveling powers of, 77; purist understanding of, 36; purposeless, 145; signification and, 203n36
Acconci, Vito, 116
acoustics, 164–65. *See also* psychoacoustics; sound
Adorno, Theodor, 80, 211n29
advertising, 31
Aeschylus: *The Eumenides*, 106
aesthetics, 18; of false totalities, 66; relational, 110, 213n21; and representation, 214n5; of the self, 111; self-knowledge in aesthetic experience, 97–98
affect: "affectless" feelings and, 85; dance and, 176; emotion and, 15, 58–59, 81, 208n7; interior, 59; and subjecthood, 200n9. *See also* affect theory; emotion
affect theory, 2, 81, 209n17, 211n34. *See also* affect
Afro-pessimism, 19, 198n13
Agamben, Giorgio, 96, 204n45, 213n19, 214n2, 215n10
All That Heaven Allows (Sirk), 154
Althusser, Louis, 6, 210n19
Ammer, Manuela, 106
anamorphosis, 101
Andre, Carl, 34
antiwar protests, 25
Antoni, Boštjan, 162, *163*, *165*
Archias, Elise, 154, 183, 190, 224n20, 231n8
Arendt, Hannah, 39, 110, 113–14, 118, 140, 213n19, 215n10, 218n32
Aristotle, 121, 217n21
Arnheim, Rudolf: *Art and Visual Perception*, 41–42
art: characterhood and, 92; Conceptualist, 210n19; expanding the field of visual, 144; frame of accessibility to self in, 89; language as used in, 89; modern, 154; modes of knowing of forms of, 9–10; postmodern, 154; promissory nature of, 4; representations of selfhood in visual, 91. *See also specific types of art*
Arte Povera, 116
art history, 4, 195n1, 196n9, 197n6; figuration in, 201n11, 201n14; modernist, 24. *See also* art
Ashforth, Blake, 222n6
Ashton, Dore, 39–40, 44

Bach, Johann Sebastian, 133–34
Bachmann, Michelle, 134
Bad Lieutenant (Ferrara), 99
Bakhtin, Mikhail, 115
Balanchine, Georges, 148, 151
ballet, 148–52, 154, 164, 189, 223n13; *Giselle*, 151; *Jewels*, 151–52; *The Nutcracker*, 151; *Serenade*, 148; story, 150, 152. *See also* dance
Balzac, Honoré de, 178
Barthes, Roland, 31, 93
Bausch, Pina, 155
Bedwell, Laurence, 176
Béjart, Maurice, 155
Bel, Jérôme, 148–49, 153; *Cédric Andrieux*, 148; *Disabled Theater*, 148; *The Show Must Go On*, 148; *Véronique Doisneau*, 148
Benjamin, Walter, 20, 55, 207n72, 215n10
Berkson, Bill, 32
Berlant, Lauren, 15, 59, 152–53
Bersani, Leo, 4
bilingualism, 118
biopic, 148–49
Black artists, 199n3

Black bodies, 122, 125
Blackmore, Susan, 132
Bois, Yve-Alain, 200n7, 204n42, 206n59
Bollas, Christopher, 4
Bourgeois, Louise, 179
Branigan, Edward, 132
Brecht, Bertolt, 94; *The Life of Galileo*, 21
Breitz, Candice, 93
Brodkey, Harold, 179
Broodthaers, Marcel, 1
Brooks, Peter, 175–76, 178
Brown, Trisha, 155, 226n6
Bryars, Gavin, 186–87, 189, 191; "The Sinking of the Titanic," 182–83
Buchloh, Benjamin: "Figures of Authority, Ciphers of Regression," 62, 66, 209n14
Bugs Bunny, 186
Butler, Judith, 2, 4, 8, 19, 110–14, 139–40, 150, 196n9, 204n45, 204n47, 221n34; *Bodies That Matter*, 19; *Giving an Account of Oneself*, 110

Cage, John, 156, 173
Cameron, James, 182
caricature, 31
cartoons, 31–32, 53, 55, 85; Disney, 169. *See also* comics
Catterson, Pat, 183
Cavarero, Adriana, 2, 4, 110, 113, 116, 139–40, 150, 196n9, 218n32, 221n32; *Relating Narratives*, 110, 113
Centre Pompidou, 157, 226n5
Cervantes, Miguel de, 105
Chaplin, Carlie, 43
character, 6–7, 88–98, 101–2, 144–48, 152–54, 183; audience's uncertain relation to, 112; category of, 92, 94, 95, 97; concept of, 199n16; conventions of, 88, 109; and figuration, 90, 212n7; problem of, 154; as vehicle for thinking about selfhood, 114. *See also* characterhood
characterhood, 88, 90–95, 118, 132, 148, 155, 159, 172, 183; and art, 92; and self-expression, 120; standards of, 123–24. *See also* character
Childs, Lucinda, 155
Chion, Michel, 220n15
choreography, 144–58, 161, 164–66, 169–78, 186–91, 228n25, 228n27, 231n8; dance notation and, 9; in time and space, 3, 174; shape in, 12–13, 152–53; ways of moving in, 8. *See also* dance
civil rights, 25
Cixous, Hélène: "The Character of 'Character,'" 88–89, 120–21, 126
Clark, T. J.: *Picasso and Truth*, 38–39, 204n43
classical drama theory, 96
cognitive science, 34
Coleman, James, 6, 90, 94–95, 214n1, 216n16; *Box (ahhareturnabout)*, 100, *101*, 117–18; *Clara and Dario*, 101; collaborations with performers of, 6, 91, 94–119, 124, 141, 214n2, 216n13; colonialism of, relation to, 100, 103–4, 108, 115–18; Conceptualism of, relation to, 116; Irishness of, relation to, 100–101, 117, 121; *Lapsus Exposure*, 102; *Ligne de foi*, 101; photography of, relation to, 99–105; *The Ploughman's Party*, 117–18; *Retake with Evidence*, 91, 95–119, *100*, *103*, *104*, *107*, 124, 141, 214n2, 215n10, 216n13; theatricality and performance in, 102–16; twinned systems of reproduction in the work of, 101
collage, 16–18, 25, 38, 65–68, 72–73, 76, 78; shape in, 17–18, 70
collectivity, 7–10, 149; horizon of, 10; individuation and, 152, 189; and relationality, 8; separability and, 5
colonialism, 100, 103–4, 204n47
color, 27, 75, 77, 89, 97, 122; in film, 124–27, 130, 132–34, 139
Color Field, 81
comedy, 54, 57. *See also* tragicomedy
comics, 9, 13, 21, 30–32, 43, 46–47, 51, 53, 55. *See also* cartoons
communication, 58; of a painting's address, 59. *See also* language
Conceptualism, 116, 195n1, 210n19
Cooper, Harry, 205n50
Crumb, R., 31
cubism, 73
Currier, Nathaniel, 101

dance, 90, 144–78; abstraction in, 152, 224n20; and affect, 176; analytic postmodern, 155; character and performer in, 148–49, 153; choreography of, 7–8, 12, 144–58, 161, 164–66, 169–78, 186–91, 228n25, 228n27, 231n8; as "drama without words," 187; European avant-garde, 155; gesture and, 12, 147–51, 166, 174, 216n17; history of, 148; individuation in, 8, 144–49, 182–84, 188, 191; modern, 153–54, 189; music and, 9, 153, 164–66, 170–72, 175–77, 182, 186, 231n8; postmodern, 149–50, 153; representation in, 175, 178; roles in, 3, 7–9, 145–48, 150–53, 162, 164, 169, 172–76, 184–91; shape in, 12–13, 152–53; social roles as form in, 175; in space, 174; and theater, 146–47, 153; unison, 187, 189. *See also* ballet; choreography; gesture; music; performance; theater
Dayan, Daniel, 126; "The Tutor-Code of Classical Cinema," 126
De Bièvre, Geert, 162
De Keersmaeker, Anne Teresa: background of, 155–56; *Cesena*, 173; choreography of, 155–78, 191, 225n27, 226n6; Childs's relation to, 155; collaborations with performers of, 155–78, 228n25; *En Attendant*, 173, 229n35; *Fase: Four Movements to the Music of Steve Reich*, 155, 173; magic cube in the work of, 161, 164, 168–69, 226n6, 226n9; and Mickey-Mousing, 169, 174, 228n26; *Mikrokosmos/Quator No. 4*, 173; music of, relation to, 164–66, 170–72, 175–77; *Ottone, Ottone*, 173; and performances in art museums, 7, 156–59, 162, 171, 226n5; Rainer's relation to, 7, 155–56; *Rosas danst Rosas*, 155, 173, 229n35; serial music of, relation to, 173; *The Six Brandenburg Concertos*, 173; *Vortex Temporum*, 7, 156–77, *159*, *165*, 184, 187–88, 225n1, 225n4, 226n6, 226n9, 228n25, 228n27; *Work/Travail/Arbeid*, 7, 156–77, *158*, *160*, *161*, *163*, *168*, *171*, 184, 187–88
Deleuze, Gilles, 127, 211n34, 212n7
de Man, Paul, 201n11, 210n25
Derrida, Jacques, 6, 196n11, 216nn18–19
Descheemaeker, Dirk, 162, *165*
Diderot, Denis, 112
digital printing, 76, 78
Dimitriou, Chryssi, 162, 228n25
Dolar, Mladen, 187
Douglas, Stan, 95; *The Secret Agent*, 93
drama. *See* theater
drawing, 9, 25, 29, 66, 84; linear, 36; and painting, 68–69, 75–76, 83; on paper, 60

Eisenman, Nicole, 24; *Weeping Woman*, 25
Eisenstein, Sergei, 144
emotion, 12–15; and affect, 15, 58–59, 81, 208n7; charges of, 178; expression and, 63, 77; idealized, 150; ideology of, 81; immediacy and, 77, 80; and painting, 81; representability of, 197n4; rhetoric of, 83; shape and, 59; structure of, 25–26, 29; as subjective content, 74. *See also* affect
Ensler, Eve, 94

Escott, Harry, 123
Expressionism, 16, 24, 62–63, 66–67, 77, 176, 208n2, 209n11, 210n25; codes of, 78, 80; gesturality of, 82–83; as a language, 63, 80; paradox of, 80–81

Fales, Cornelia, 166–67
Fassbender, Michael, 97, 121, 125, *126*, *128*, *129*, *130*, *131*, *137*
feeling. *See* emotion
figuration, 6, 15, 19, 24–31, 38–39, 51, 201n11, 201n14; and abstraction, 5, 38; character and, 90, 212n7; representation and, 25, 39; shape and, 84–85; simple, 32. *See also* representation
film, 9, 105, 125–27, 153–56; character in, 3, 6–7, 89, 92–94; classical, 96, 123, 126–27; documentary, 149; editing technique of, 124, 126; Hollywood, 96, 127, 153; "show qualities" of, 102; structuralist, 221n2
film theory, 132
floor sculpture, 60
Foreman, Richard, 94
formalism, 24, 153; ahistorical, 100; of dance, 145, 149, 151, 175
formlessness, 5, 18–19, 77–78, 82–83; gestural, 46; as rhetorical form, 80. *See also* shape
Forsythe, William, 155
Forti, Simone, 231n16; *Huddle*, 188, 231n16
Foster, Hal, 63, 77, 81, 195n1
Foster, Susan Leigh, 147
Foucault, Michel, 111, 211n34
Fouéré, Olwen, 101
Frampton, Hollis, 34
François, Jean-Charles, 167
Freud, Sigmund, 47, 58, 95, 104, 198n15, 215n6
Freytag, Gustav, 146–47, 217n21
Fried, Michael, 36, 39
Frow, John, 212n7
Frye, Northrop, 9–10; "First Essay," 9

Garbin, Carlos, *159*, 162, *163*, *170*, *171*, 226n9
gender, 2; structures of, 88. *See also* sexuality
geometric rationalism, 24
Gestalt theory, 18, 33–34, 36, 42, 198n9
gesture: in dance, 12, 145–51, 166, 174, 216n17; in Expressionism, 82–83; in painting, 50, 62, 78, 83; shape as both structure and, 69; as the "unary" trait, 20. *See also* dance
Gilligan, Melanie, 95; *Popular Unrest*, 92–93
Godard, Jean-Luc, 179
Goffman, Erving, 145, 222n5
Gombrich, Ernst, 31
Gordon, Douglas: *24 Hour Psycho*, 93
Goudot, Marie, 162, *163*, *165*
Gould, Glenn, 133, 135–36, 139, 220n29
Gould, John, 106
Graham, Dan, 116
Graham, Martha, 149, 189
Grand Union, 154, 230n6, 231n9
Greenberg, Clement, 36, 39
Grieg, Edvard: *Arietta*, 181
Grisey, Gérard, 157–58, 164–69, 172, 176–77, 180
guilt, 96; of Oedipus, 97
Gunning, Tom, 202n17
Guston, Philip, 5–6, 9, 15–21, 23–56, *40*, 61–65, 71–72; *Ancient Wall*, 40, 47, *49*; *Back View*, 51; *Cabal*, 51; *The Coat*, 26–27, *27*, 29–32, 50–51; comics and illustrative work of, 31; *Dawn*, 21, 52–53, *53*; *A Day's Work*, 52; *Deluge III*, 51; *Discipline*, 50; *The Door*, 51; *Driving Around*, 45; *Entrance*, 50; *Flatlands*, 21, 52; *Green Rug*, 40, 47, *48*, 49–51; *Group in Sea*, 51; hapticity of, relation to, 205n56; *Monument*, 51; multiplicatory canvases of, 85; *Painting, Smoking, Eating*, 40; paintings of "common objects," 39–47, 50, 55; *Pit*, 51; *Plain*, 51; *Poor Richard*, 31; *Room*, 50–51; *Scared Stiff*, 52; as shape painter, 15–21, 37–39, 46–47, 50–51, 64–65, 201n11, 202n15, 209n15; *Shoe*, 42–43, *42*, 45; *Sleeping*, 50; *Source*, 47; *The Street*, 51, *52*; and the subfigural, 28, 31, 54, 201n11; *Tomb*, 51; and unrecognizability, 16, 85; *Untitled (Light Bulb)*, 40–41, *41*; *Untitled (Nail)*, 44–45, *44*; *Untitled (Shoe)*, 40, 42–43, *43*; *Waking Up*, 50; *Wharf*, 51; *Yellow Light*, 26–30, *26*, 32, 51

Hamlet (Olivier), 112
Haraway, Donna, 229n38
Hare, Denise: Guston's studio, 40, *40*
Hawking, Stephen: *A Brief History of Time*, 196n8
Hegel, Georg Wilhelm Friedrich, 217n21; "Love," 8
Heidegger, Martin, 43
historicism, 62–63, 66
history, 8, 16, 25, 29, 85–86; expressivity and, 85; modes of, 9
Hoffbauer, Patricia, 179, 181–83, 188, 190
Hofstadter, Alfred, 52, 206n64
holocaust, 25
Holzer, Jenny, 89
Honig, Bonnie, 136, 138
Hoxby, Blair, 135, 206n66, 217n21, 220n21
Husserl, Edmund, 6, 196n11

identity: class, 146; group, 85; questions of, 4, 85; racialized, 146; signification and, 182
ideology, 6, 213n13; Gestaltist, 33
imagination, 58, 136, 167, 169, 176
Institute of Contemporary Art (London), 117
intension, 15, 30, 36, 197n6
interior conversations, 6, 58, 95, 98, 119. *See also* interiority
interiority, 1–2, 14, 19, 22, 46, 56, 66, 74, 82–83, 93, 96, 124–25, 139, 144; as a battle between emotion and affect, 58; dramas of, 172–73; painterly investigations of, 25; publicness and, 58–59; and separability, 5. *See also* interior conversations
interpretation, 35; of human facial exterior, 144
intersubjectivity, 97–98, 112, 114–15, 153
Islamic history, 179
Ives, James Merritt, 101
Izzo, Vincent, 181

Jackson, Michael, 186–88
James, Henry, 175
Jameson, Fredric, 93, 95, 179
Jinhua, Dai, 136
Johns, Jasper, 81
Jonas, Joan, 227n18, 229n38
Judson Dance Theater, 154
Julien, Isaac: *Baltimore*, 91; *Ten Thousand Waves*, 91

Kandinsky, Wassily, 77, 210n27
Kant, Immanuel, 149
Keitel, Harvey, 6, 91, 95–120, *100*, *103*, *104*, 124, 214n2, 216n13, 216n19
Kelly, Ellsworth, 23–24, 27, 61; *Green Curve with White Panel*, 61, *63*
Klein, Melanie, 47, 196n8
Köhler, Wolfgang, 197n8
Krauss, Rosalind, 73
Kremer, Johann Paul, 189
Kristeva, Julia, 5, 19; *Pouvoirs de l'horreur*, 19
Kruger, Barbara, 81

Lacan, Jacques, 6, 47, 198n15
Lambert-Beatty, Carrie, 154
language, 2–3, 6, 31–32, 113, 149; in art, 89, 91–92;

blindness and, 108; Expressionism as a, 63, 80; impersonal operations of, 73–74; as master narrative of subjecthood, 6; materiality of, 216nn18–19; metaphorical, 81; psychoanalytic, 32; and the self, 89–90, 94; and self-reflection, 121; in social life, 112; structures of, 74, 88–89; structuring of the brain by, 118; transparency and immediacy of, 90; and visuality, 47; Wittgenstein's investigations of, 34; world view of a particular, 115–17. *See also* communication; speech acts
Last Temptation of Christ, The (Scorsese), 99
Lemon, Ralph, 148, 153
Levine, Sherrie, 81
Lichtenstein, Roy, 75, 210n22
literature: character in, 89; fiction, 89, 92. *See also* art
Loemij, Cynthia, 144, *159*, 162, *163*, *165*, 170
Louis, Morris, 83
Lux, Deedee, *130*

Magritte, René, 30
Mama, La, 94
Manning, Erin, 150, 173
Martin, Agnes, 61, 178
Marx, Karl, 58, 203n26
mass media, 31
Massumi, Brian, 58–59, 74, 197n4
Mayer, Musa, 202n20
McCloud, Scott, 31
McLane, Maureen, 179
McQueen, Steve, 7, 90–91, 94–96; *End Credits*, 121–22; *Girls, Tricky*, 121–22; *Hunger*, 90, 121, *131*, 132; *Illuminer*, 122, 125, 219n4; *Shame*, 90–91, 96–98, 120–41, *126*, *128*, *129*, *130*, *131*, *137*, 219n5; *Twelve Years a Slave*, 91; *Western Deep*, 121–22
meaning: concrete meaning of dance, 8; figural, 31; in the image, 34–35; semiotic, 43, 45; of shape, 14; subfigural, 31; symbol and, 32. *See also* representation
Mean Streets (Scorsese), 99
melodrama, 10, 134–38, 151–55, 158, 169, 172–78, 183, 187; feminist literature on, 220n25; individuation and, 173–78; of signification, 182
Meltzer, Eve: *Systems We Have Loved*, 210n19
Michelson, Sarah, 12–13; *May 2018 /*, 12, 197n2
Minimalism, 116
Miró, Joan, 30
modernism, 23, 38, 54, 62–63; in dance, 172, 186; late, 61
modernity, 104; Oedipus as the title character for Western, 95; supreme tragedy of, 55; tragicomedy in, 207n67
modes. *See* art
Molesworth, Helen, 67, 70, 209n13
Molière (Jean-Baptiste Poquelin): *Amphitryon*, 54–55
Monty, Julien, 162
Morris, Robert, 198n9, 231n16; "Notes on Sculpture," 34
Morris, Rosalind C., 203n25
Moten, Fred, 19
Mudam, 157
Mudra, 155
Mulligan, Carey, *128*, 133, 136
Munch, Edvard: *The Scream*, 93
Münter, Gabriele, 16; *Portrait of a Young Woman*, 16, *17*
Murail, Tristan, 164
mural, 60–61. *See also* painting
Murray, Elizabeth, 61; *Her Story*, 61–62, *62*
Museum of Modern Art (New York), 59, 157, 179, 186, 214n1, 226n5, 230n1, 230n4
music: and dance, 9, 153, 164–66, 170–72, 175–77, 182, 186, 231n8; melodies of, 33; spectral, 164, 167, 226n10, 227n20. *See also* dance; opera
myth, 31–32; Greek, 216n13; in pictorial art, 91–92; tragicomedy and, 51–56

narrative theory, 95
Nauman, Bruce, 116
Neo-Expressionism, 61–62, 66, 77
New York City, 130, 155
New York Times, 180
Ngai, Sianne, 211n30
Nietzsche, Friedrich, 225n2
Nixon, Richard, 21, 31
Nolde, Emil: *The Burial*, *78*, *80*

Obama, Barack, 179
Octors, Georges-Elie, *165*
Oedipal complex, 104, 109
Olitski, Jules, 36–38, 60; *Demikovsky Green*, 36; *Unlocked*, 36; *Wet Heat Company*, 36–37, *37*
Olivier, Laurence, 112
One Thousand and One Nights, 152
opera, 147, 155. *See also* music
Oudart, Jean-Pierre, 126, 212n12

painting: abstract, 20–21; acts of reference in, 5; cartoonish, 31–32; of common objects, 39–46; communicative, 58; constant crisis of morbidity of, 28; drawing and, 68–69, 83; expressivity of, 16, 21; figurative, 15, 24–25, 27–32, 38–39, 43, 47; history, 5–6, 15, 25, 30, 37–38, 46, 52, 55–56, 84–86; language in, 89; "Minimalist" tendencies in, 90; Old Master, 127; painterly "space" in, 9; rules of, 16; shape, 3, 5–6, 14–46, 50–67, 75, 203n36; signifying work of, 5–6; the "subfigural" in, 200n10; subjective relations to others permitted by, 59. *See also* mural
Parkinson, Chrysa, 144
patriarchy, 141
perception: and shape, 29, 41, 60; the "what" of a, 132
performance: choreography and, 145–47, 173–75, 184; marking and, 107; neutral, 231n13; "post-performance," 106; reading during a dance, 180; rehearsal and, 216n17; space of, 9, 12, 174, 230n4. *See also* dance
performance art, 145, 222n3, 227n18
Performance Space, 197n3
Phillips, Adam, 4
Phillips, Jayne Anne: *Lark and Termite*, 67
philosophy, 8; feminist, 4; moral, 4; readings in phenomenology, 198n9
photography, 60, 102–4, 115, 214n3
Phuon, Emmanuèle, 181–82, 190
Picasso, Pablo: *Guernica*, 38, 204n41, 204n45
Pictures Generation, 116
Plouvier, Jean-Luc, 162, 165, *165*, *170*, *171*, 177–78
poetry, 59, 89
Pomero, Michaël, 161–62, *165*, 226n9
postmodernism, 1, 3, 54, 93, 187, 195n1; musical, 173; postmodern literary criticism, 175
poststructuralism, 89, 199n2, 211n30
printmaking, 6, 9, 14–15, 18, 25, 59, 65–66, 70; reinvention of painting through processes of, 14–15
psychoacoustics, 164–65. *See also* acoustics
psychoanalysis, 4, 20, 32–33, 47, 89
psychology, 18, 58

Quandt, James, 134, 138
Quaytman, Rebecca, 72–73

Rainer, Yvonne, 7–8, 90, 94, 97, 144, 154–55, 231n16; *AG Indexical*, 190; aging and time in the work of,

155; *At My Body's House*, 154; choreography of, 179–91; *The Concept of Dust*, 155–56, 179–91, *180*, *181*, *184*, *185*, *188*, 230n1, 230nn5–6; and ensemble dancing, 182, 184, 187–88, 191; *Inner Appearances*, 144; *Lives of Performers*, 8, 88, 155; movement references in the work of, 8, 90, 154, 186–91; and music, 182, 186–91, 231n8; and the "neutral doer," 90, 183; *Ordinary Dance*, 154; "A Quasi Survey of Some 'Minimalist' Tendencies in the Quantitatively Minimal Dance Activity Midst the Plethora, or an Analysis of *Trio A*," 90, *91*, 154; *RoS Indexical*, 190; *Spiraling Down*, 183, 190; *Three Seascapes*, 154; *Trio A*, 154, 224n20; voice and narration in the work of, 179–81, 187–90
Ratcliff, Carter, 23–25, 27, 35
Rauschenberg, Robert, 156
Read, Herbert, 176
Rear Window (Hitchcock), 130
Reich, Steve, 173
Reina Sofia (Madrid), 214n1
representation, 57, 172–78, 200n6; aesthetics and, 214n5; connotative or intensive depths of, 16; in dance, 175, 178; and figuration, 25, 39; limits of, 20–21; myth of, 103; in painting, 210n27; questions of, 40. *See also* figuration; meaning
reproduction, 67–68; twinned systems of, 101
Richter, Gerhard, 61
Robbe-Grillet, Alain, 144
Robbrecht, Jeroen, 162
Robeson, Paul, 121–22
Rorschach tests, 19
Rose, Jacqueline, 196n8
Ross, Alex, 179
Rousseau, Henri: *The Sleeping Gypsy*, 179, 186
Rousseau, Jean-Jacques, 6, 196n11

Saccoccio, Jackie, 58
Said, Edward: *Orientalism*, 212n4
Sands, Bobby, 121, 132
Saussure, Ferdinand de, 28; *Cours de linguistique générale*, 28
Schmitt, Carl: *Politische Theologie*, 215n10
sculpture, 89; "Minimalist," 90, 221n2
Sedgwick, Eve, 96
Segal, Charles, 96, 217n20
self, 1–4, 7, 18, 85, 92, 113, 156; aesthetics of the, 111; and collective, 94; concept of, 196n7; in dance, 150, 175, 191; ideas of the, 25; interior, 14, 25; internal monologue as access to the, 116–17; intuitive, 14; knowledge of the, 78; language and the, 89–90, 94; making of the, 114; perceptive, 14; promissory nature of the, 1, 4; separable and collective, 7; and shape, 18, 33; structures that seem to threaten the autonomy of the, 5; and subjecthood, 18; unfolding, 110; unity of the, 18. *See also* selfhood; subjectivity
self-accounting, 110–11, 113–14
selfhood: art as a vehicle for experiences of, 1, 114; in dance, 145, 149–50, 152, 174; in the ethics of a face-to-face encounter, 4; figures of, 10; improvement of, 85; interiority as a repository of, 58; in narratability, 113; operation of, 22; politics of, 173; psychoanalytic references to, 4; revisionary discourse on, 25; shape and, 18, 29; understanding, 89. *See also* self; subjecthood
Semenoff, Igor, 162
separability/separateness, 1–2, 5; and collectivity, 5; difference and, 7; interiority and, 5
sex addiction, 96, 125, 127, 130, 132, 136, 219n7. *See also* sexuality
Sexton, Jared, 198n13
sexuality, 2, 123; civic management of, 13; in dance, 12–13, 147; gay, 219n5; sex panics, 134–39. *See also* gender; sex addiction
Shakespeare, William: *Hamlet*, 111, 203n26
shame, 96, 209n17
shape, 12–14, 76, 82, 84–85; in collage, 17–18, 70; comic potential of, 72; in dance, 12–13, 152–53; and emotion, 59; expressivity of, 14, 19; and figuration, 84–85; and formlessness, 19; as object of perception, 29; in painting, 3, 5–6, 14–46, 50–67, 75, 201n14; problem of the totalized, 61; psychology and, 208n3; of sadness, 12–13; selfhood and, 18, 29; simplicity of, 41; theory of, 23–24, 33, 35; as wholes, 33, 35–36; Wittgenstein on, 35–36. *See also* formlessness
Shape of Shape, The (exhibition, Museum of Modern Art), 59–60, *60*
Sherman, Cindy, 81, 95; *Untitled Film Stills*, 92
silkscreen, 75–76, 78
Sillman, Amy, 6, 9, 14–18, 24–25, 37, 57–86, 204n39, 208n3, 208n8; collage practices in painting of, 65–68, 70–74, 76; *Dub Stamp*, 84–85, *85*; and expressivity/expression, 6, 16, 18, 63–67, 70, 73–74, 77–78, 82, 85; *Fatso*, 64, *64*, 72; formlessness in the work of, 77–78, 82–83; and Guston, 6, 9, 15, 18, 24–25, 37, 61–65, 71–72, 84–85, 209n13; installation practices of, 59–61, 75–84; interiority and domestic scenes in the work of, 14, 58–59, 66, 74, 82–83, 207n1; *Mostly Drawing* (exhibition, Gladstone Gallery), 75–84, *75*, *77*; *Nose Job*, 25; *The Plumbing*, 64; *The Shape of Shape*, 59–60; shapes and affect/emotion in the work of, 14–15, 58–59, 61, 63, 74, 84–85, 208n3; shapes and figuration in the work of, 24–25, 63–64, 67–74, 76, 84–85; shapes and replication/duplication/multiplication in the work of, 6, 60, 72–73, 84; shapes and signification in the work of, 14, 70, 72–74; *A Shape That Stands Up and Listens #8*, 67–68, *68*, 70–74; *A Shape That Stands Up and Listens #10*, 67, 69–70, *69*, 72–74; *A Shape That Stands Up and Listens #11*, 70, *71*, 72–74; *A Shape That Stands Up and Listens #48*, 70, 72–74; *A Shape That Stands Up and Listens #57*, 70, 72–74; *SK42*, 78, *79*; *Them*, 64; *Untitled*, 65, *65*; *XL-18-1*, 76
Sirk, Douglas, 153–54
Slifkin, Robert, 37, 200n4, 201n11, 202n23, 206n61
social life, 29; tragic, 95
soliloquy, 6, 95–98, 102, 108–13, 123, 138, 141, 147
song, 89
Sophocles, 104–5, 115, 119, 139–41, 146, 214n6, 215n9, 221n30; *Antigone*, 136, 138, 141; *Oedipus at Kolonnus*, 95–96, 105–9, 111, 138, 215n10
sound, 89, 97, 122, 174, 227n15; in film, 124–27, 133–34, 139; and musical color, 164–66; timbre of, 166–67. *See also* acoustics
space: embeddedness in a shared, 13; linguistic, 30; mythographic, 202n17; negative, 49; ontological, 52; pictorial, 30–31; recessive, 49–50; and time, 175. *See also* time
spectralism, 164, 167, 227n20
speech acts, 113. *See also* language
Spiegelman, Art: *Portrait of the Artist as a Young Man*, 32
Spivak, Gayatri, 199n2
Stone, Edward Durell, 76, 210n23
Stravinsky, Igor, 186
structuralism, 8, 15, 23, 25, 33, 172, 195n1, 198n9, 210n19
structure, 6, 66, 74, 80, 83, 88
subfigural, the, 27–28
subjecthood, 3, 54; affect and, 200n9; conditions of, 16; individuating terms of, 186; as master narrative of, 6; relationality and, 111; self and, 18; theories of, 1–3. *See also* selfhood; subjectivity

subjectivity, 2, 13, 136, 153, 197n5; "full," 54; illusion of, 63; individual, 93; modernist, 24; phenomenological concepts of, 8; structuralist concepts of, 8; terms of, 175. *See also* self; subjecthood
suture theory, 89, 126, 133

Tate Modern, 157, 171
Tati, Jacques, 186–88; *Playtime*, 185, 186–87
Taxi Driver (Scorsese), 99
Taylor, Charles: *Sources of the Self*, 3–4, 88–90, 92, 94
television, 93
Terada, Rei, 63, 81, 211n30
Thatcher, Margaret, 121
theater, 9, 89, 102, 105–8; character in, 92, 94; classical, 95; conventions of Anglophone, 216n13; dance and, 146–47, 153; experimental, 94; sociality of, 112–13. *See also* dance
theism, 4
time: musical, 167–68, 228n22; sense or perception of, 169; space and, 175; spectrum of, 190; and temporality, 181; three categories of, 167; of tragedy, 25. *See also* space
Tomkins, Silvan, 209n17, 210n20
totalization: capacity of shape for, 47; celebration of, 46; problem of, 36; and repetition, 47–51
tragedy, 10, 16, 21, 26, 95, 134–36, 138–39, 223n9; Greek, 95–96, 106–9, 135, 146–47; heroes of, 95–96; representation of, 25; revolution as, 199n18. *See also* tragicomedy
tragicomedy, 10, 16, 26, 29, 32, 206n65, 207n67; or the burlesque, 76; and myth, 51–56. *See also* comedy; tragedy
Trecartin, Ryan, 92, 95, 212n8
Trochimczyk, Maja, 182–83

uniqueness, 2, 10, 66, 125; of experience, 80; and group identity, 85; shape and, 14; and substitutability, 5
universalism, narratives of, 95

van Gogh, Vincent, 43
van Goyen, Jan, 200n10
video, 6, 59, 91–92, 99, 120; music, 148
Vietnam war, 21
violence: layers of, 103; structural, 2; tyranny and violence in Sophocles, 214n6
Volksbühne, 157
von Sternberg, Josef, 127

Walker, Dorothy, 117
Walker, Kara, 92
Walpole, Horace, 54
Warhol, Andy: *Screen Tests*, 92
Weil, Simone, 105
Werner and Elaine Dannheiser Lobby Gallery, 179
Wertheimer, Max: "Gestalt Theory," 33–35
Wiels, 157, 162, 171, 226n5, 228n25
Williams, Bernard: *Problems of the Self*, 3–4
Williams, Raymond, 21, 25, 95
Winnicott, Donald W., 47
Wittgenstein, Ludwig: *Philosophical Investigations*, 34–36, 72
Wöfflin, Heinrich, 20, 46, 55, 198n14, 205n54
Wooster Group, 94
Written on the Wind (Sirk), 154

Zupani, Alenka, 53–55